FIRE FORCE

30

ATSUSHI
OHKUBO

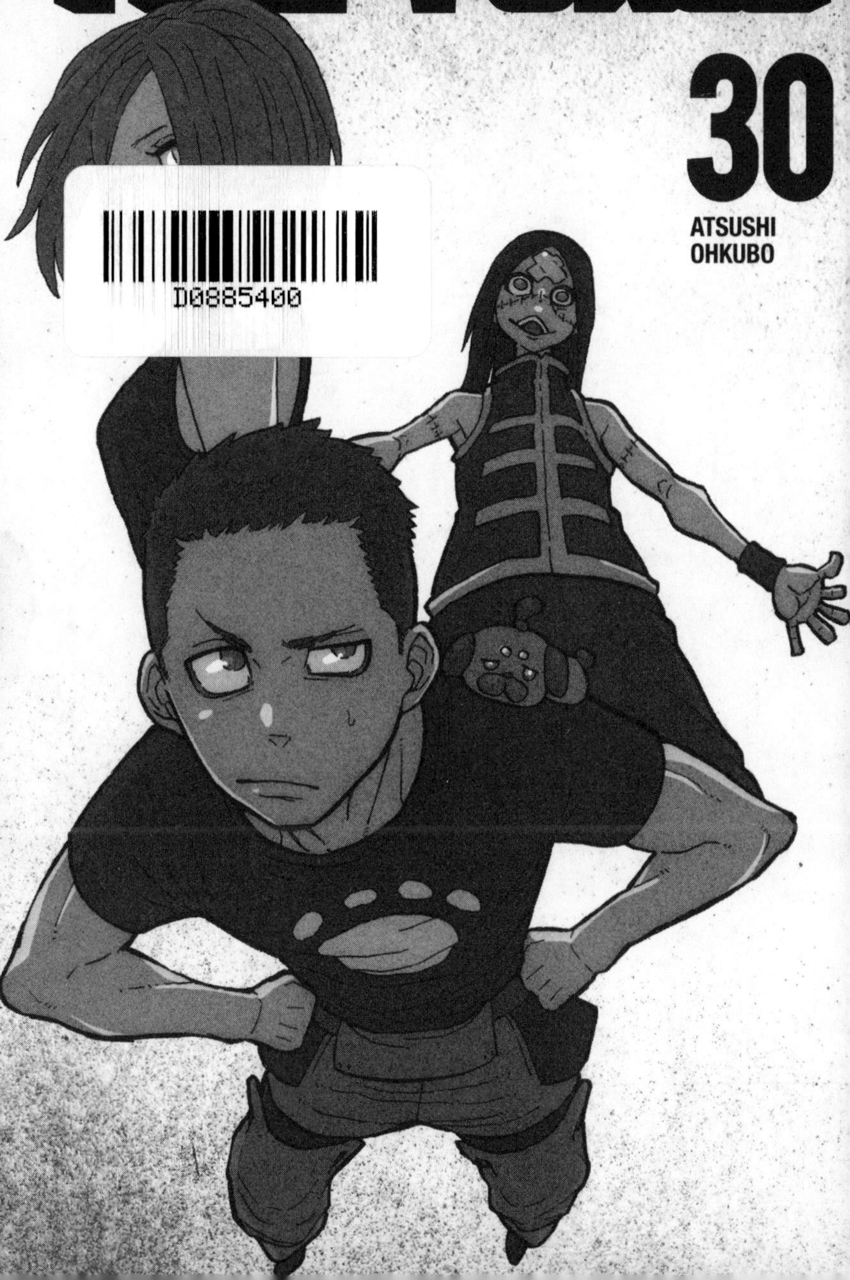

-on

ntation.

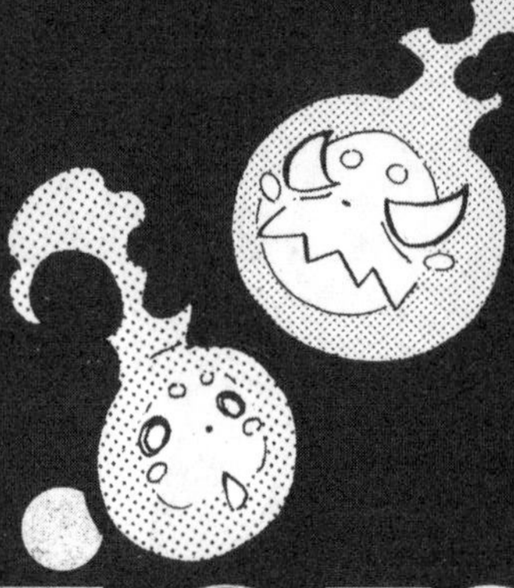

VOL.30

ATSUSHI OHKUBO

a head
confro

FIRE FORCE

SPECIAL FIRE FORCE COMPANY 8

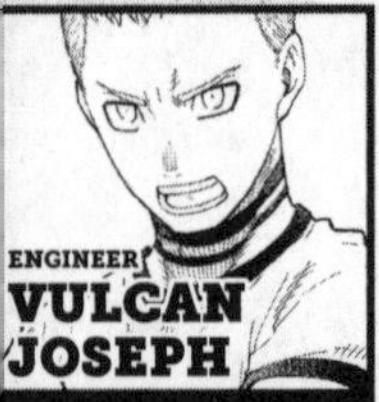

ENGINEER
VULCAN JOSEPH

The greatest engineer of the day, renowned as the God of Fire and the Forge. He accompanies Arthur to the cathedral and watches over him in his trial.

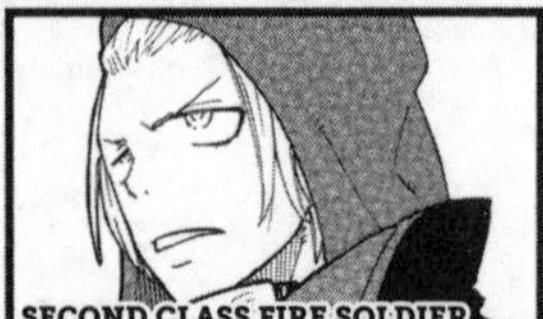

SECOND CLASS FIRE SOLDIER (THIRD GENERATION PYROKINETIC)
ARTHUR BOYLE

Trained at the academy with Shinra. He follows his own personal code of chivalry as the self-proclaimed Knight King. He's a blockhead who is bad at mental exercise. He's a weirdo who grows stronger the more delusional he gets. To overcome the trial that he had left unfinished, he returns to Special Fire Cathedral 8 and breaks out the Special Mintendo.

WATCHES OUT FOR

TRUSTS

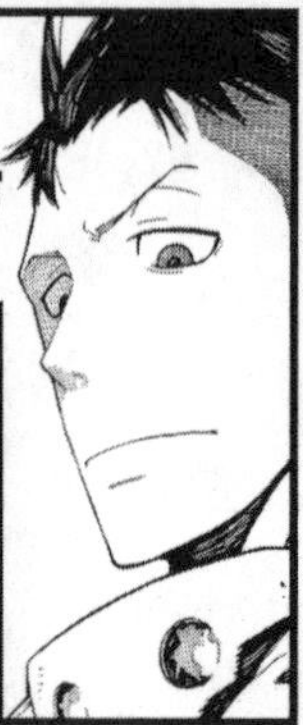

CAPTAIN (NON-POWERED)
AKITARU ŌBI

The caring leader of the newly established Company 8. He has no powers, but uses his finely honed muscles as a weapon in a battle style that makes him worthy of the Captain title. He energizes the other companies with a transmission telling them not to give up hope.

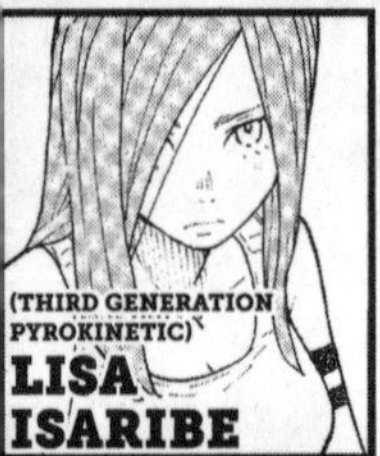

(THIRD GENERATION PYROKINETIC)
LISA ISARIBE

Formerly a spy sent by Dr. Giovanni, she is now a member of Company 8. She controls tentacles of flame.

IDIOT!!

WATCHES OUT FOR

TRUSTS

STRONG BOND

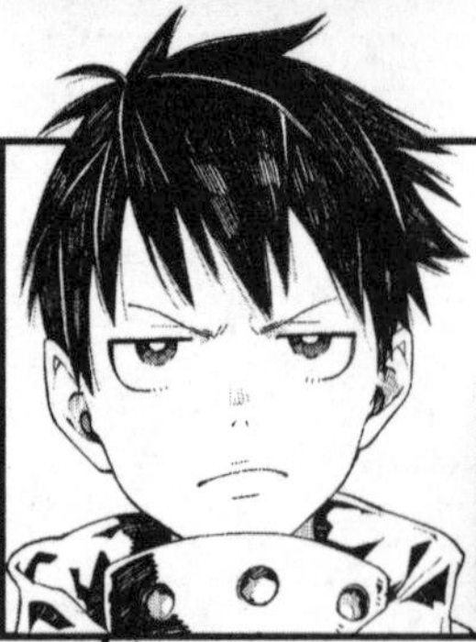

SECOND CLASS FIRE SOLDIER (THIRD GENERATION PYROKINETIC)
SHINRA KUSAKABE

Dreams of becoming a hero who saves people from spontaneous combustion! His weapon is a fiery kick. He wields a special flame called the Adolla Burst. He defeats Raffles I at Tama Bay, but the civilians start murmuring that he is a devil, and a moment later, he vanishes.

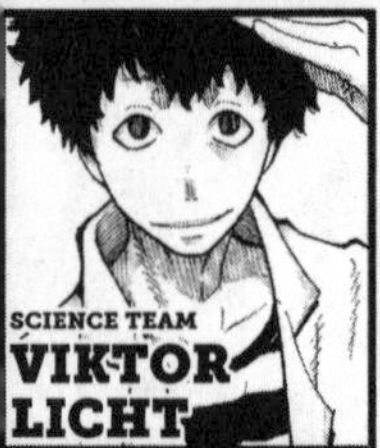

SCIENCE TEAM
VIKTOR LICHT

A genius deployed to Company 8 from Haijima Industries. Has confessed to being a Haijima spy.

A NICE GIRL

LOOKS AWESOME ON THE JOB

A TOUGH BUT WEIRD LADY

HANG IN THERE, ROOKIE!

TERRIFIED

STRICT DISCIPLINARIAN

HAS HIM ON HER MIND

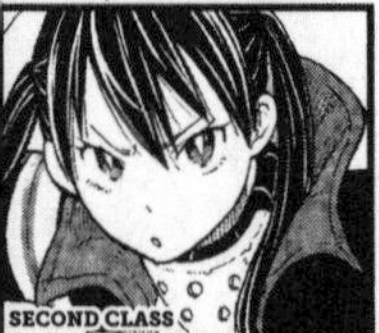

SECOND CLASS FIRE SOLDIER (THIRD GENERATION PYROKINETIC)
TAMAKI KOTATSU

A rookie from Company 1 currently in Company 8's care. She controls nekomata-like flames.

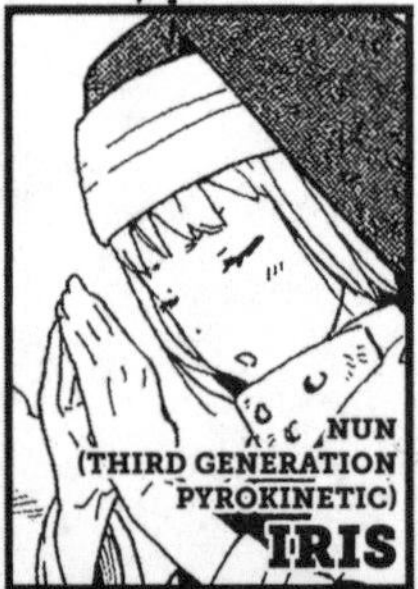

NUN (THIRD GENERATION PYROKINETIC)
IRIS

A sister of the Holy Sol Temple, her prayers are an indispensable part of extinguishing Infernals. Her ignition powers have recently manifested. She disappeared at the same time as Shinra.

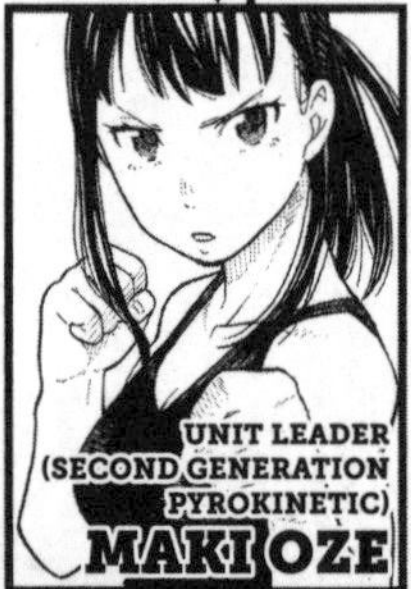

UNIT LEADER (SECOND GENERATION PYROKINETIC)
MAKI OZE

A former member of the military, she is an excellent fighter who controls fire. She's a cool lady, but is mad about love stories, and her beauty is overshadowed by her "head full of flowers and wedding bells."

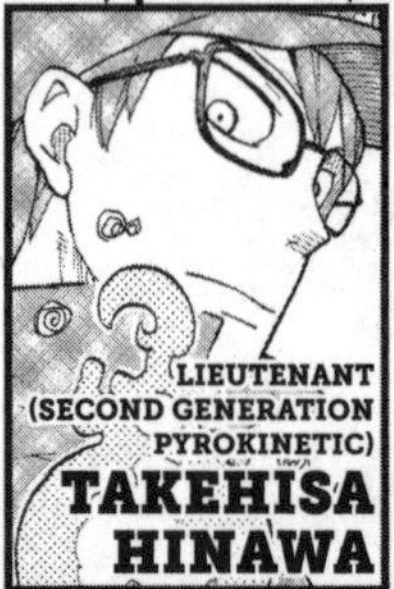

LIEUTENANT (SECOND GENERATION PYROKINETIC)
TAKEHISA HINAWA

A dry, unemotional ex-military man, whose stern discipline is feared among the new recruits. The gun he uses is a cherished memento from his friend who became an Infernal.

THE GIRLS' CLUB

RESPECTS

SPECIAL FIRE FORCE COMPANY 1

REKKA HÓSHIMIYA

A hot-blooded jackass, formerly a lieutenant in Company 1. He died long ago, but now appears in front of his company as a doppelganger. He calls out to his fellow fire soldiers, asking them to destroy the world with him in an effort to give them despair.

LIEUTENANT, PRIEST (SECOND GENERATION PYROKINETIC) KARIM FLAM

Uses an ability called thermoacoustic cooling, which can chill any type of heat. When Rekka returns, he asks his friend about the actions he took and the dreams he had when he was alive. He still can't see his old friend as an enemy.

LIEUTENANT, PRIEST (THIRD GENERATION PYROKINETIC) HUO YAN LI

Concentrates heat into his fingertips and fights with the Tōrō-ken (Lantern Fist) style of martial arts. He lost his arm shielding Karim during the Rekka incident. Believing his friend Rekka to already be dead, he proclaims that the returned Rekka is an impostor and attacks.

HOLY SOL TEMPLE + "EVANGELIST"

DESTROYER DRAGON

An overpowering presence, breath that burns with a single exhale, adamantine scales...with powers equal to his name, the dragon battled with Arthur. Never finding anyone equal to his strength and despairing over the vanity of it all, for a time he considered merely drifting through space for eternity, but now the memory of the defiant look in Arthur's eyes brings him back to Earth.

COMPANY 8 WARD

YŪ
POSSESSED

A self-proclaimed apprentice of Vulcan's. While infiltrating Amaterasu with Vulcan and Lisa, Dr. Giovanni appeared out of nowhere and eventually possessed him. After metamorphosing into a grotesque creature, he turned the key to the Great Cataclysm...

SUMMARY☺

Possessing Yū's body, Dr. Giovanni has turned the key to the Great Cataclysm. And with Shinra gone, Company 8 attempts a battle to defend Amaterasu. The Guardian Charon unleashes the last of his strength in an attack that is full of unconditional love for Haumea. Large-scale fires break out across the Empire. While "despair" fuels the flames that burn up the world, the power to fight against it is "hope." As Special Fire Force Company 8 calls out for hope, the late Rekka appears before Company 1 as a doppelganger... Meanwhile, Arthur has taken Vulcan to Special Fire Cathedral 8. He begins what he claims is the final trial he must overcome: the Special Mintendo!

SPUTT
SPUTT

FIRE FORCE 30
CONTENTS

CHAPTER 259: MY FRIEND

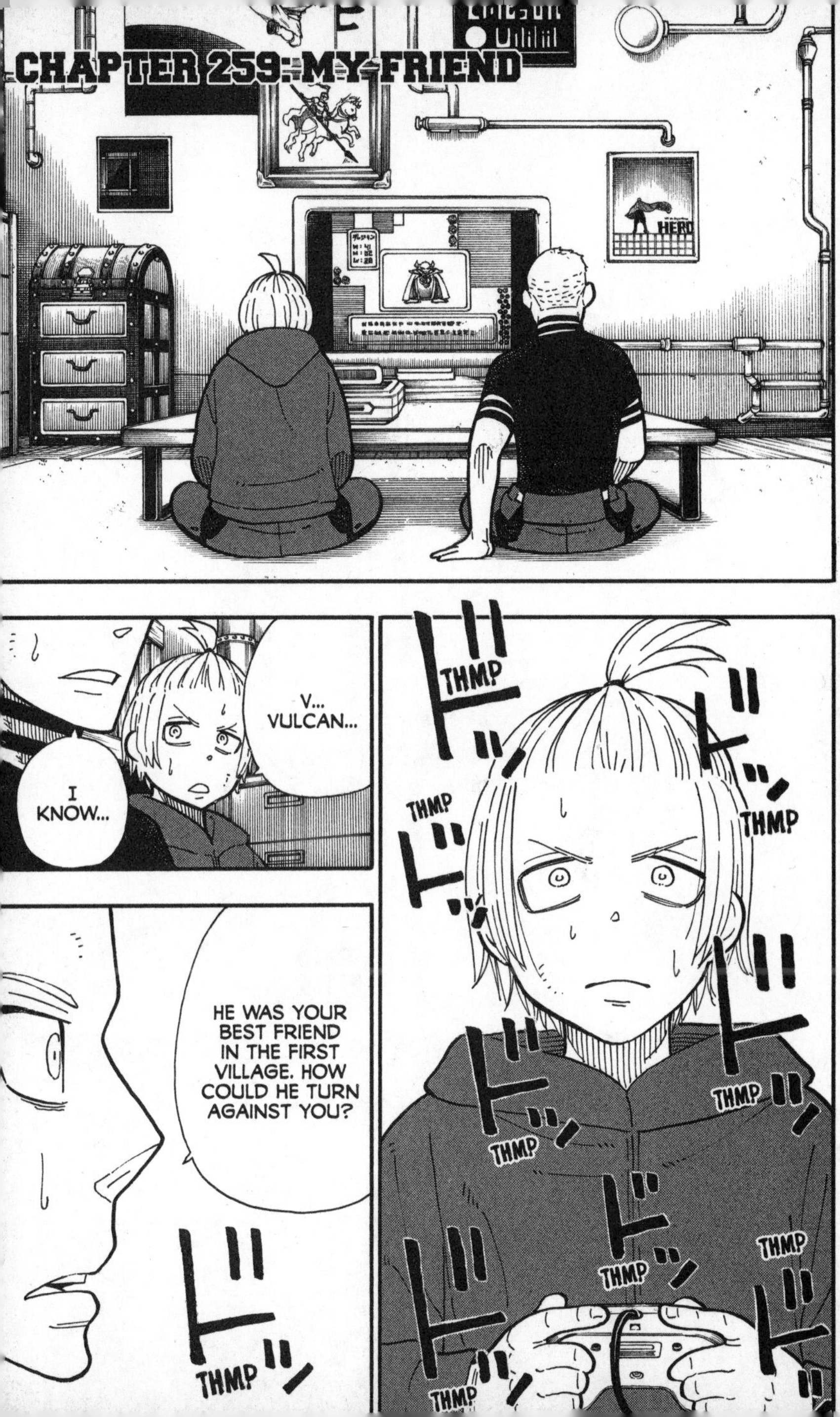
HERO
THMP
THMP
THMP
THMP
THMP
THMP
THMP
THMP
V... VULCAN...
I KNOW...
HE WAS YOUR BEST FRIEND IN THE FIRST VILLAGE. HOW COULD HE TURN AGAINST YOU?
THMP

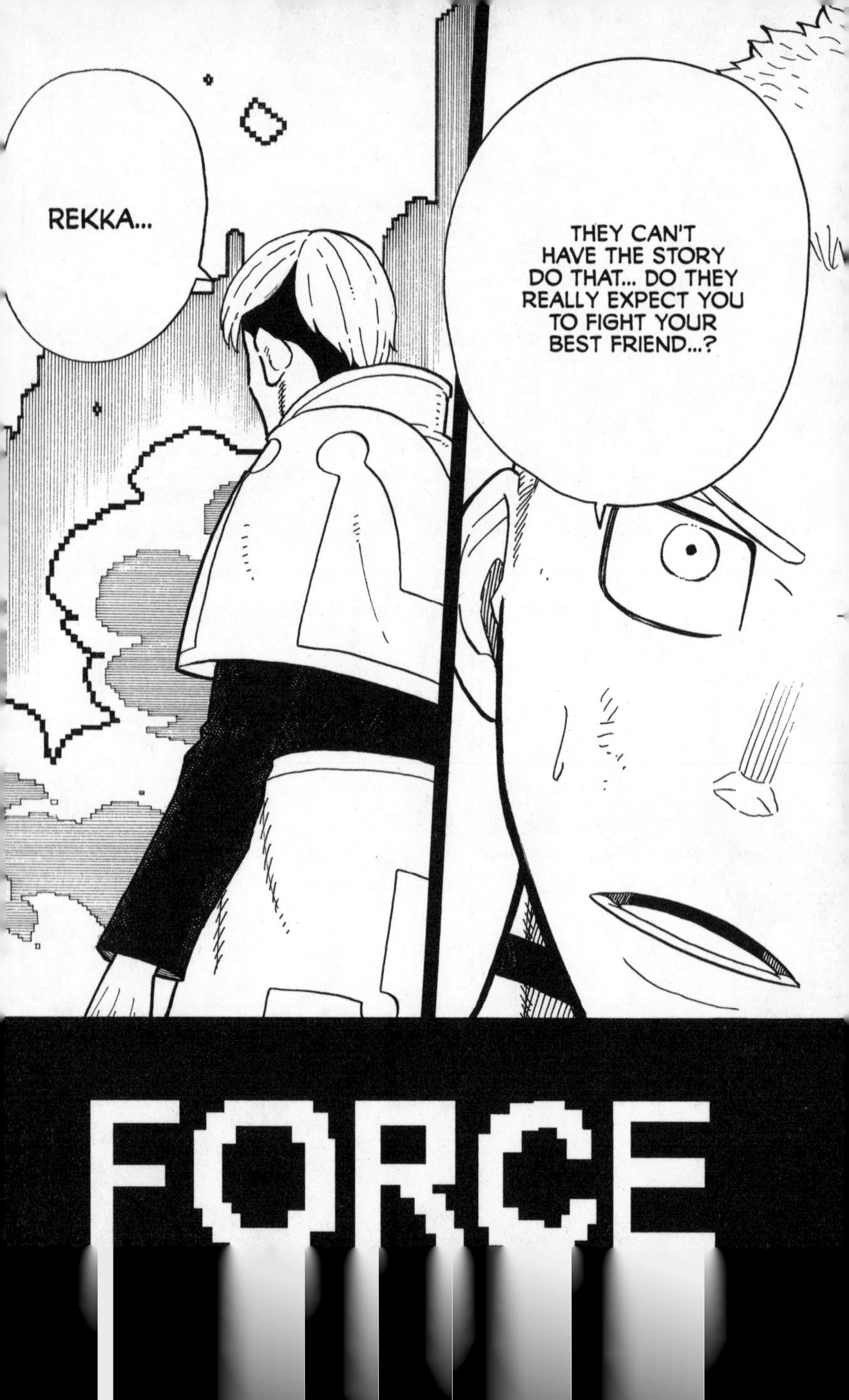
THEY CAN'T HAVE THE STORY DO THAT... DO THEY REALLY EXPECT YOU TO FIGHT YOUR BEST FRIEND...?
REKKA...
FORCE

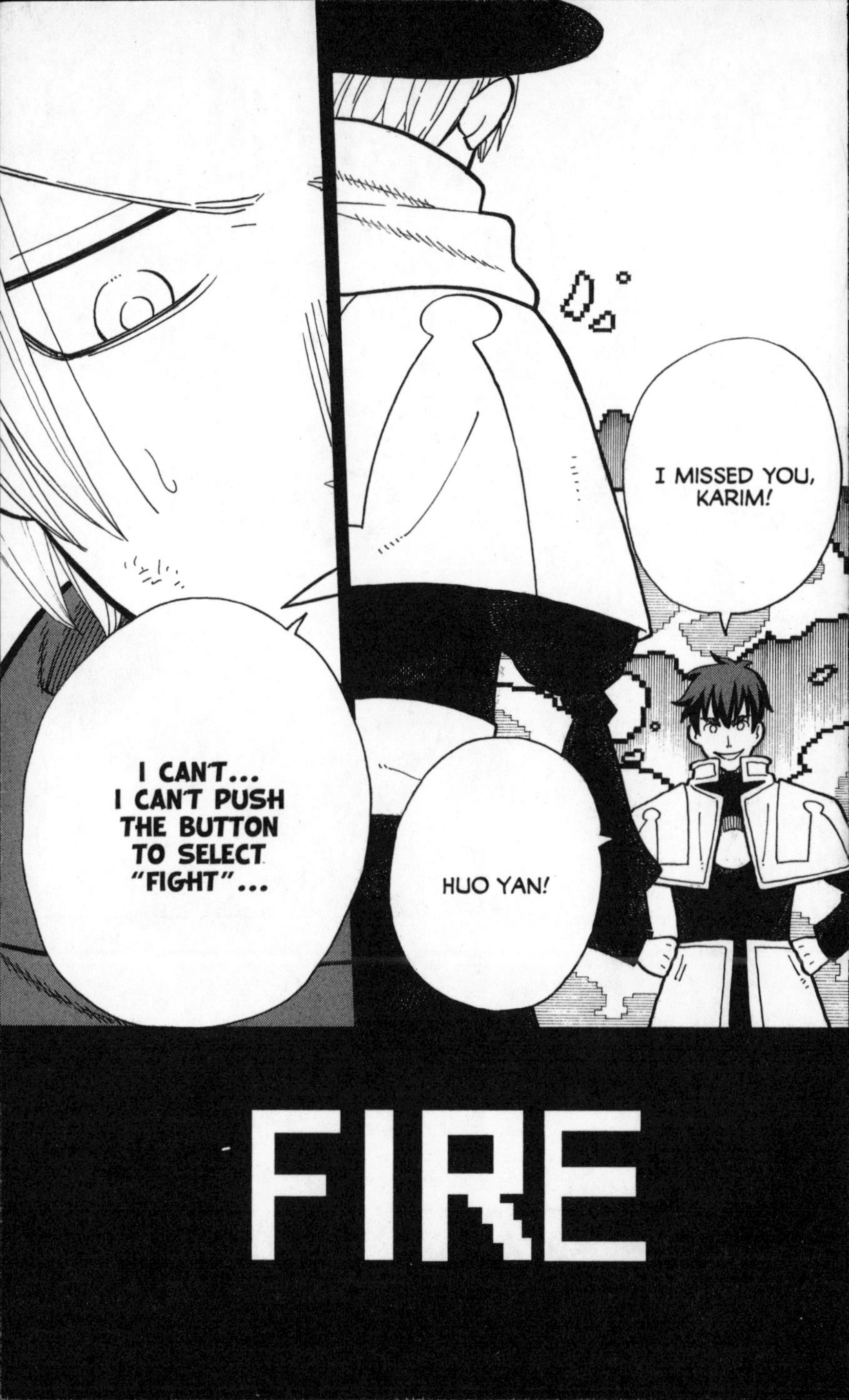
I MISSED YOU, KARIM!
HUO YAN!
I CAN'T... I CAN'T PUSH THE BUTTON TO SELECT "FIGHT"...
FIRE

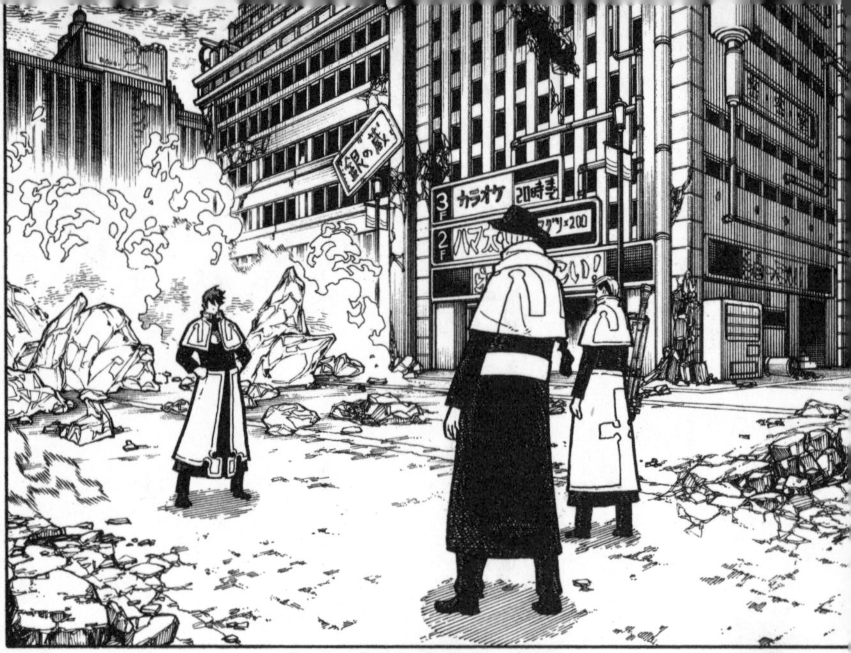
銀の蔵
カラオケ

Sign: Gin no Kura Sign: Karaoke open until 20:00
Sign: Hamata
Sign: Oily!

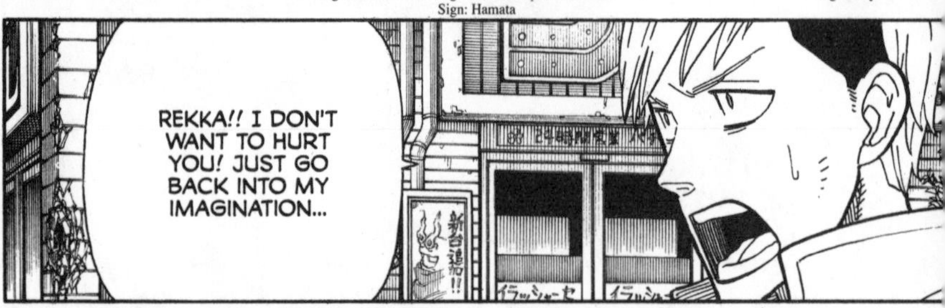
REKKA!! I DON'T WANT TO HURT YOU! JUST GO BACK INTO MY IMAGINATION...

Sign: New machines added!! Sign: Open 24 hours Pachinko
Sign: Come on in

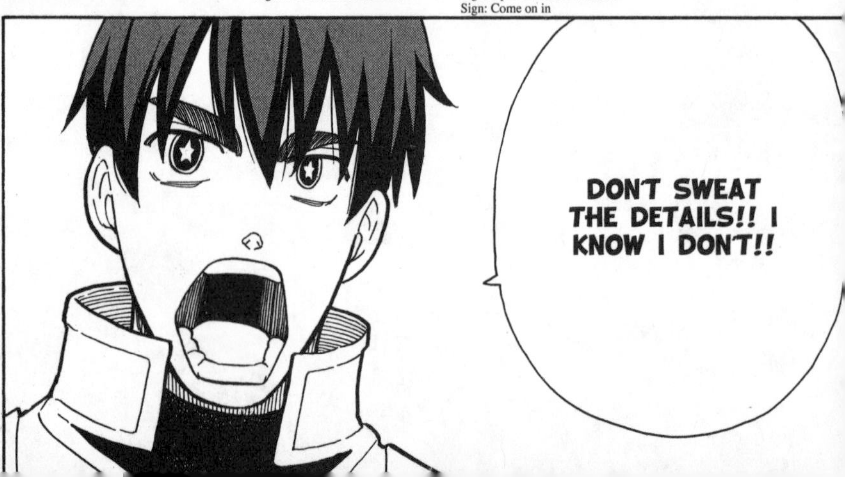
DON'T SWEAT THE DETAILS!! I KNOW I DON'T!!

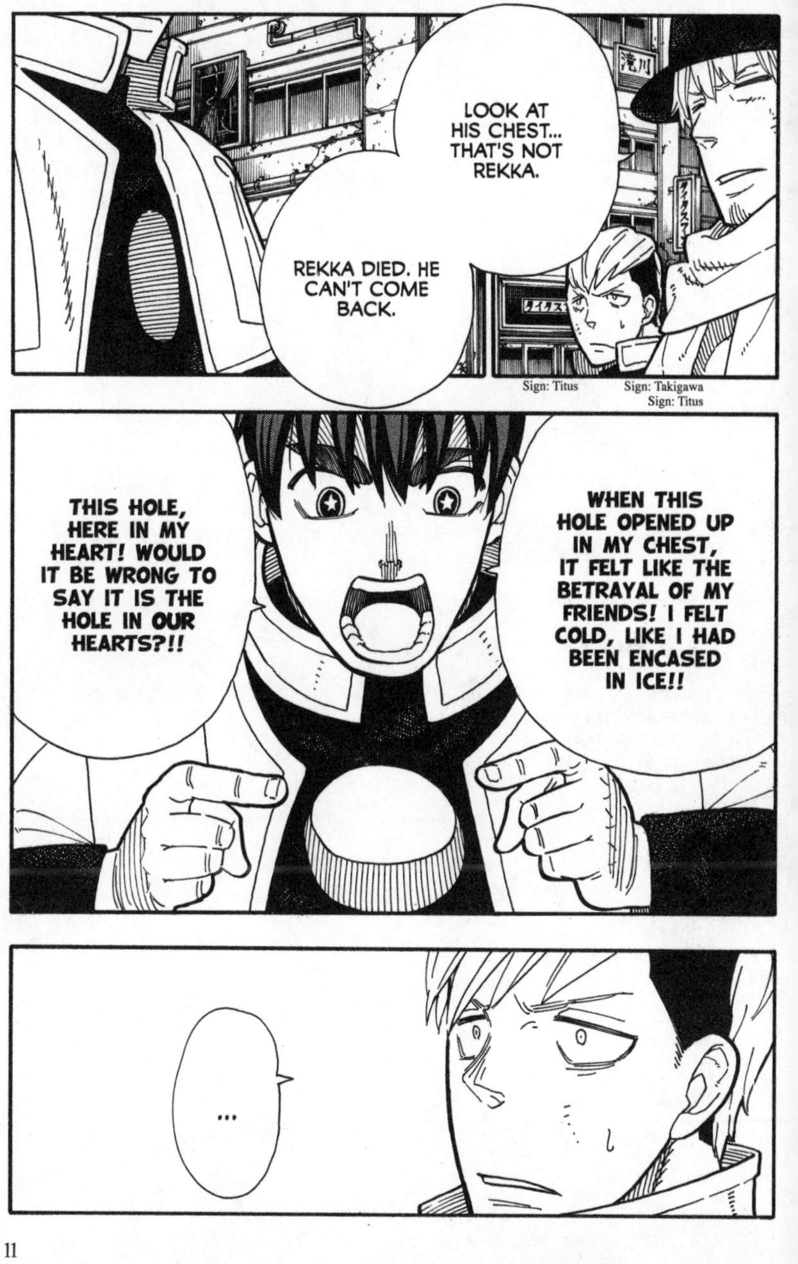
LOOK AT HIS CHEST... THAT'S NOT REKKA.
REKKA DIED. HE CAN'T COME BACK.
WHEN THIS HOLE OPENED UP IN MY CHEST, IT FELT LIKE THE BETRAYAL OF MY FRIENDS! I FELT COLD, LIKE I HAD BEEN ENCASED IN ICE!!
THIS HOLE, HERE IN MY HEART! WOULD IT BE WRONG TO SAY IT IS THE HOLE IN OUR HEARTS?!!
...

Sign: Takigawa
Sign: Titus
Sign: Titus

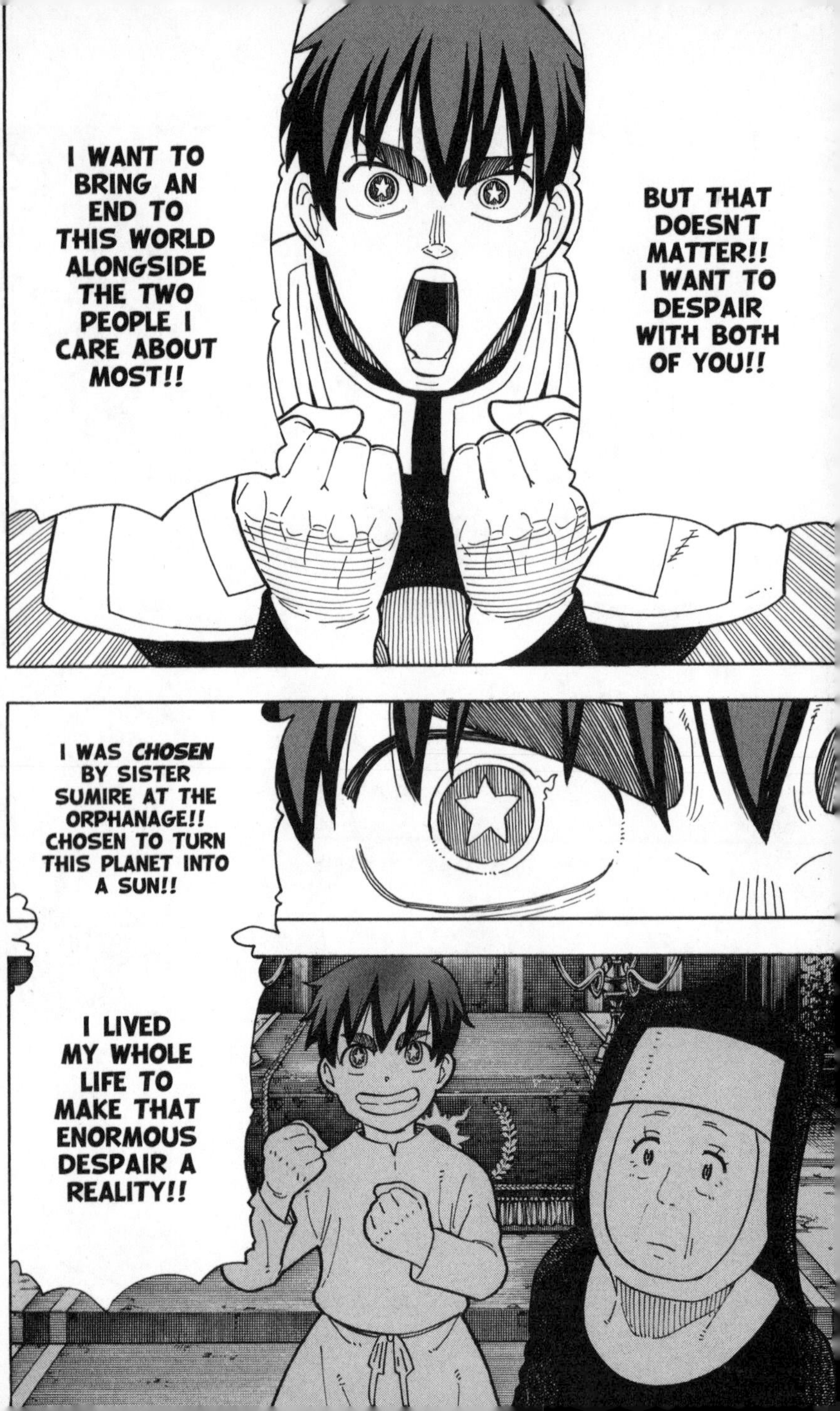
BUT THAT DOESN'T MATTER!! I WANT TO DESPAIR WITH BOTH OF YOU!!
I WANT TO BRING AN END TO THIS WORLD ALONGSIDE THE TWO PEOPLE I CARE ABOUT MOST!!
I WAS *CHOSEN* BY SISTER SUMIRE AT THE ORPHANAGE!! CHOSEN TO TURN THIS PLANET INTO A SUN!!
I LIVED MY WHOLE LIFE TO MAKE THAT ENORMOUS DESPAIR A REALITY!!

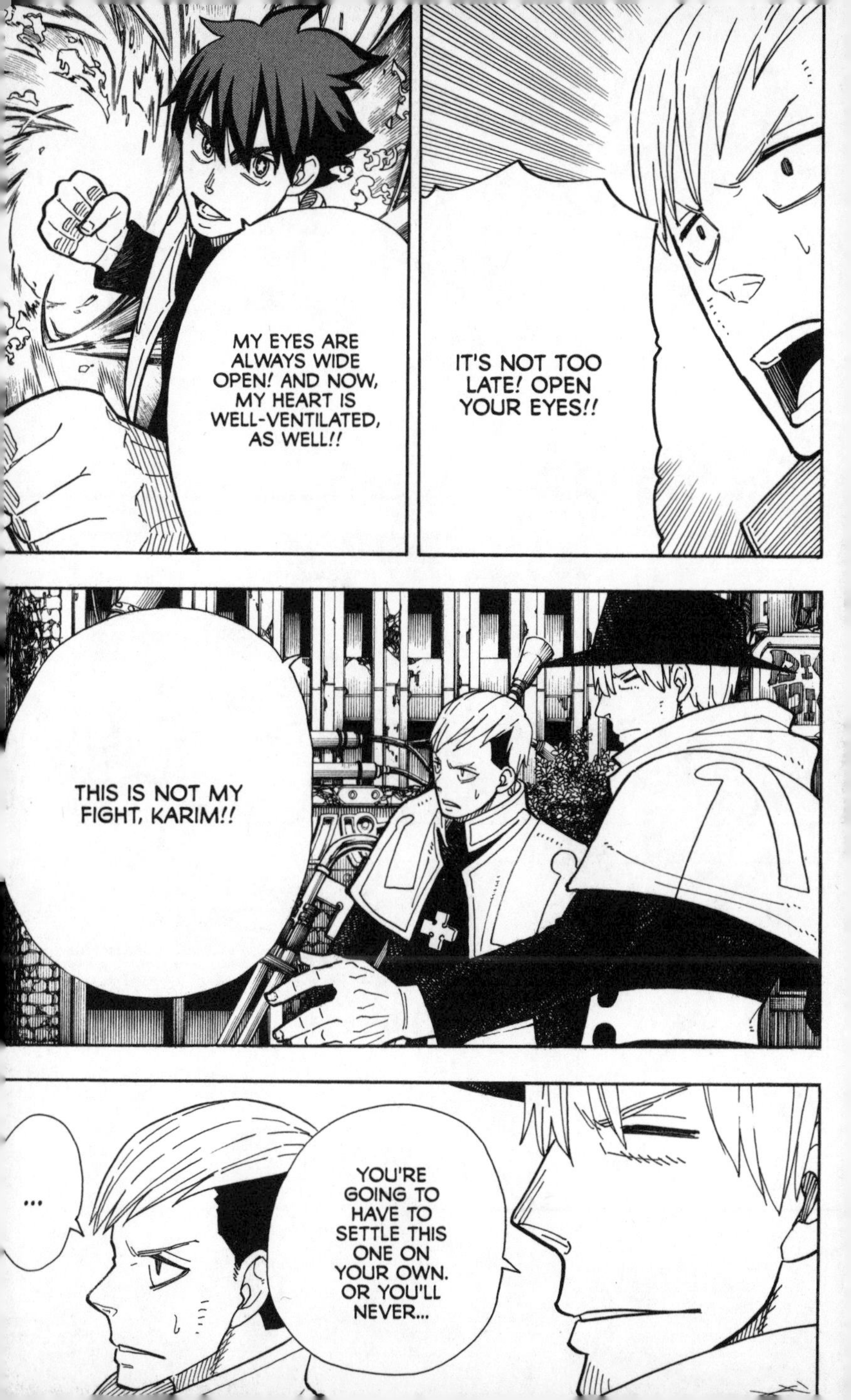
IT'S NOT TOO LATE! OPEN YOUR EYES!!
MY EYES ARE ALWAYS WIDE OPEN! AND NOW, MY HEART IS WELL-VENTILATED, AS WELL!!
THIS IS NOT MY FIGHT, KARIM!!
YOU'RE GOING TO HAVE TO SETTLE THIS ONE ON YOUR OWN. OR YOU'LL NEVER...
...

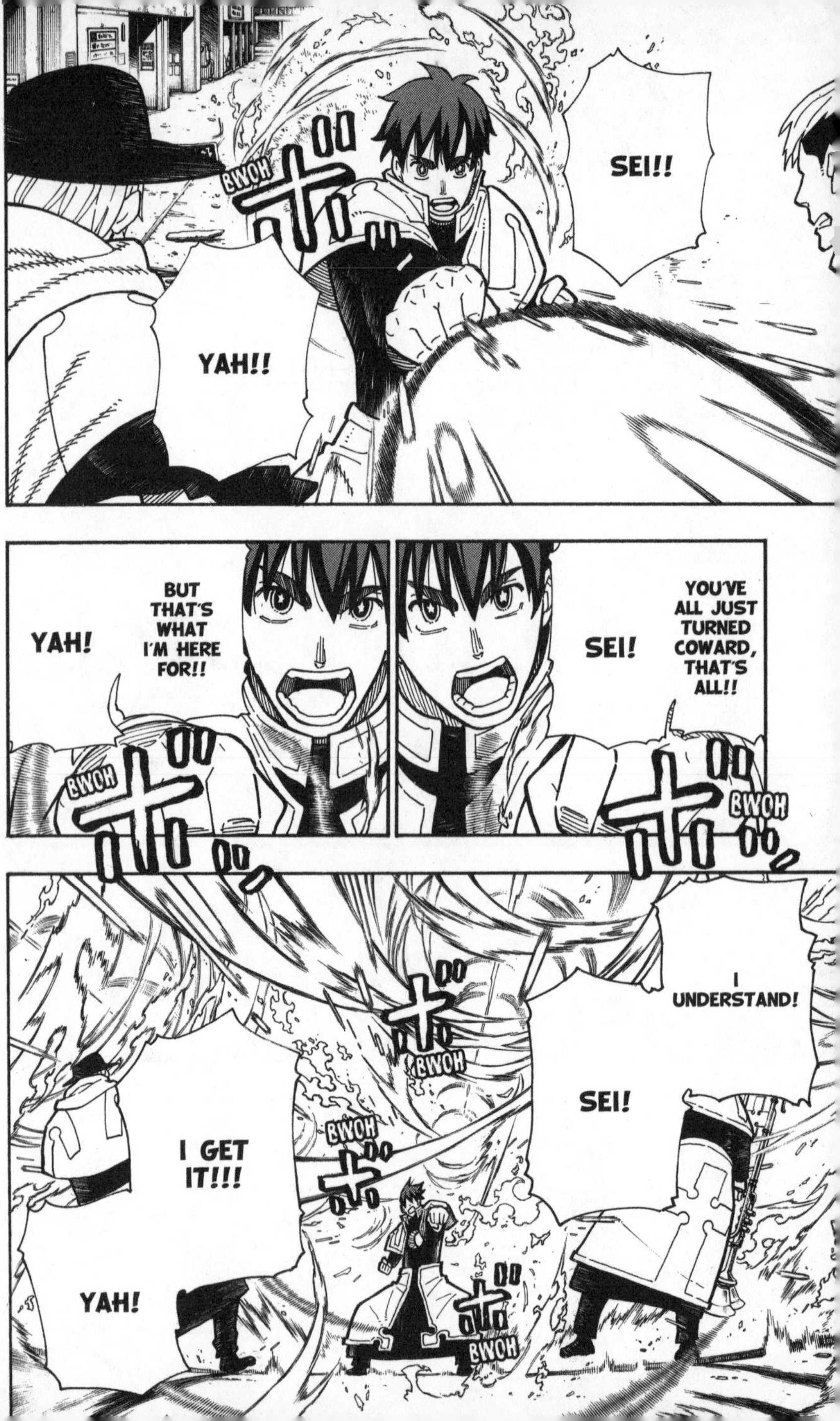
SEI!!
BWOH
YAH!!
YOU'VE ALL JUST TURNED COWARD, THAT'S ALL!!
SEI!
BWOH
BUT THAT'S WHAT I'M HERE FOR!!
YAH!
BWOH
I UNDERSTAND!
SEI!
BWOH
BWOH
BWOH
I GET IT!!!
YAH!

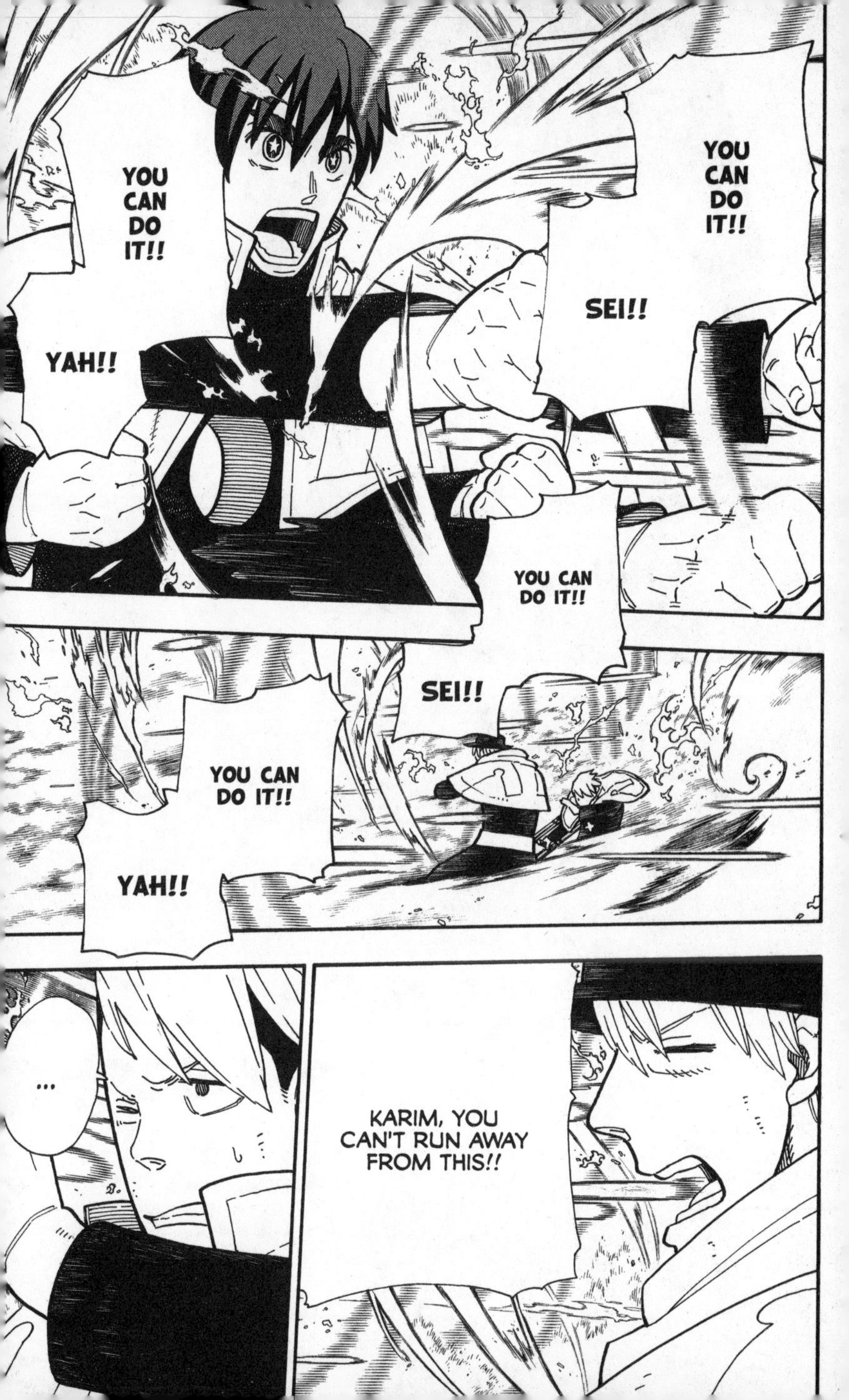
YOU CAN DO IT!!
SEI!!
YOU CAN DO IT!!
YAH!!
YOU CAN DO IT!!
SEI!!
YOU CAN DO IT!!
YAH!!
KARIM, YOU CAN'T RUN AWAY FROM THIS!!
...

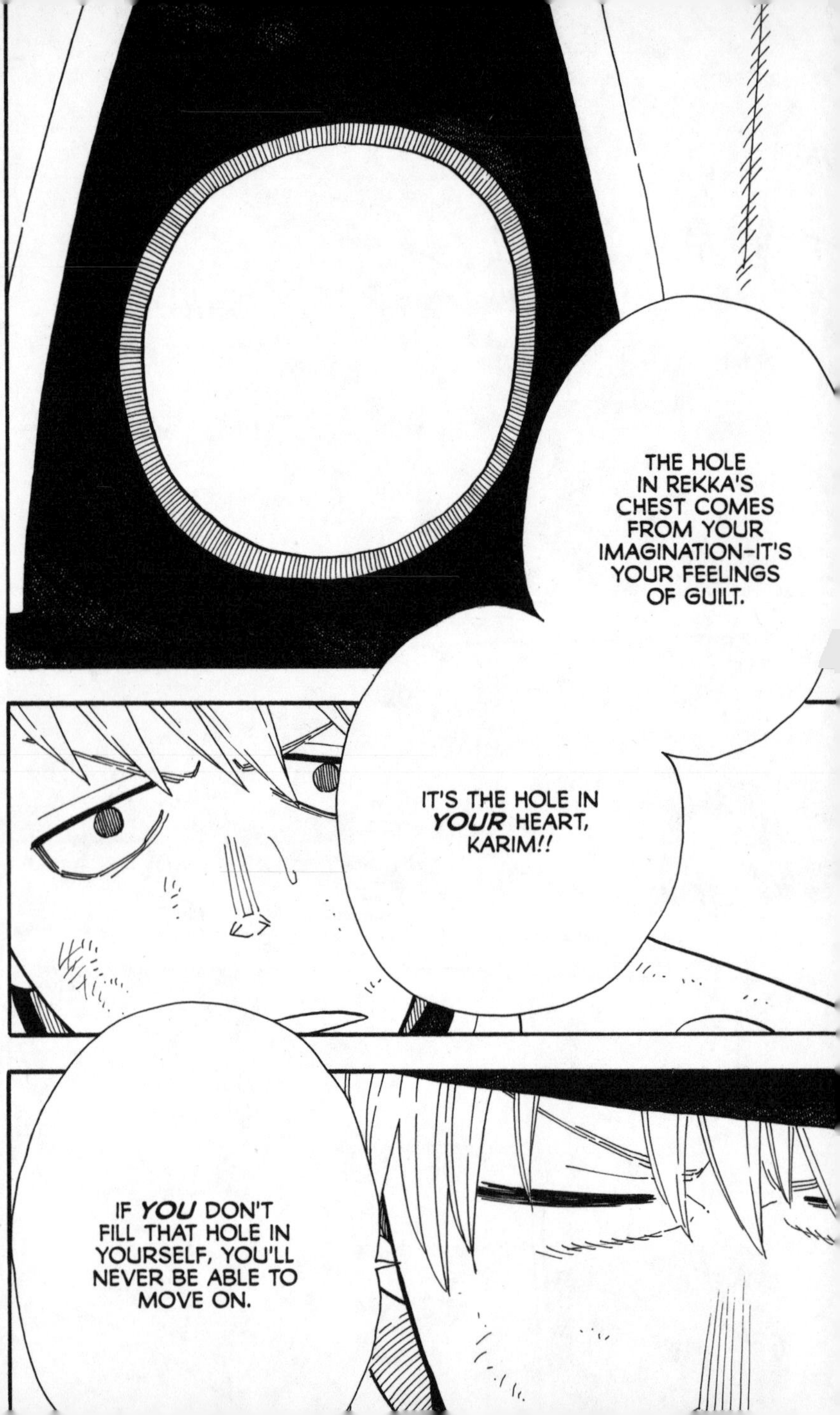
THE HOLE IN REKKA'S CHEST COMES FROM YOUR IMAGINATION–IT'S YOUR FEELINGS OF GUILT.
IT'S THE HOLE IN *YOUR* HEART, KARIM!!
IF *YOU* DON'T FILL THAT HOLE IN YOURSELF, YOU'LL NEVER BE ABLE TO MOVE ON.

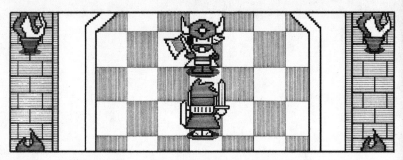

VULCAN, IS IT REALLY OKAY FOR ME TO ATTACK HIM...?
IF YOU DON'T BEAT THIS GUY, YOU CAN'T MOVE ON.
THIS PART OF THE GAME IS DESIGNED TO HELP THE HERO POWER UP.
YOUR ONLY CHOICE IS TO GET THROUGH IT!!
BUT WE... WE'RE BEST FRIENDS...

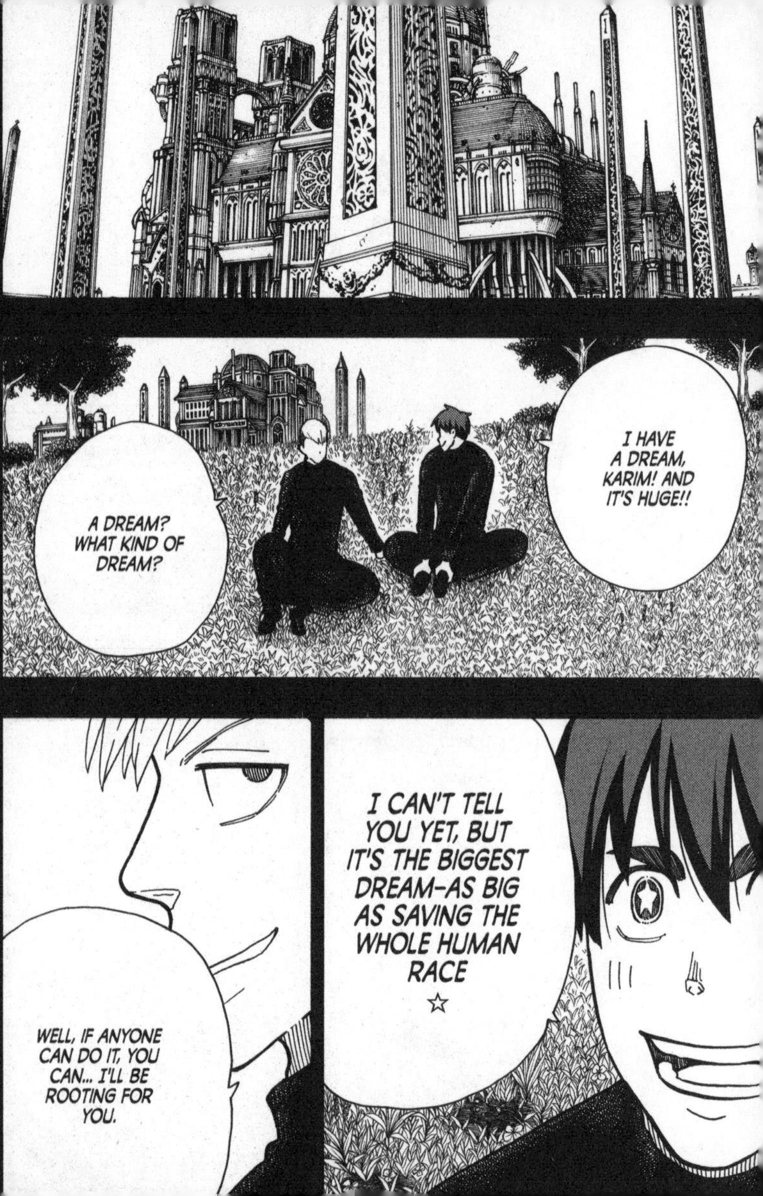
I HAVE A DREAM, KARIM! AND IT'S HUGE!!
A DREAM? WHAT KIND OF DREAM?
I CAN'T TELL YOU YET, BUT IT'S THE BIGGEST DREAM—AS BIG AS SAVING THE WHOLE HUMAN RACE ☆
WELL, IF ANYONE CAN DO IT, YOU CAN... I'LL BE ROOTING FOR YOU.

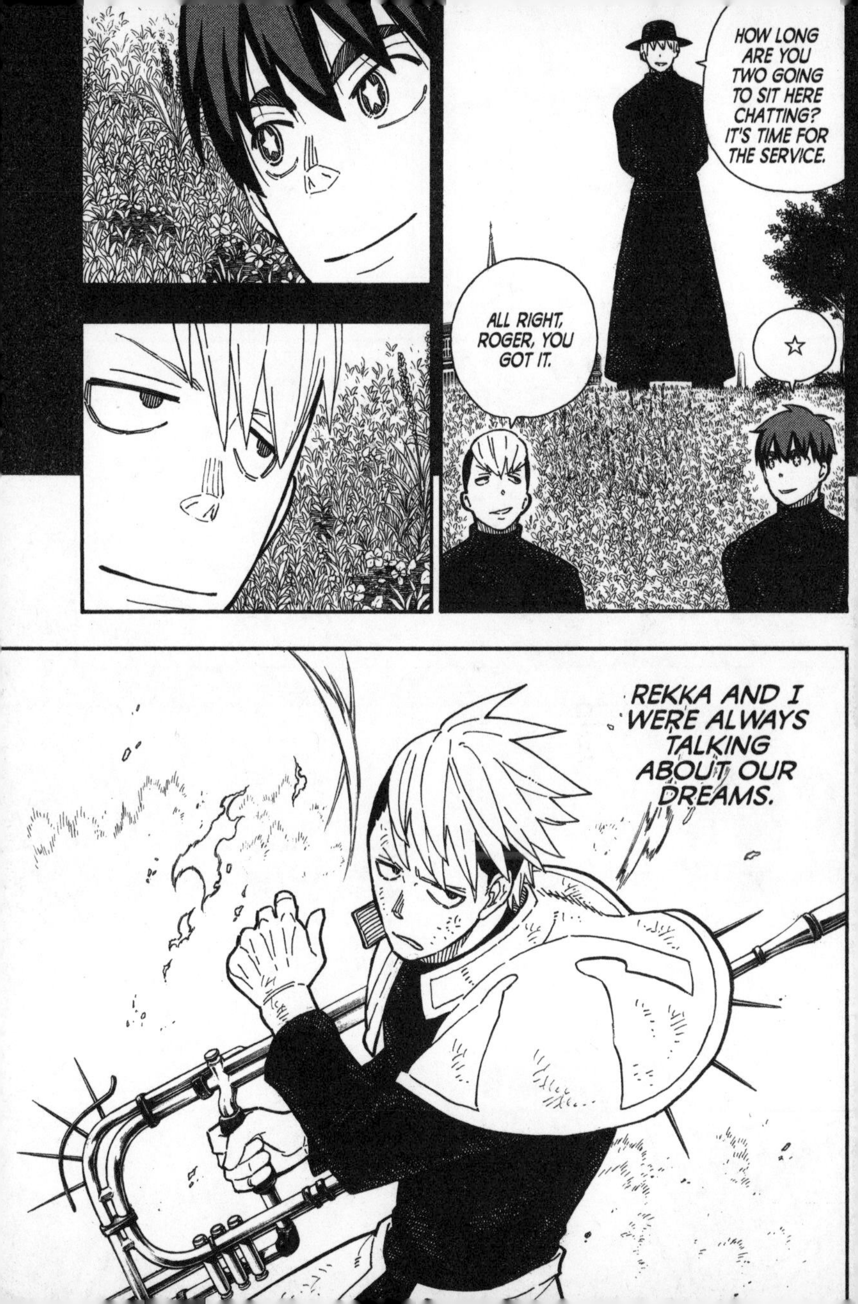
HOW LONG ARE YOU TWO GOING TO SIT HERE CHATTING? IT'S TIME FOR THE SERVICE.
☆
ALL RIGHT, ROGER, YOU GOT IT.
REKKA AND I WERE ALWAYS TALKING ABOUT OUR DREAMS.

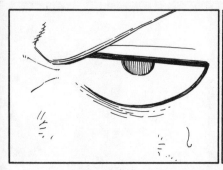

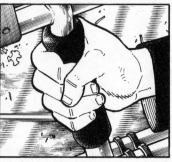

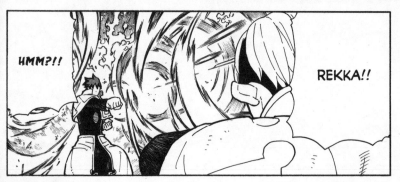

REKKA!!
HMM?!!
I WANTED TO HELP YOU WITH YOUR DREAM, WITH ALL MY HEART AND EVERYTHING IN MY POWER!!
THANK YOU!! KARIM!! YOU ALWAYS WERE MY BEST FRIEND ☆

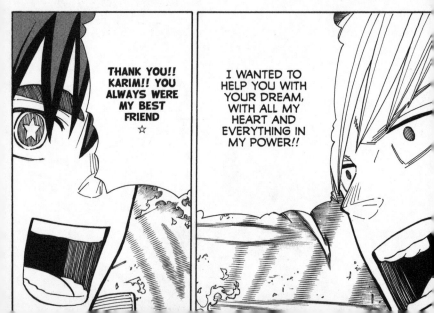

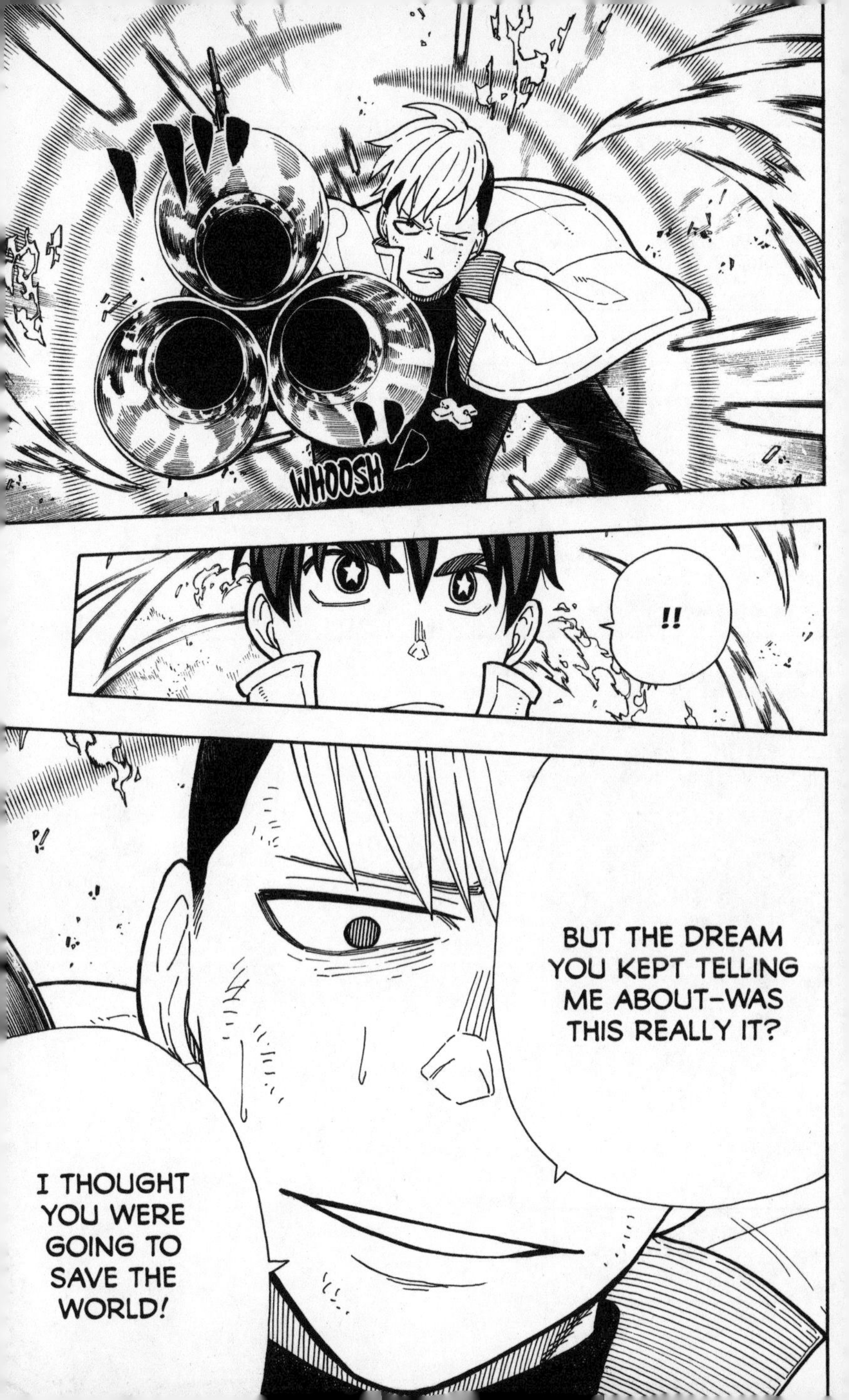
WHOOSH
!!
BUT THE DREAM YOU KEPT TELLING ME ABOUT—WAS THIS REALLY IT?
I THOUGHT YOU WERE GOING TO SAVE THE WORLD!

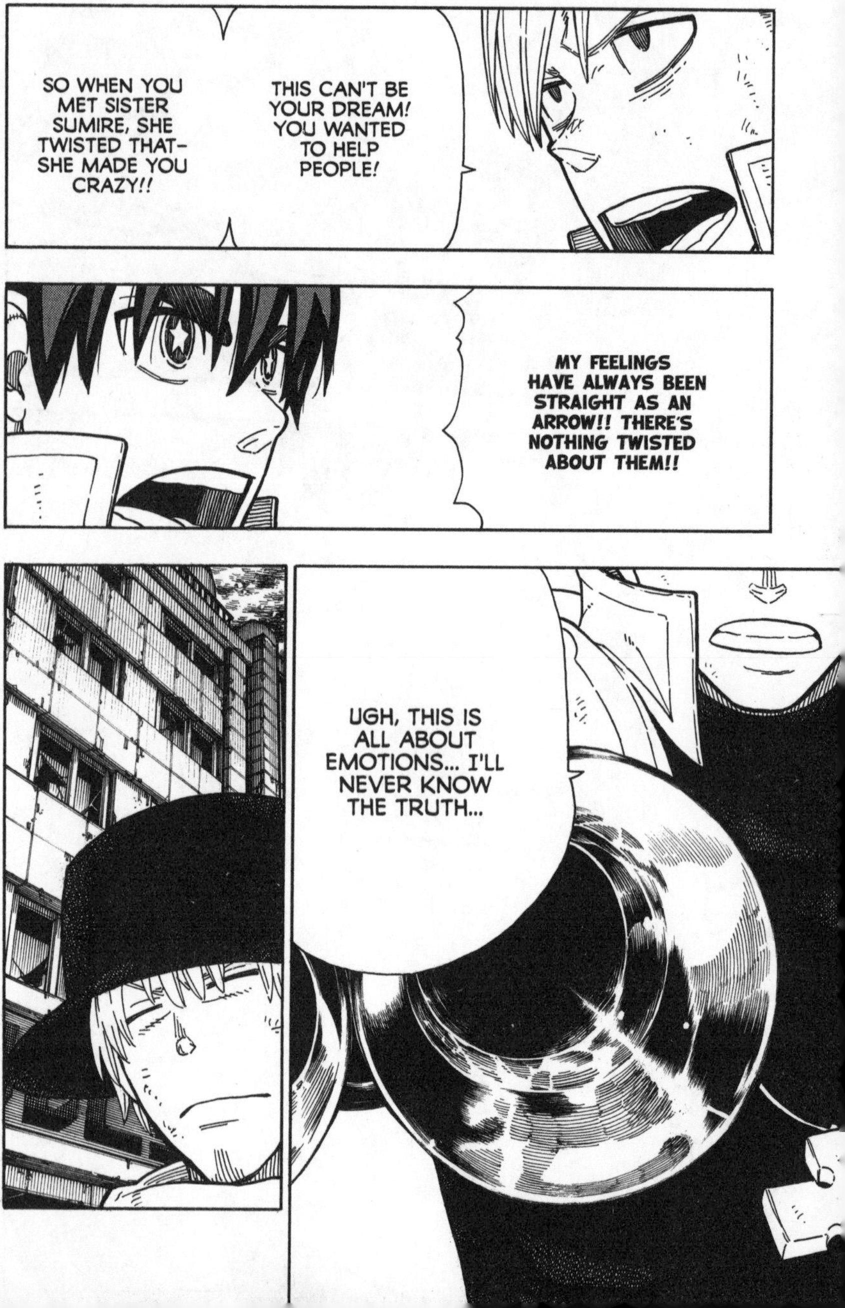
THIS CAN'T BE YOUR DREAM! YOU WANTED TO HELP PEOPLE!
SO WHEN YOU MET SISTER SUMIRE, SHE TWISTED THAT-SHE MADE YOU CRAZY!!
MY FEELINGS HAVE ALWAYS BEEN STRAIGHT AS AN ARROW!! THERE'S NOTHING TWISTED ABOUT THEM!!
UGH, THIS IS ALL ABOUT EMOTIONS... I'LL NEVER KNOW THE TRUTH...

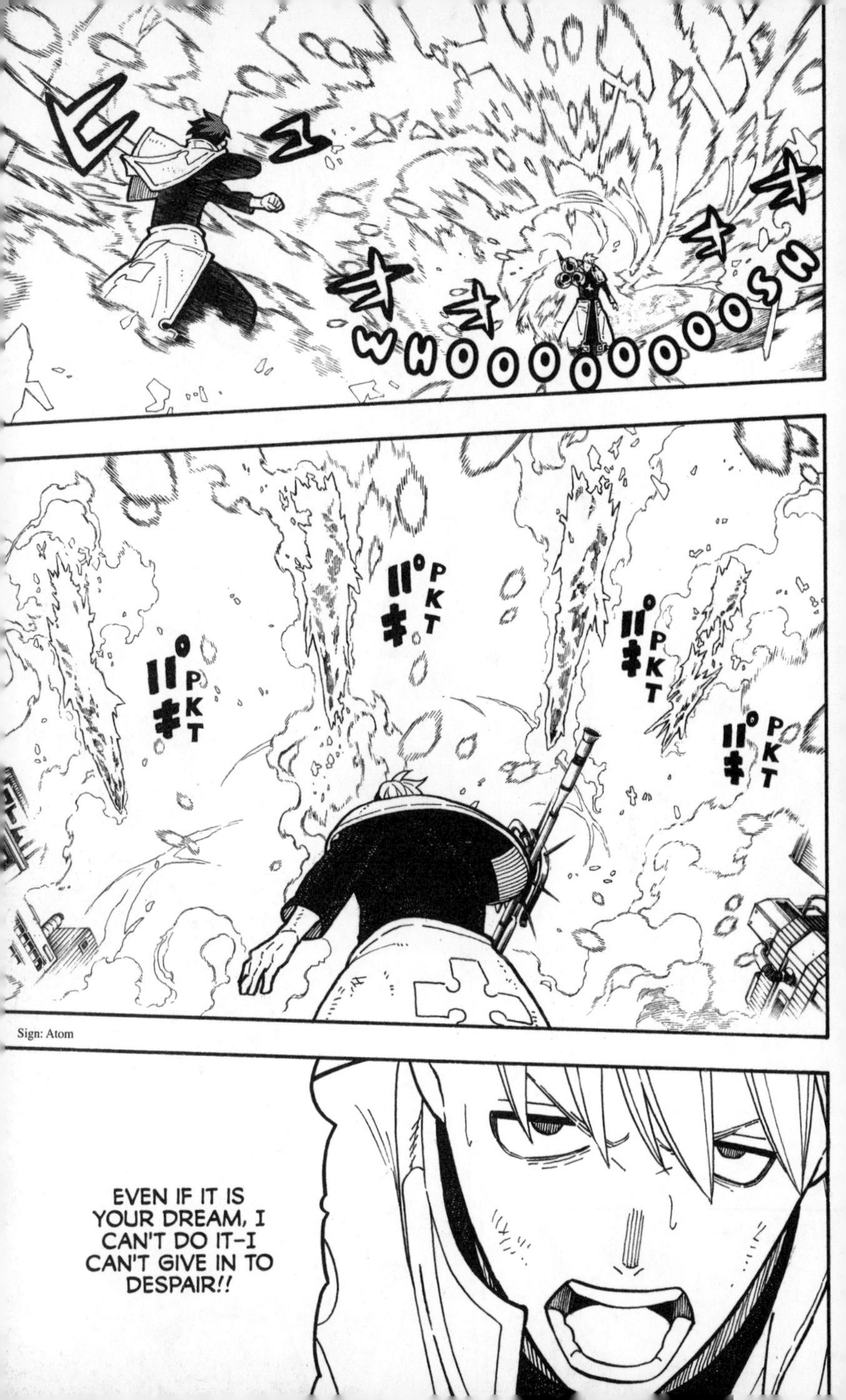
WHOOOOOOOOSH
PKT
PKT
PKT
PKT
Sign: Atom
EVEN IF IT IS YOUR DREAM, I CAN'T DO IT—I CAN'T GIVE IN TO DESPAIR!!

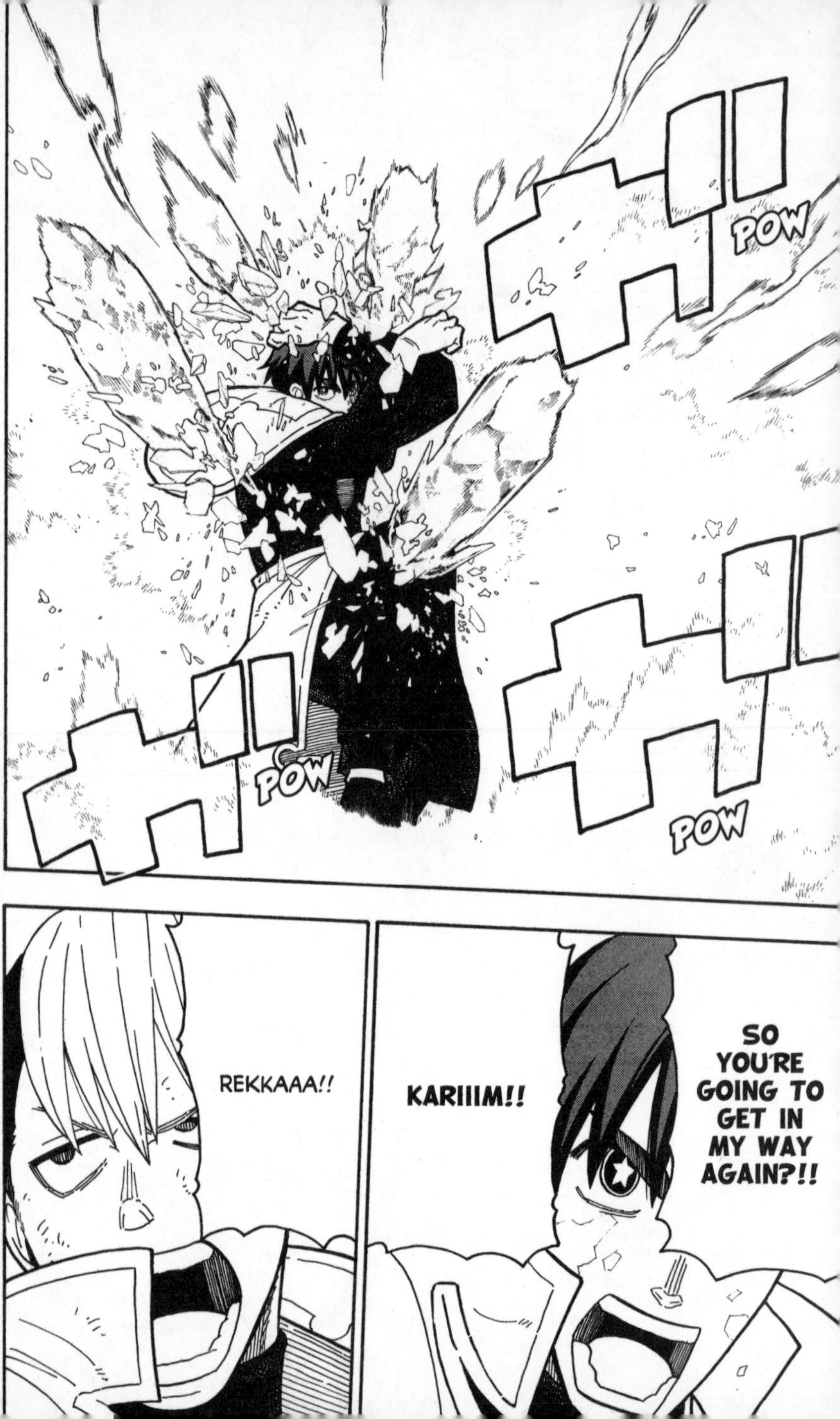
POW
POW
POW
SO YOU'RE GOING TO GET IN MY WAY AGAIN?!!
KARIIIM!!
REKKAAA!!

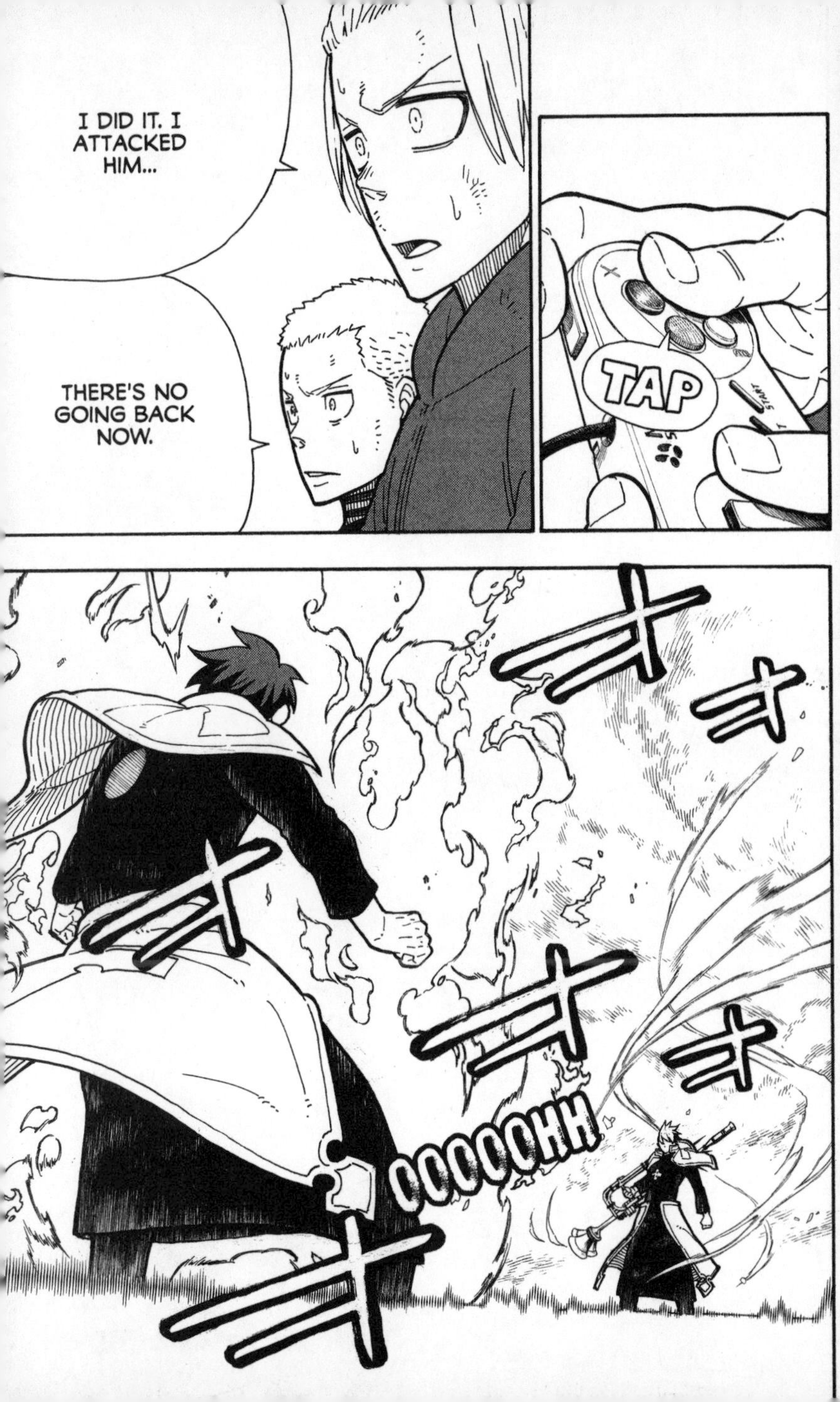
TAP
I DID IT. I ATTACKED HIM...
THERE'S NO GOING BACK NOW.
OOOOOOHH

FIRE FORCE

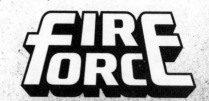

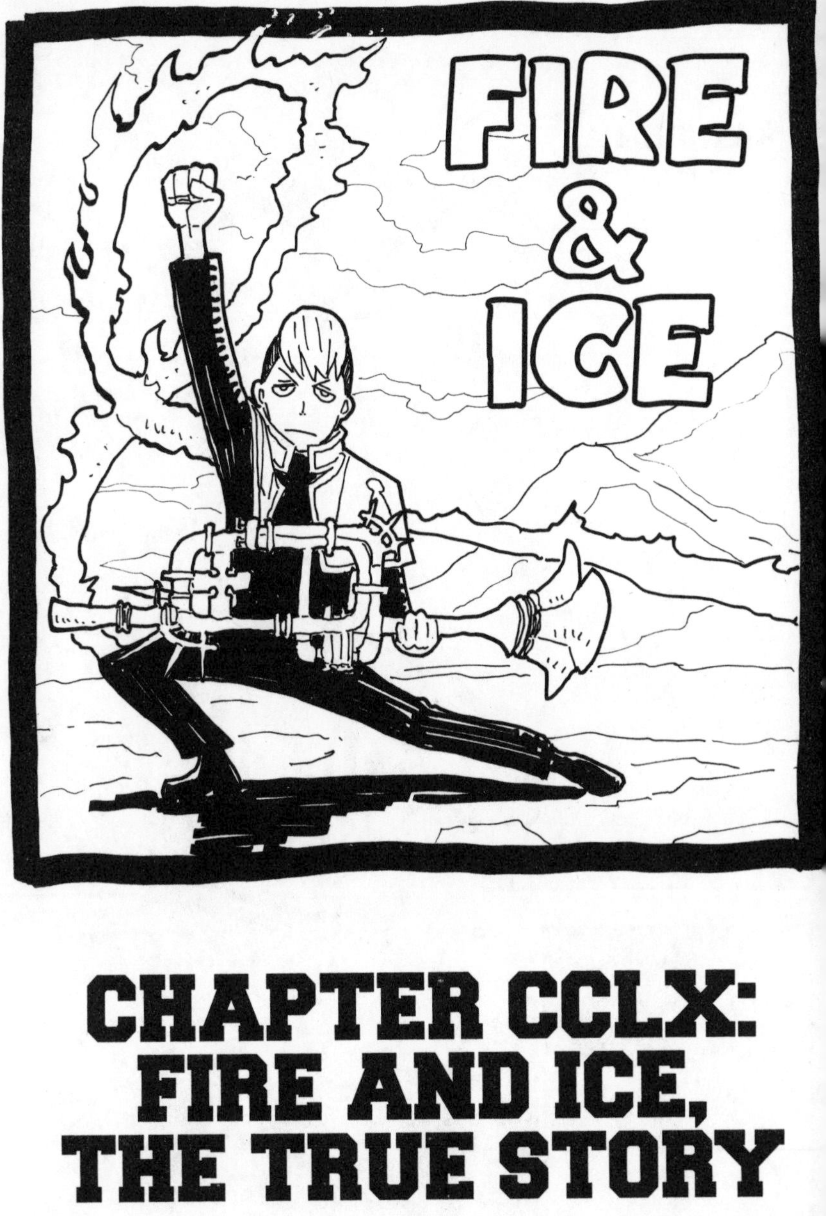
FIRE
&
ICE

CHAPTER CCLX: FIRE AND ICE, THE TRUE STORY

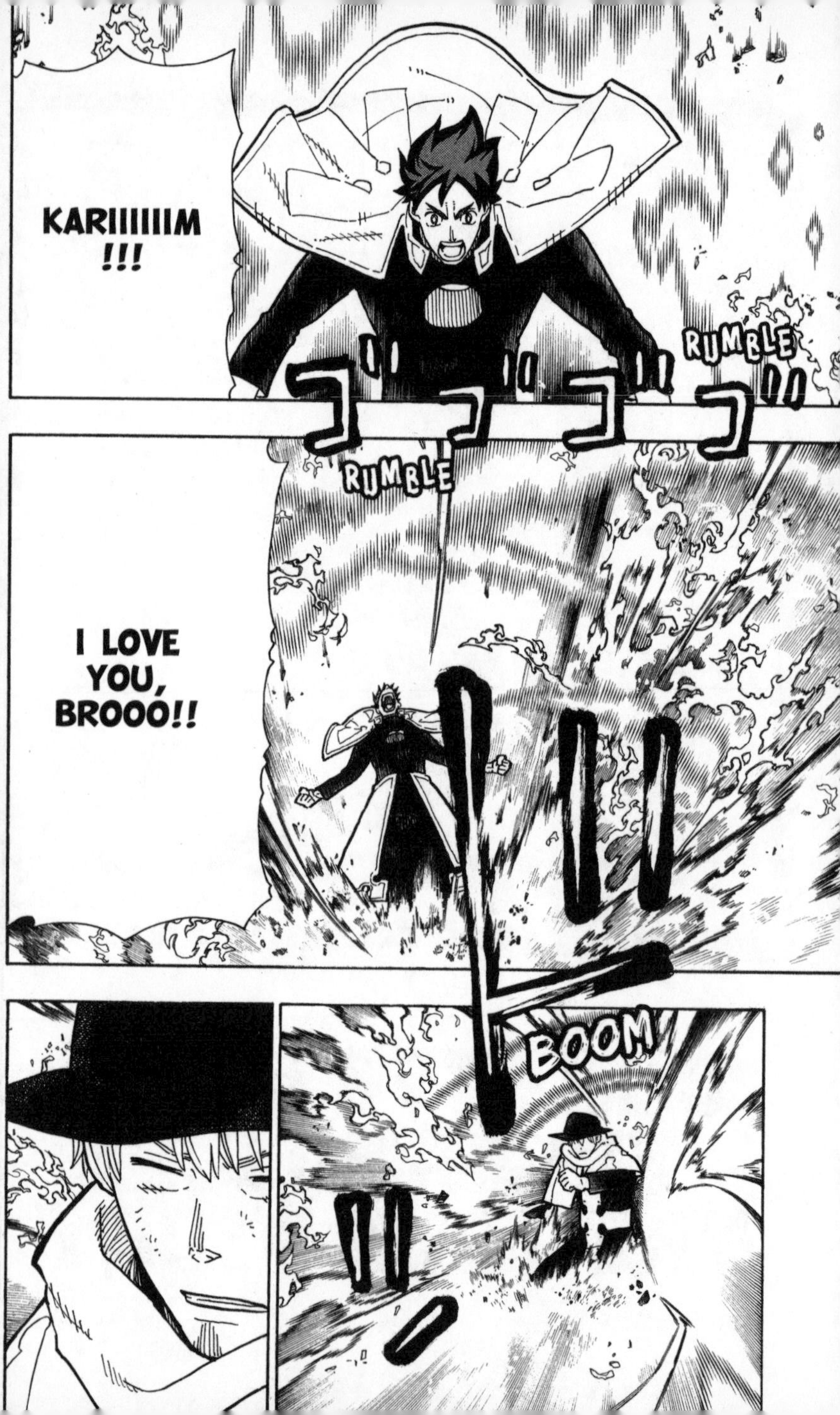
KARIIIIIIM
!!!
RUMBLE
ゴゴゴゴ
RUMBLE
I LOVE YOU, BROOÓ!!
BOOM

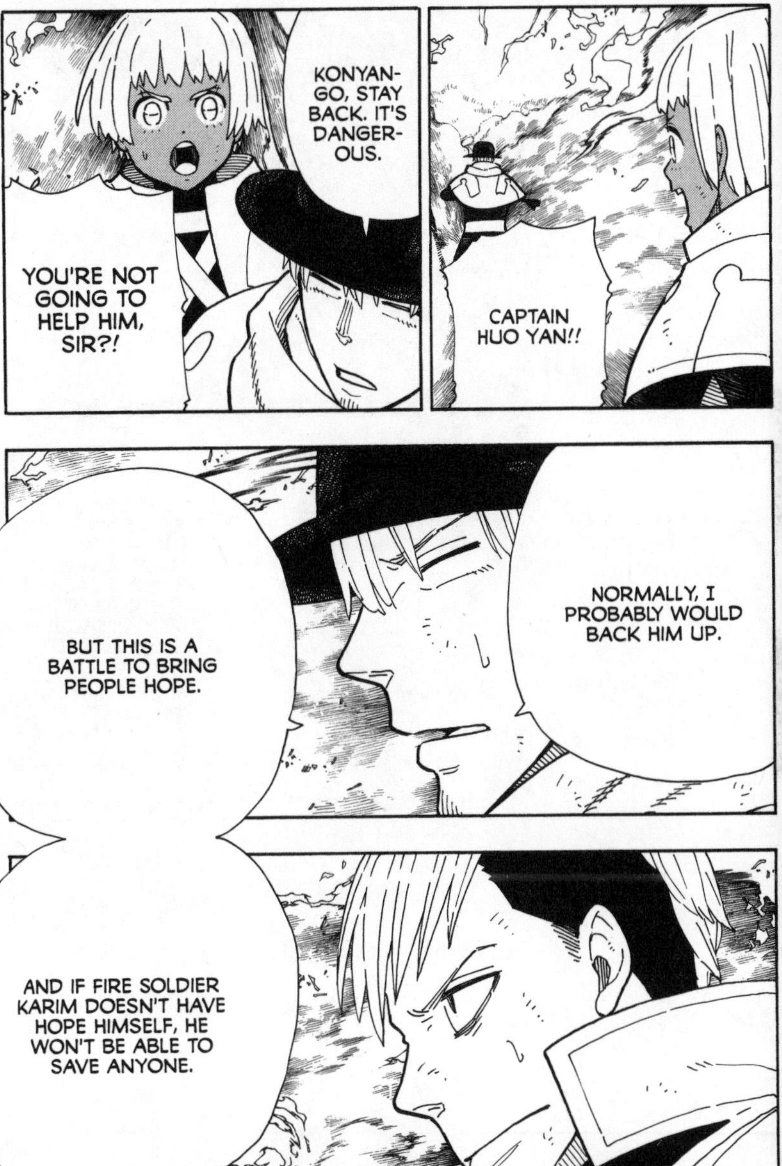
CAPTAIN HUO YAN!!
KONYAN-GO, STAY BACK. IT'S DANGER-OUS.
YOU'RE NOT GOING TO HELP HIM, SIR?!
NORMALLY, I PROBABLY WOULD BACK HIM UP.
BUT THIS IS A BATTLE TO BRING PEOPLE HOPE.
AND IF FIRE SOLDIER KARIM DOESN'T HAVE HOPE HIMSELF, HE WON'T BE ABLE TO SAVE ANYONE.

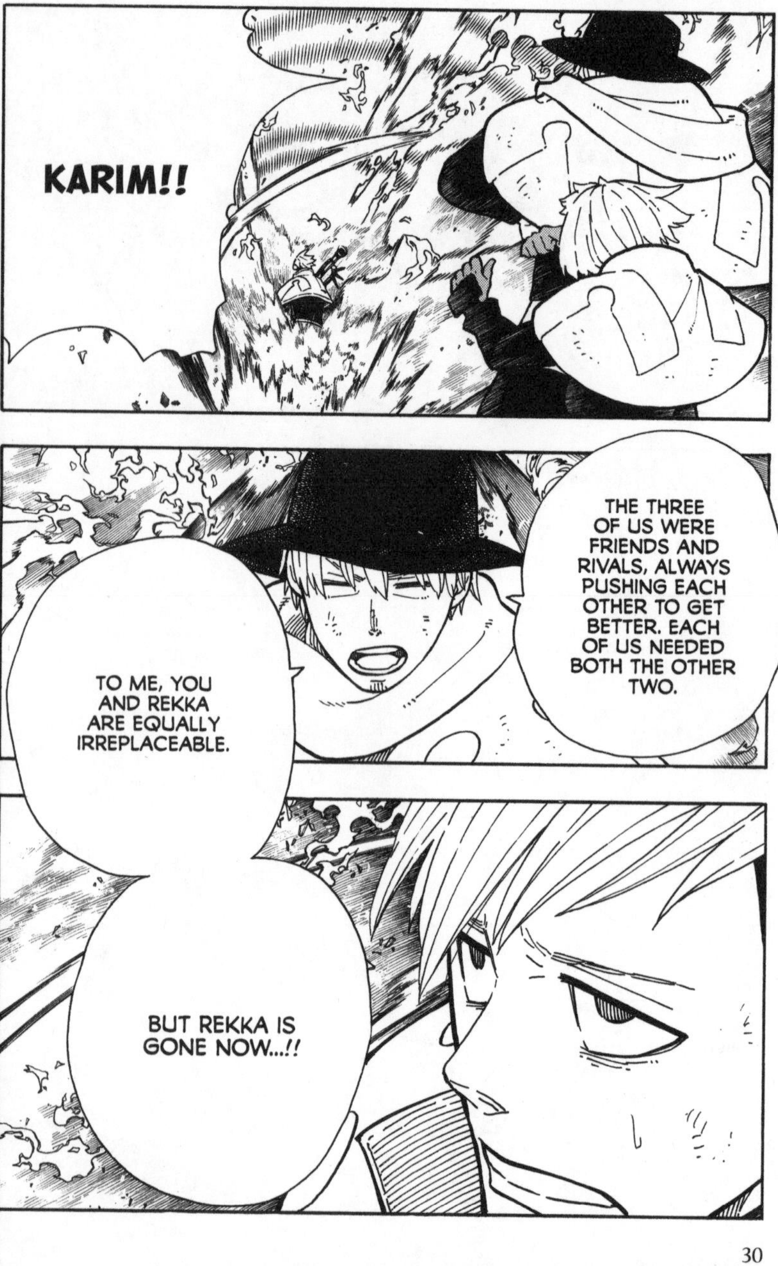
KARIM!!
THE THREE OF US WERE FRIENDS AND RIVALS, ALWAYS PUSHING EACH OTHER TO GET BETTER. EACH OF US NEEDED BOTH THE OTHER TWO.
TO ME, YOU AND REKKA ARE EQUALLY IRREPLACEABLE.
BUT REKKA IS GONE NOW...!!

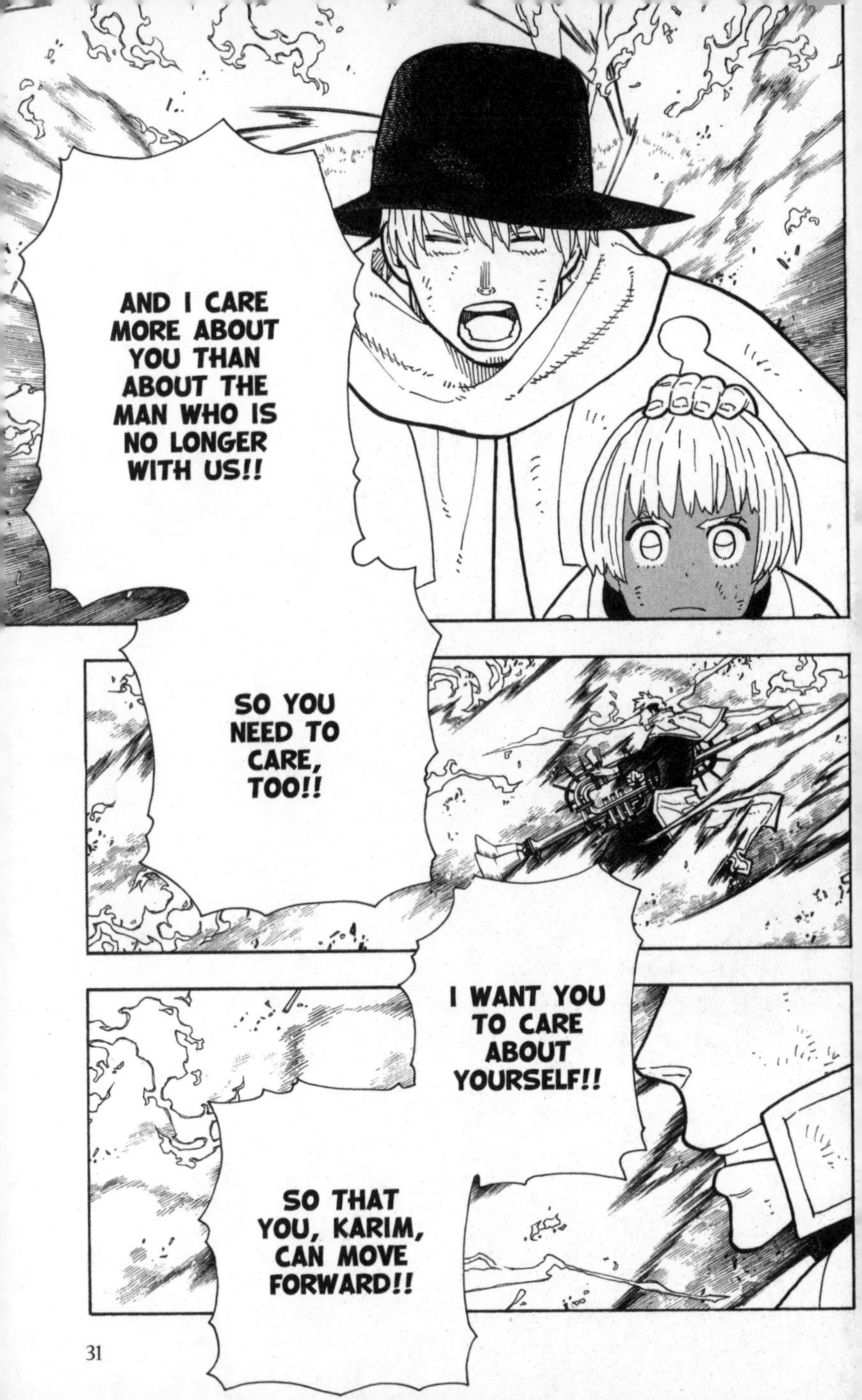
AND I CARE MORE ABOUT YOU THAN ABOUT THE MAN WHO IS NO LONGER WITH US!!
SO YOU NEED TO CARE, TOO!!
I WANT YOU TO CARE ABOUT YOURSELF!!
SO THAT YOU, KARIM, CAN MOVE FORWARD!!

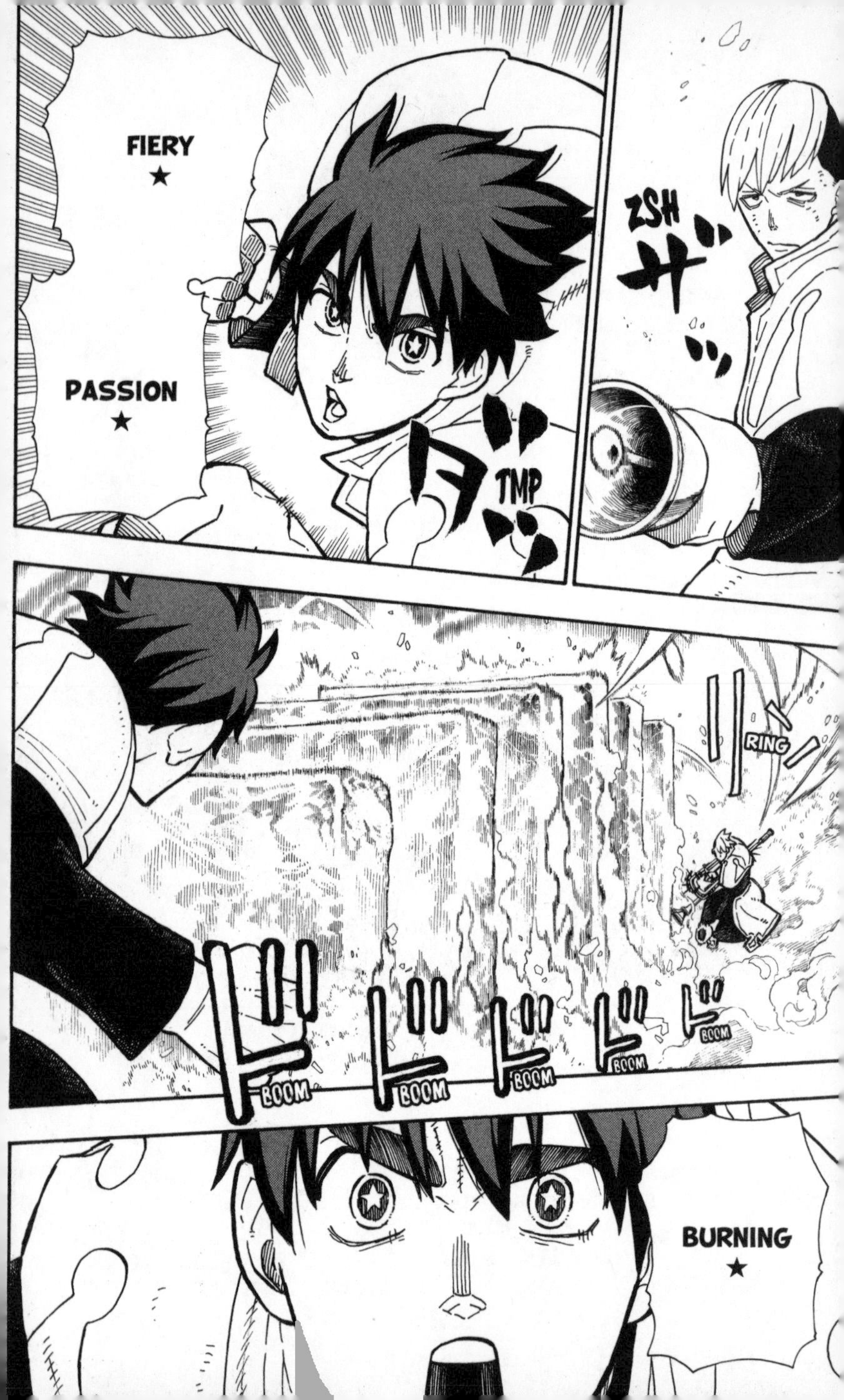
ZSH
FIERY ★
PASSION ★
TMP
RING
BOOM
BOOM
BOOM
BOOM
BOOM
BURNING ★

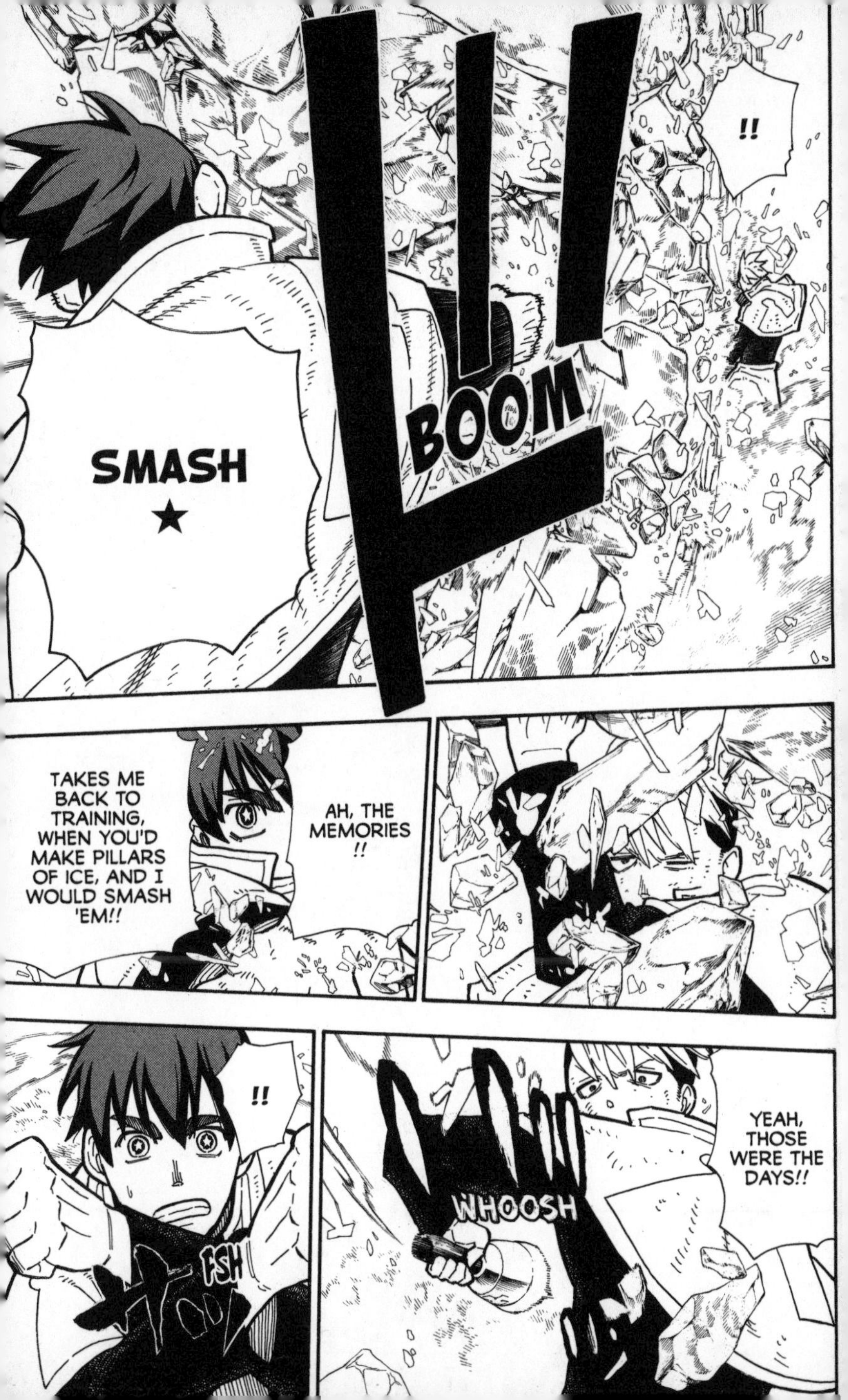
!!
BOOM
SMASH ★
AH, THE MEMORIES !!
TAKES ME BACK TO TRAINING, WHEN YOU'D MAKE PILLARS OF ICE, AND I WOULD SMASH 'EM!!
YEAH, THOSE WERE THE DAYS!!
WHOOSH
!!
FSH

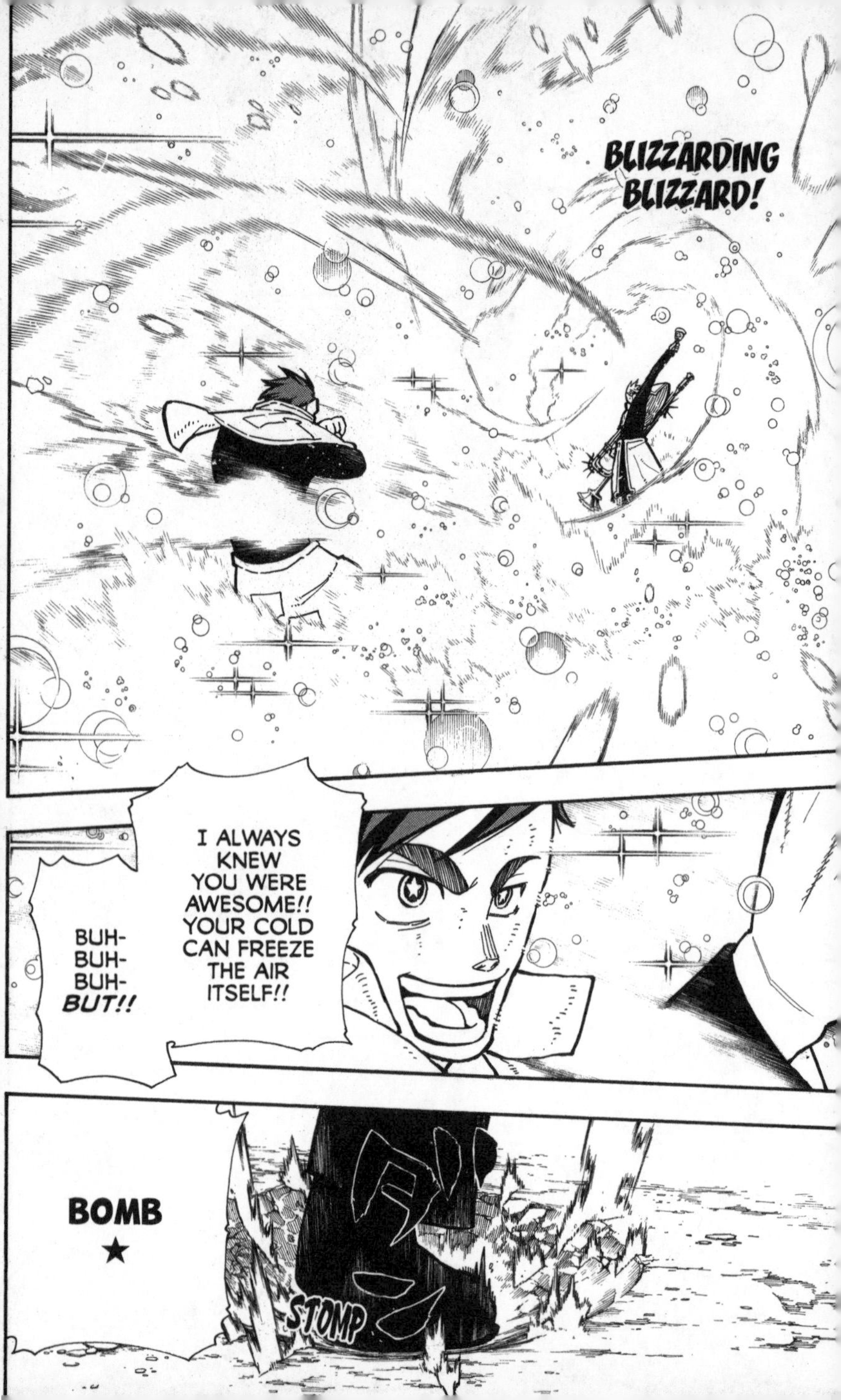
BLIZZARDING BLIZZARD!
I ALWAYS KNEW YOU WERE AWESOME!! YOUR COLD CAN FREEZE THE AIR ITSELF!!
BUH-BUH-BUH-*BUT!!*
BOMB ★
STOMP

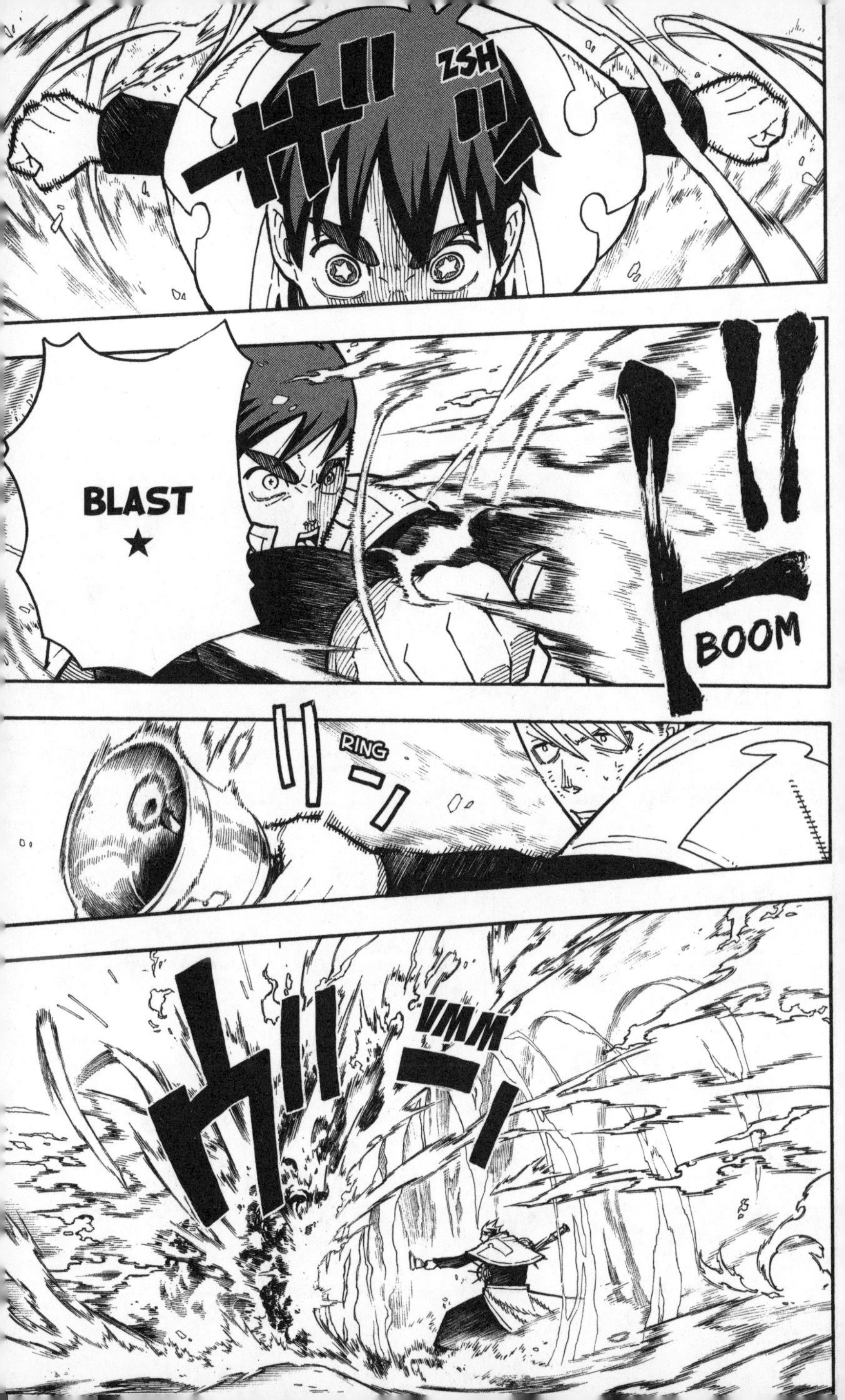
ZSH
BOOM
BLAST ★
RING
VMM

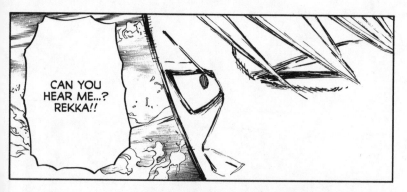

CAN YOU HEAR ME...? REKKA!!
I HEAR YOU, KARIM!! I WOULD NEVER LET YOUR WORDS ESCAPE ME!!
WE WERE EXACT OPPOSITES IN EVERYTHING...
WHENEVER WE BUTTED HEADS, OR WE TALKED ABOUT OUR DREAMS, IT WAS ALWAYS EXACTLY HEAD-ON.
YEAH, THAT'S RIGHT!
WHATEVER WE DID, WE WENT AT IT WITH EVERYTHING WE HAD!

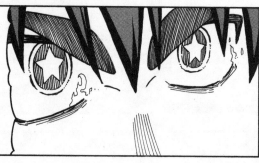

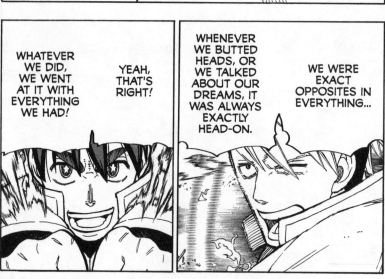

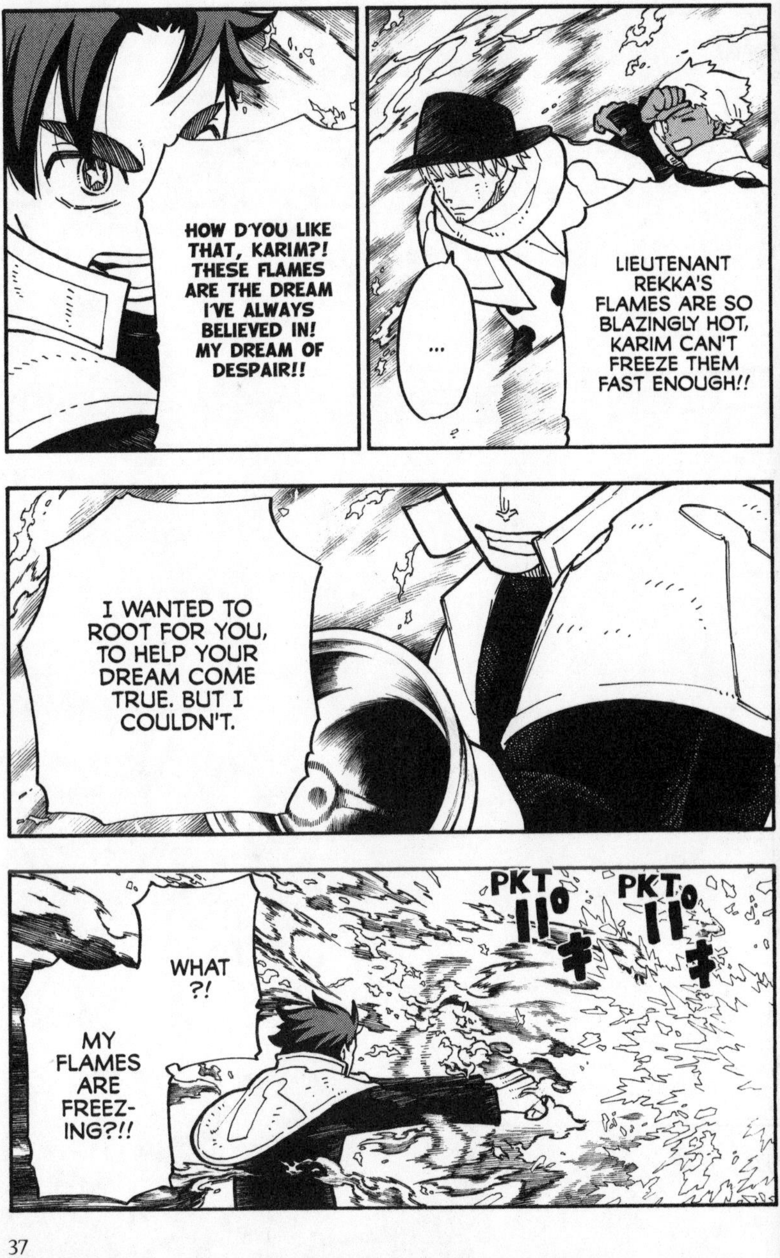
LIEUTENANT REKKA'S FLAMES ARE SO BLAZINGLY HOT, KARIM CAN'T FREEZE THEM FAST ENOUGH!!
...
HOW D'YOU LIKE THAT, KARIM?! THESE FLAMES ARE THE DREAM I'VE ALWAYS BELIEVED IN! MY DREAM OF DESPAIR!!
I WANTED TO ROOT FOR YOU, TO HELP YOUR DREAM COME TRUE. BUT I COULDN'T.
PKT
PKT
WHAT?!
MY FLAMES ARE FREEZ-ING?!!

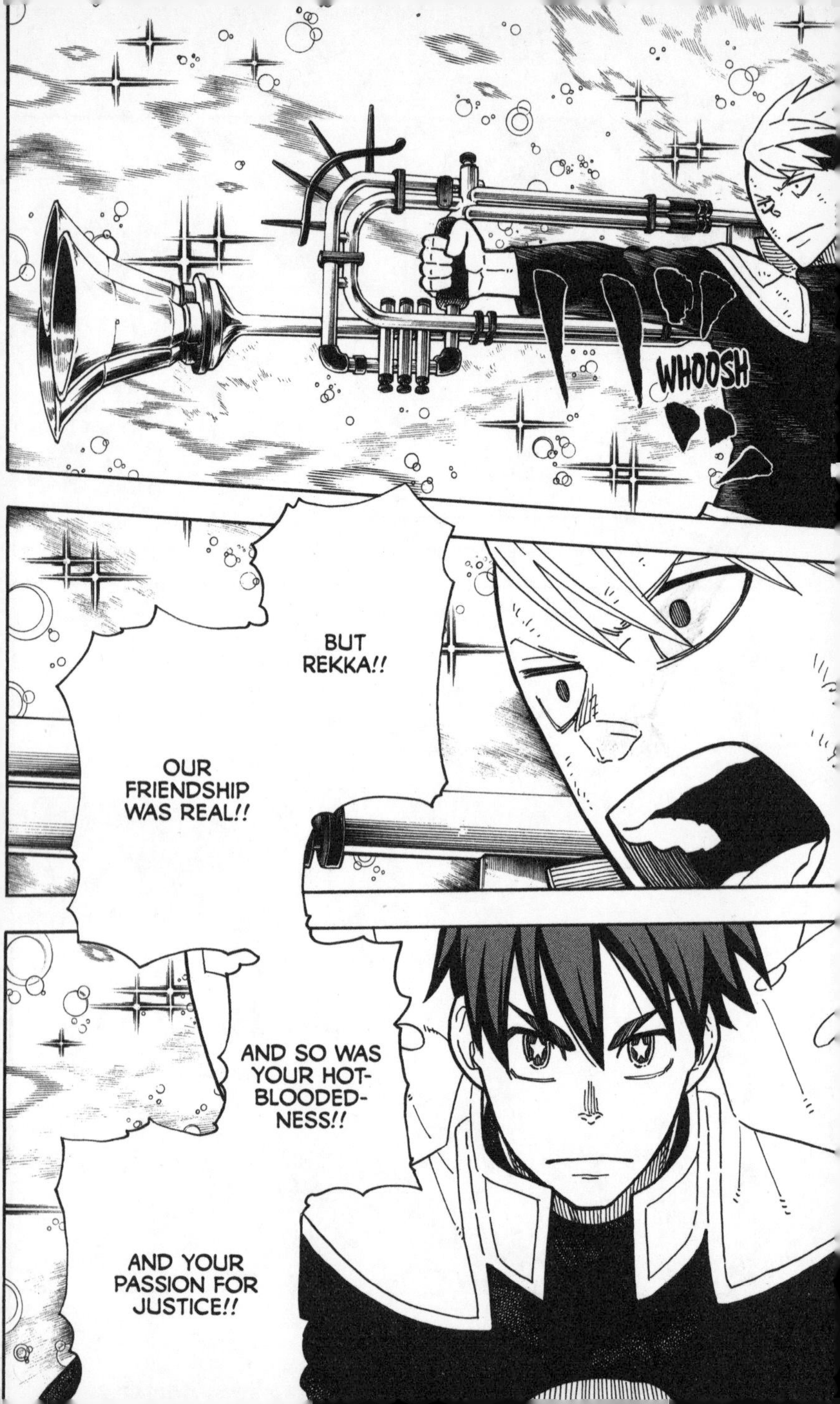
WHOOSH
BUT REKKA!!
OUR FRIENDSHIP WAS REAL!!
AND SO WAS YOUR HOT-BLOODED-NESS!!
AND YOUR PASSION FOR JUSTICE!!

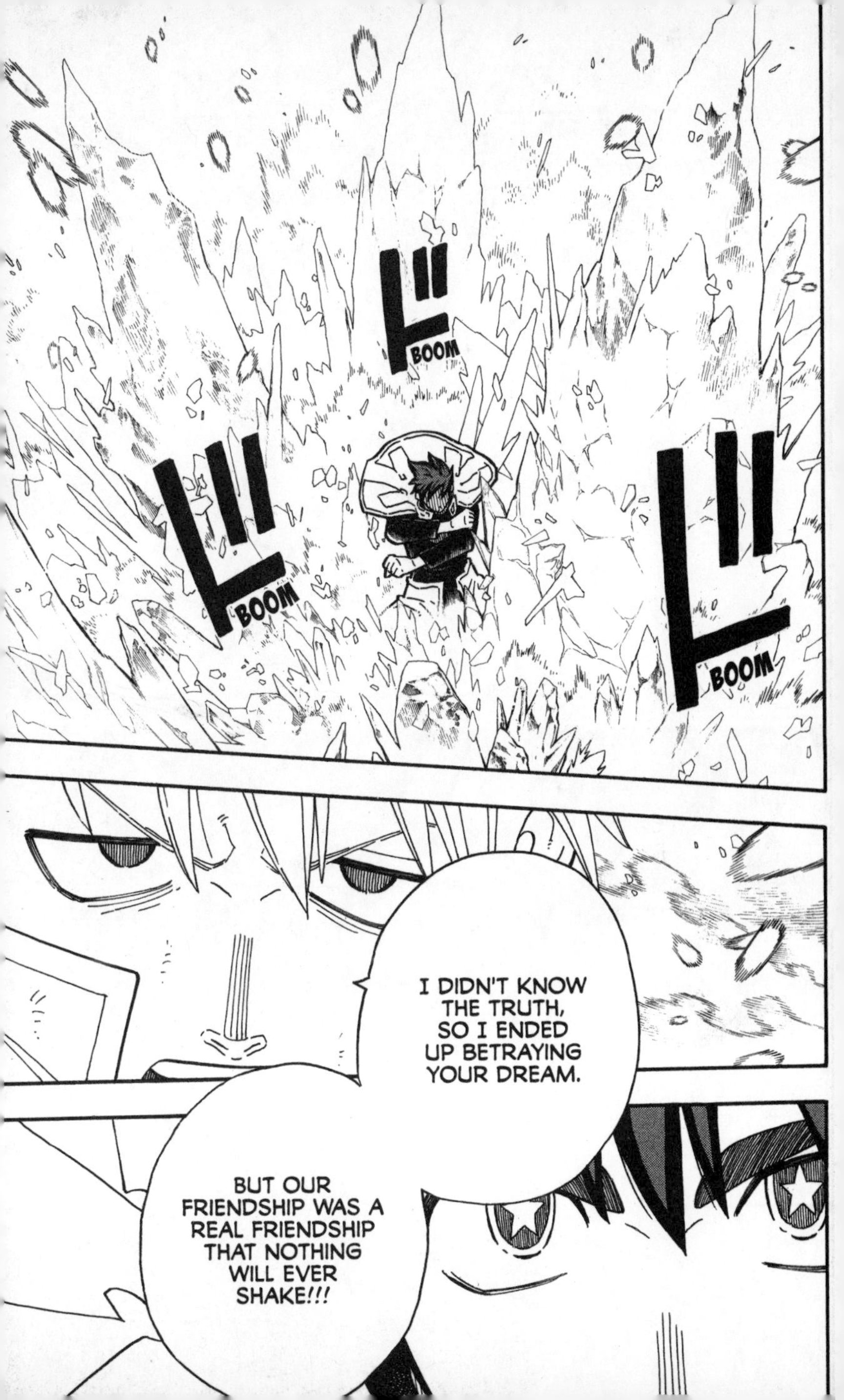
BOOM
BOOM
BOOM
I DIDN'T KNOW THE TRUTH, SO I ENDED UP BETRAYING YOUR DREAM.
BUT OUR FRIENDSHIP WAS A REAL FRIENDSHIP THAT NOTHING WILL EVER SHAKE!!!

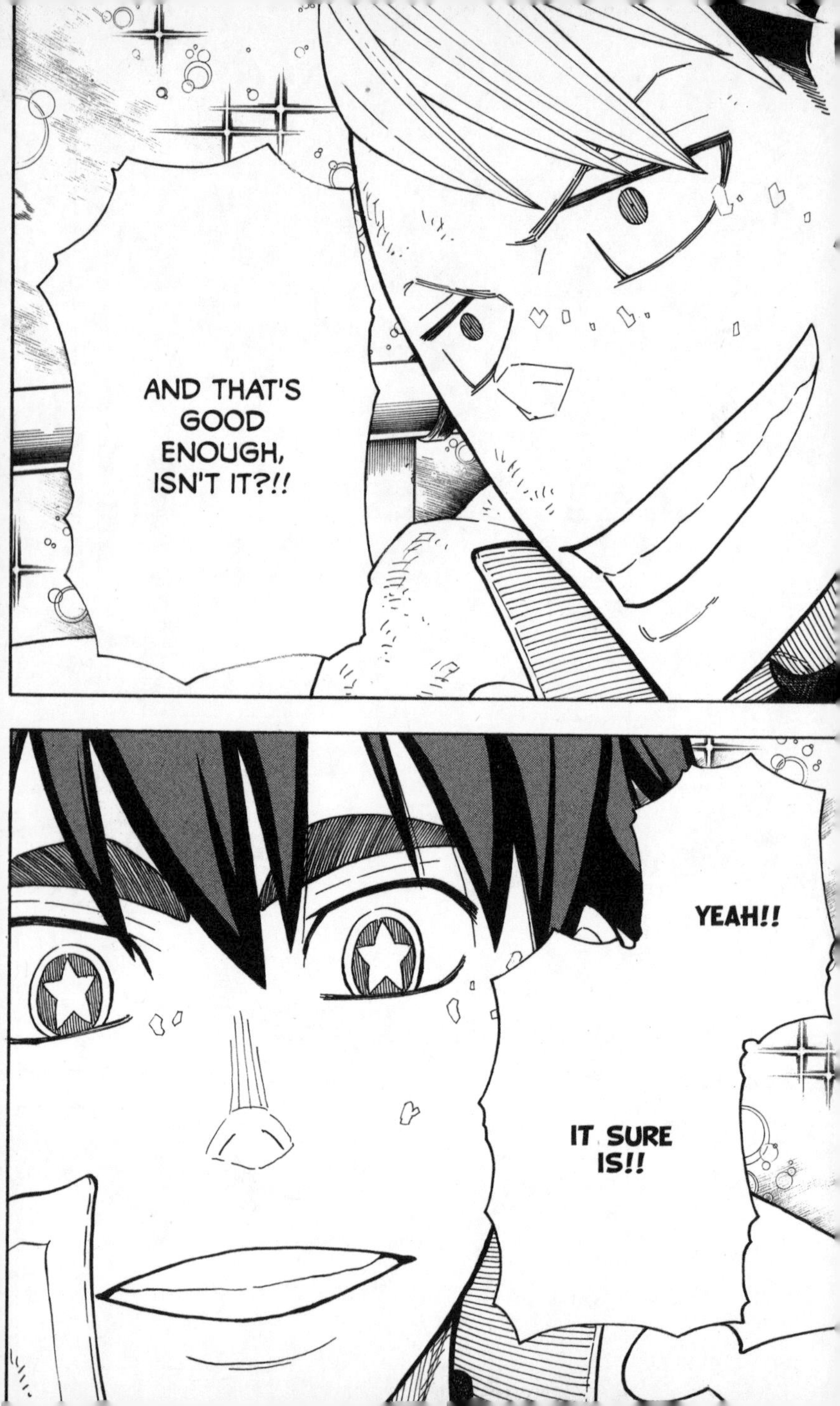
AND THAT'S GOOD ENOUGH, ISN'T IT?!!
YEAH!!
IT SURE IS!!

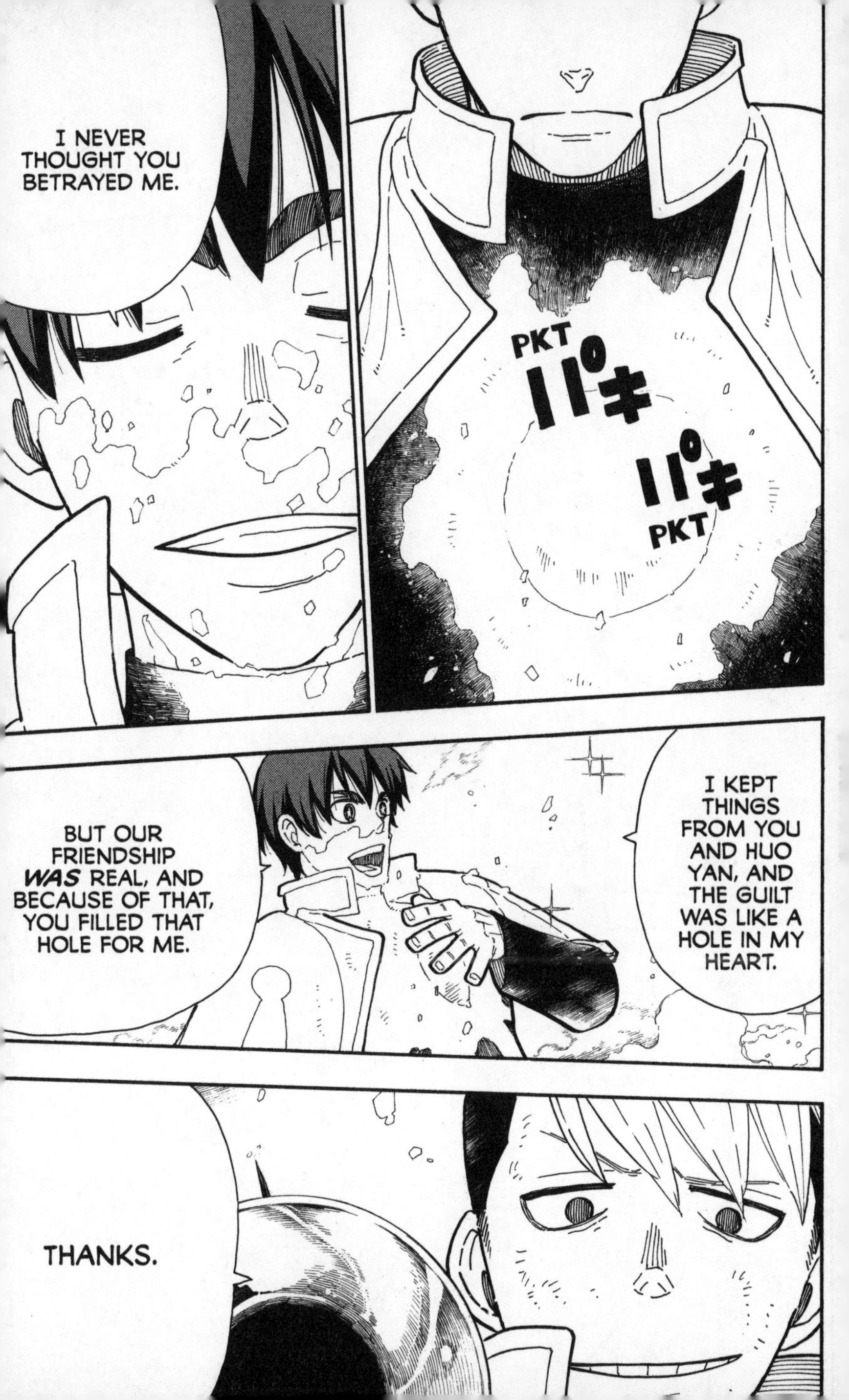
PKT
パキ
パキ
PKT
I NEVER THOUGHT YOU BETRAYED ME.
I KEPT THINGS FROM YOU AND HUO YAN, AND THE GUILT WAS LIKE A HOLE IN MY HEART.
BUT OUR FRIENDSHIP *WAS* REAL, AND BECAUSE OF THAT, YOU FILLED THAT HOLE FOR ME.
THANKS.

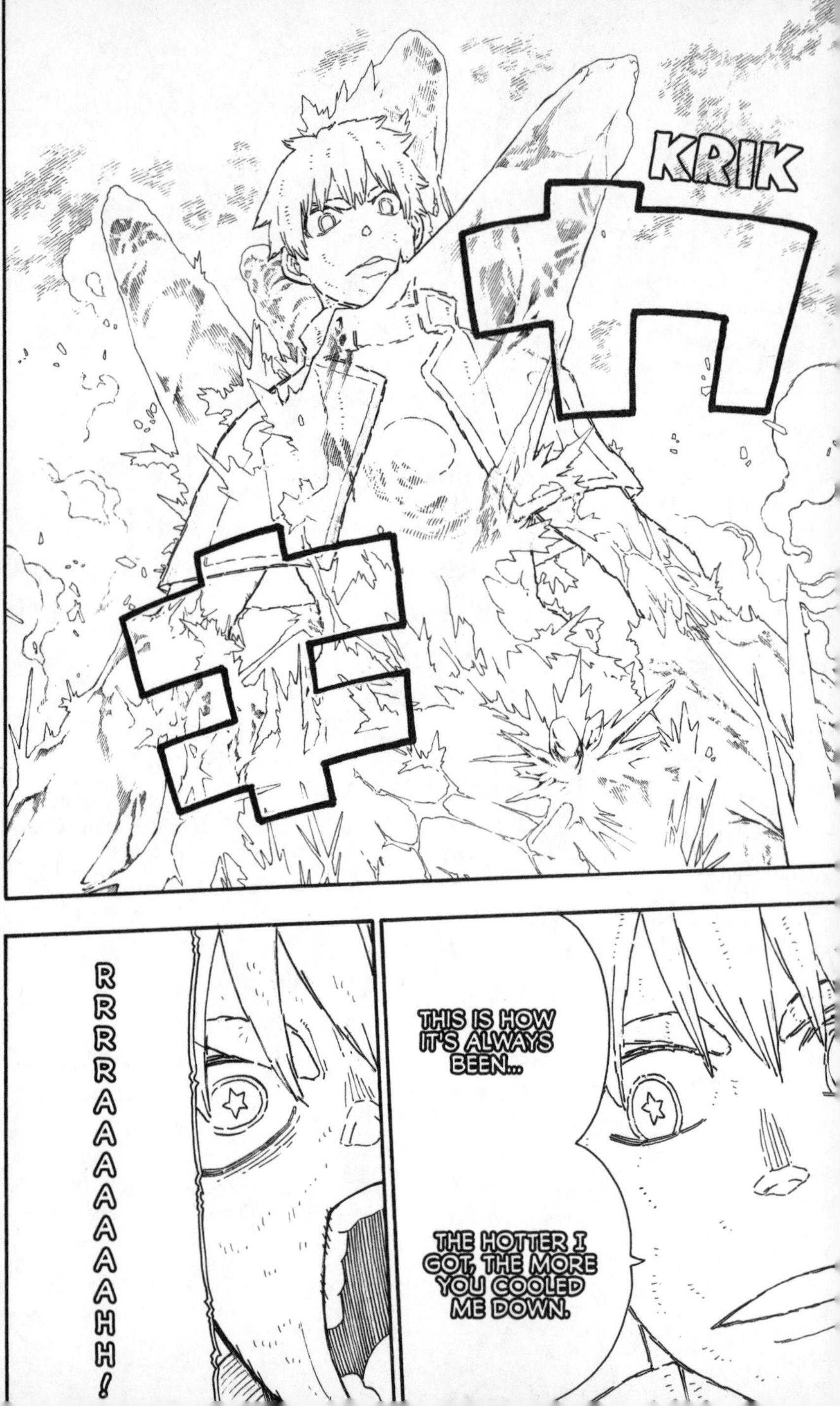
KRIK
THIS IS HOW IT'S ALWAYS BEEN...
THE HOTTER I GOT, THE MORE YOU COOLED ME DOWN.
RRRRAAAAAAAHH!

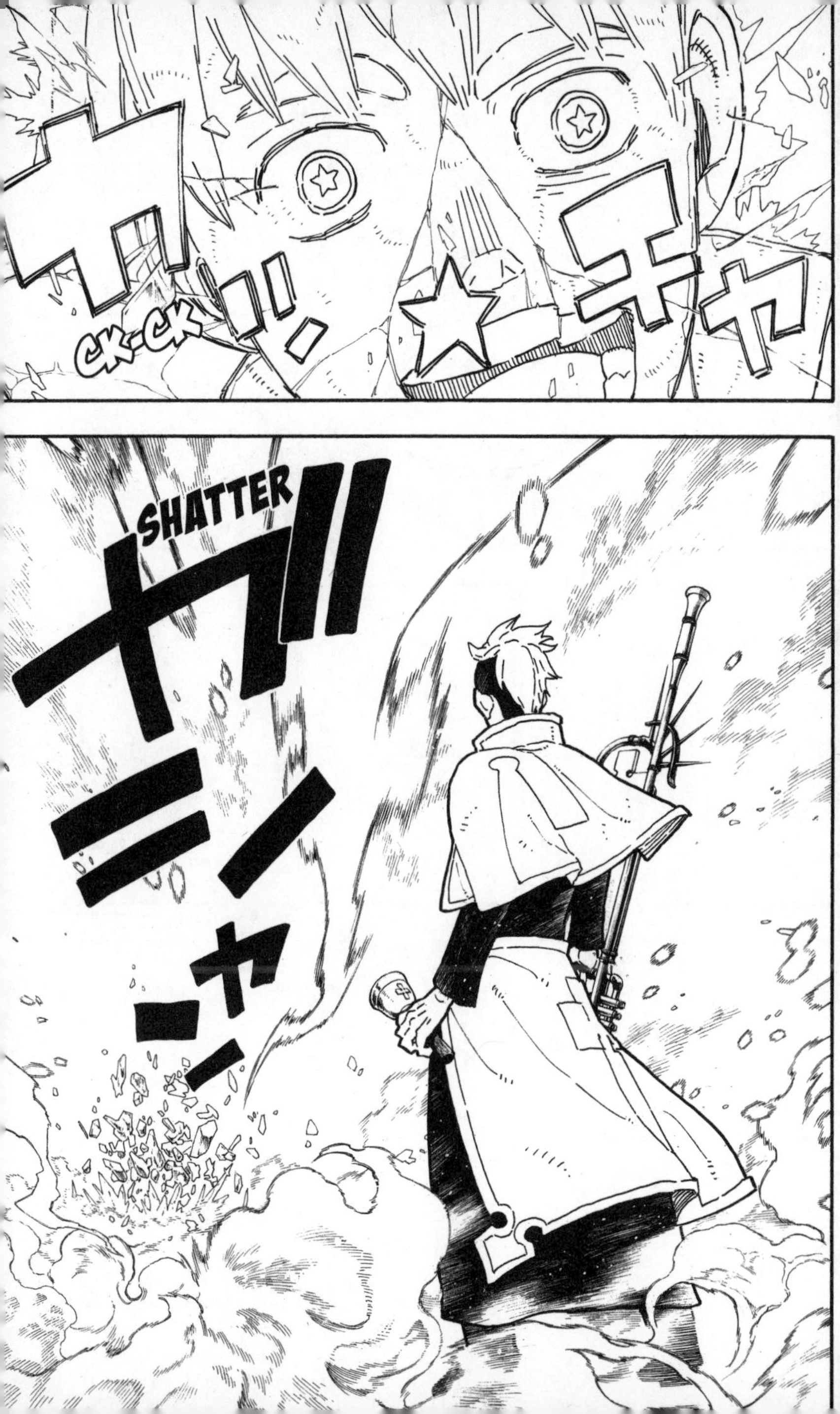
CK-CK
SHATTER

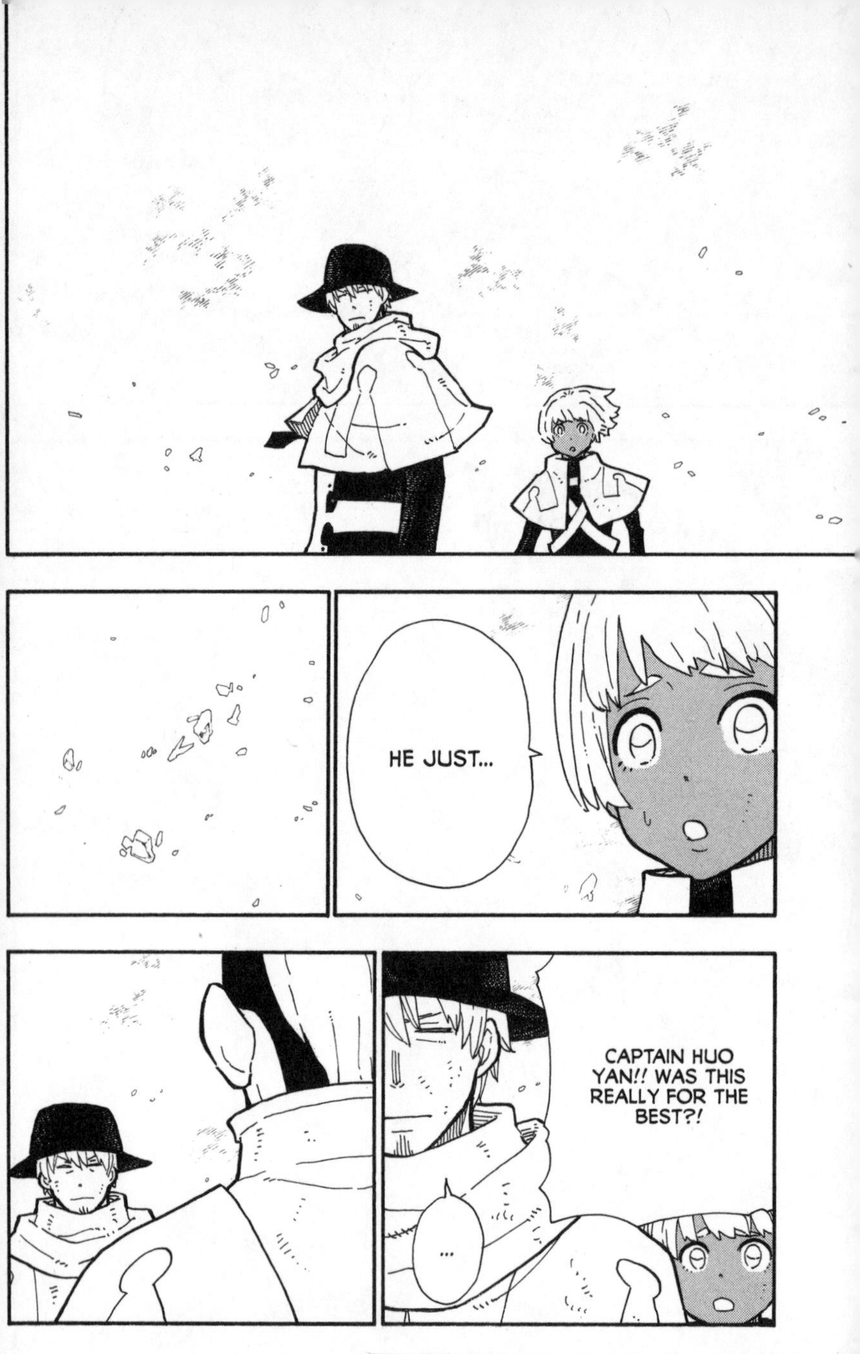
HE JUST...
CAPTAIN HUO YAN!! WAS THIS REALLY FOR THE BEST?!
...

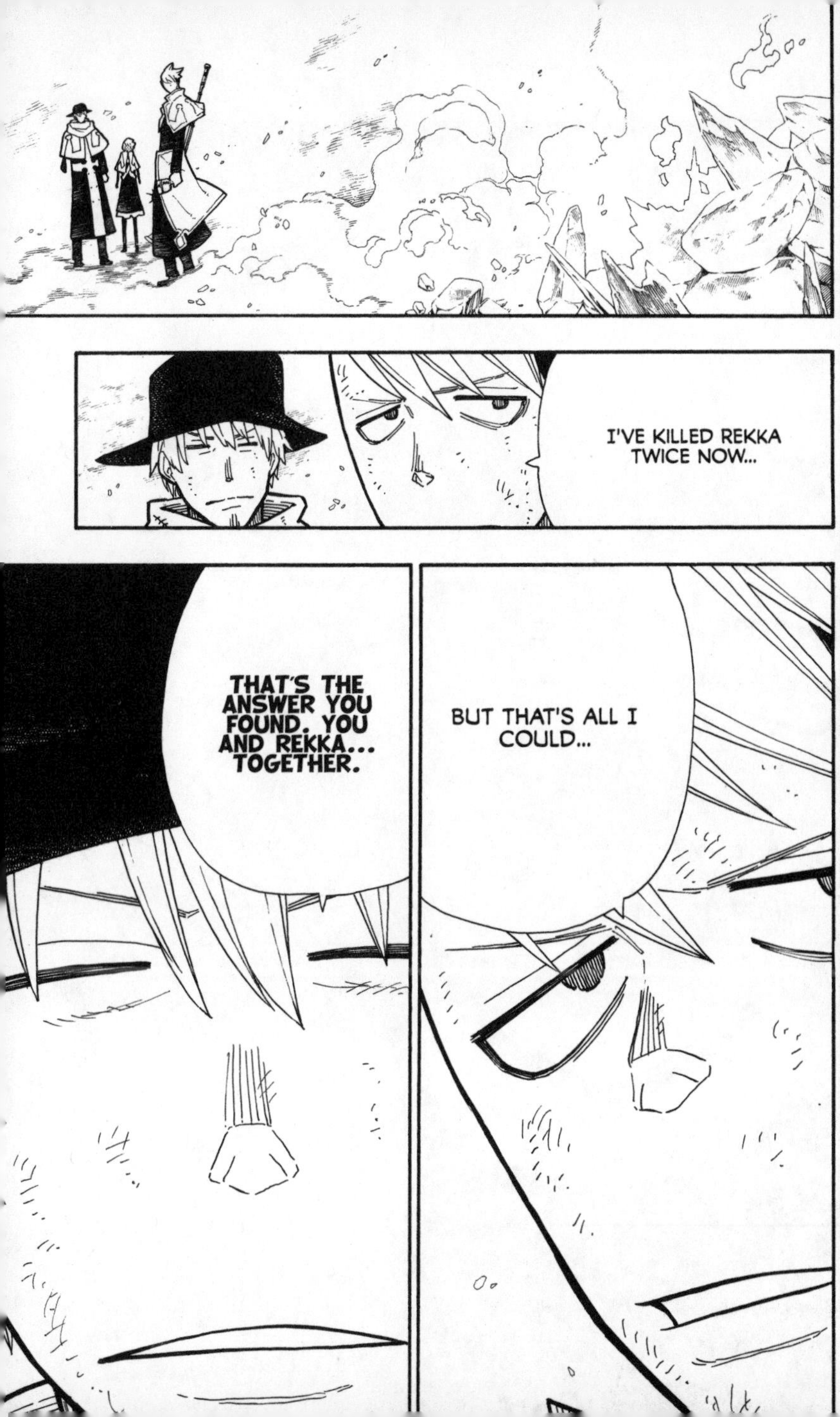
I'VE KILLED REKKA TWICE NOW...
BUT THAT'S ALL I COULD...
THAT'S THE ANSWER YOU FOUND. YOU AND REKKA... TOGETHER.

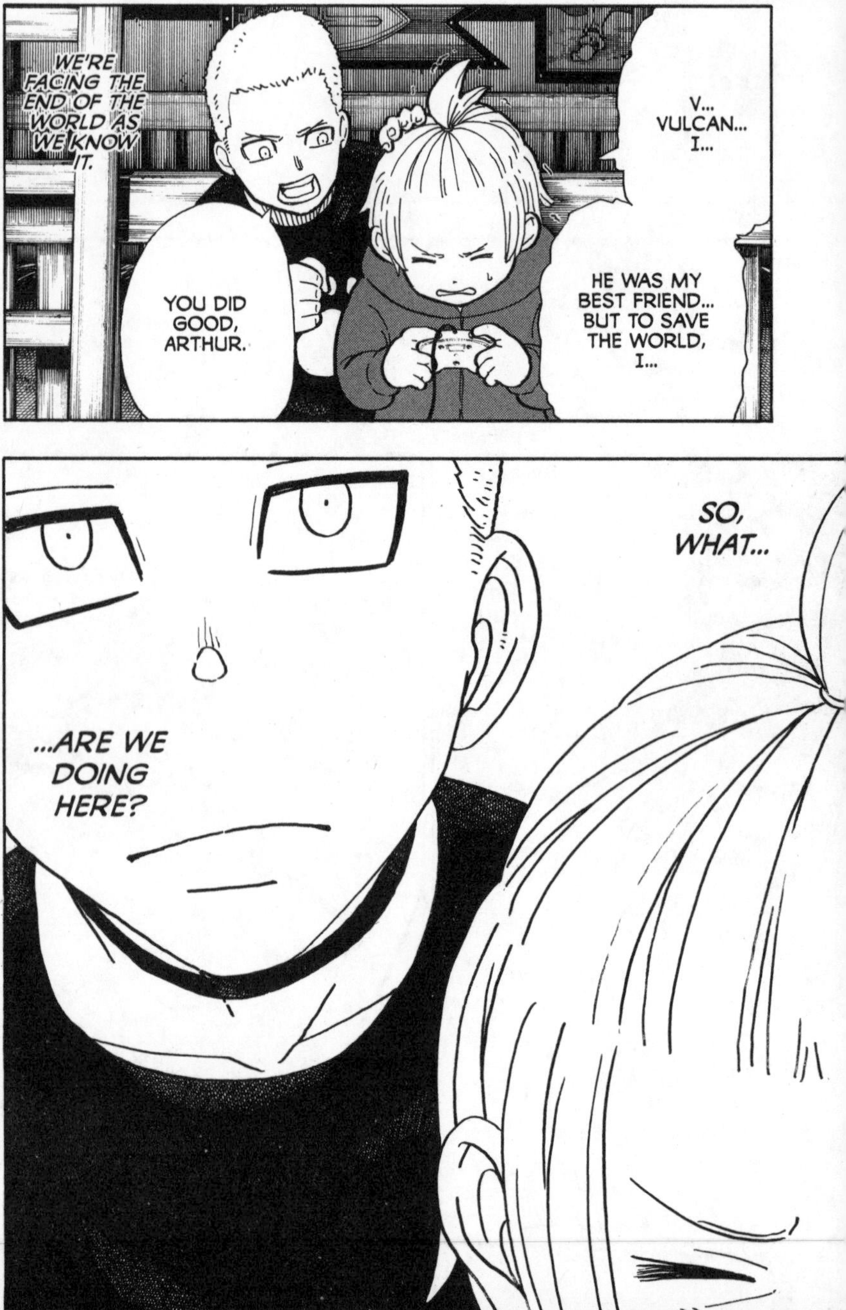
V... VULCAN... I...
HE WAS MY BEST FRIEND... BUT TO SAVE THE WORLD, I...
WE'RE FACING THE END OF THE WORLD AS WE KNOW IT.
YOU DID GOOD, ARTHUR.
SO, WHAT...
...ARE WE DOING HERE?

FIRE FORCE

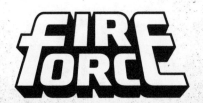

FIRE FORCE

CHAPTER CCLXI: THE KNIGHT KING RISES

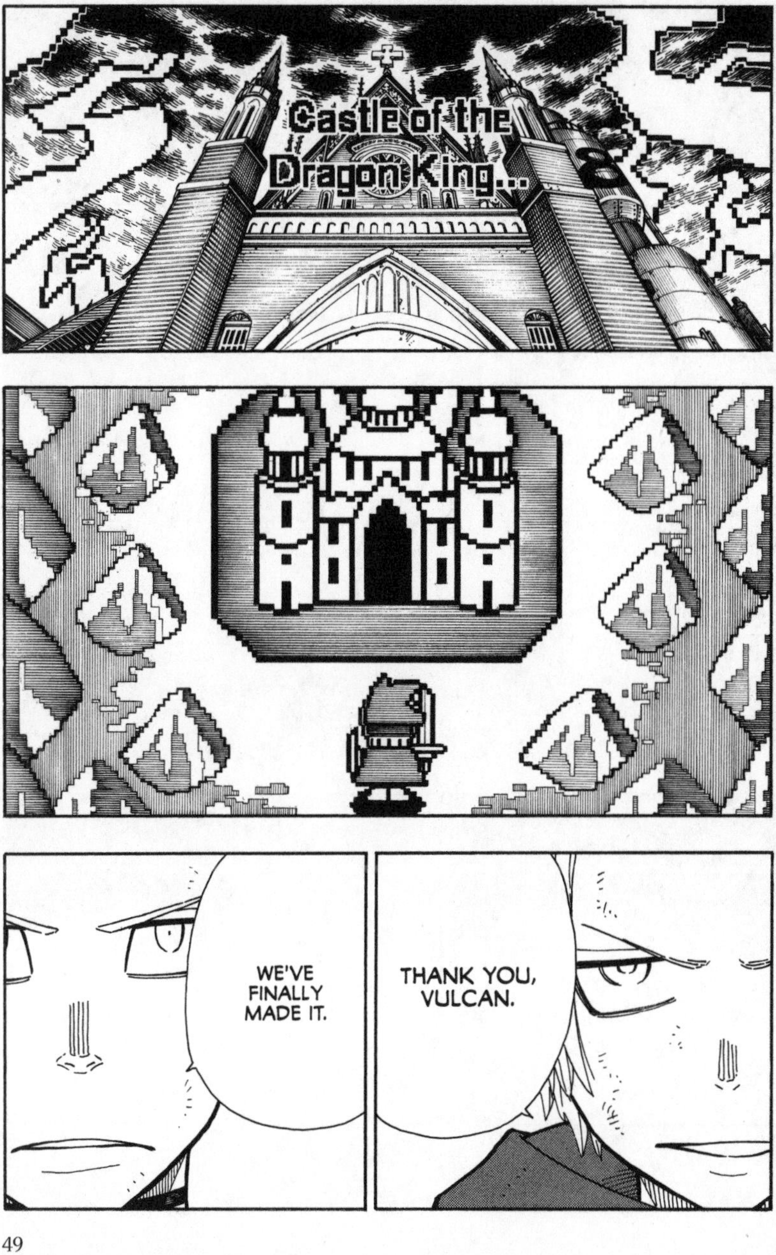
Castle of the Dragon King...
THANK YOU, VULCAN.
WE'VE FINALLY MADE IT.

Final Chapter

Dragon King Dracon
The Hero's party has at last arrived at the Castle of the Dragon King.

The Hero's final battle is about to begin.

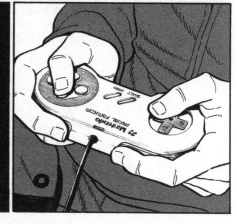

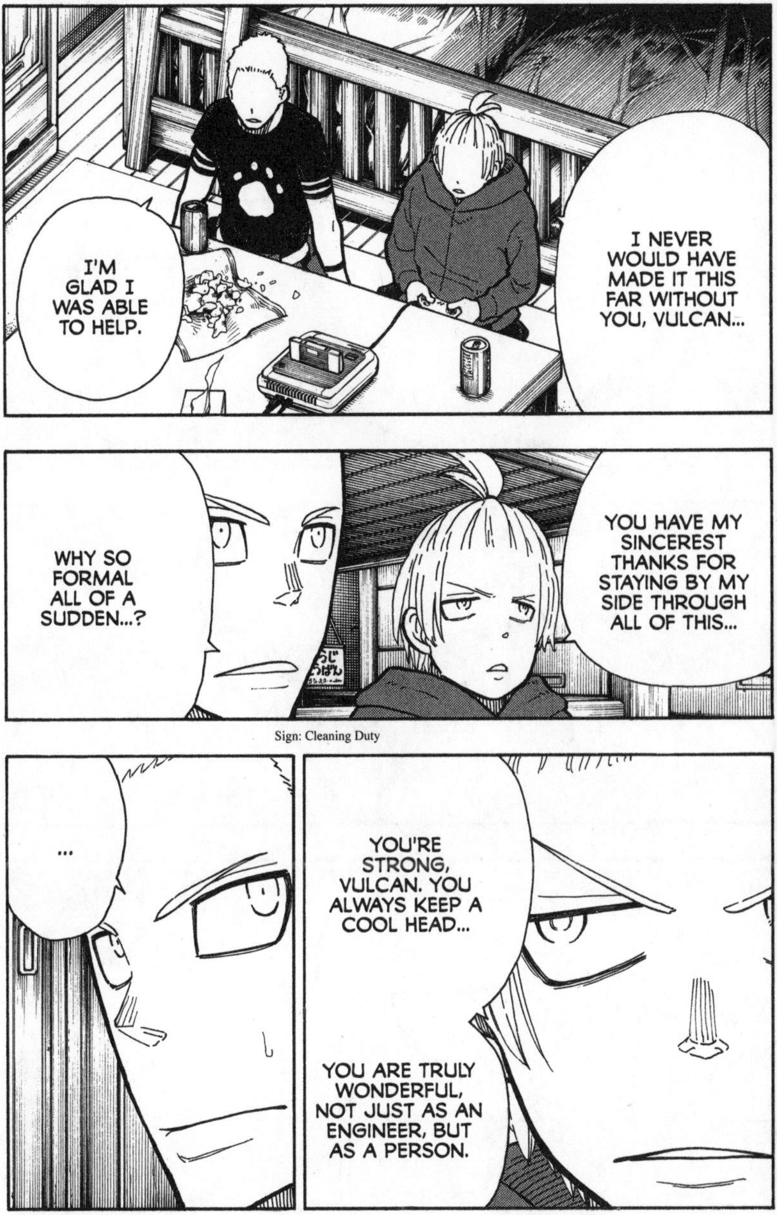
I NEVER WOULD HAVE MADE IT THIS FAR WITHOUT YOU, VULCAN...
I'M GLAD I WAS ABLE TO HELP.
YOU HAVE MY SINCEREST THANKS FOR STAYING BY MY SIDE THROUGH ALL OF THIS...
WHY SO FORMAL ALL OF A SUDDEN...?
YOU'RE STRONG, VULCAN. YOU ALWAYS KEEP A COOL HEAD...
YOU ARE TRULY WONDERFUL, NOT JUST AS AN ENGINEER, BUT AS A PERSON.
...

Sign: Cleaning Duty

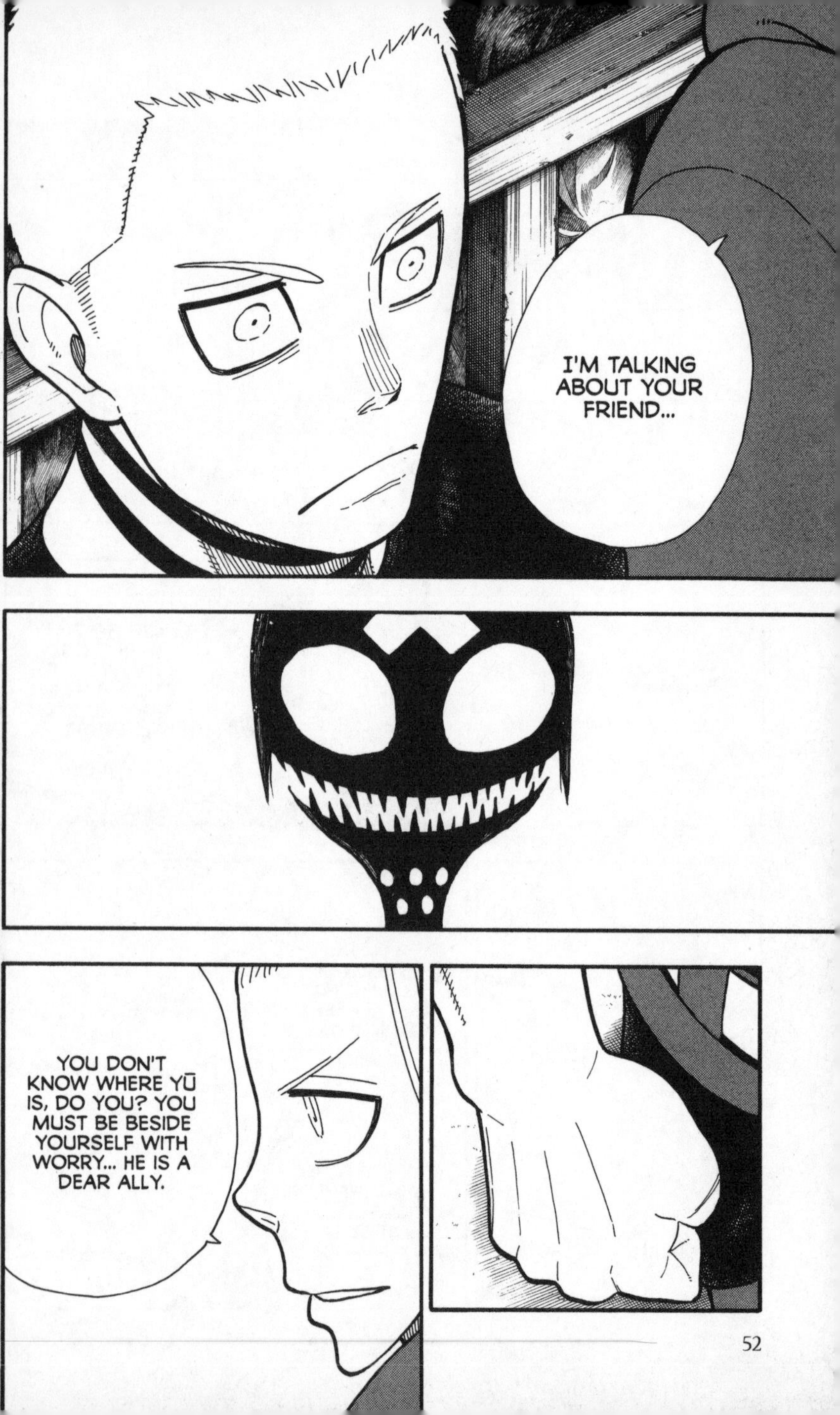
I'M TALKING ABOUT YOUR FRIEND...
YOU DON'T KNOW WHERE YŪ IS, DO YOU? YOU MUST BE BESIDE YOURSELF WITH WORRY... HE IS A DEAR ALLY.

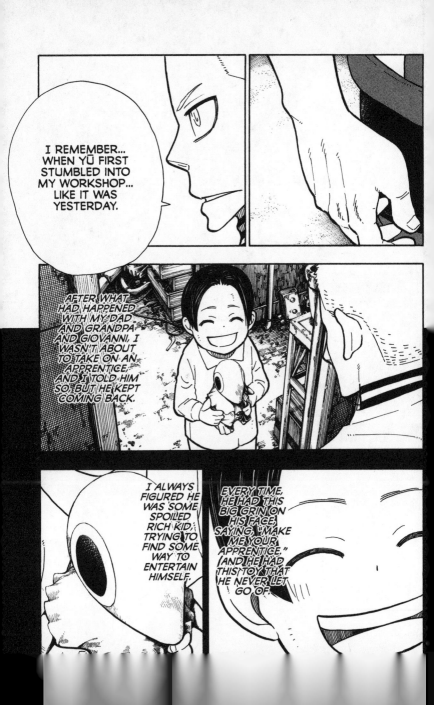

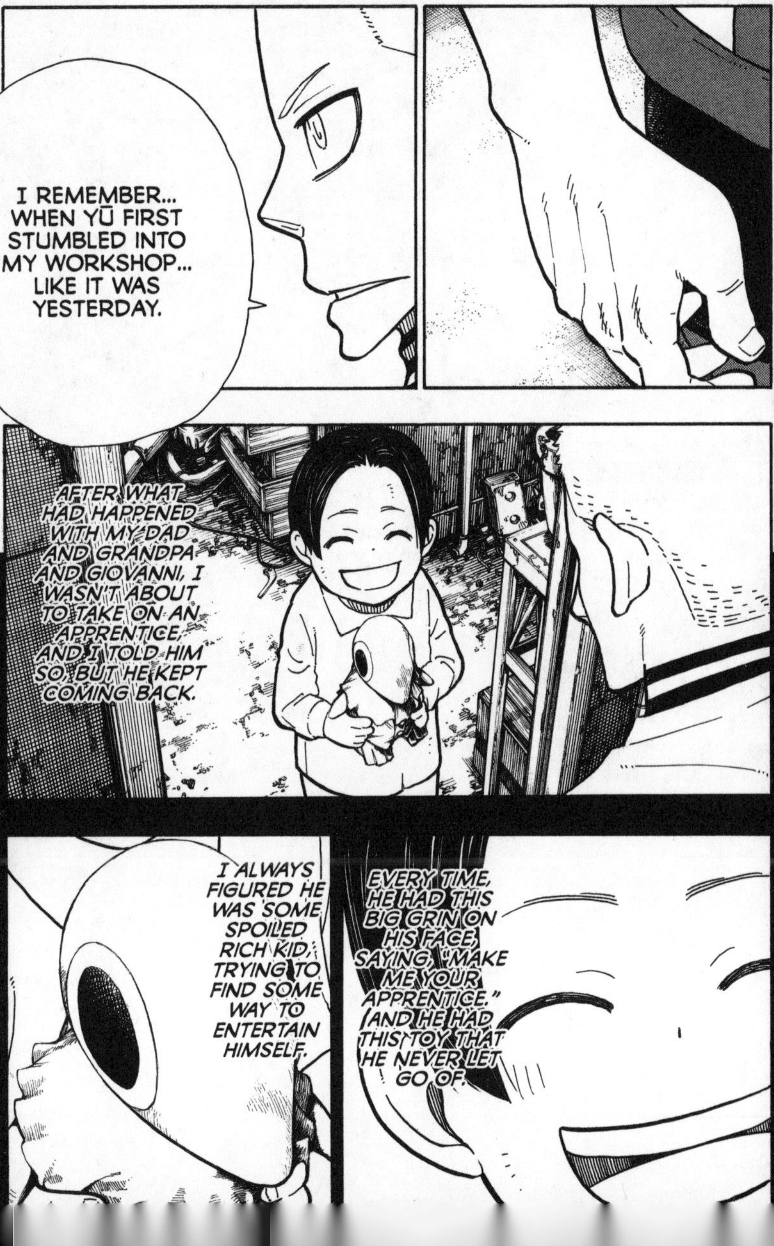
I REMEMBER... WHEN YŪ FIRST STUMBLED INTO MY WORKSHOP... LIKE IT WAS YESTERDAY.
AFTER WHAT HAD HAPPENED WITH MY DAD AND GRANDPA AND GIOVANNI, I WASN'T ABOUT TO TAKE ON AN APPRENTICE, AND I TOLD HIM SO, BUT HE KEPT COMING BACK.
EVERY TIME, HE HAD THIS BIG GRIN ON HIS FACE, SAYING, "MAKE ME YOUR APPRENTICE." AND HE HAD THIS TOY THAT HE NEVER LET GO OF.
I ALWAYS FIGURED HE WAS SOME SPOILED RICH KID, TRYING TO FIND SOME WAY TO ENTERTAIN HIMSELF.

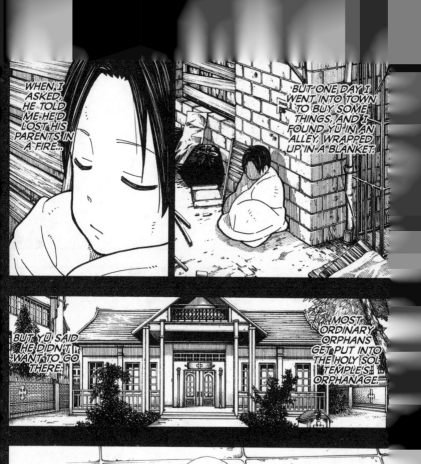

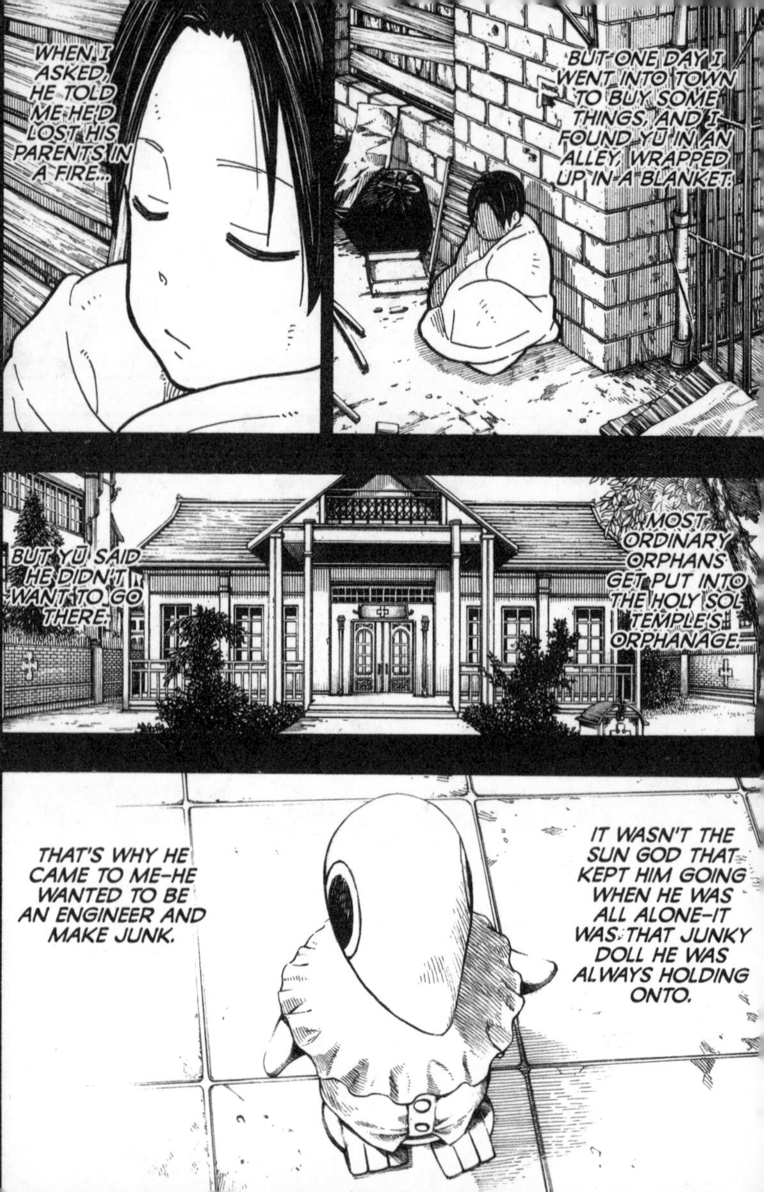
BUT ONE DAY I WENT INTO TOWN TO BUY SOME THINGS, AND I FOUND YŪ IN AN ALLEY, WRAPPED UP IN A BLANKET.
WHEN I ASKED, HE TOLD ME HE'D LOST HIS PARENTS IN A FIRE...
MOST ORDINARY ORPHANS GET PUT INTO THE HOLY SOL TEMPLE'S ORPHANAGE.
BUT YŪ SAID HE DIDN'T WANT TO GO THERE.
IT WASN'T THE SUN GOD THAT KEPT HIM GOING WHEN HE WAS ALL ALONE—IT WAS THAT JUNKY DOLL HE WAS ALWAYS HOLDING ONTO.
THAT'S WHY HE CAME TO ME—HE WANTED TO BE AN ENGINEER AND MAKE JUNK.

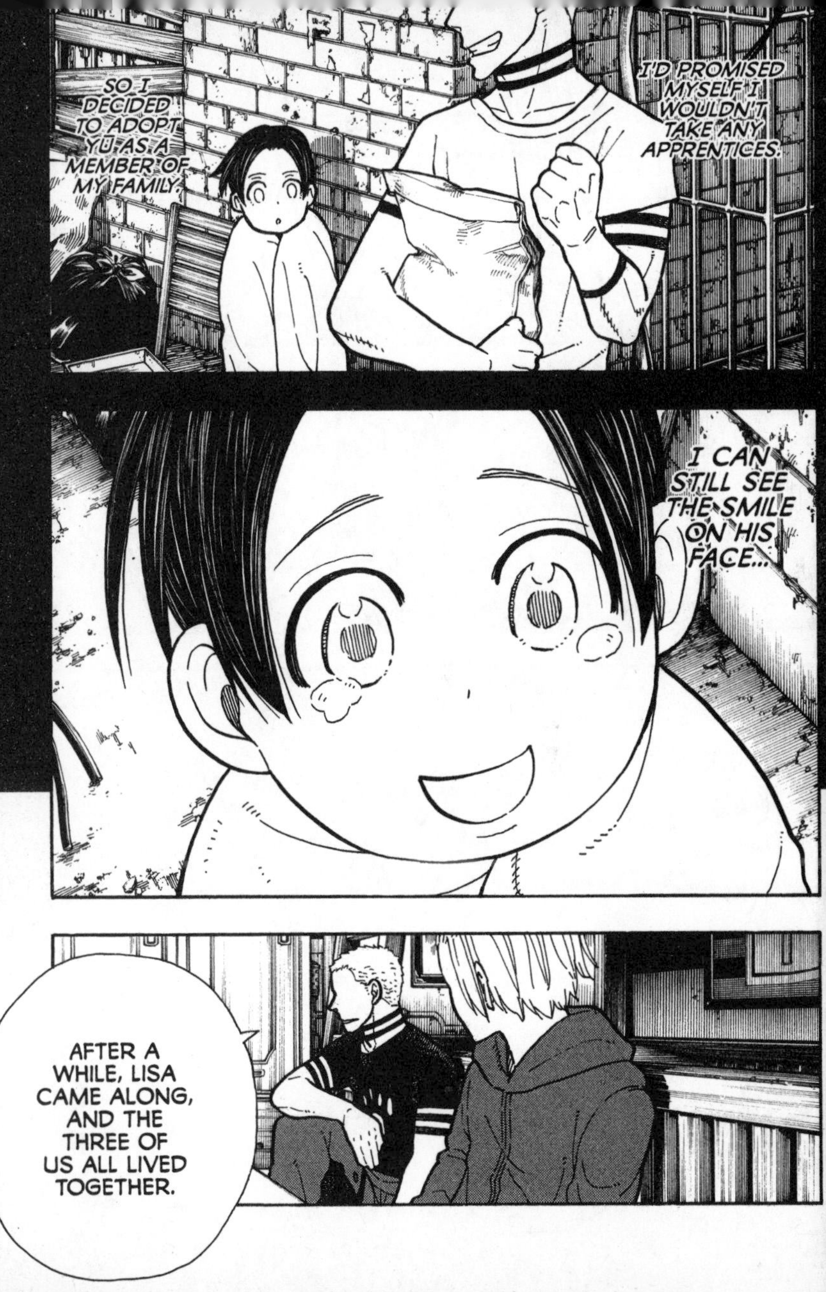
I'D PROMISED MYSELF I WOULDN'T TAKE ANY APPRENTICES.
SO I DECIDED TO ADOPT YŪ AS A MEMBER OF MY FAMILY.
I CAN STILL SEE THE SMILE ON HIS FACE...
AFTER A WHILE, LISA CAME ALONG, AND THE THREE OF US ALL LIVED TOGETHER.

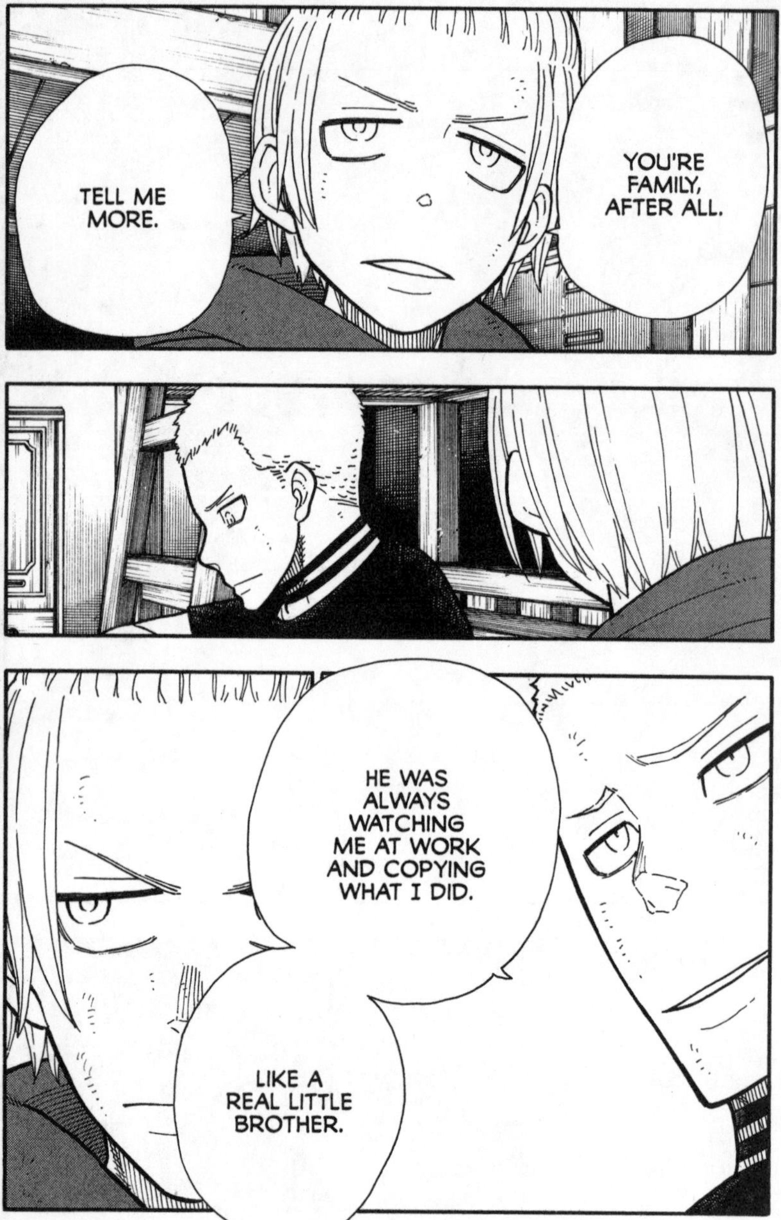
YOU'RE FAMILY, AFTER ALL.
TELL ME MORE.
HE WAS ALWAYS WATCHING ME AT WORK AND COPYING WHAT I DID.
LIKE A REAL LITTLE BROTHER.

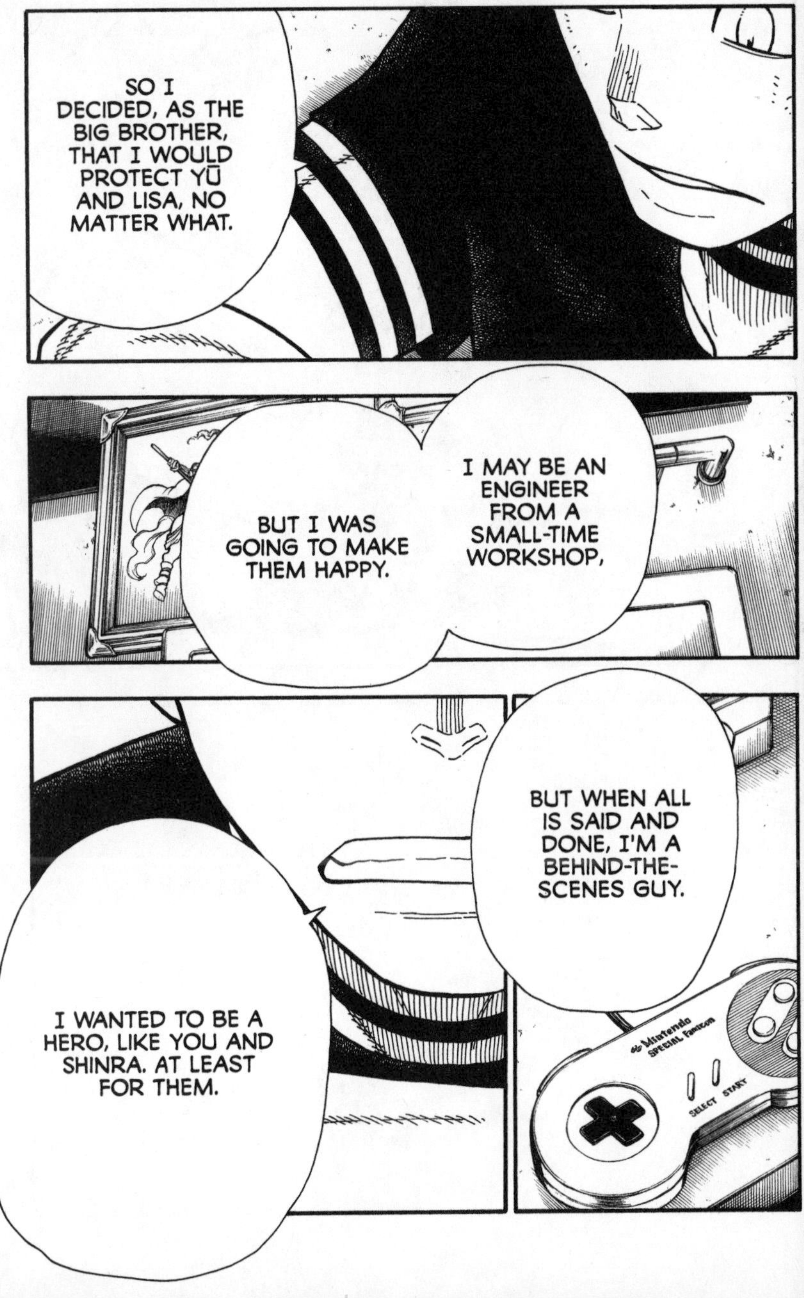
SO I DECIDED, AS THE BIG BROTHER, THAT I WOULD PROTECT YŪ AND LISA, NO MATTER WHAT.
I MAY BE AN ENGINEER FROM A SMALL-TIME WORKSHOP,
BUT I WAS GOING TO MAKE THEM HAPPY.
BUT WHEN ALL IS SAID AND DONE, I'M A BEHIND-THE-SCENES GUY.
Nintendo
SPECIAL Famicom
SELECT START
I WANTED TO BE A HERO, LIKE YOU AND SHINRA. AT LEAST FOR THEM.

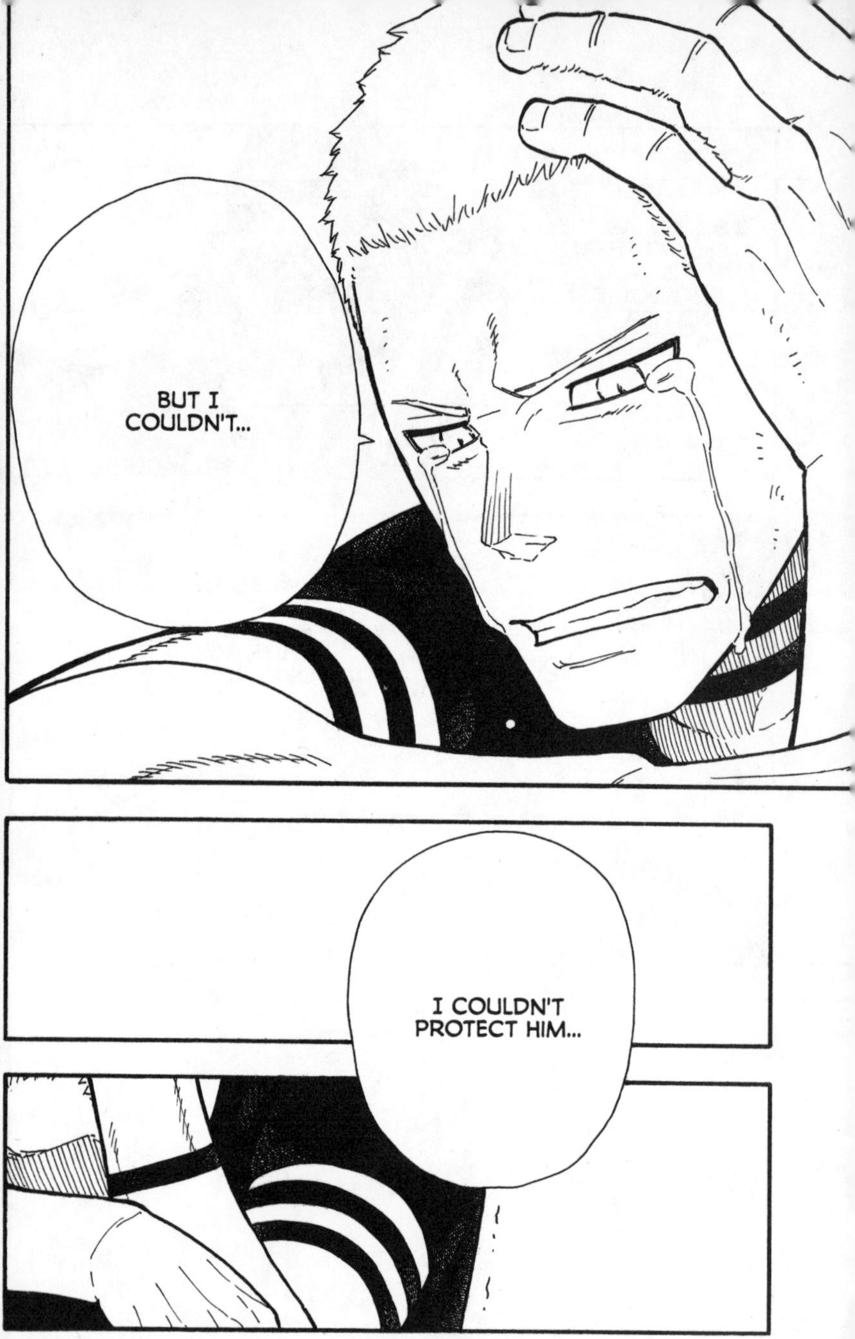
BUT I COULDN'T...
I COULDN'T PROTECT HIM...

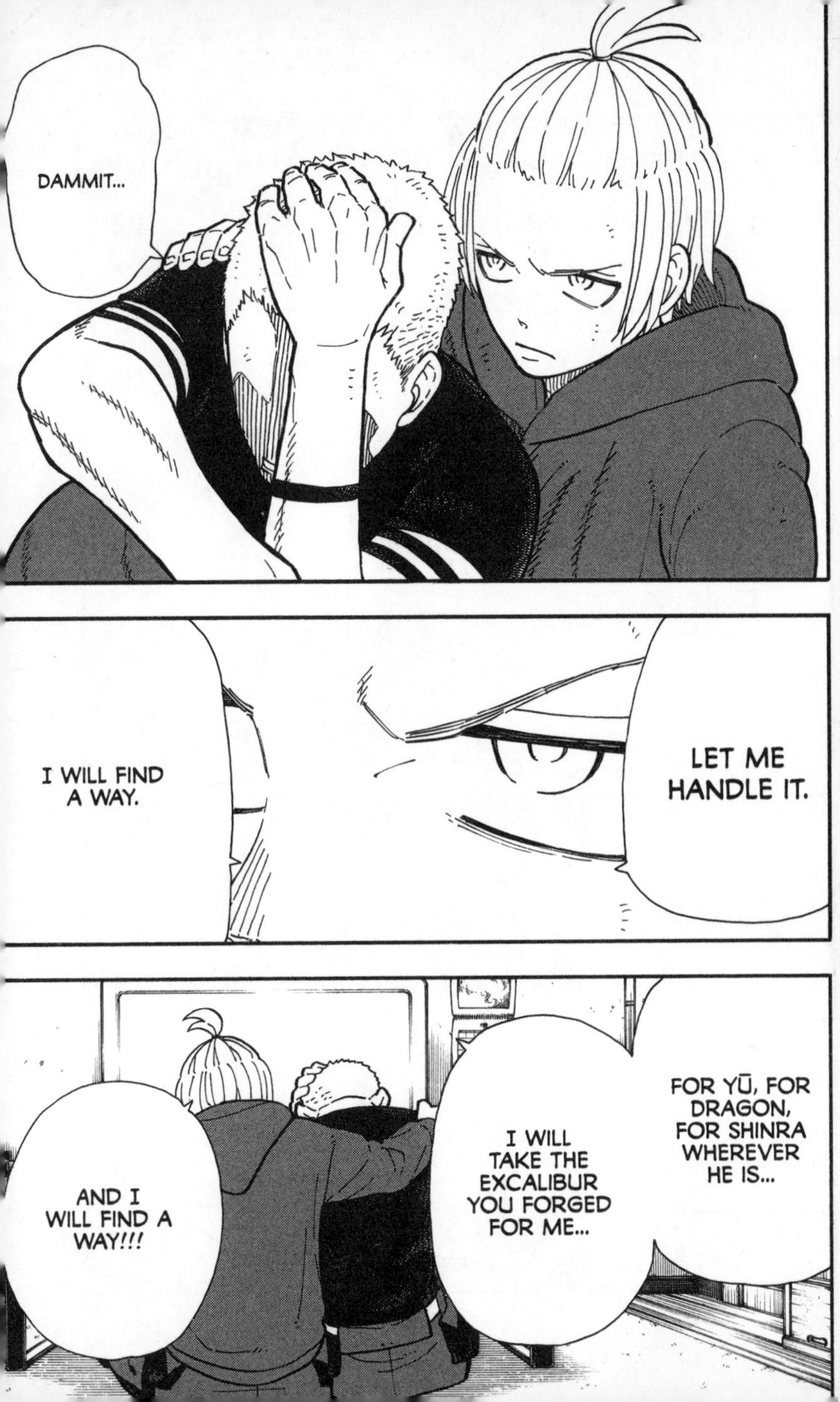
DAMMIT...
LET ME HANDLE IT.
I WILL FIND A WAY.
FOR YŪ, FOR DRAGON, FOR SHINRA WHEREVER HE IS...
I WILL TAKE THE EXCALIBUR YOU FORGED FOR ME...
AND I WILL FIND A WAY!!!

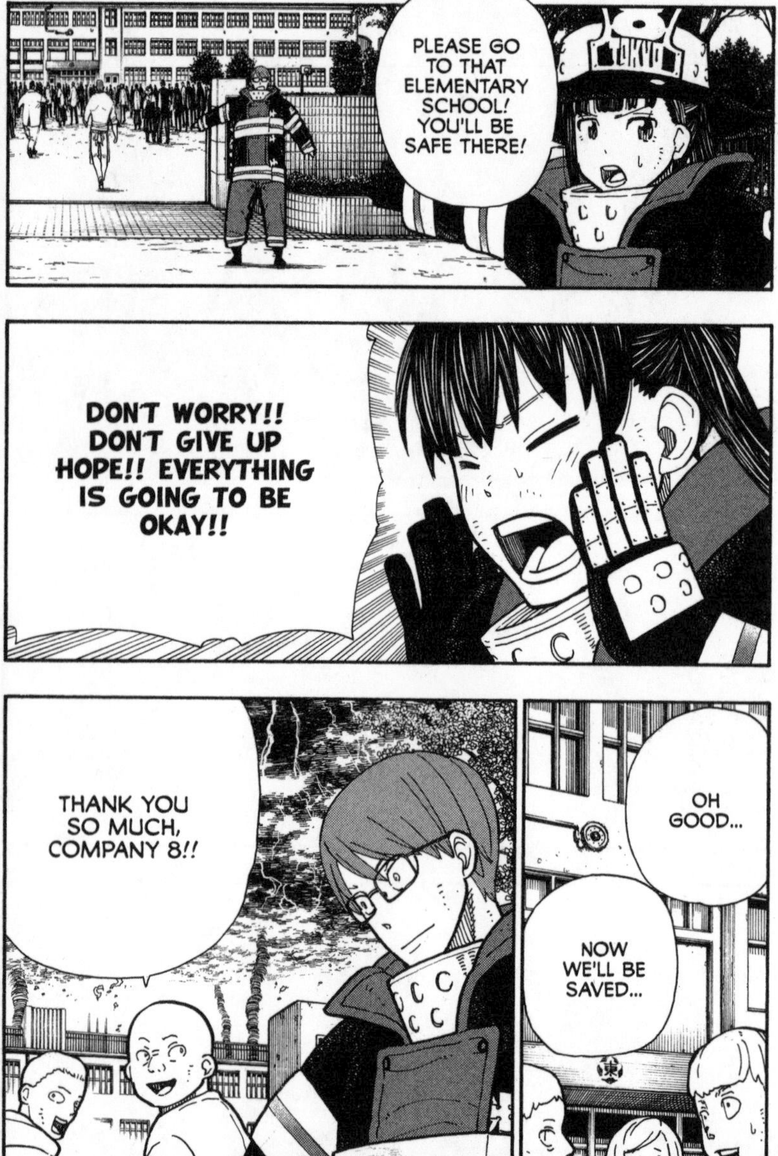
PLEASE GO TO THAT ELEMENTARY SCHOOL! YOU'LL BE SAFE THERE!
TOKYO
DON'T WORRY!! DON'T GIVE UP HOPE!! EVERYTHING IS GOING TO BE OKAY!!
OH GOOD...
NOW WE'LL BE SAVED...
THANK YOU SO MUCH, COMPANY 8!!

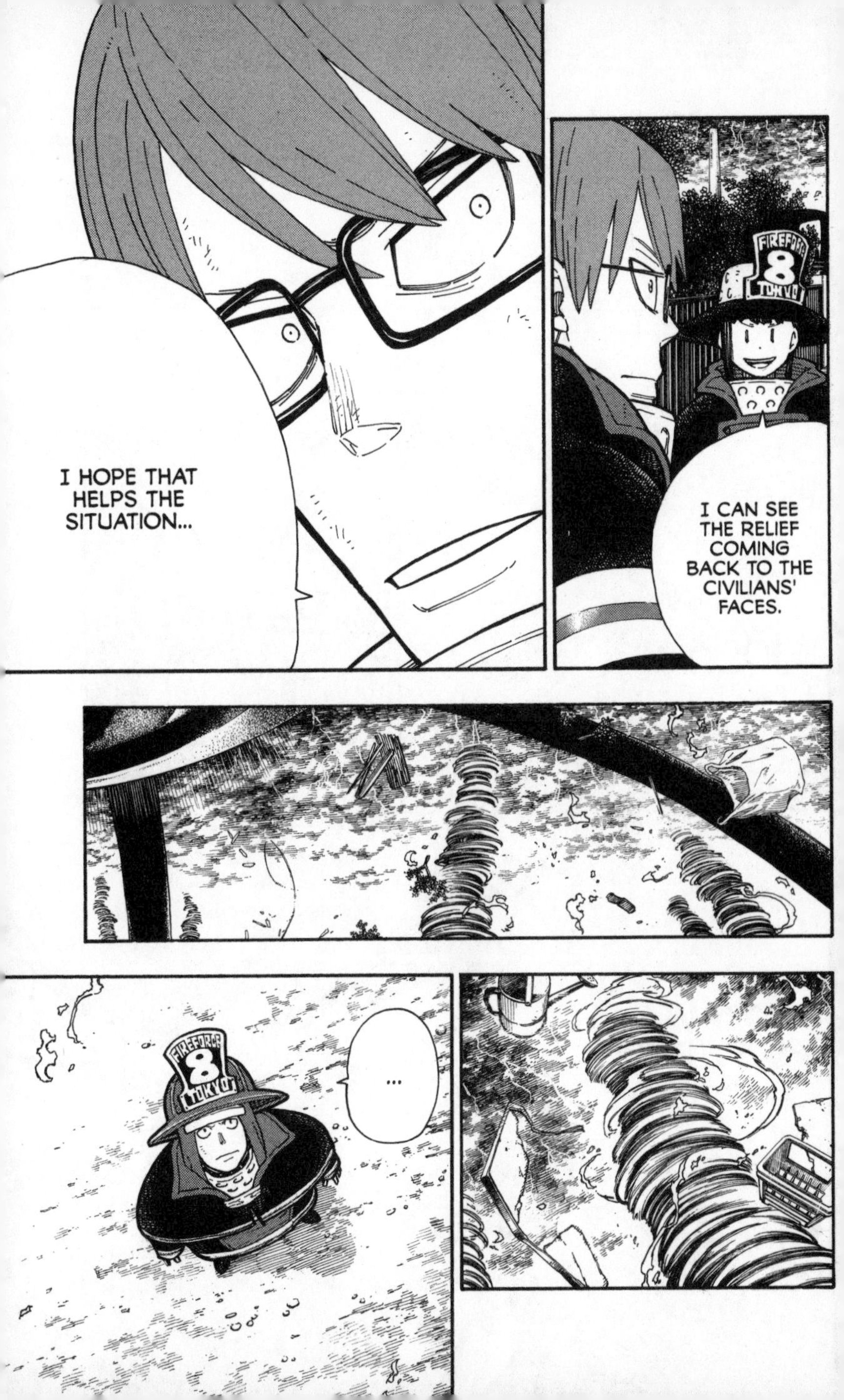
I CAN SEE THE RELIEF COMING BACK TO THE CIVILIANS' FACES.
I HOPE THAT HELPS THE SITUATION...
...

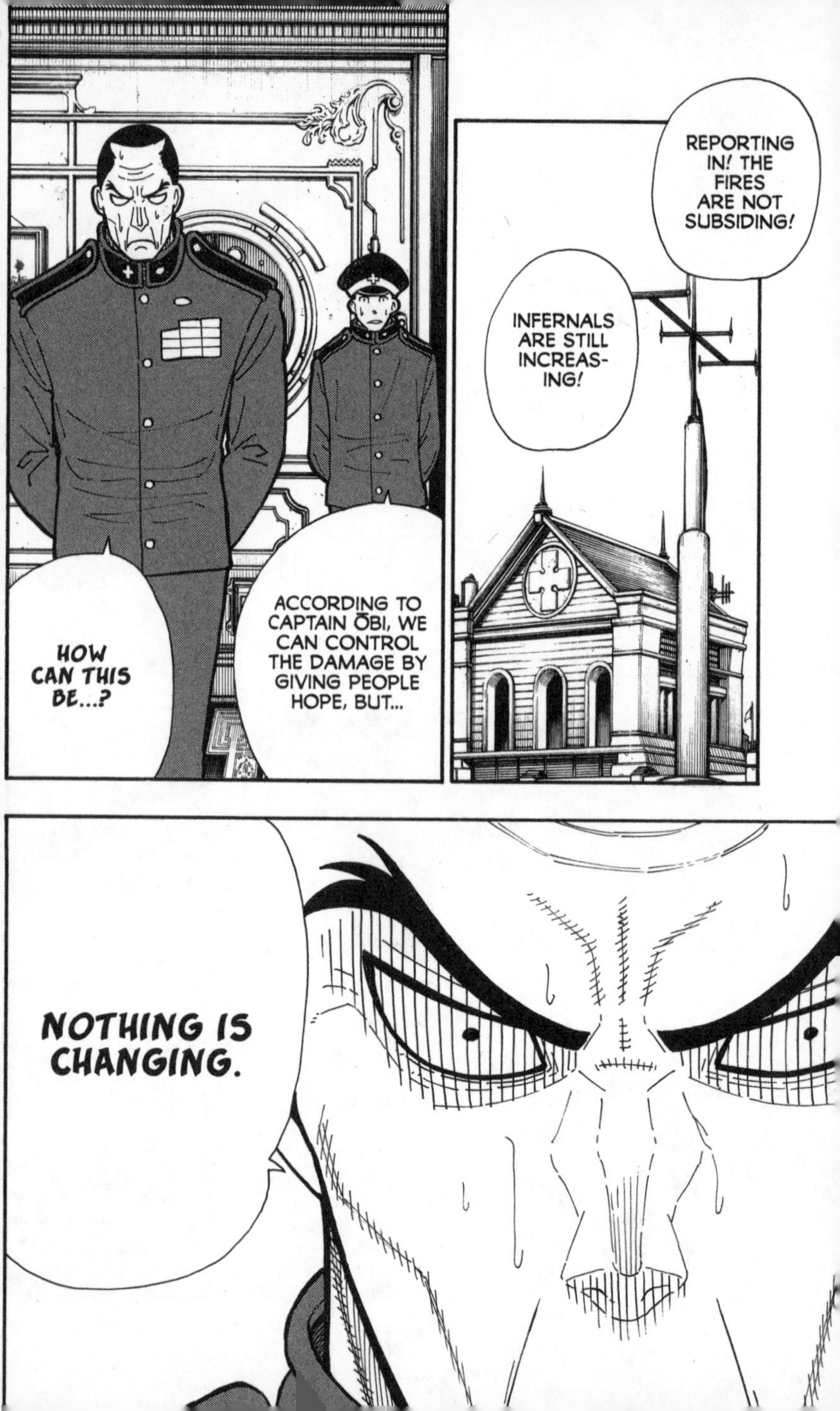
REPORTING IN! THE FIRES ARE NOT SUBSIDING!
INFERNALS ARE STILL INCREAS-ING!
ACCORDING TO CAPTAIN ŌBI, WE CAN CONTROL THE DAMAGE BY GIVING PEOPLE HOPE, BUT...
HOW CAN THIS BE...?
NOTHING IS CHANGING.

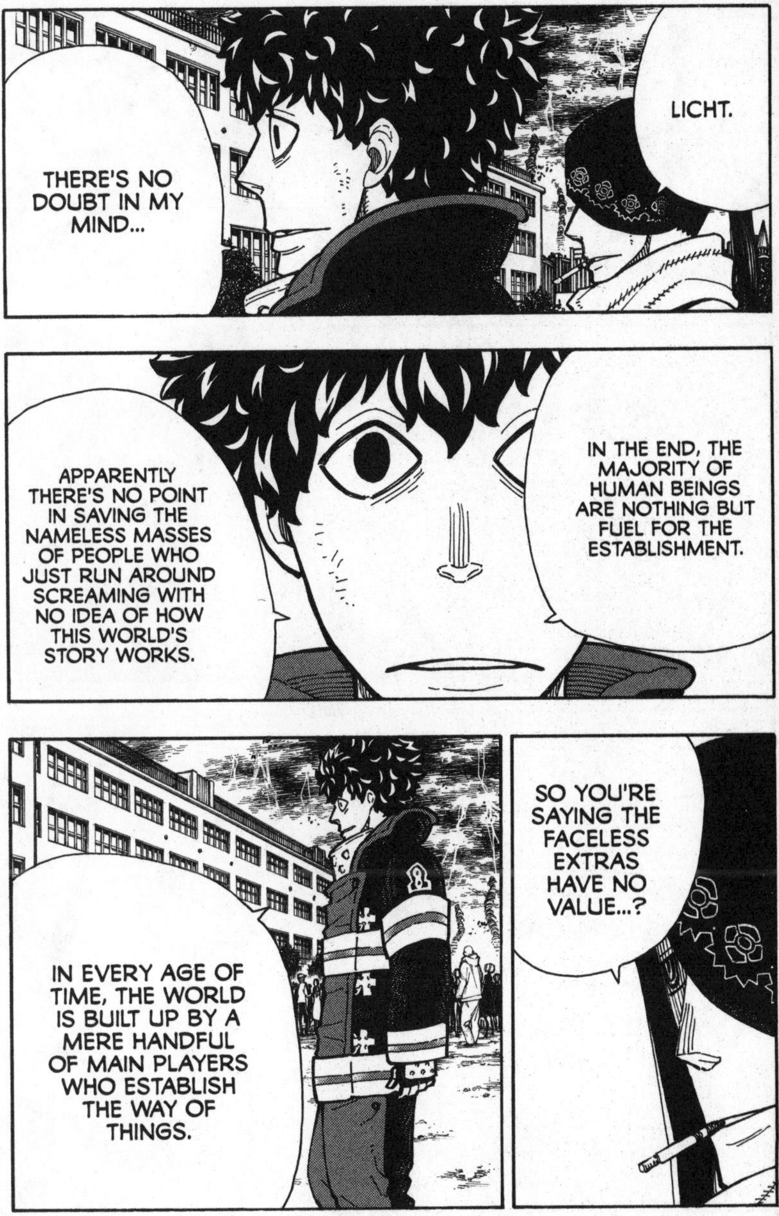
LICHT.
THERE'S NO DOUBT IN MY MIND...
IN THE END, THE MAJORITY OF HUMAN BEINGS ARE NOTHING BUT FUEL FOR THE ESTABLISHMENT.
APPARENTLY THERE'S NO POINT IN SAVING THE NAMELESS MASSES OF PEOPLE WHO JUST RUN AROUND SCREAMING WITH NO IDEA OF HOW THIS WORLD'S STORY WORKS.
SO YOU'RE SAYING THE FACELESS EXTRAS HAVE NO VALUE...?
IN EVERY AGE OF TIME, THE WORLD IS BUILT UP BY A MERE HANDFUL OF MAIN PLAYERS WHO ESTABLISH THE WAY OF THINGS.

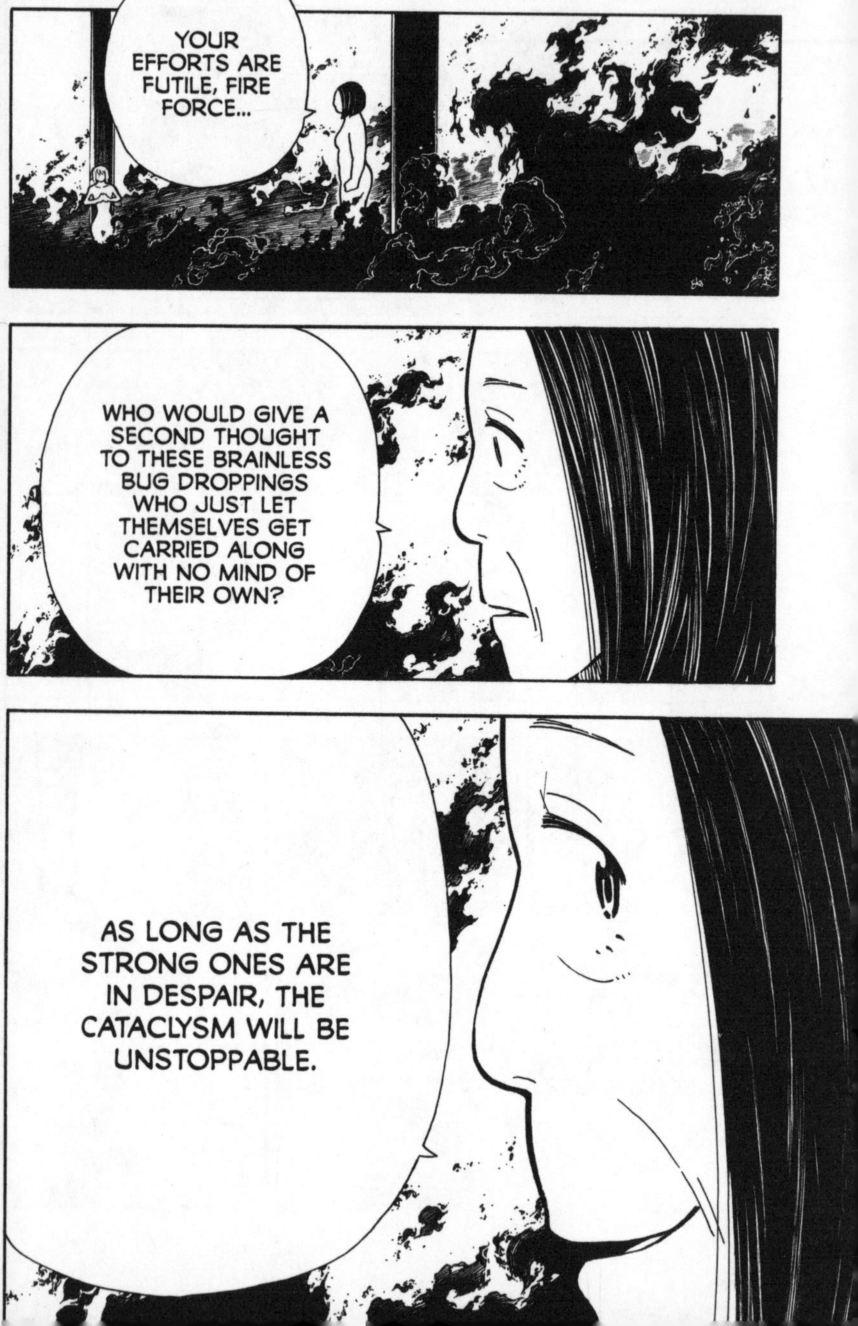
YOUR EFFORTS ARE FUTILE, FIRE FORCE...
WHO WOULD GIVE A SECOND THOUGHT TO THESE BRAINLESS BUG DROPPINGS WHO JUST LET THEMSELVES GET CARRIED ALONG WITH NO MIND OF THEIR OWN?
AS LONG AS THE STRONG ONES ARE IN DESPAIR, THE CATACLYSM WILL BE UNSTOPPABLE.

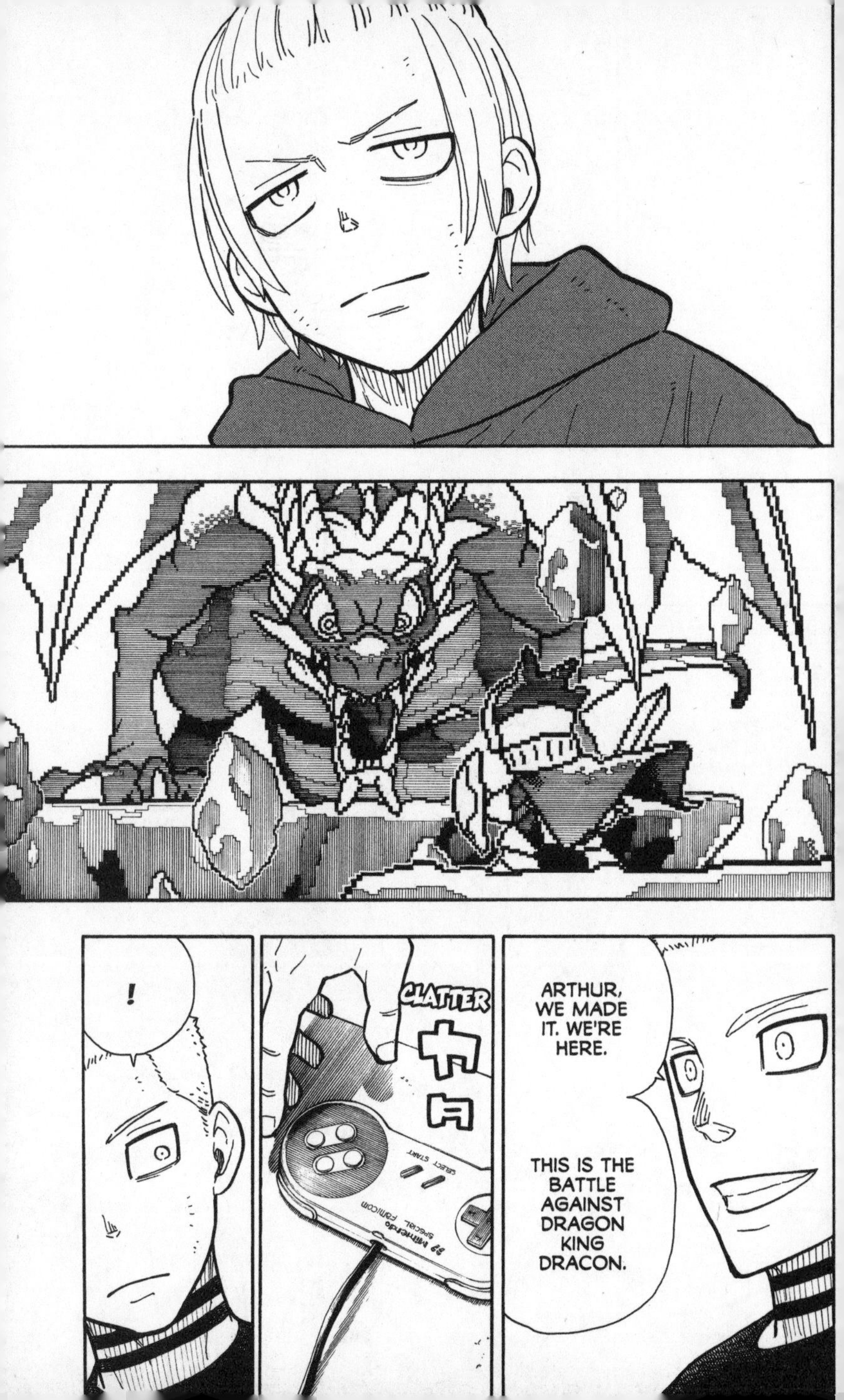
ARTHUR, WE MADE IT. WE'RE HERE.
THIS IS THE BATTLE AGAINST DRAGON KING DRACON.
CLATTER
!

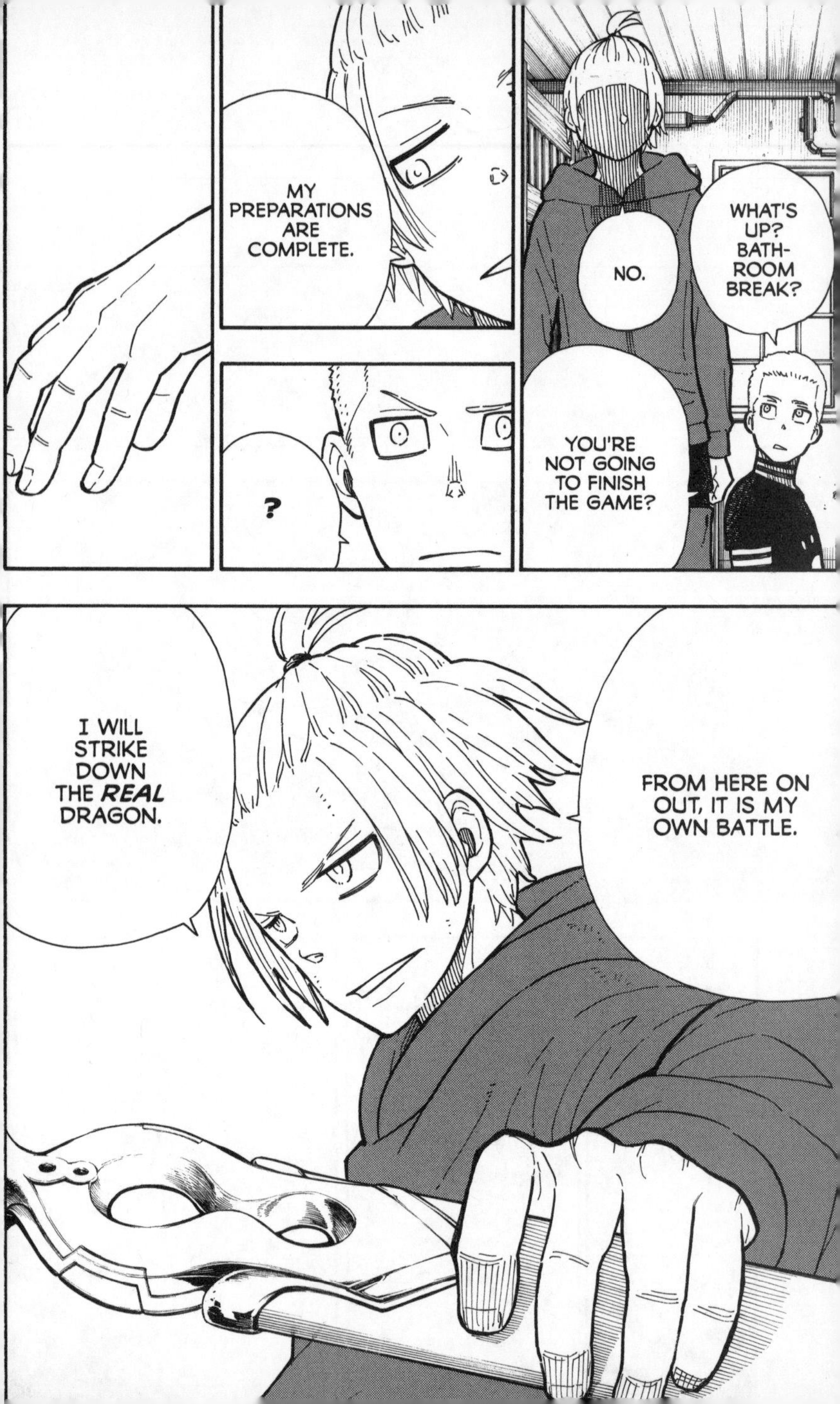
WHAT'S UP? BATH-ROOM BREAK?
NO.
YOU'RE NOT GOING TO FINISH THE GAME?
MY PREPARATIONS ARE COMPLETE.
?
FROM HERE ON OUT, IT IS MY OWN BATTLE.
I WILL STRIKE DOWN THE *REAL* DRAGON.

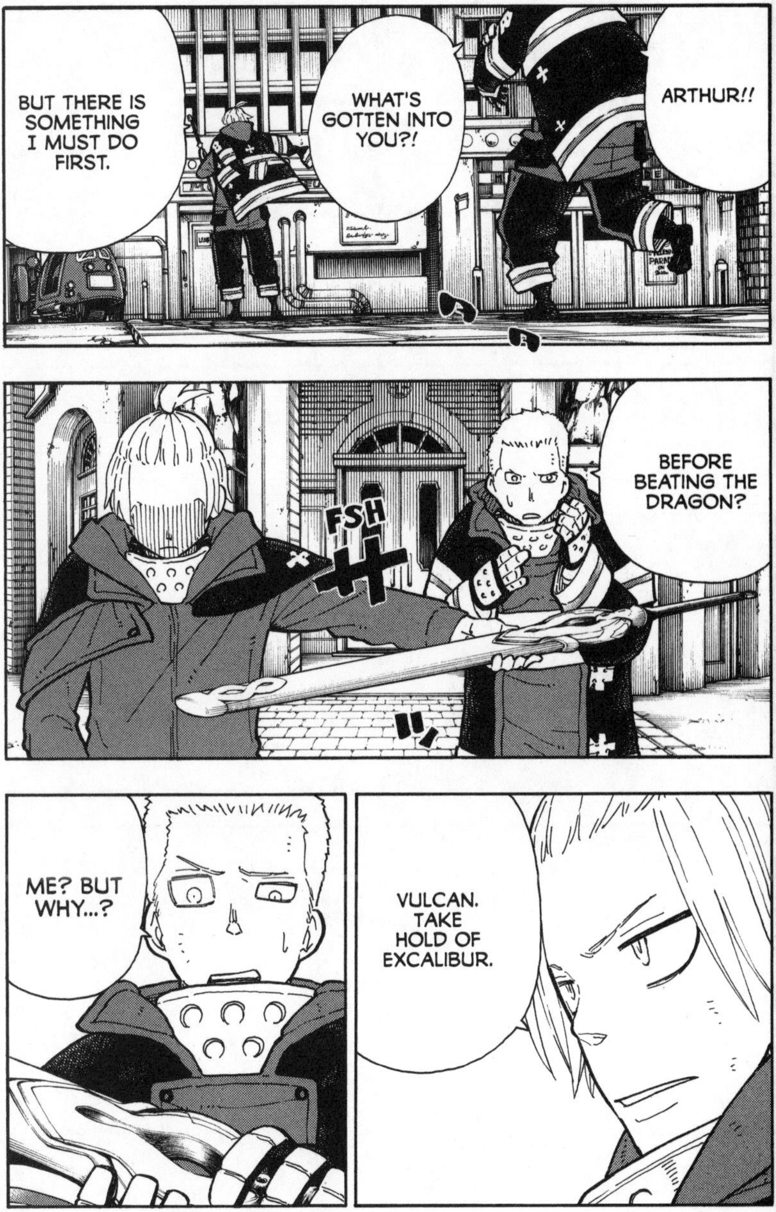
ARTHUR!!
WHAT'S GOTTEN INTO YOU?!
BUT THERE IS SOMETHING I MUST DO FIRST.
BEFORE BEATING THE DRAGON?
FSH
VULCAN. TAKE HOLD OF EXCALIBUR.
ME? BUT WHY...?

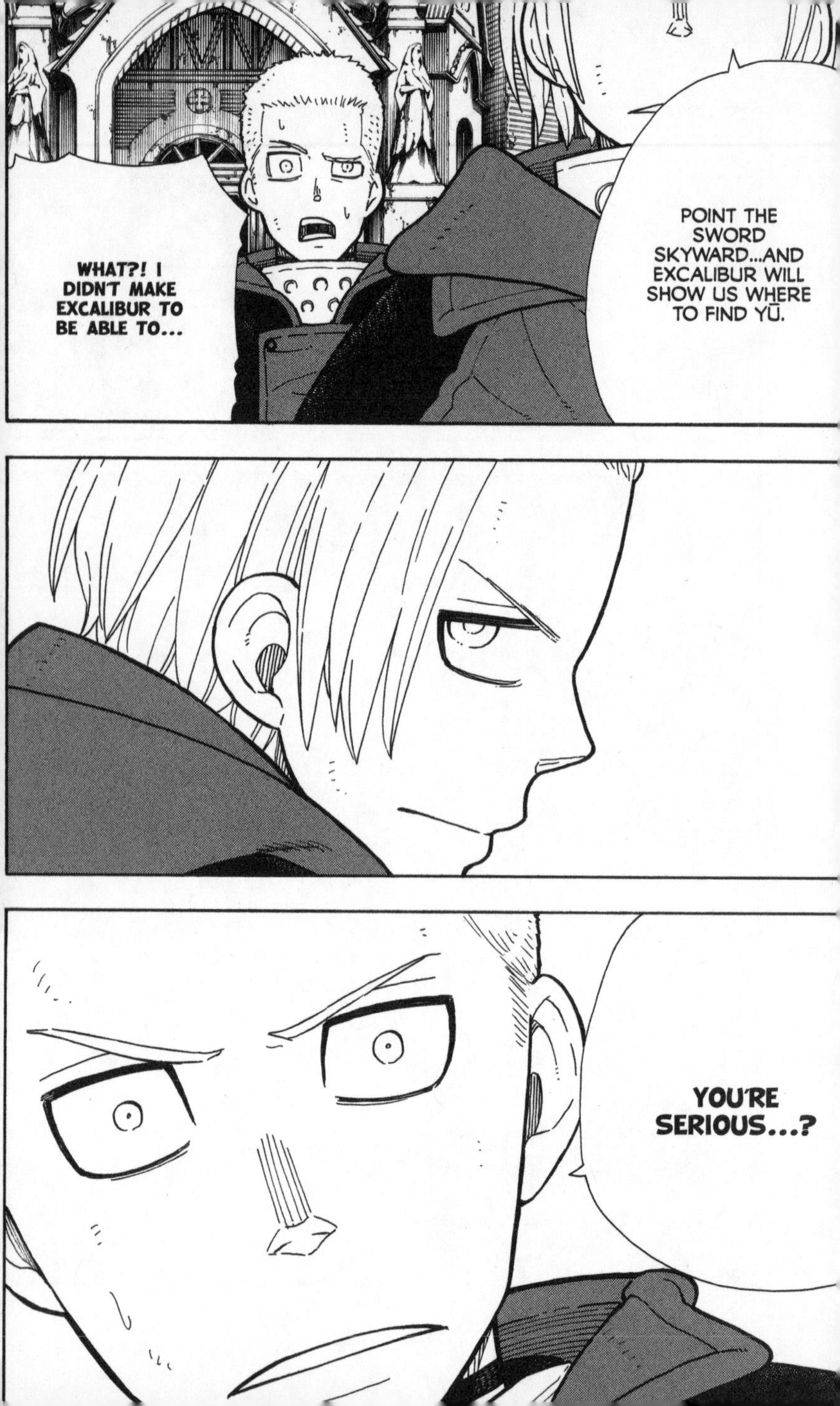
POINT THE SWORD SKYWARD...AND EXCALIBUR WILL SHOW US WHERE TO FIND YŪ.
WHAT?! I DIDN'T MAKE EXCALIBUR TO BE ABLE TO...
YOU'RE SERIOUS...?

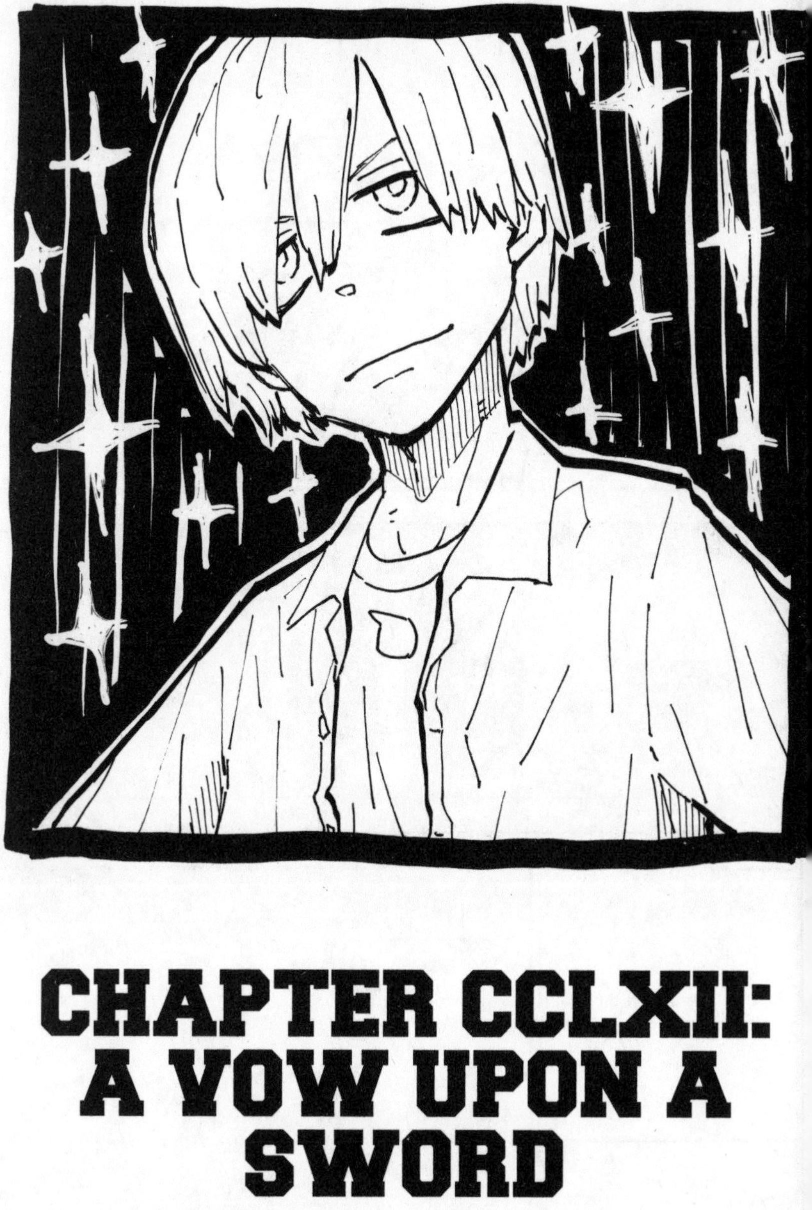

CHAPTER CCLXII: A VOW UPON A SWORD

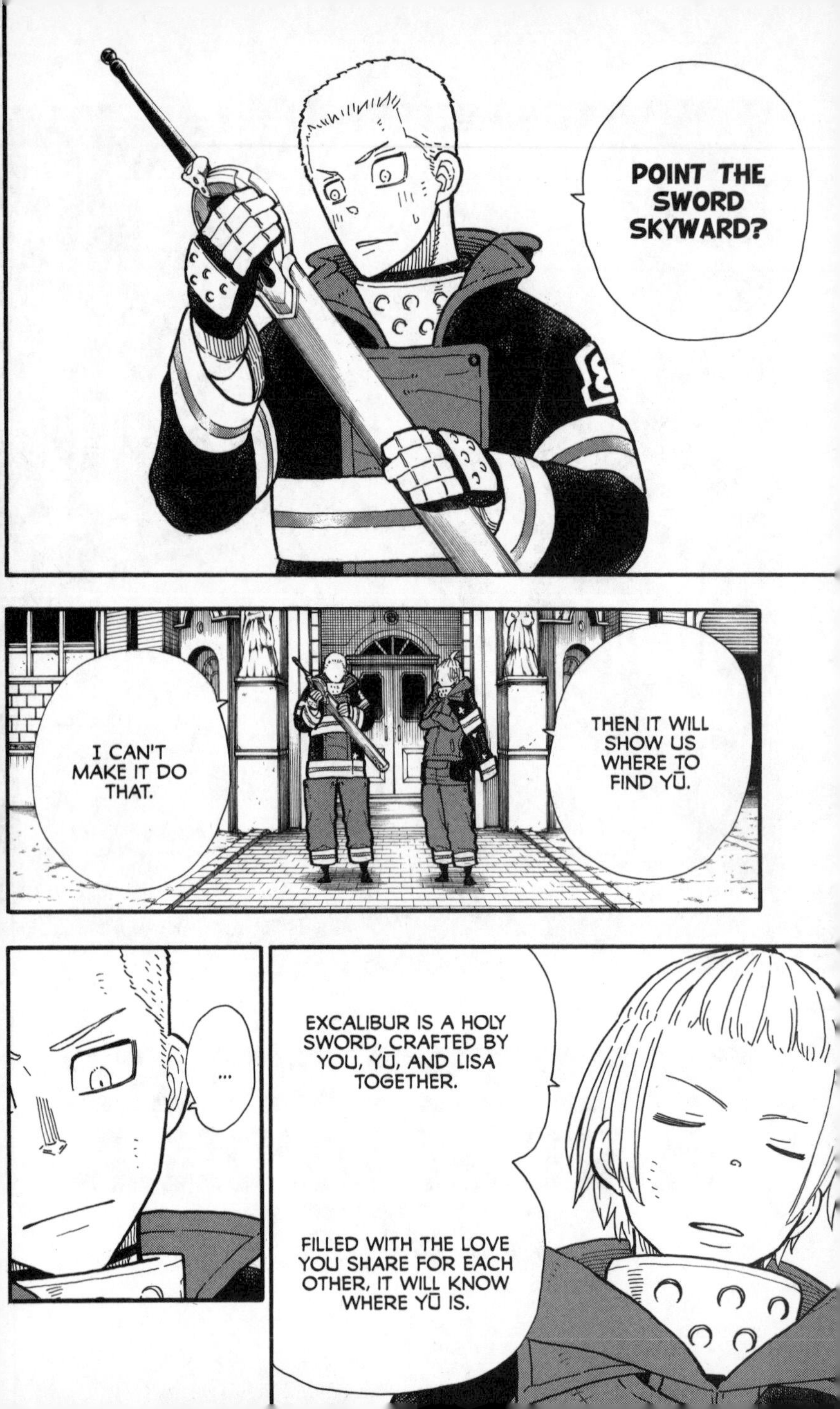
POINT THE SWORD SKYWARD?
THEN IT WILL SHOW US WHERE TO FIND YŪ.
I CAN'T MAKE IT DO THAT.
EXCALIBUR IS A HOLY SWORD, CRAFTED BY YOU, YŪ, AND LISA TOGETHER.
FILLED WITH THE LOVE YOU SHARE FOR EACH OTHER, IT WILL KNOW WHERE YŪ IS.
...

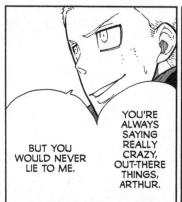

カチ
CLANK
YOU'RE ALWAYS SAYING REALLY CRAZY, OUT-THERE THINGS, ARTHUR.
BUT YOU WOULD NEVER LIE TO ME.
STILL, IF NOTHING HAPPENS, THIS IS GONNA BE *REALLY* EMBARRASSING!!
YOUR FEELINGS FOR YŪ WILL GUIDE YOU TO OUR DESTINATION.
MY FEELINGS FOR YŪ...

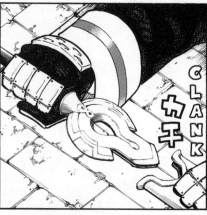

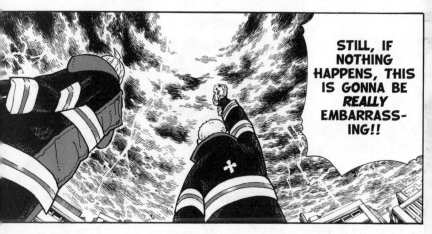

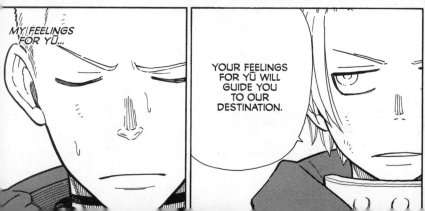

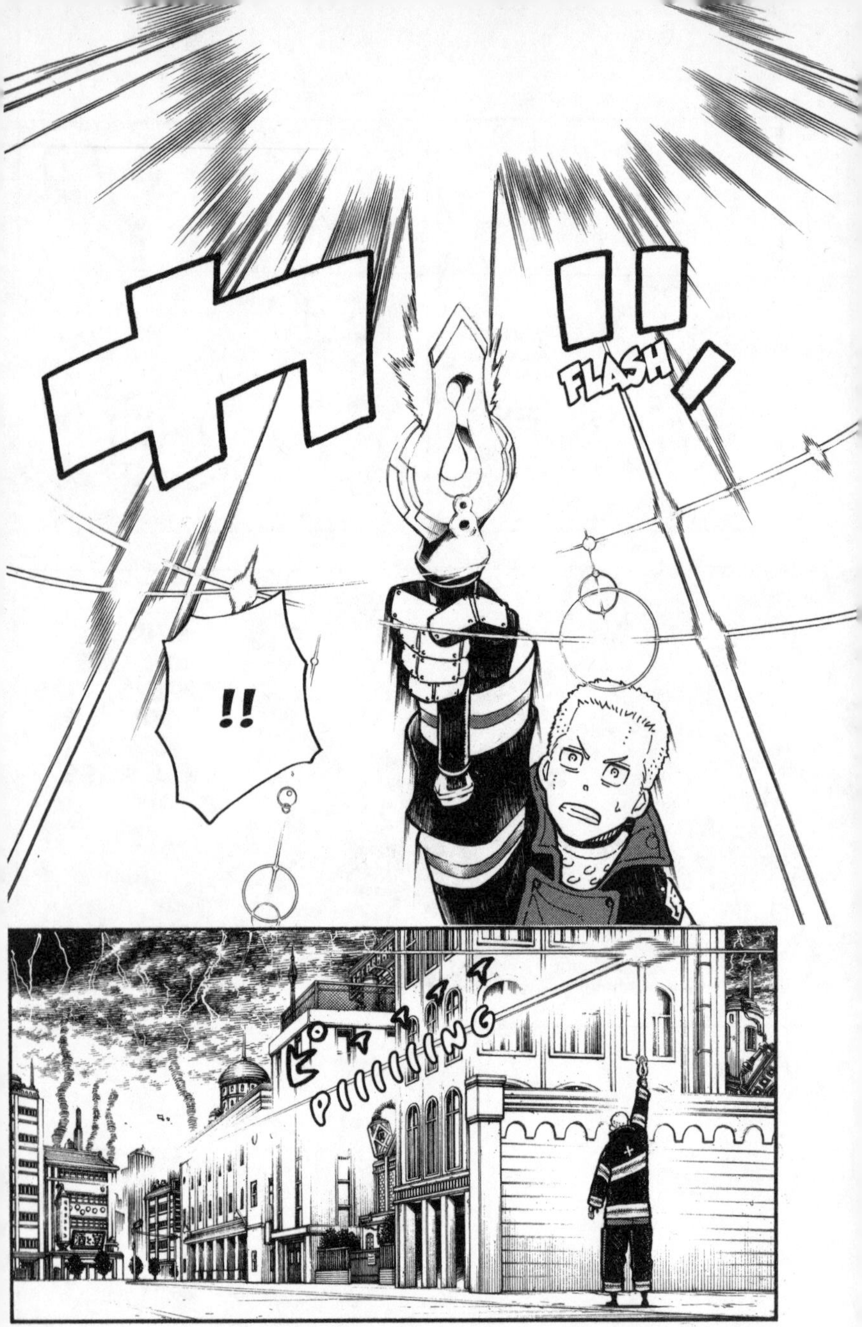
FLASH
!!
PIIIIIING

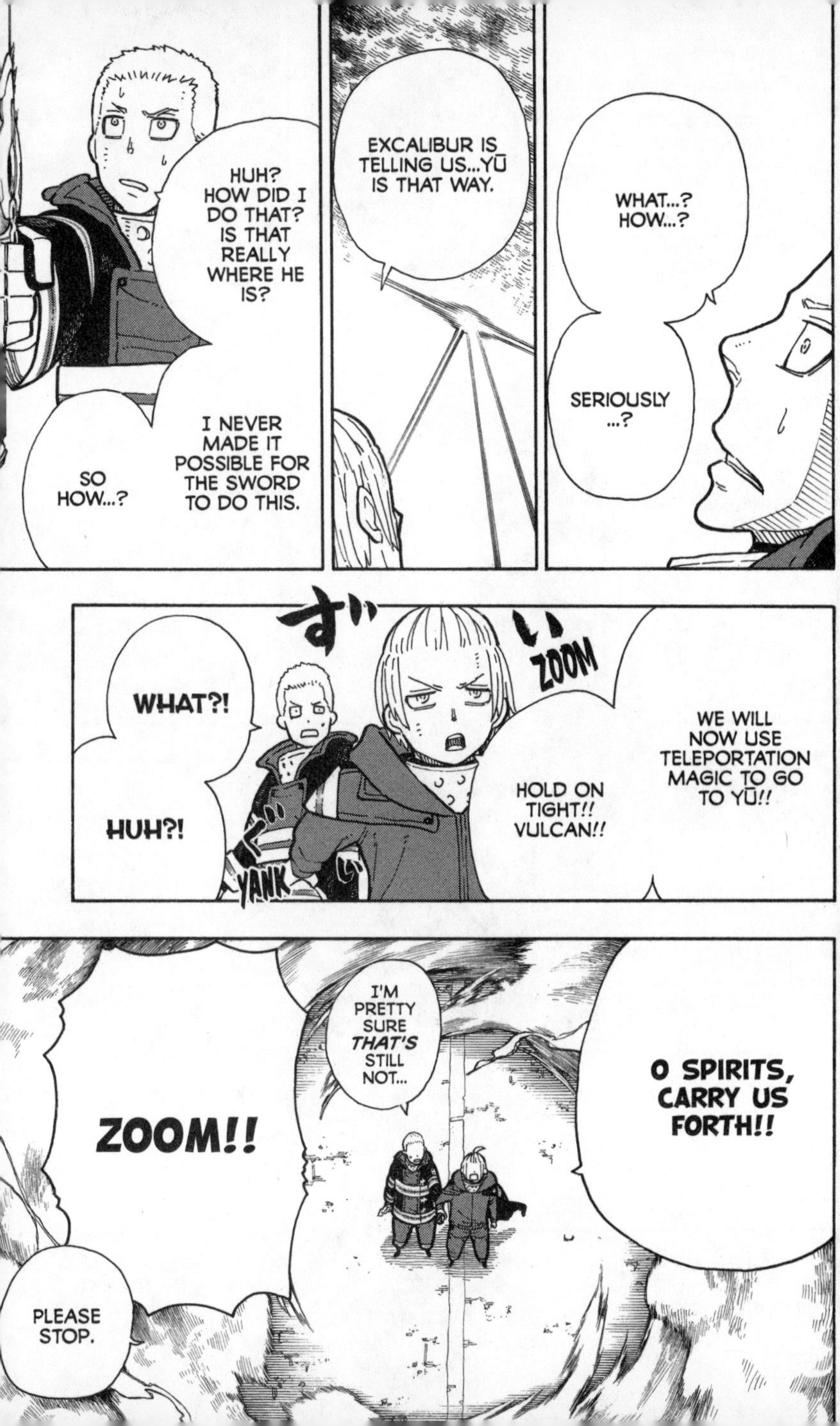
WHAT...? HOW...?
SERIOUSLY ...?
EXCALIBUR IS TELLING US...YŪ IS THAT WAY.
HUH? HOW DID I DO THAT? IS THAT REALLY WHERE HE IS?
I NEVER MADE IT POSSIBLE FOR THE SWORD TO DO THIS.
SO HOW...?
WE WILL NOW USE TELEPORTATION MAGIC TO GO TO YŪ!!
ZOOM
HOLD ON TIGHT!! VULCAN!!
YANK
WHAT?!
HUH?!
O SPIRITS, CARRY US FORTH!!
I'M PRETTY SURE *THAT'S* STILL NOT...
ZOOM!!
PLEASE STOP.

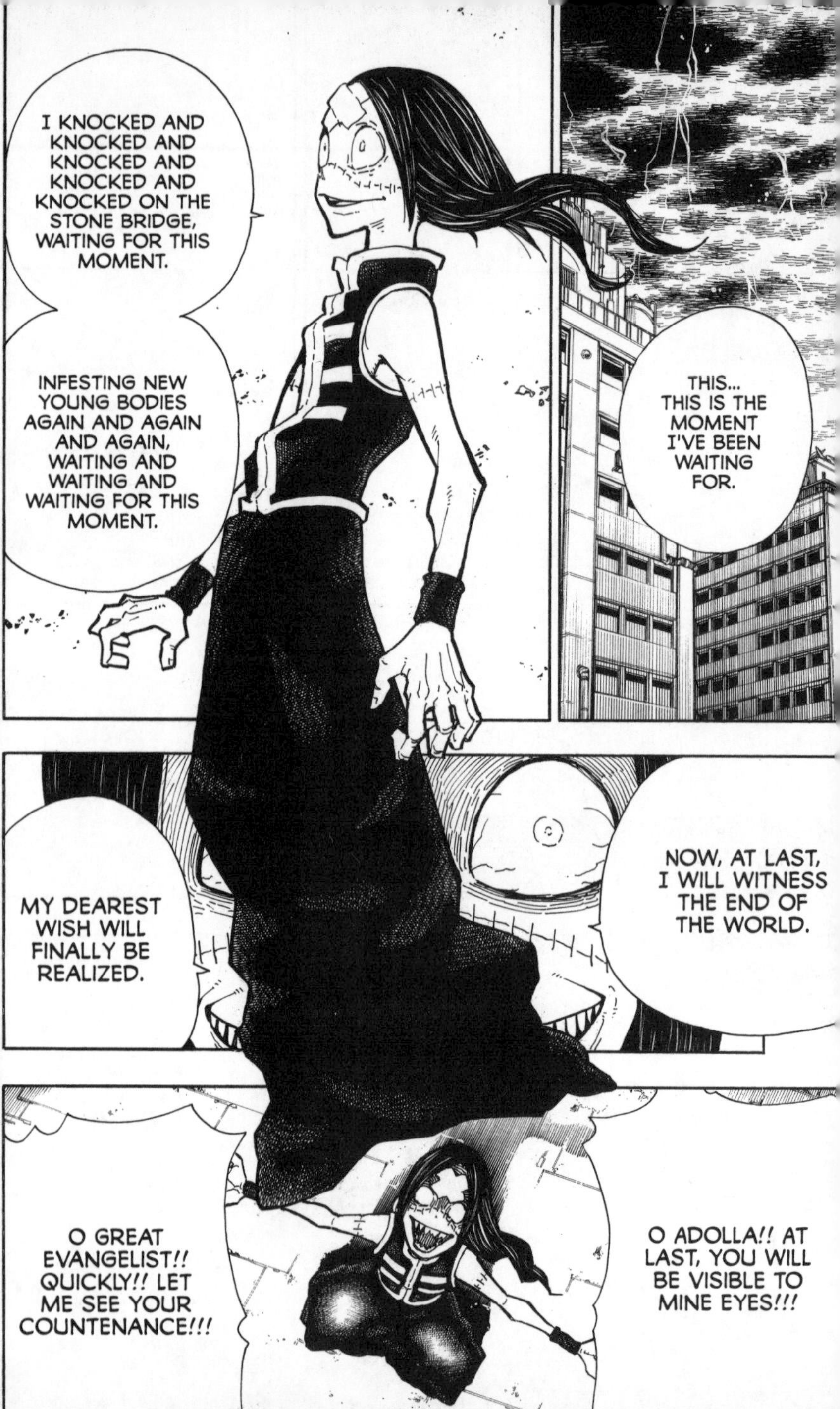
THIS... THIS IS THE MOMENT I'VE BEEN WAITING FOR.
I KNOCKED AND KNOCKED AND KNOCKED AND KNOCKED AND KNOCKED ON THE STONE BRIDGE, WAITING FOR THIS MOMENT.
INFESTING NEW YOUNG BODIES AGAIN AND AGAIN AND AGAIN, WAITING AND WAITING AND WAITING FOR THIS MOMENT.
NOW, AT LAST, I WILL WITNESS THE END OF THE WORLD.
MY DEAREST WISH WILL FINALLY BE REALIZED.
O ADOLLA!! AT LAST, YOU WILL BE VISIBLE TO MINE EYES!!!
O GREAT EVANGELIST!! QUICKLY!! LET ME SEE YOUR COUNTENANCE!!!

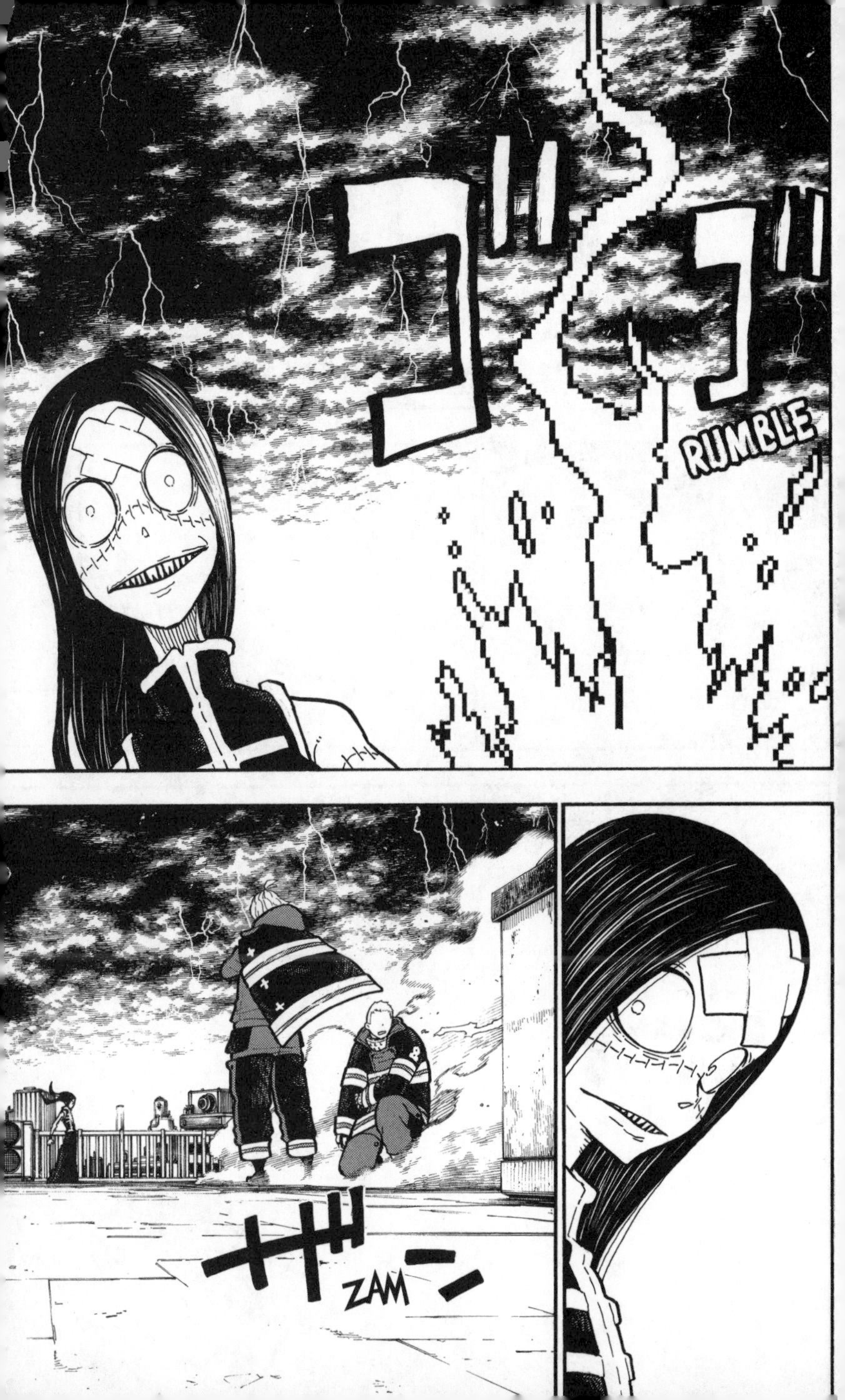
RUMBLE
ZAM

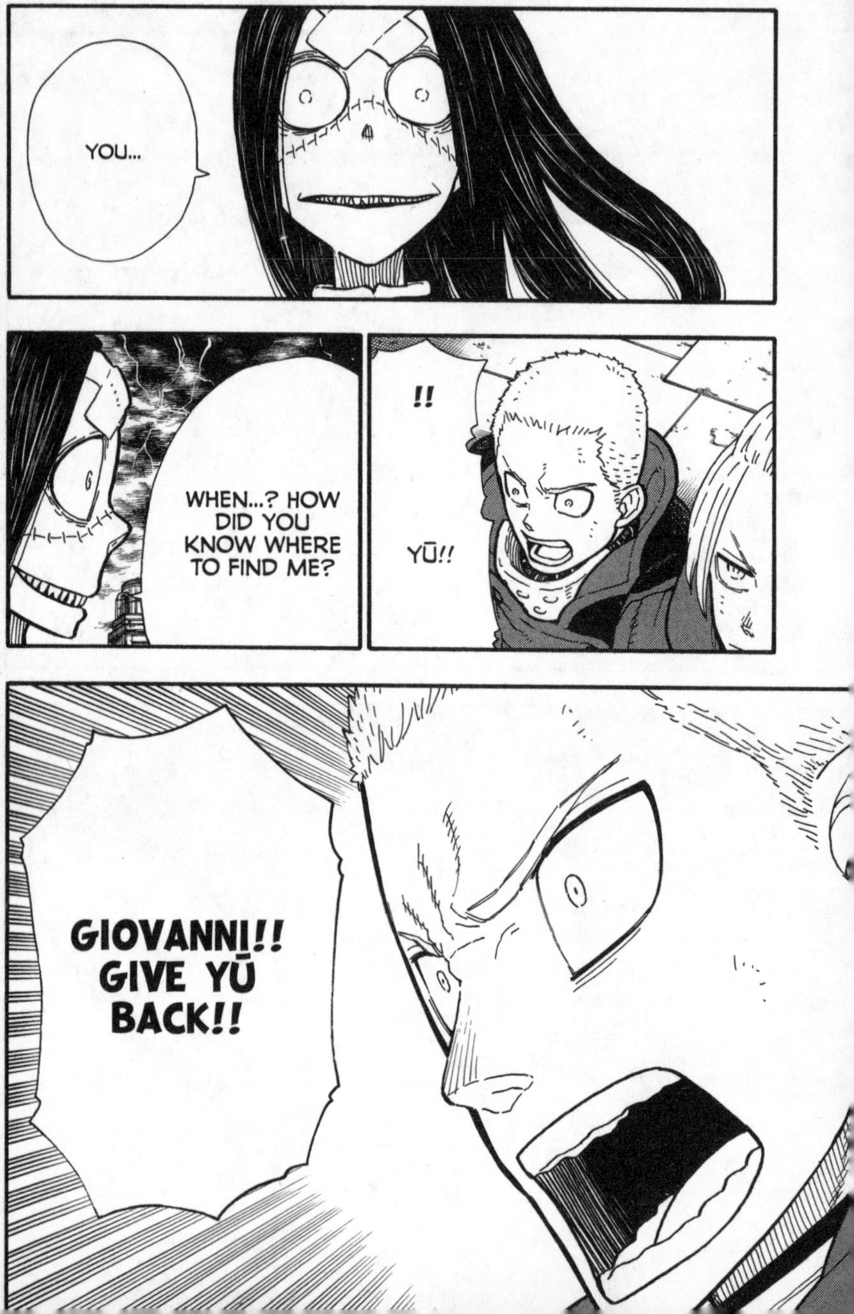
YOU...
!!
YŪ!!
WHEN...? HOW DID YOU KNOW WHERE TO FIND ME?
GIOVANNI!! GIVE YŪ BACK!!

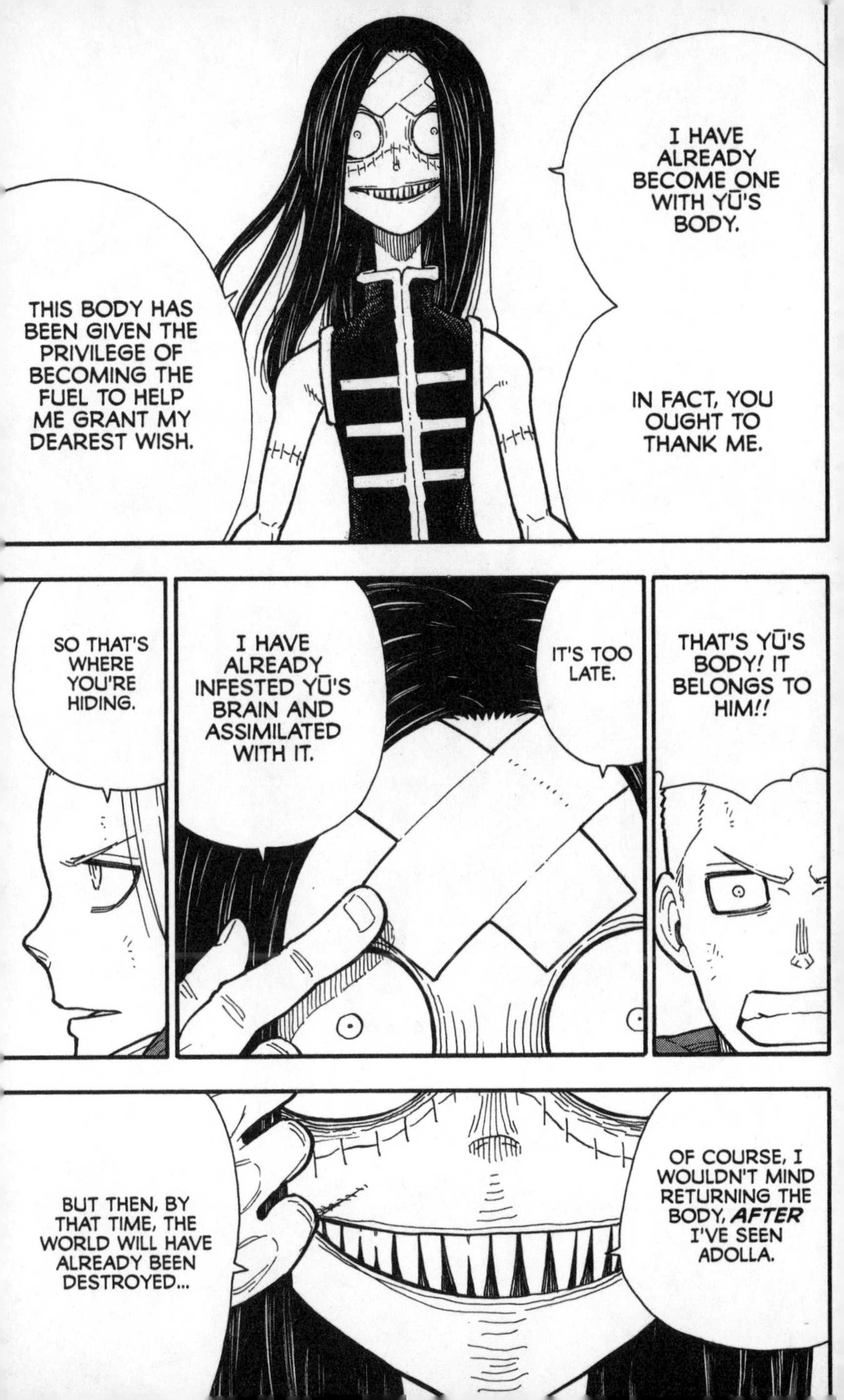
I HAVE ALREADY BECOME ONE WITH YŪ'S BODY.
IN FACT, YOU OUGHT TO THANK ME.
THIS BODY HAS BEEN GIVEN THE PRIVILEGE OF BECOMING THE FUEL TO HELP ME GRANT MY DEAREST WISH.
THAT'S YŪ'S BODY! IT BELONGS TO HIM!!
IT'S TOO LATE.
I HAVE ALREADY INFESTED YŪ'S BRAIN AND ASSIMILATED WITH IT.
SO THAT'S WHERE YOU'RE HIDING.
OF COURSE, I WOULDN'T MIND RETURNING THE BODY, ***AFTER*** I'VE SEEN ADOLLA.
BUT THEN, BY THAT TIME, THE WORLD WILL HAVE ALREADY BEEN DESTROYED...

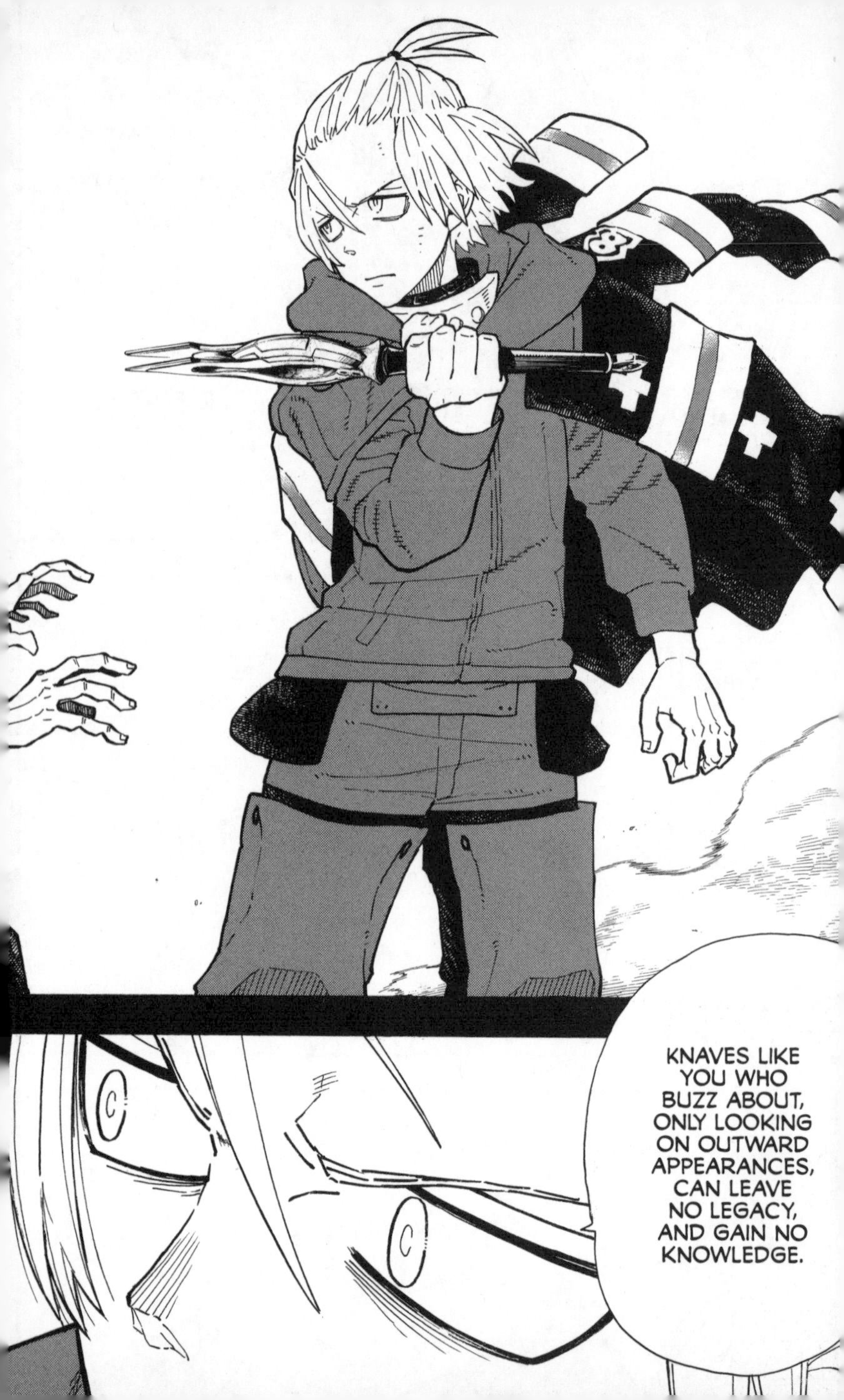
KNAVES LIKE YOU WHO BUZZ ABOUT, ONLY LOOKING ON OUTWARD APPEARANCES, CAN LEAVE NO LEGACY, AND GAIN NO KNOWLEDGE.

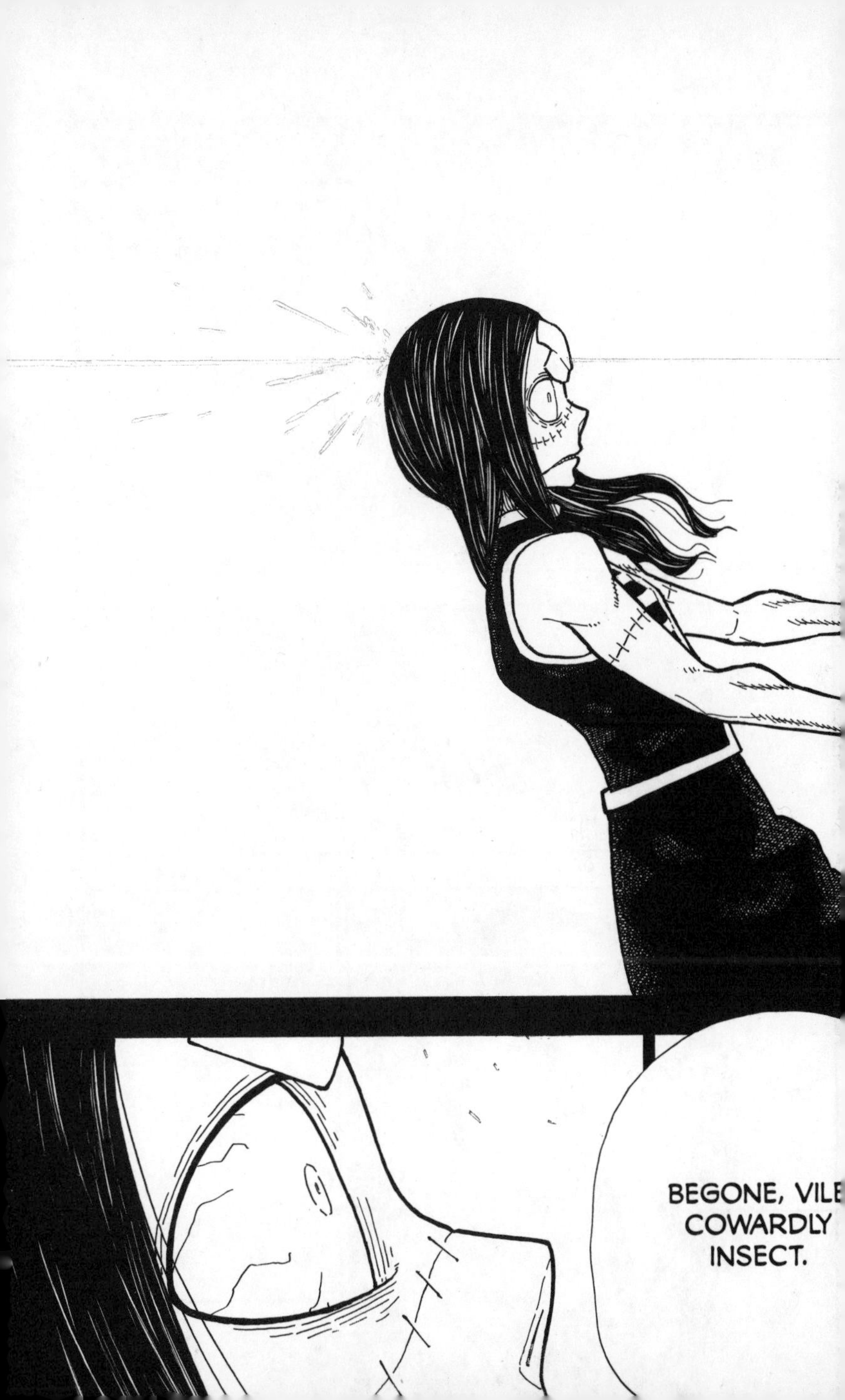
BEGONE, VILE COWARDLY INSECT.

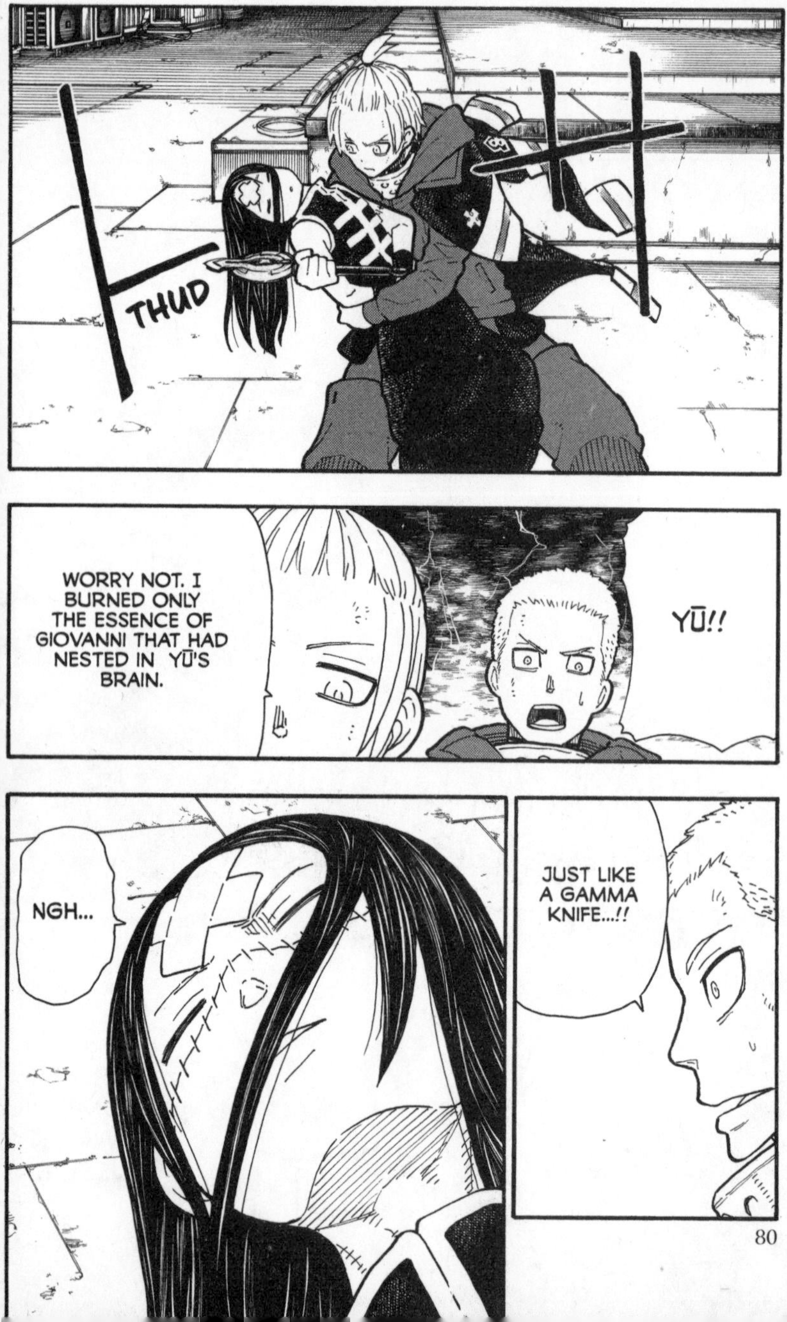
THUD
YŪ!!
WORRY NOT. I BURNED ONLY THE ESSENCE OF GIOVANNI THAT HAD NESTED IN YŪ'S BRAIN.
JUST LIKE A GAMMA KNIFE...!!
NGH...

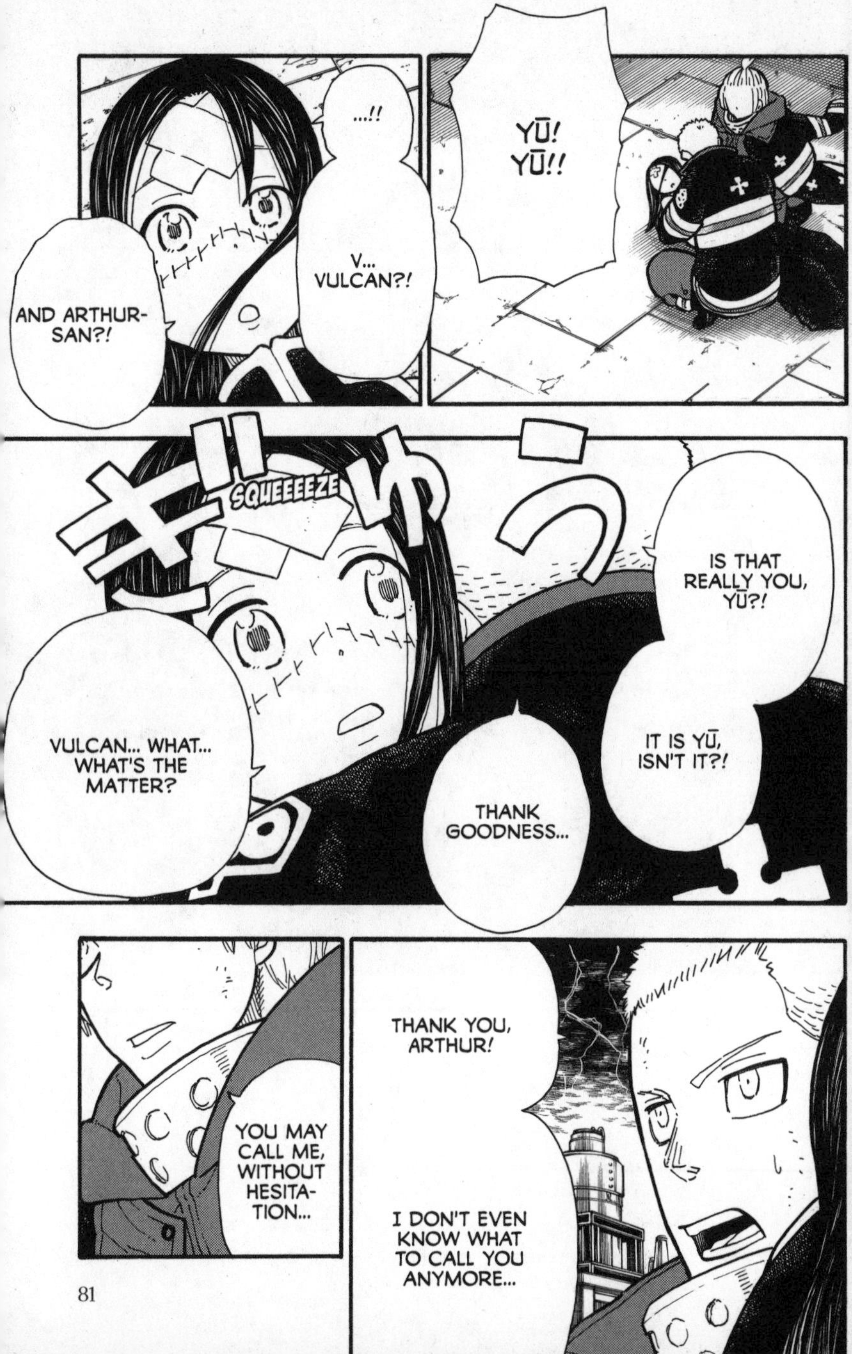
YŪ! YŪ!!
...!!
V... VULCAN?!
AND ARTHUR-SAN?!
SQUEEEEEZE
IS THAT REALLY YOU, YŪ?!
IT IS YŪ, ISN'T IT?!
THANK GOODNESS...
VULCAN... WHAT... WHAT'S THE MATTER?
THANK YOU, ARTHUR!
I DON'T EVEN KNOW WHAT TO CALL YOU ANYMORE...
YOU MAY CALL ME, WITHOUT HESITATION...

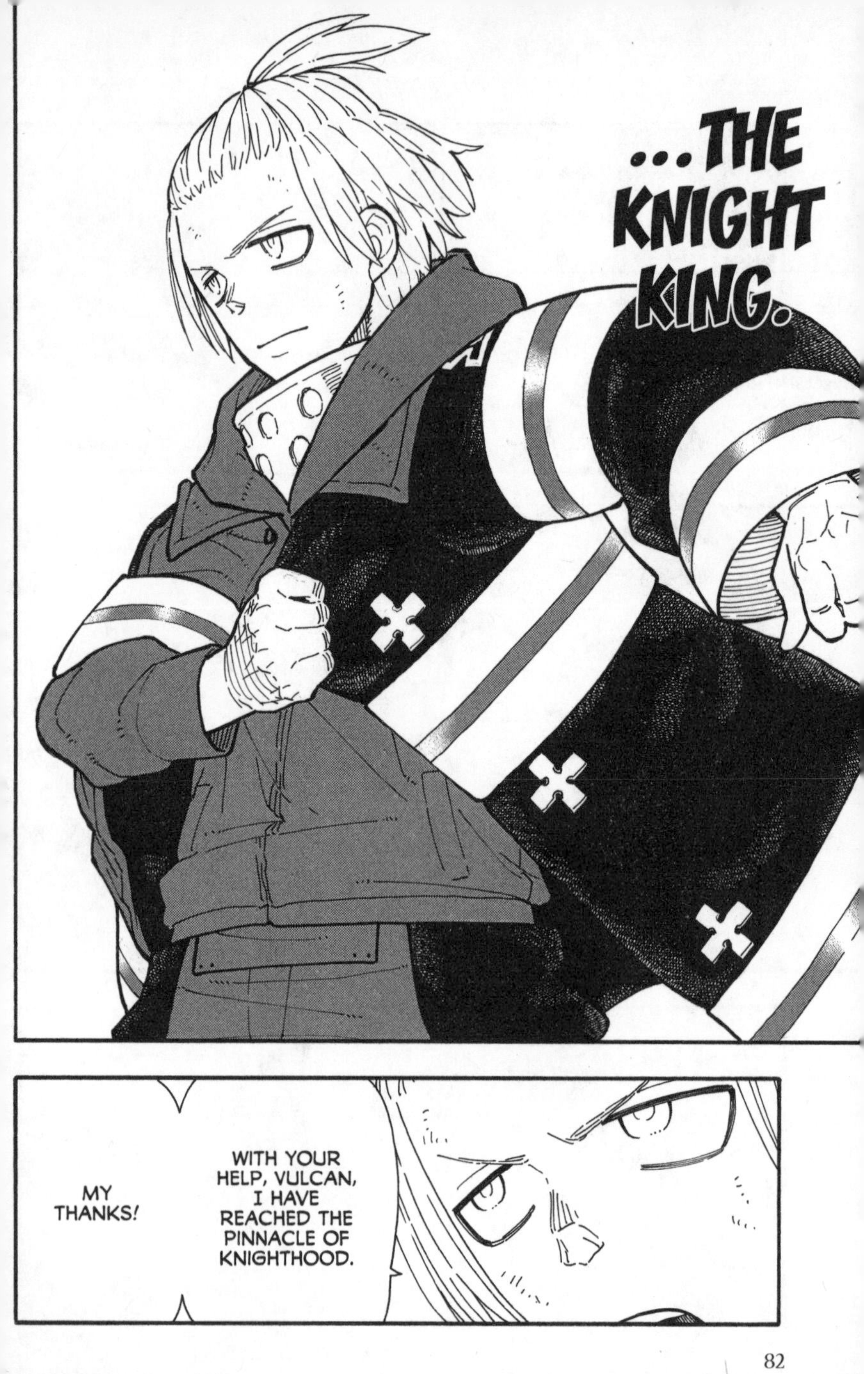
...THE KNIGHT KING.
WITH YOUR HELP, VULCAN, I HAVE REACHED THE PINNACLE OF KNIGHTHOOD.
MY THANKS!

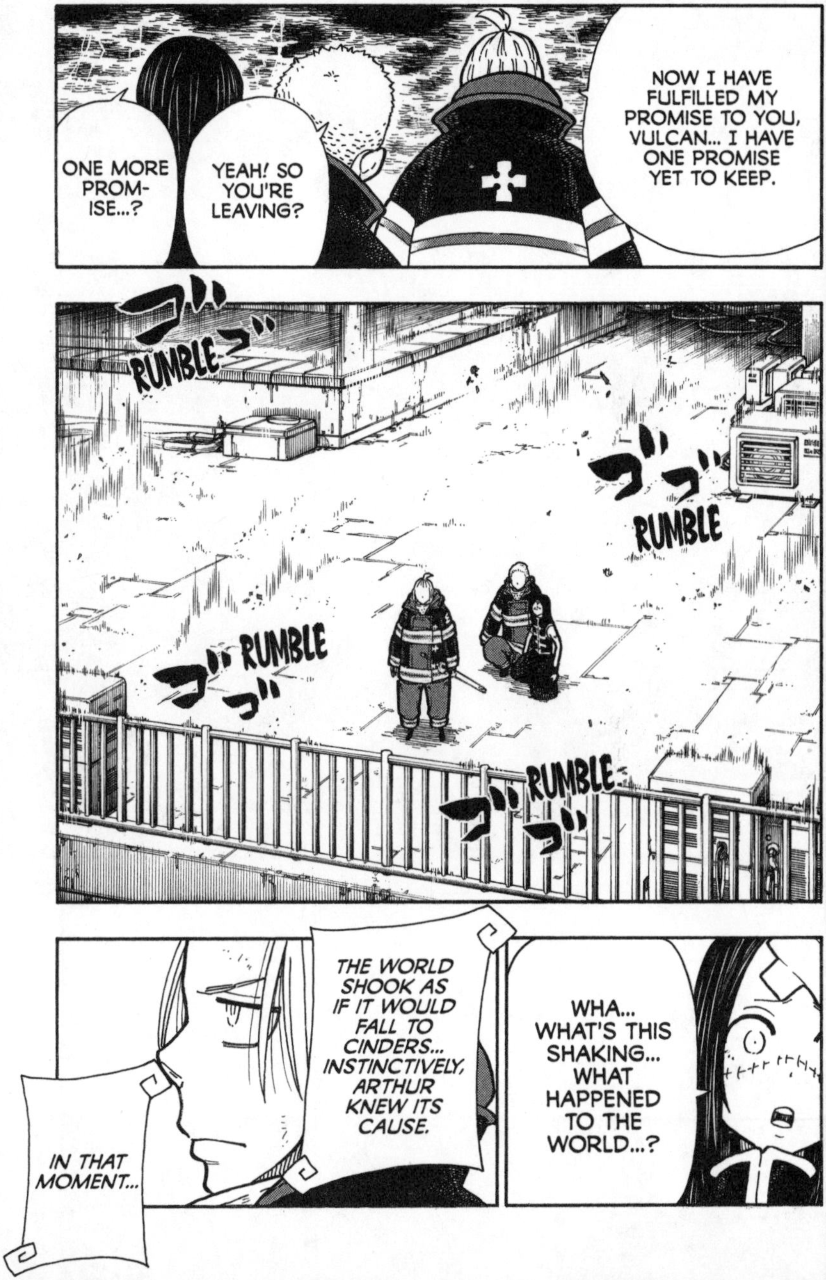
NOW I HAVE FULFILLED MY PROMISE TO YOU, VULCAN... I HAVE ONE PROMISE YET TO KEEP.
YEAH! SO YOU'RE LEAVING?
ONE MORE PROM-ISE...?
RUMBLE
RUMBLE
RUMBLE
RUMBLE
WHA... WHAT'S THIS SHAKING... WHAT HAPPENED TO THE WORLD...?
THE WORLD SHOOK AS IF IT WOULD FALL TO CINDERS... INSTINCTIVELY, ARTHUR KNEW ITS CAUSE.
IN THAT MOMENT...

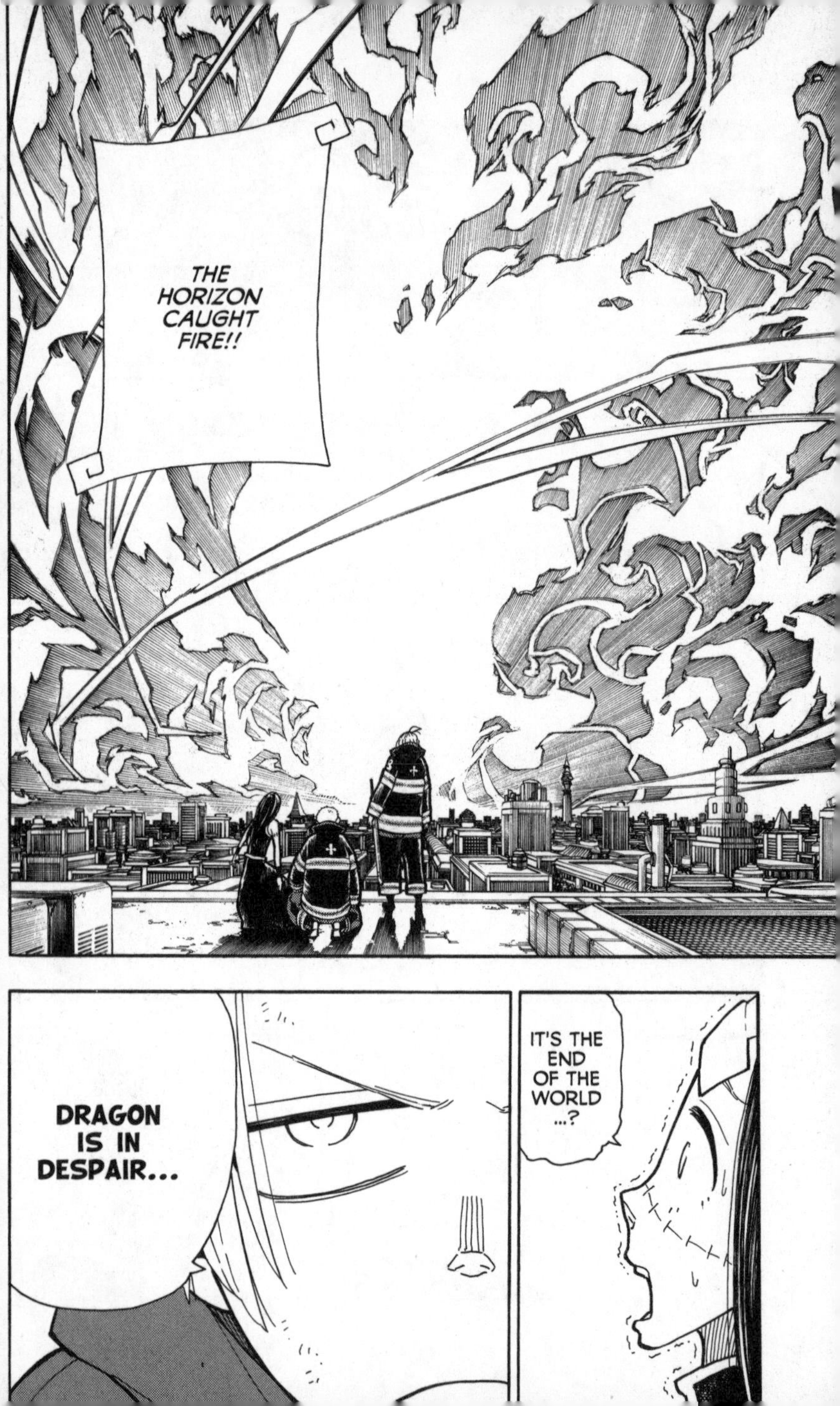
THE HORIZON CAUGHT FIRE!!
IT'S THE END OF THE WORLD ...?
DRAGON IS IN DESPAIR...

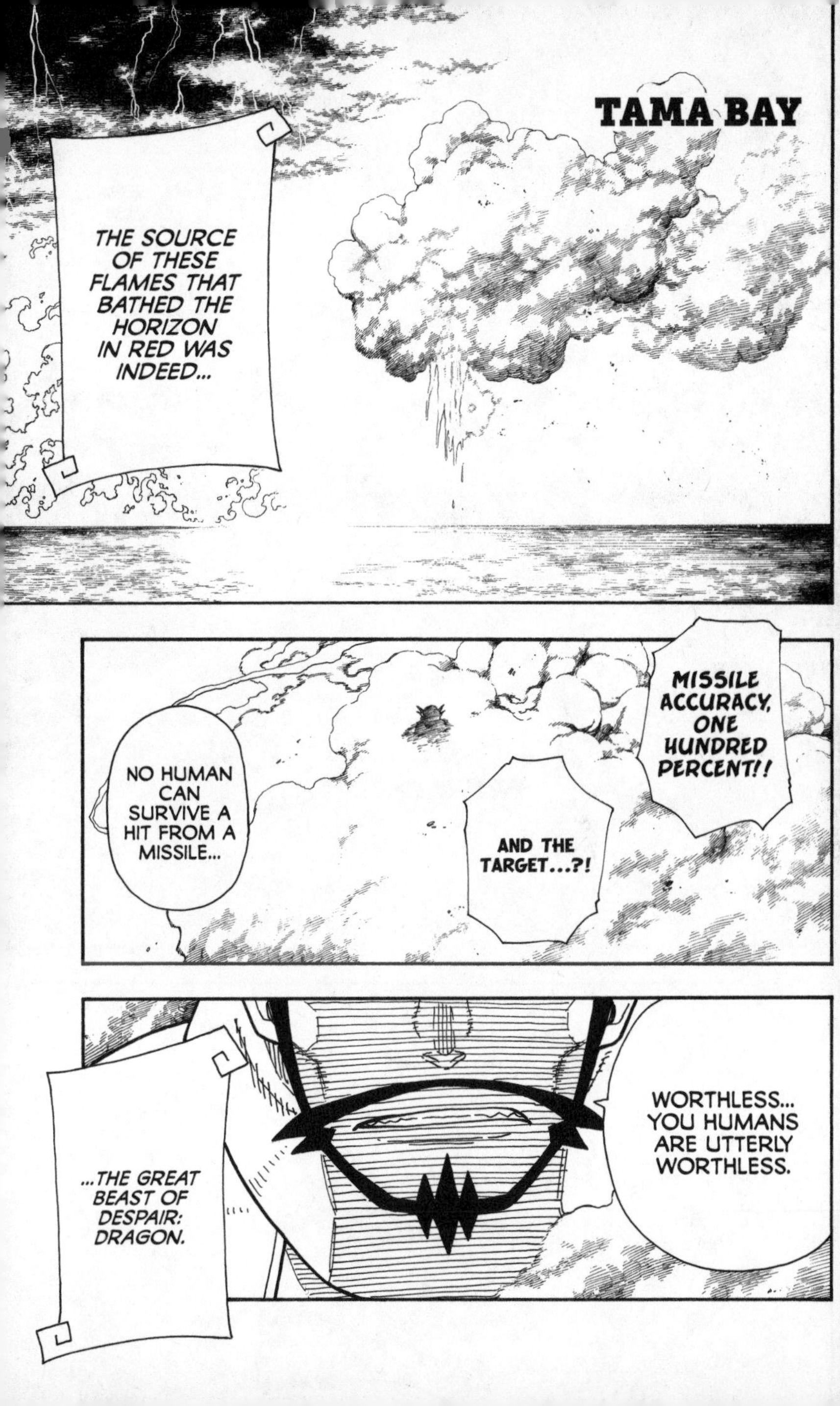
TAMA BAY
THE SOURCE OF THESE FLAMES THAT BATHED THE HORIZON IN RED WAS INDEED...
MISSILE ACCURACY, ONE HUNDRED PERCENT!!
AND THE TARGET...?!
NO HUMAN CAN SURVIVE A HIT FROM A MISSILE...
WORTHLESS... YOU HUMANS ARE UTTERLY WORTHLESS.
...THE GREAT BEAST OF DESPAIR: DRAGON.

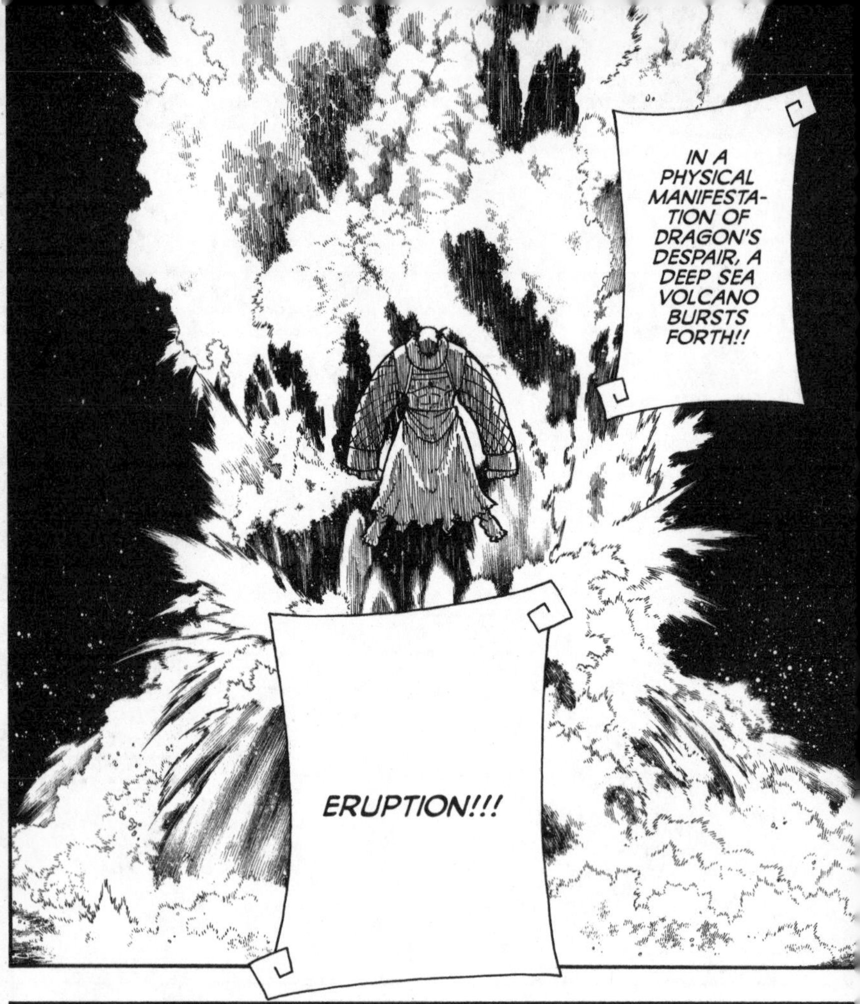
IN A PHYSICAL MANIFESTATION OF DRAGON'S DESPAIR, A DEEP SEA VOLCANO BURSTS FORTH!!
ERUPTION!!!
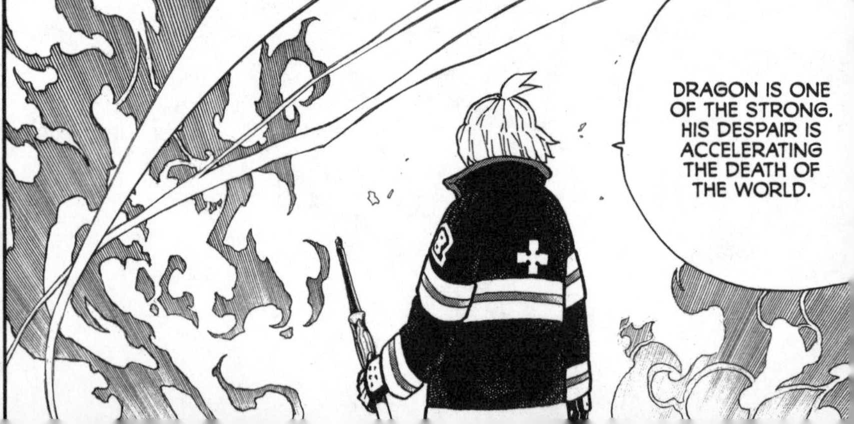
DRAGON IS ONE OF THE STRONG. HIS DESPAIR IS ACCELERATING THE DEATH OF THE WORLD.

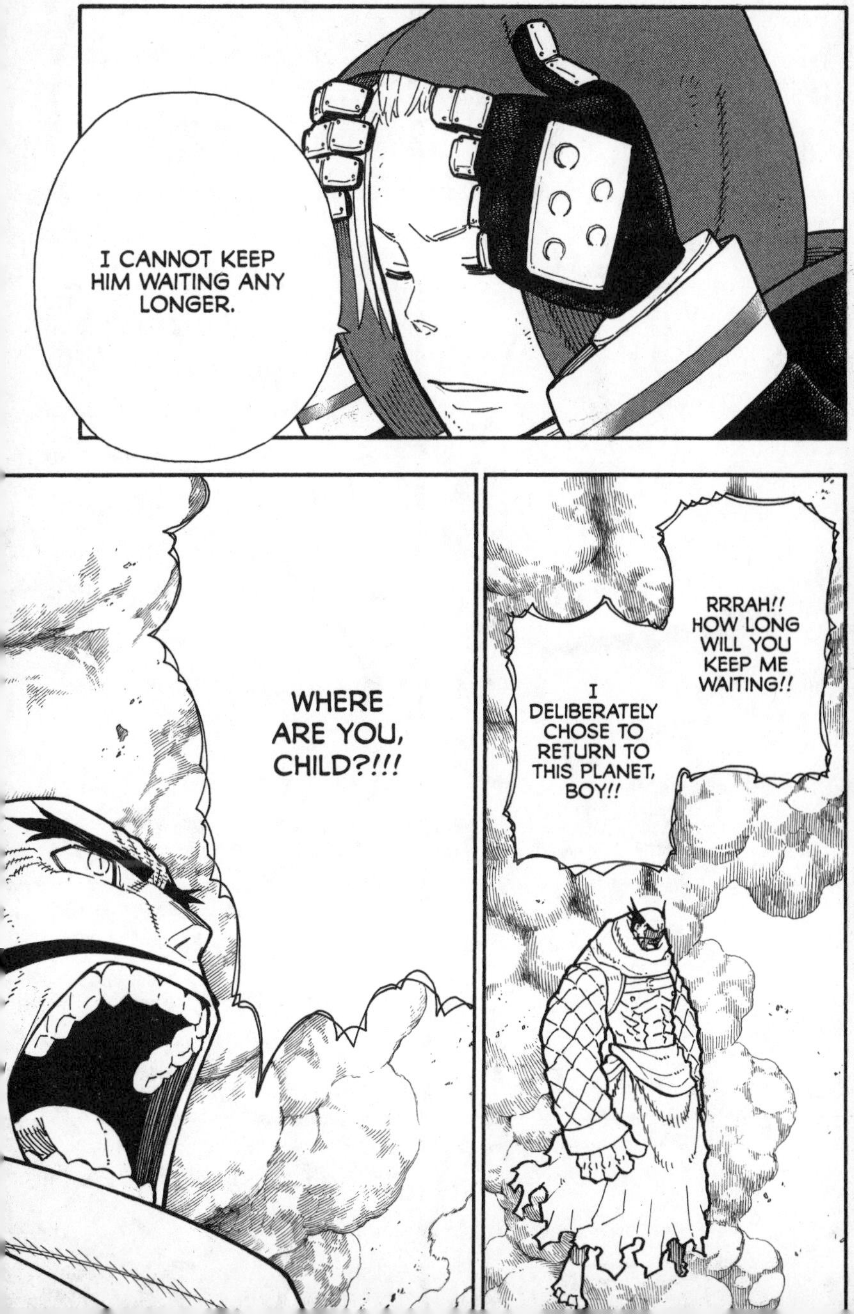
I CANNOT KEEP HIM WAITING ANY LONGER.
RRRAH!! HOW LONG WILL YOU KEEP ME WAITING!!
I DELIBERATELY CHOSE TO RETURN TO THIS PLANET, BOY!!
WHERE ARE YOU, CHILD?!!!

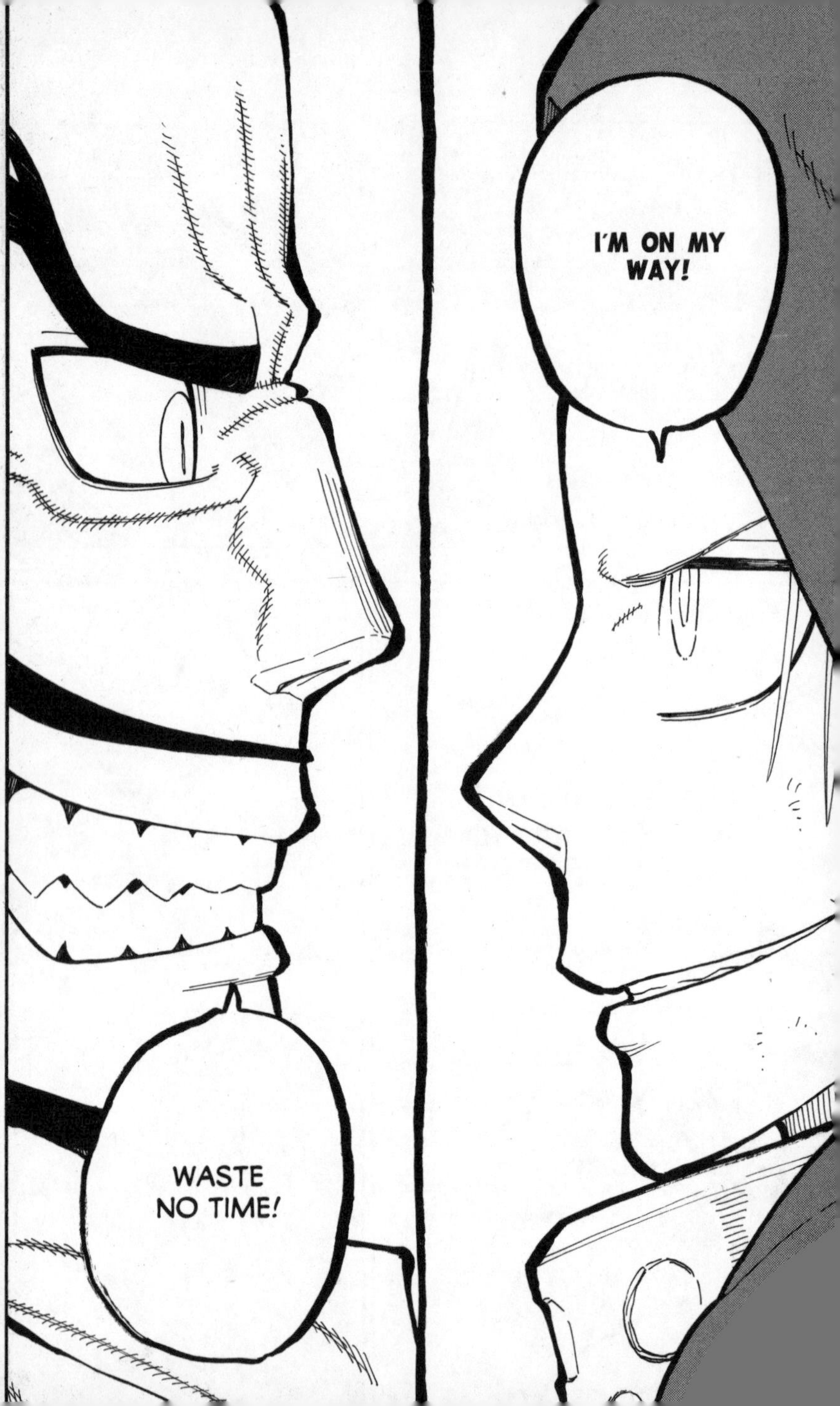
I'M ON MY WAY!
WASTE NO TIME!

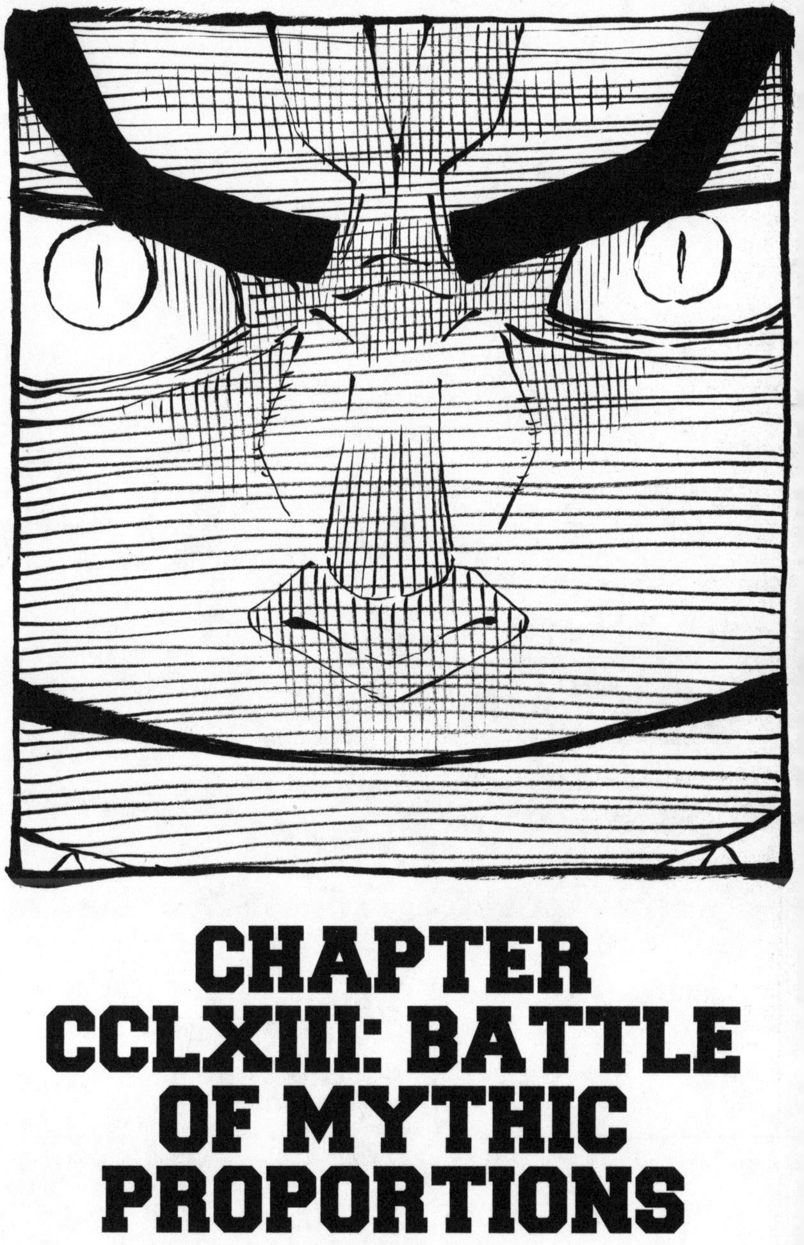

CHAPTER CCLXIII: BATTLE OF MYTHIC PROPORTIONS

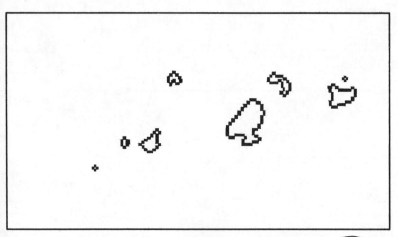

HE...

HE DISAP-PEARED...

HE WENT TO SETTLE HIS SCORE WITH DRAGON...

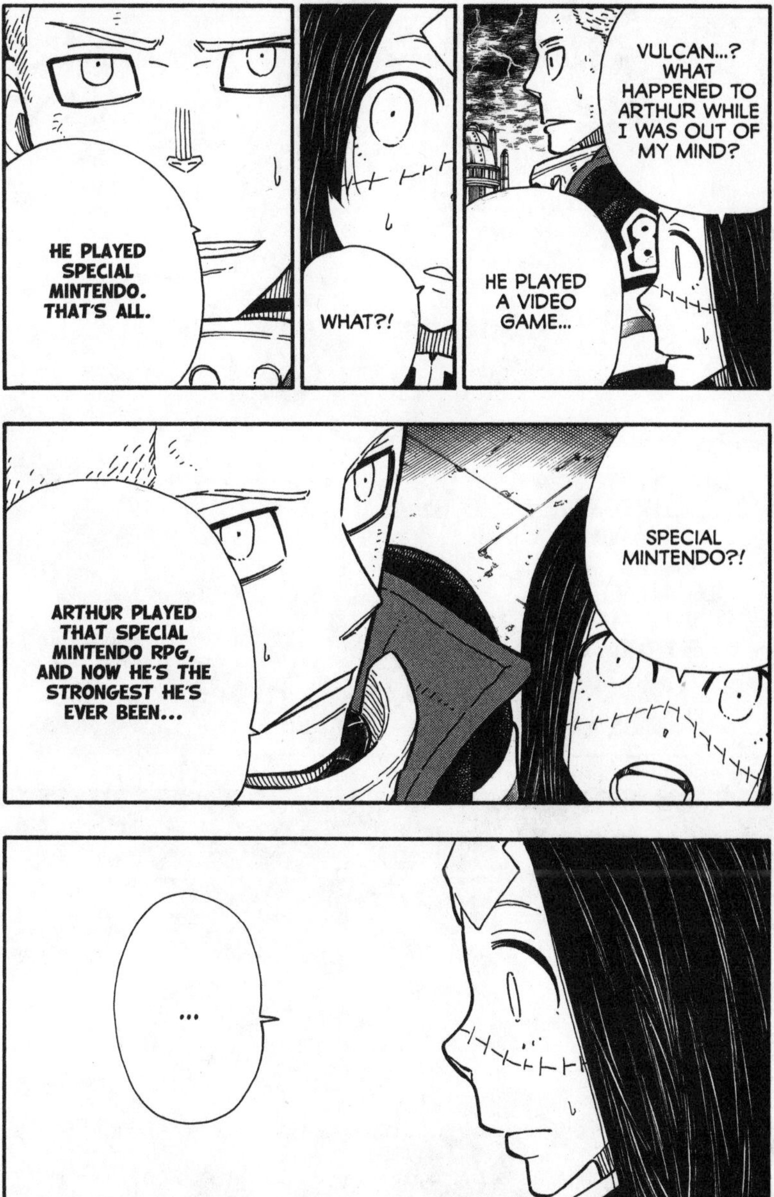
VULCAN...? WHAT HAPPENED TO ARTHUR WHILE I WAS OUT OF MY MIND?
HE PLAYED A VIDEO GAME...
WHAT?!
HE PLAYED SPECIAL MINTENDO. THAT'S ALL.
SPECIAL MINTENDO?!
ARTHUR PLAYED THAT SPECIAL MINTENDO RPG, AND NOW HE'S THE STRONGEST HE'S EVER BEEN...
...

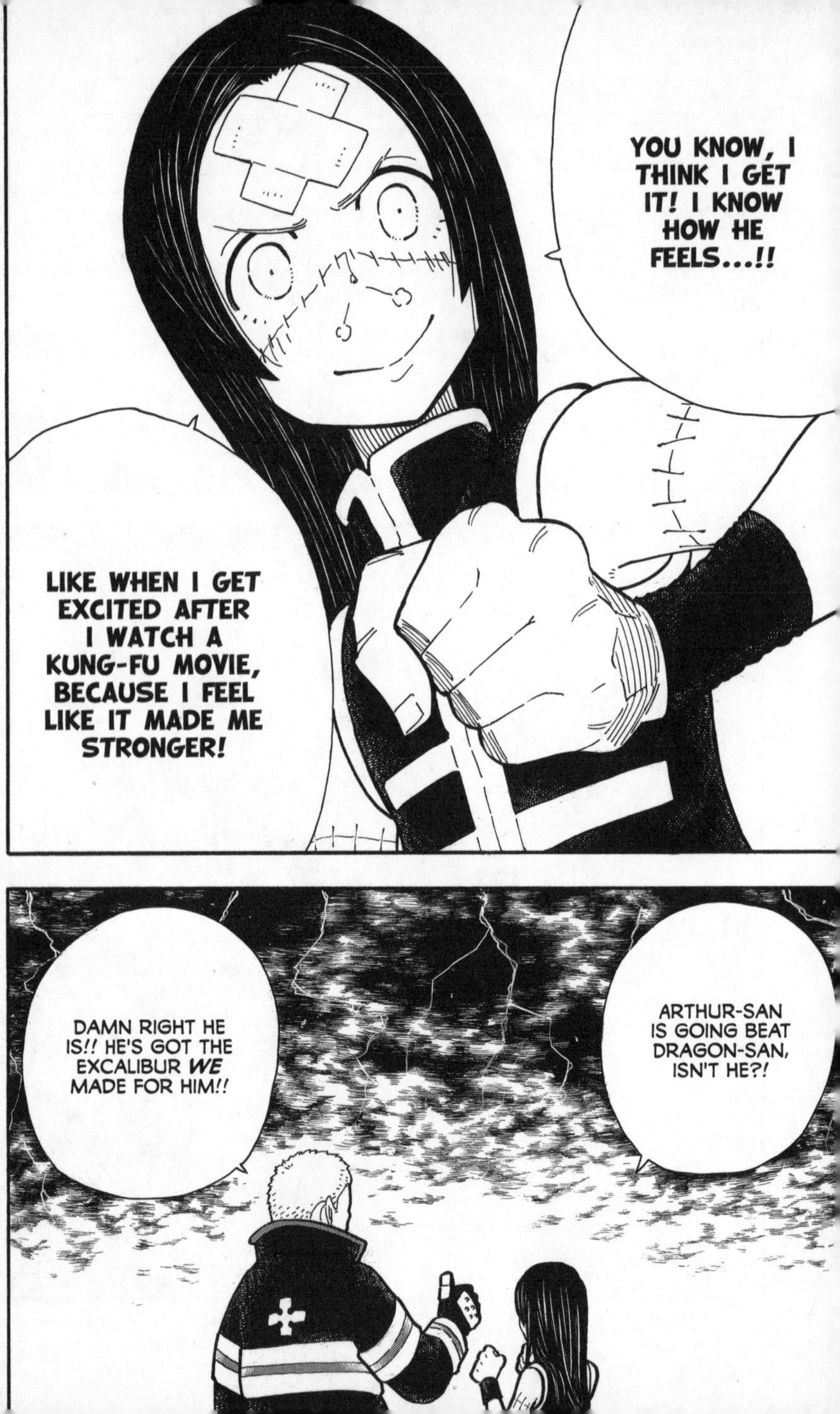
YOU KNOW, I THINK I GET IT! I KNOW HOW HE FEELS...!!
LIKE WHEN I GET EXCITED AFTER I WATCH A KUNG-FU MOVIE, BECAUSE I FEEL LIKE IT MADE ME STRONGER!
ARTHUR-SAN IS GOING BEAT DRAGON-SAN, ISN'T HE?!
DAMN RIGHT HE IS!! HE'S GOT THE EXCALIBUR *WE* MADE FOR HIM!!

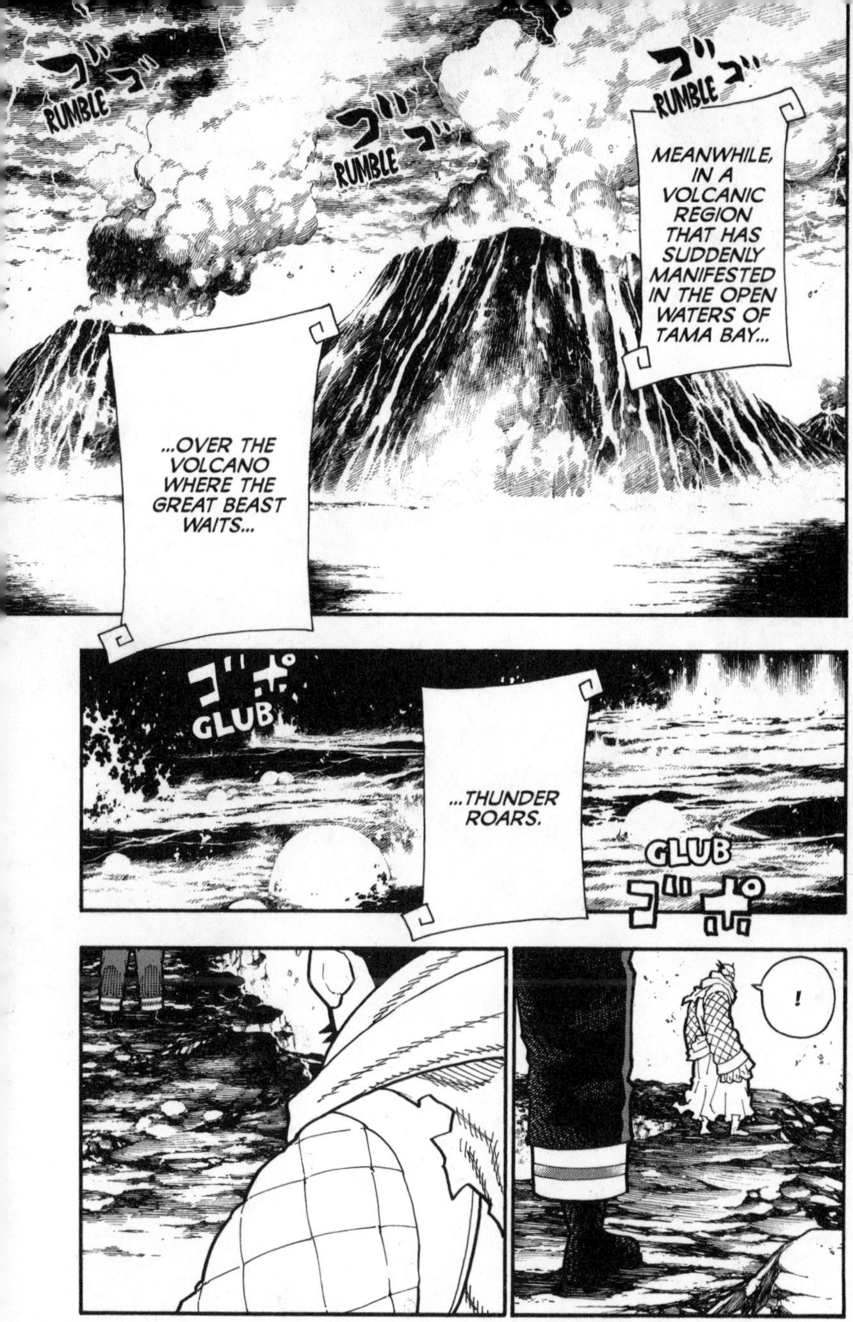
MEANWHILE, IN A VOLCANIC REGION THAT HAS SUDDENLY MANIFESTED IN THE OPEN WATERS OF TAMA BAY...
RUMBLE
RUMBLE
RUMBLE
...OVER THE VOLCANO WHERE THE GREAT BEAST WAITS...
GLUB
...THUNDER ROARS.
GLUB
!

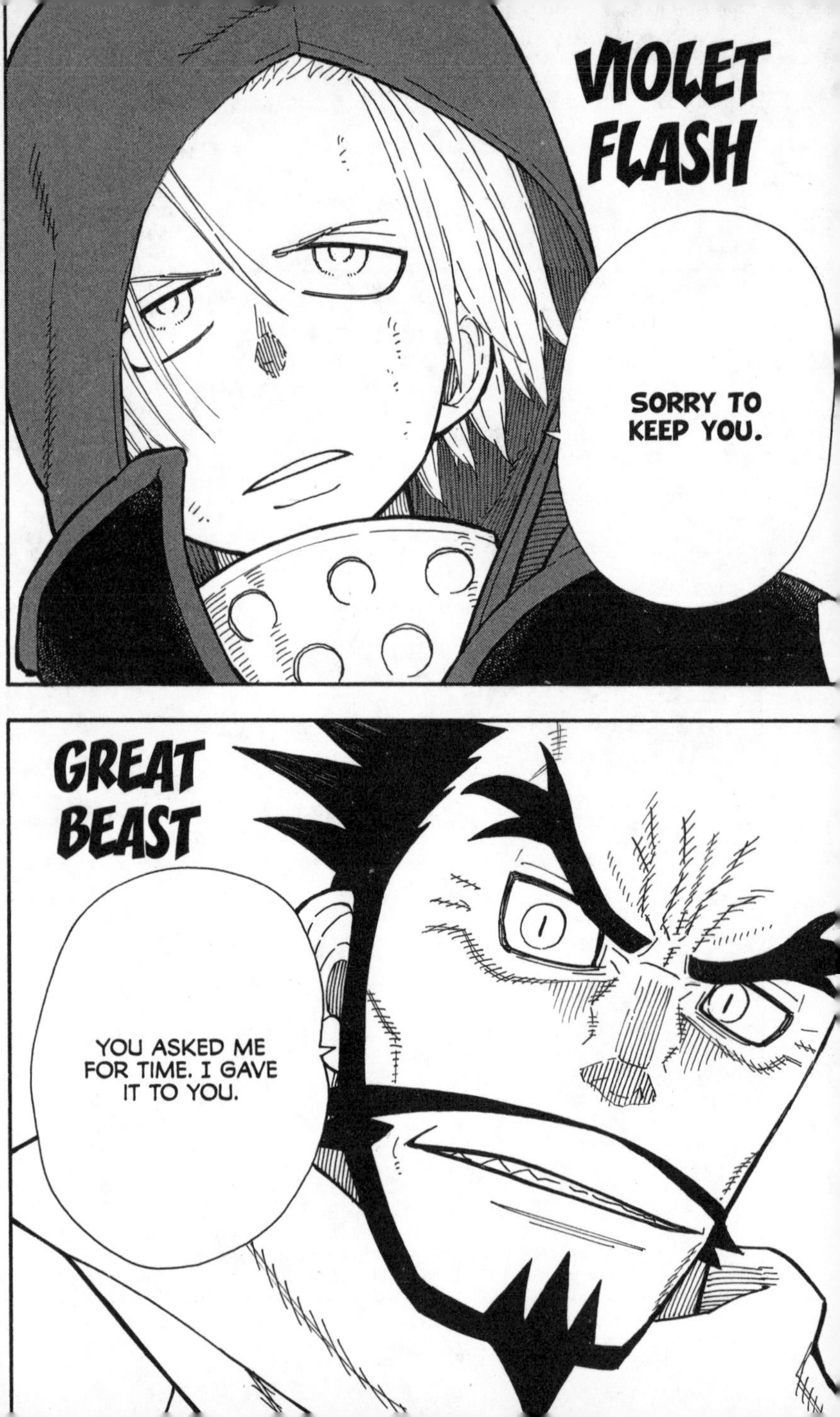
VIOLET FLASH
SORRY TO KEEP YOU.
GREAT BEAST
YOU ASKED ME FOR TIME. I GAVE IT TO YOU.

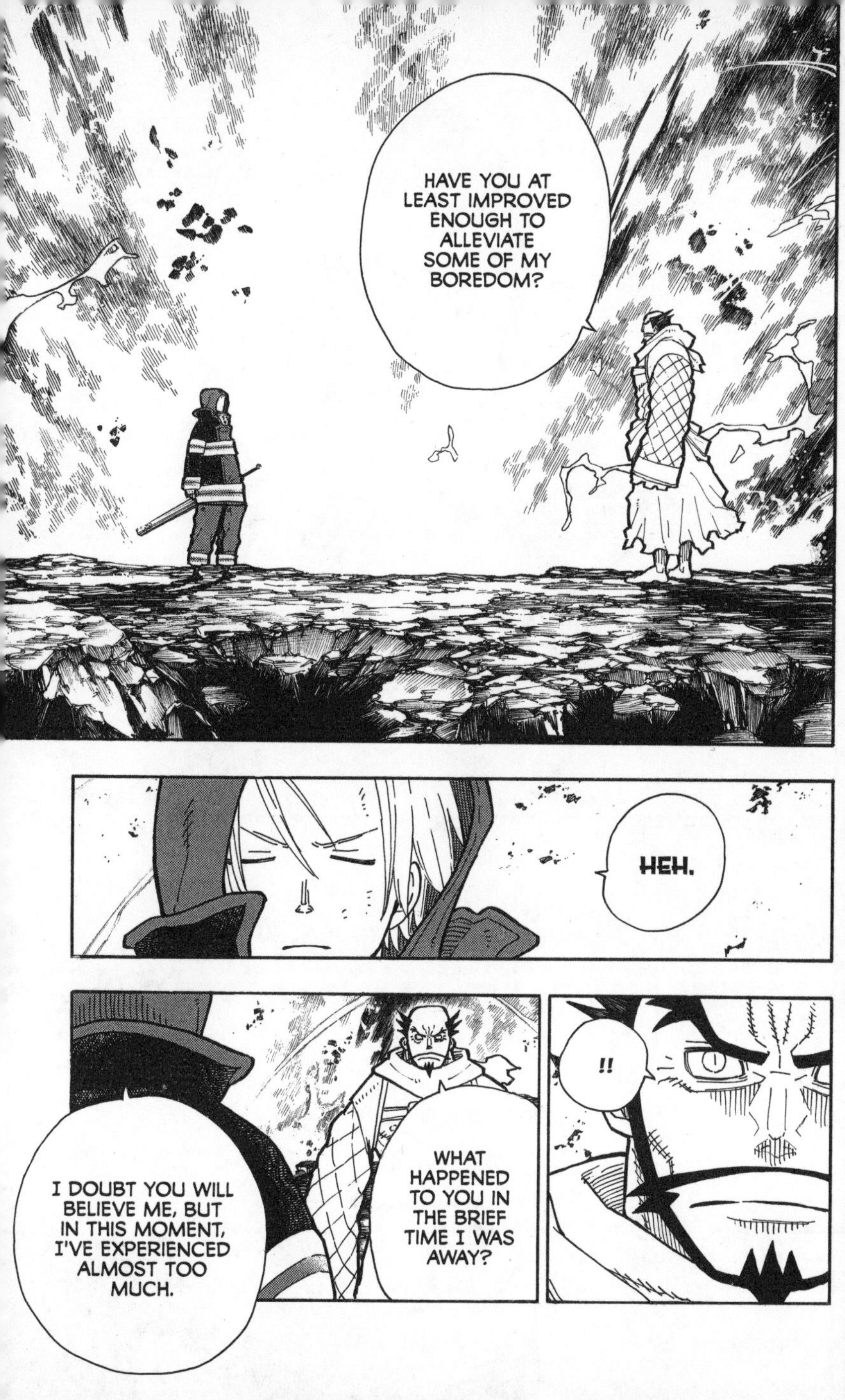
HAVE YOU AT LEAST IMPROVED ENOUGH TO ALLEVIATE SOME OF MY BOREDOM?
HEH.
!!
WHAT HAPPENED TO YOU IN THE BRIEF TIME I WAS AWAY?
I DOUBT YOU WILL BELIEVE ME, BUT IN THIS MOMENT, I'VE EXPERIENCED ALMOST TOO MUCH.

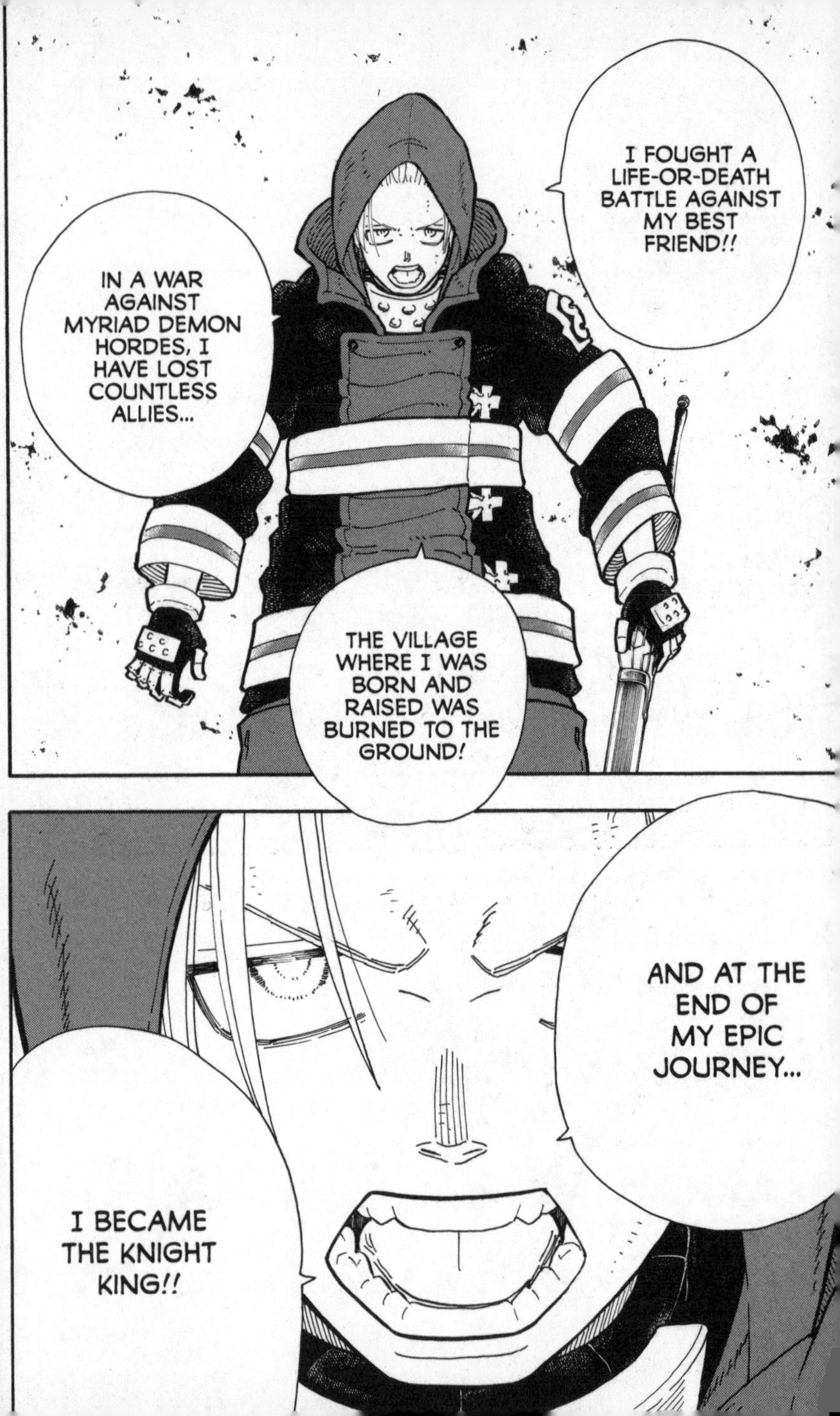
I FOUGHT A LIFE-OR-DEATH BATTLE AGAINST MY BEST FRIEND!!
IN A WAR AGAINST MYRIAD DEMON HORDES, I HAVE LOST COUNTLESS ALLIES...
THE VILLAGE WHERE I WAS BORN AND RAISED WAS BURNED TO THE GROUND!
AND AT THE END OF MY EPIC JOURNEY...
I BECAME THE KNIGHT KING!!

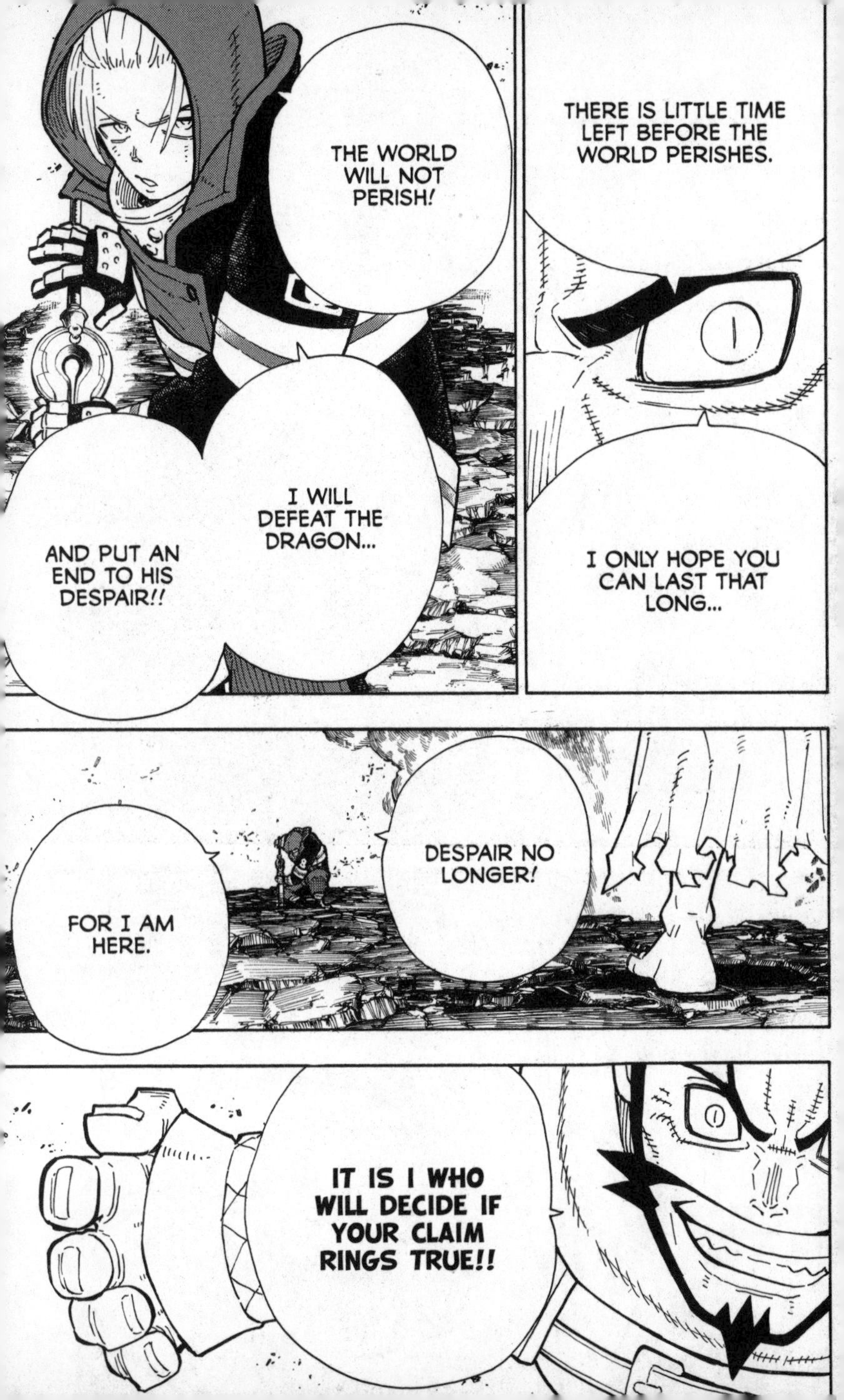
THERE IS LITTLE TIME LEFT BEFORE THE WORLD PERISHES.
I ONLY HOPE YOU CAN LAST THAT LONG...
THE WORLD WILL NOT PERISH!
I WILL DEFEAT THE DRAGON...
AND PUT AN END TO HIS DESPAIR!!
DESPAIR NO LONGER!
FOR I AM HERE.
IT IS I WHO WILL DECIDE IF YOUR CLAIM RINGS TRUE!!

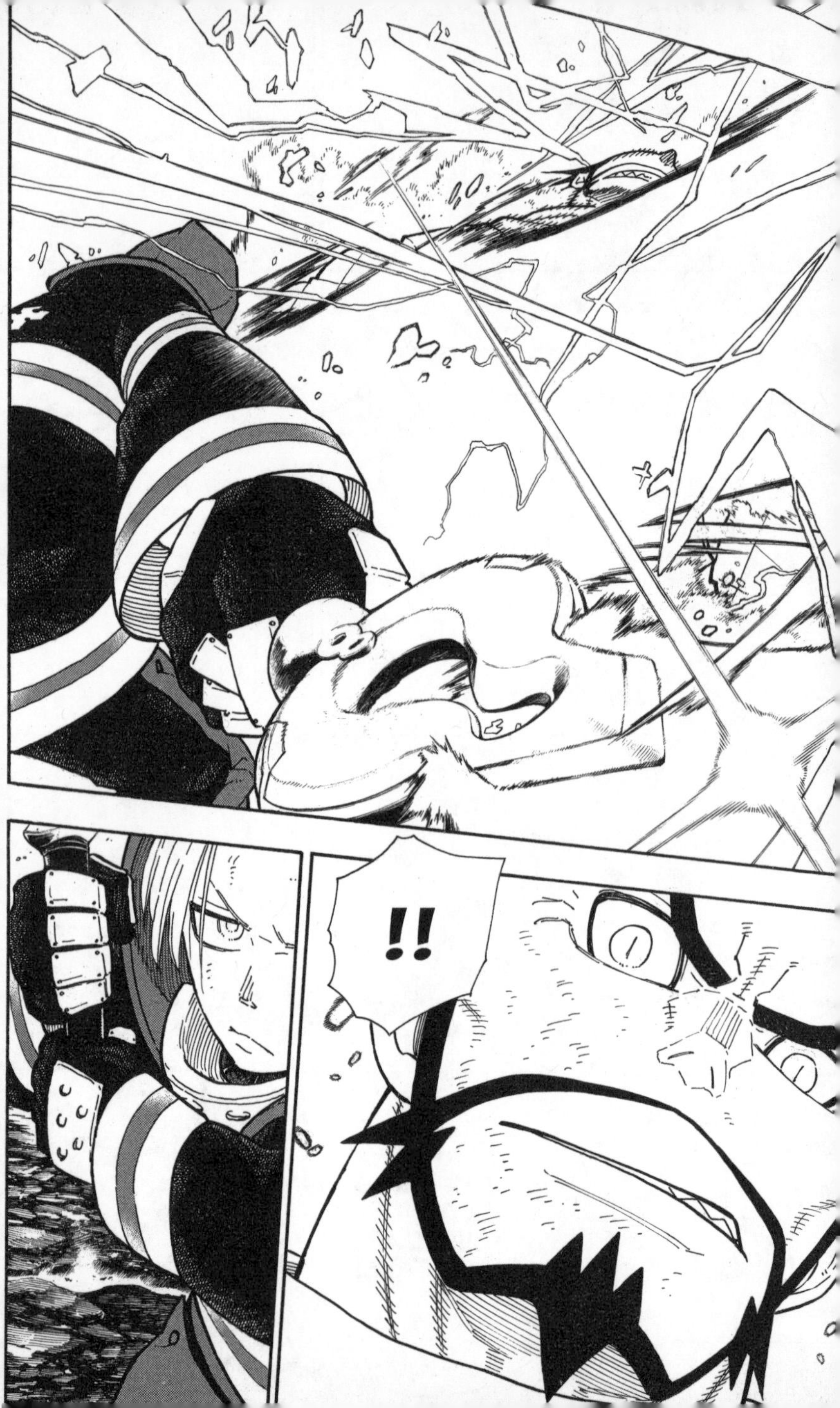
!!

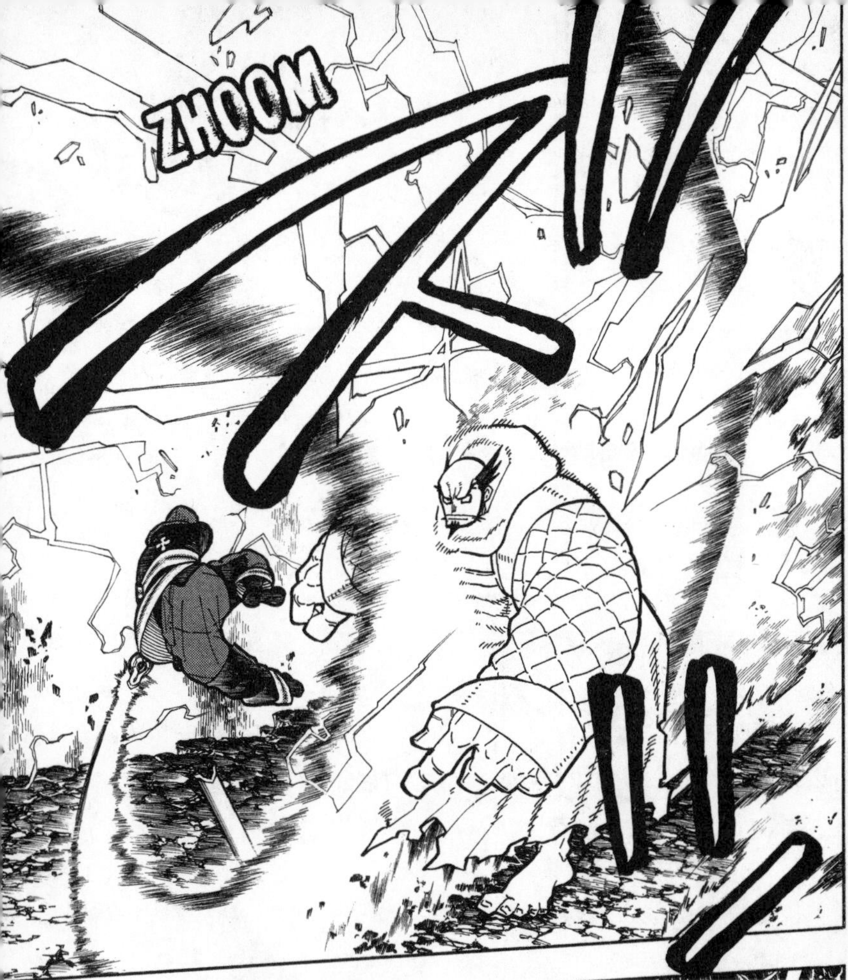
ZHOOM

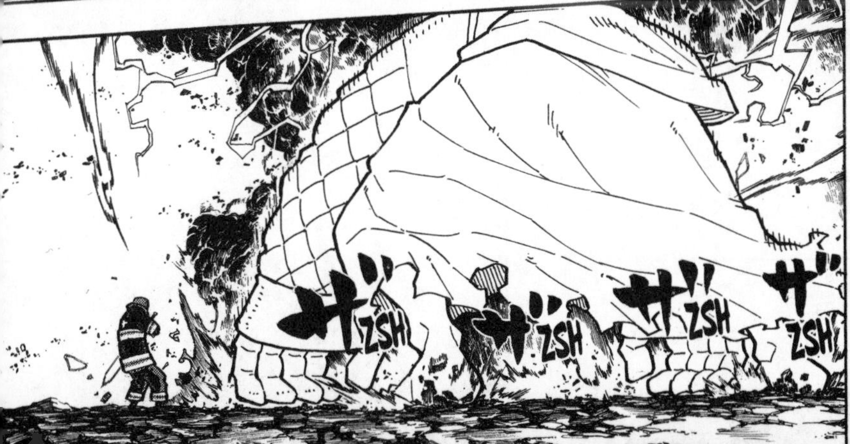
ZSH
ZSH
ZSH
ZSH

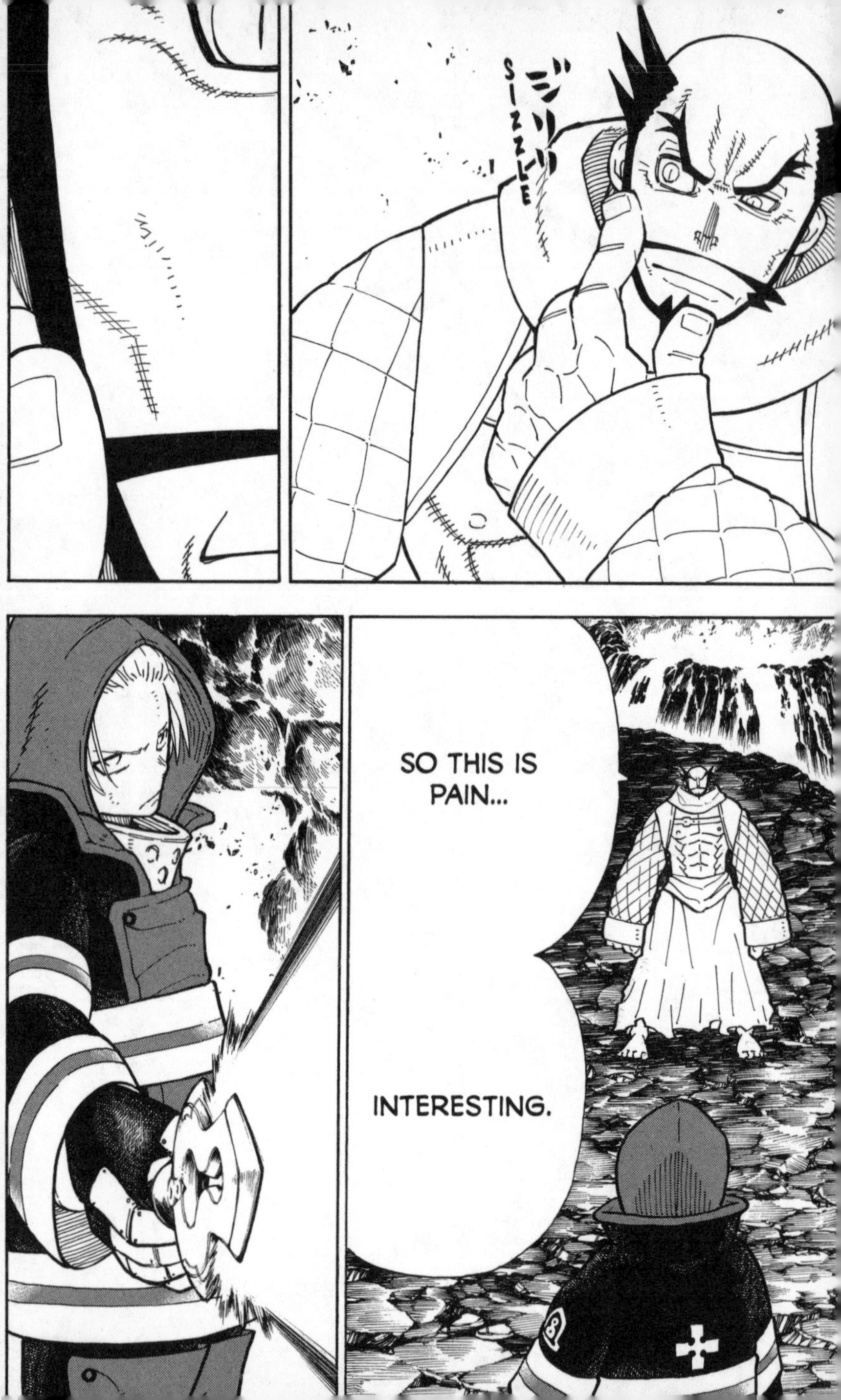
SIZZLE
SO THIS IS PAIN...
INTERESTING.

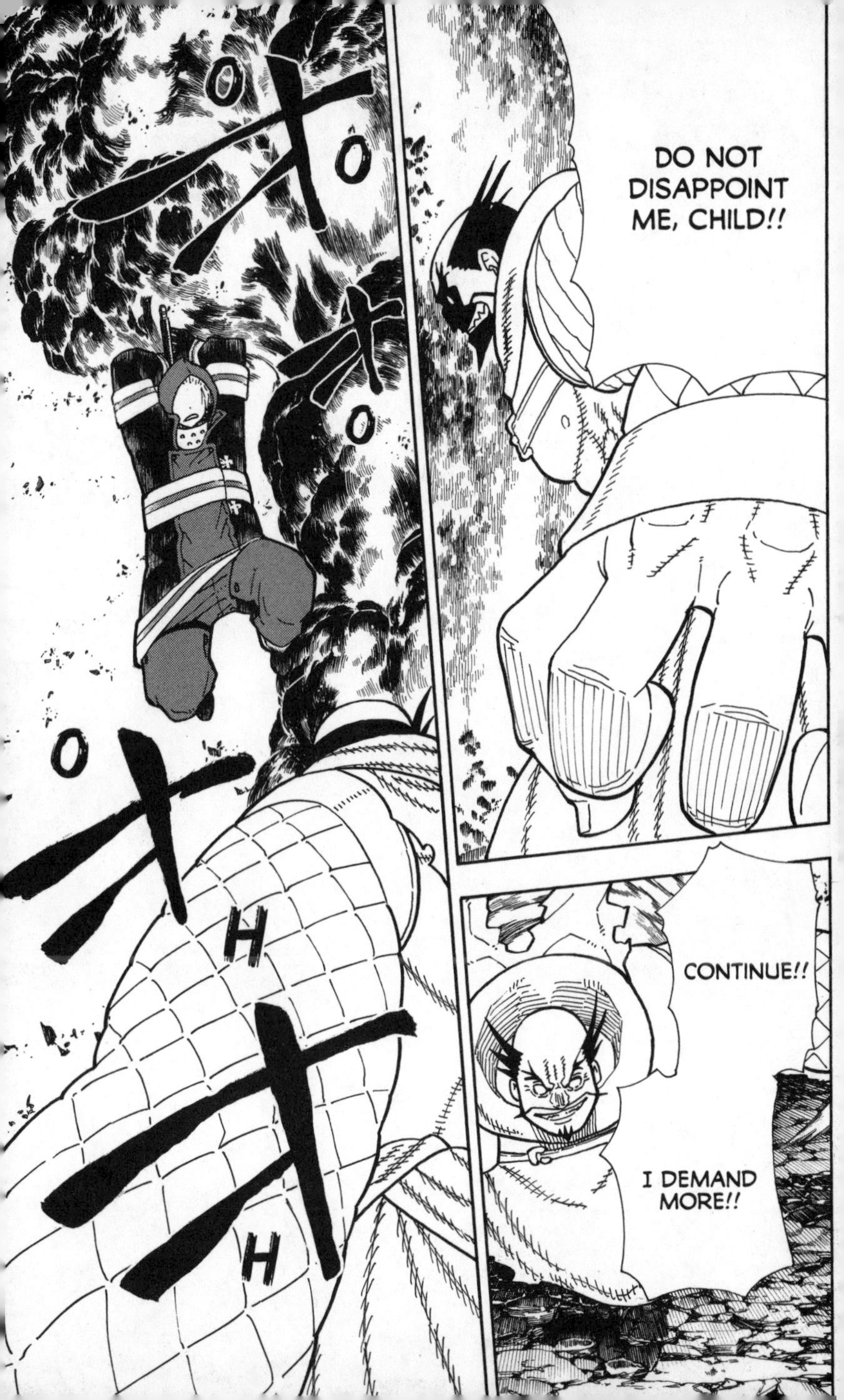
DO NOT DISAPPOINT ME, CHILD!!
CONTINUE!!
I DEMAND MORE!!
OOOOHH

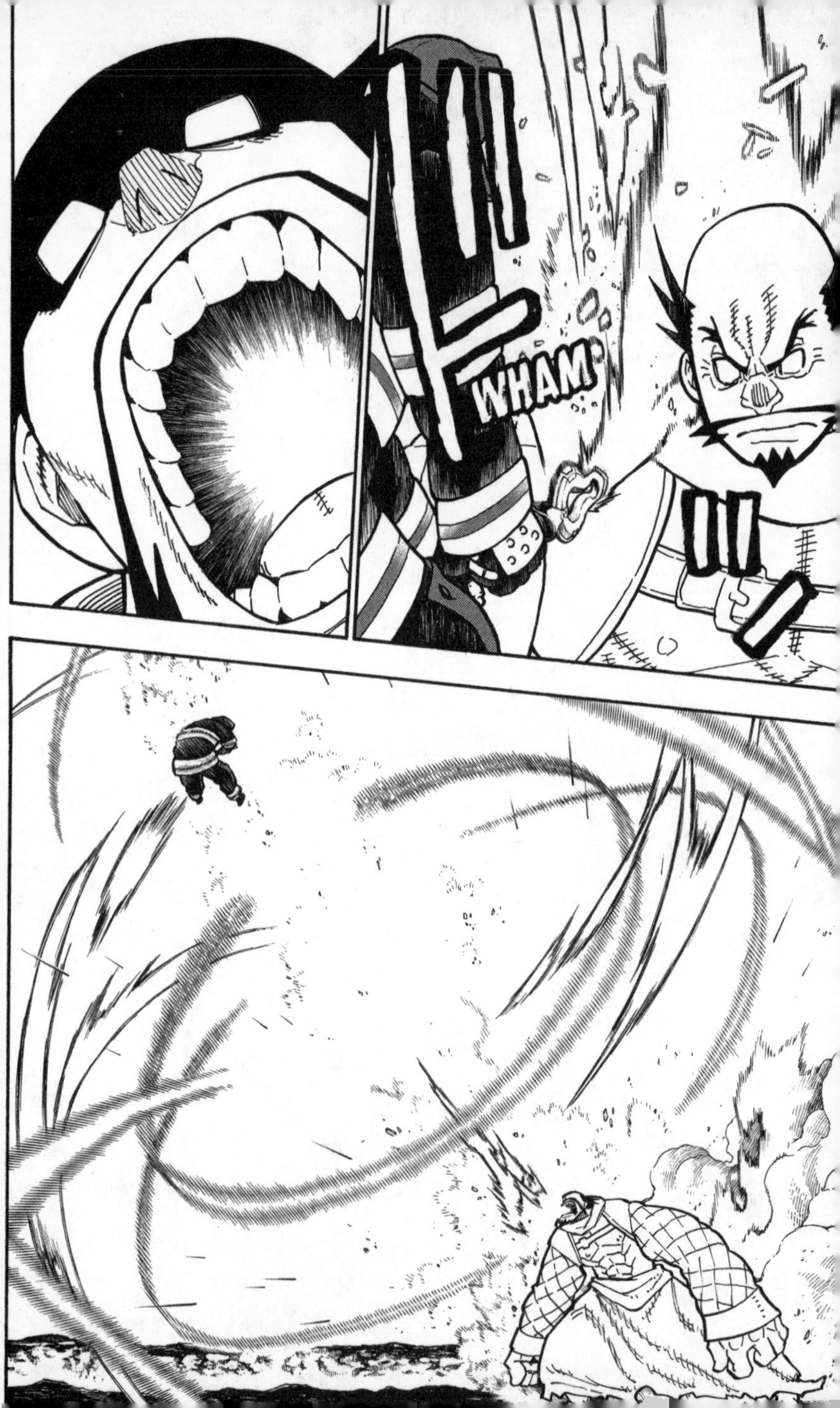
WHAM

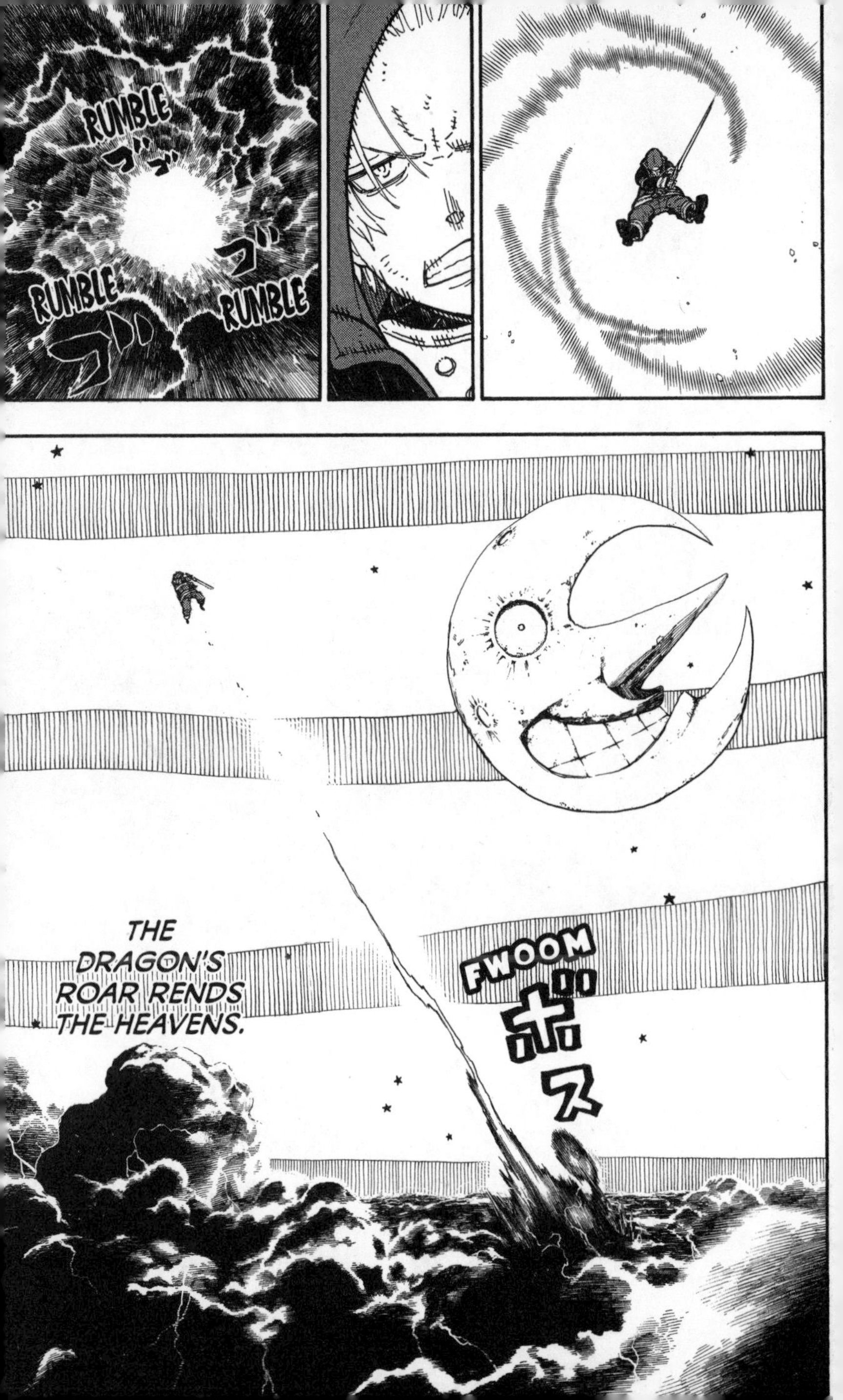
RUMBLE
RUMBLE
RUMBLE
THE DRAGON'S ROAR RENDS THE HEAVENS.
FWOOM
ボス

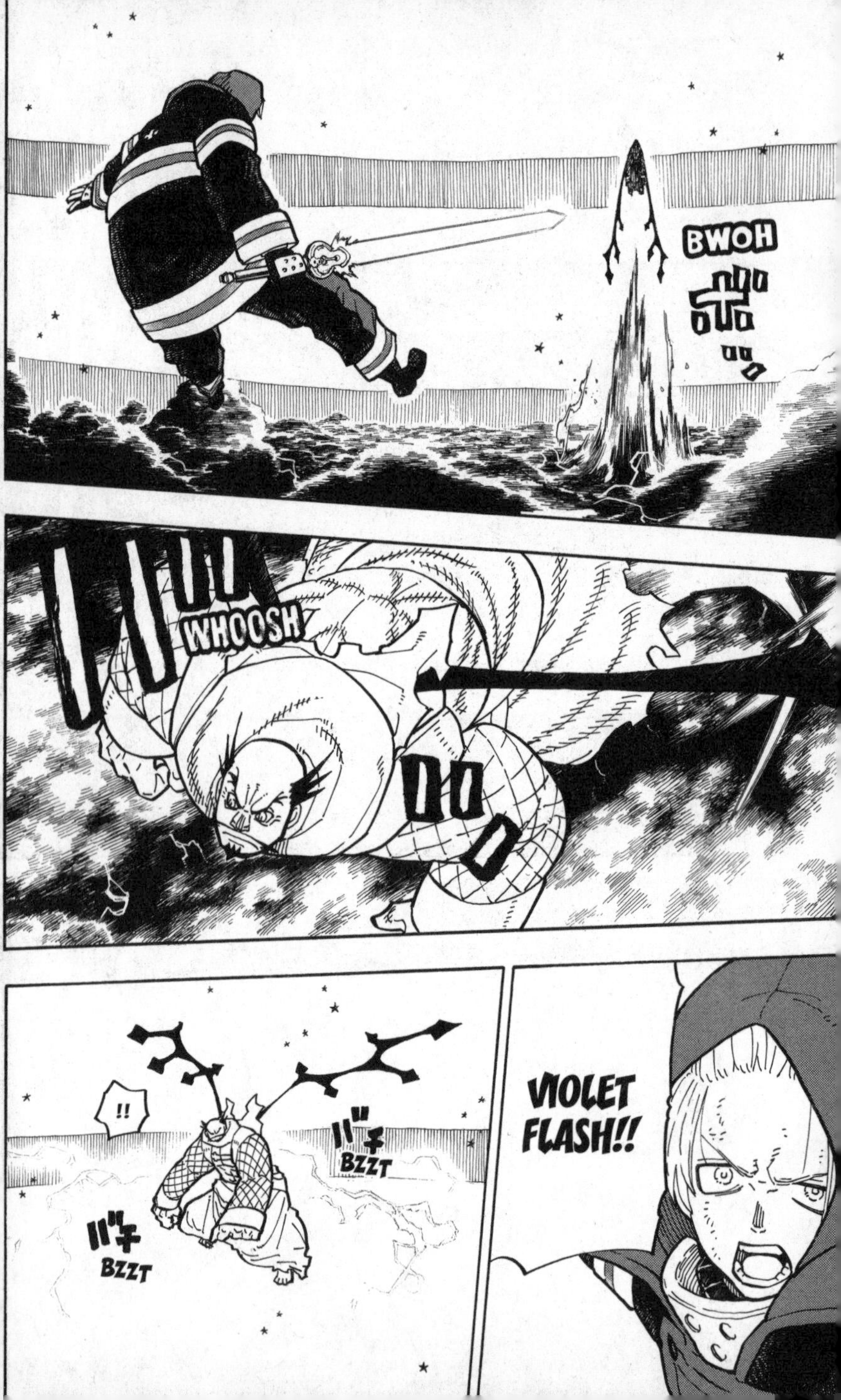
BWOH
WHOOSH
VIOLET FLASH!!
!!
BZZT
BZZT

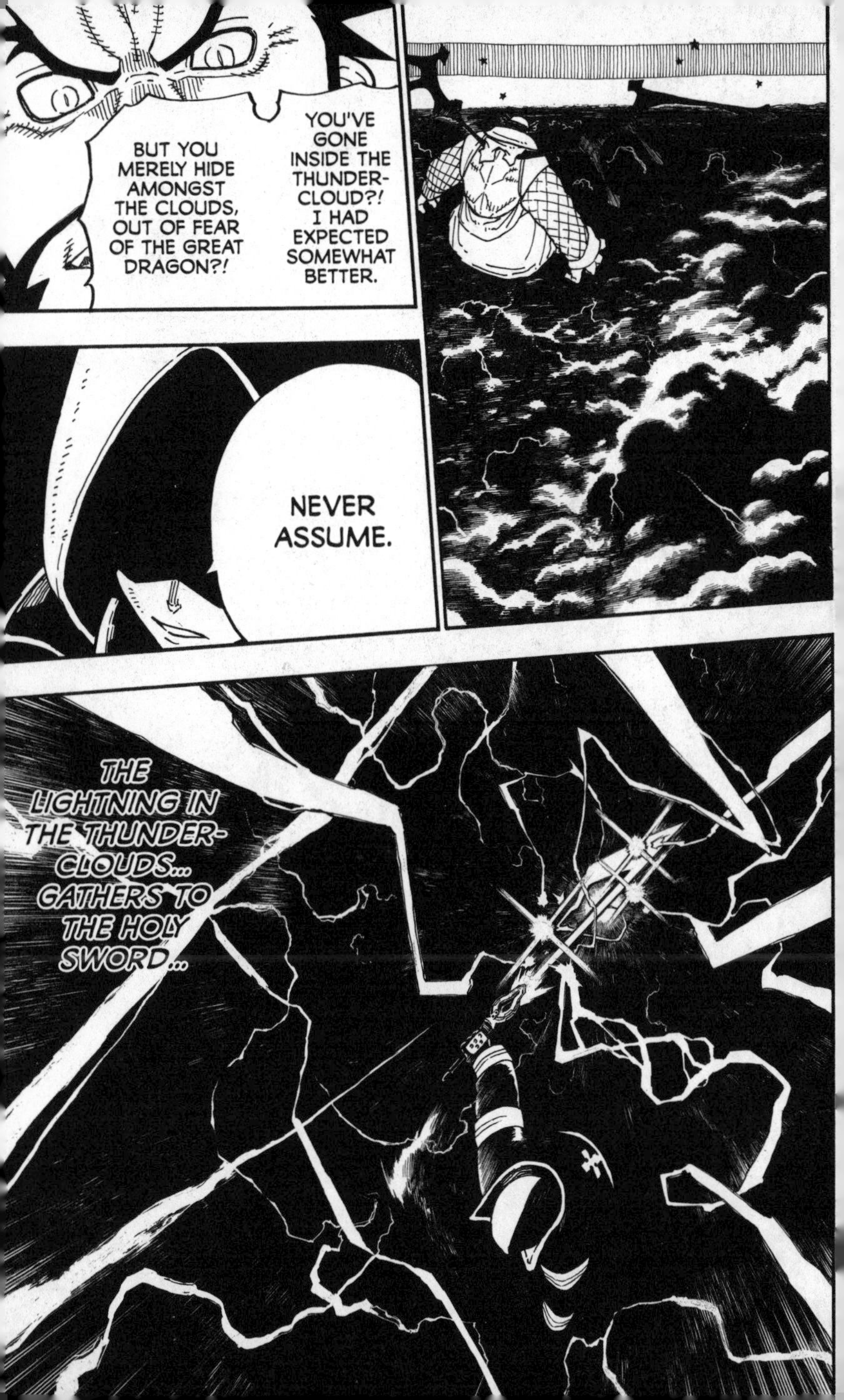
YOU'VE GONE INSIDE THE THUNDER-CLOUD?! I HAD EXPECTED SOMEWHAT BETTER.
BUT YOU MERELY HIDE AMONGST THE CLOUDS, OUT OF FEAR OF THE GREAT DRAGON?!
NEVER ASSUME.
THE LIGHTNING IN THE THUNDER-CLOUDS... GATHERS TO THE HOLY SWORD...

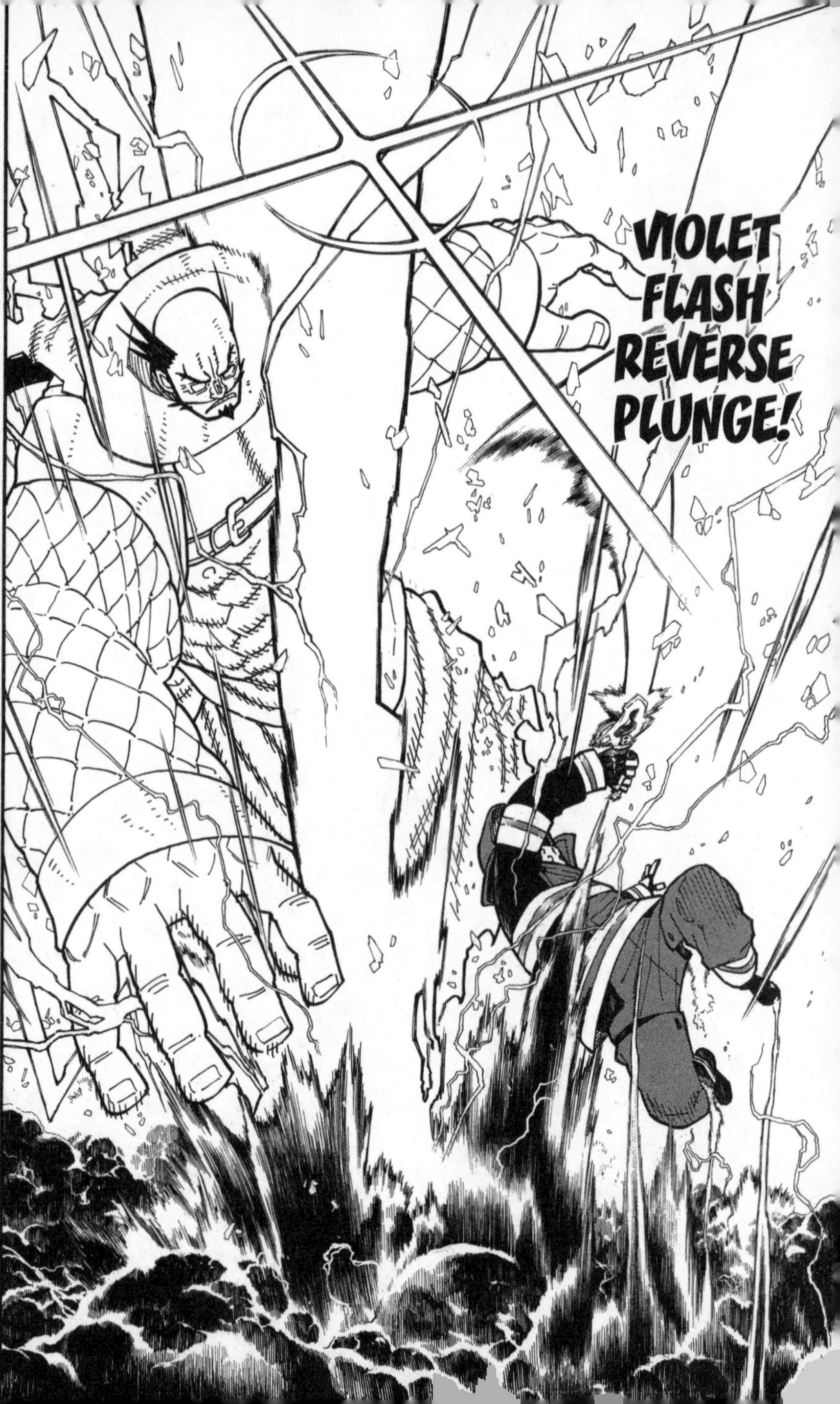
VIOLET FLASH REVERSE PLUNGE!

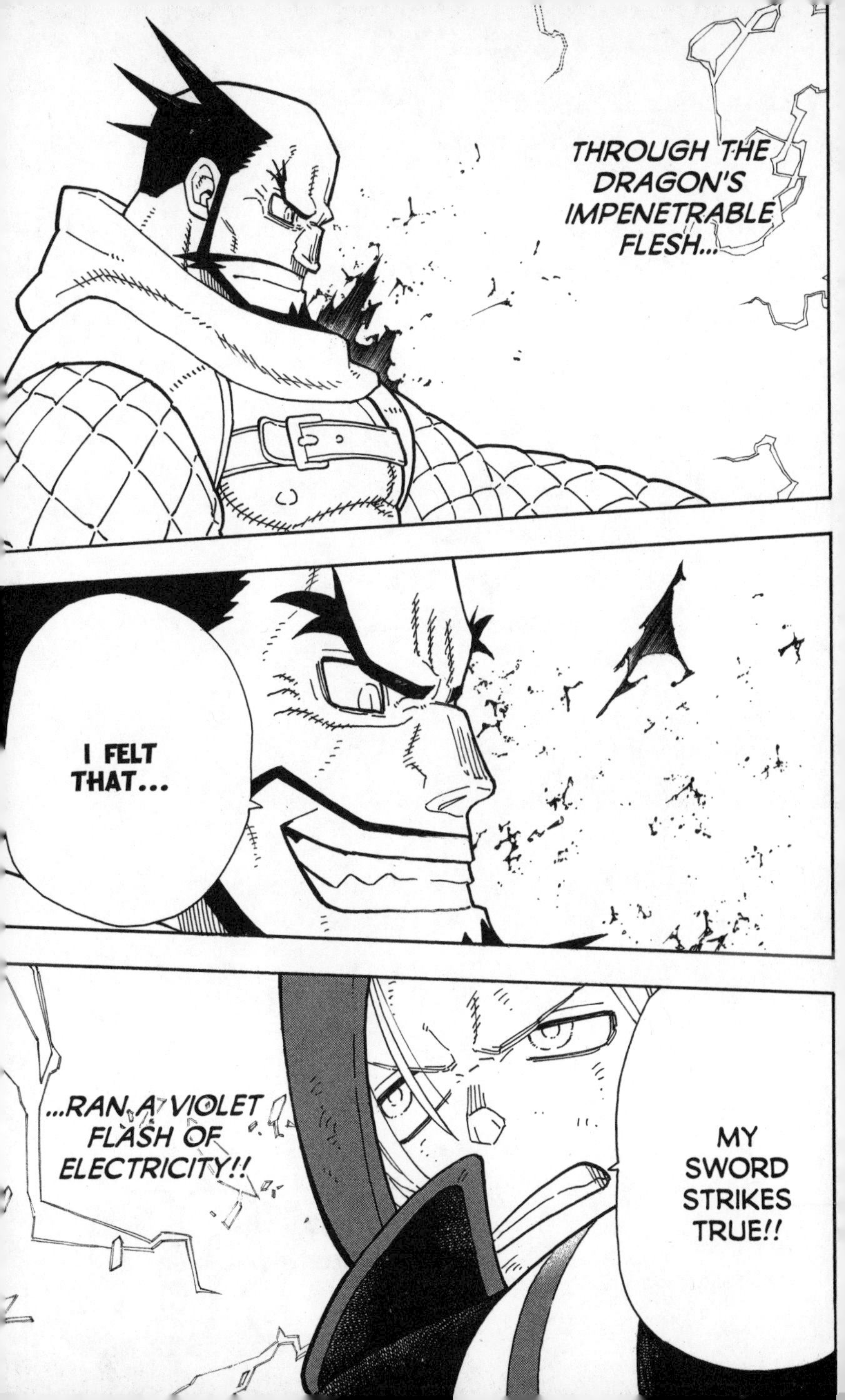
THROUGH THE DRAGON'S IMPENETRABLE FLESH...
I FELT THAT...
MY SWORD STRIKES TRUE!!
...RAN A VIOLET FLASH OF ELECTRICITY!!

FIRE FORCE

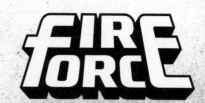

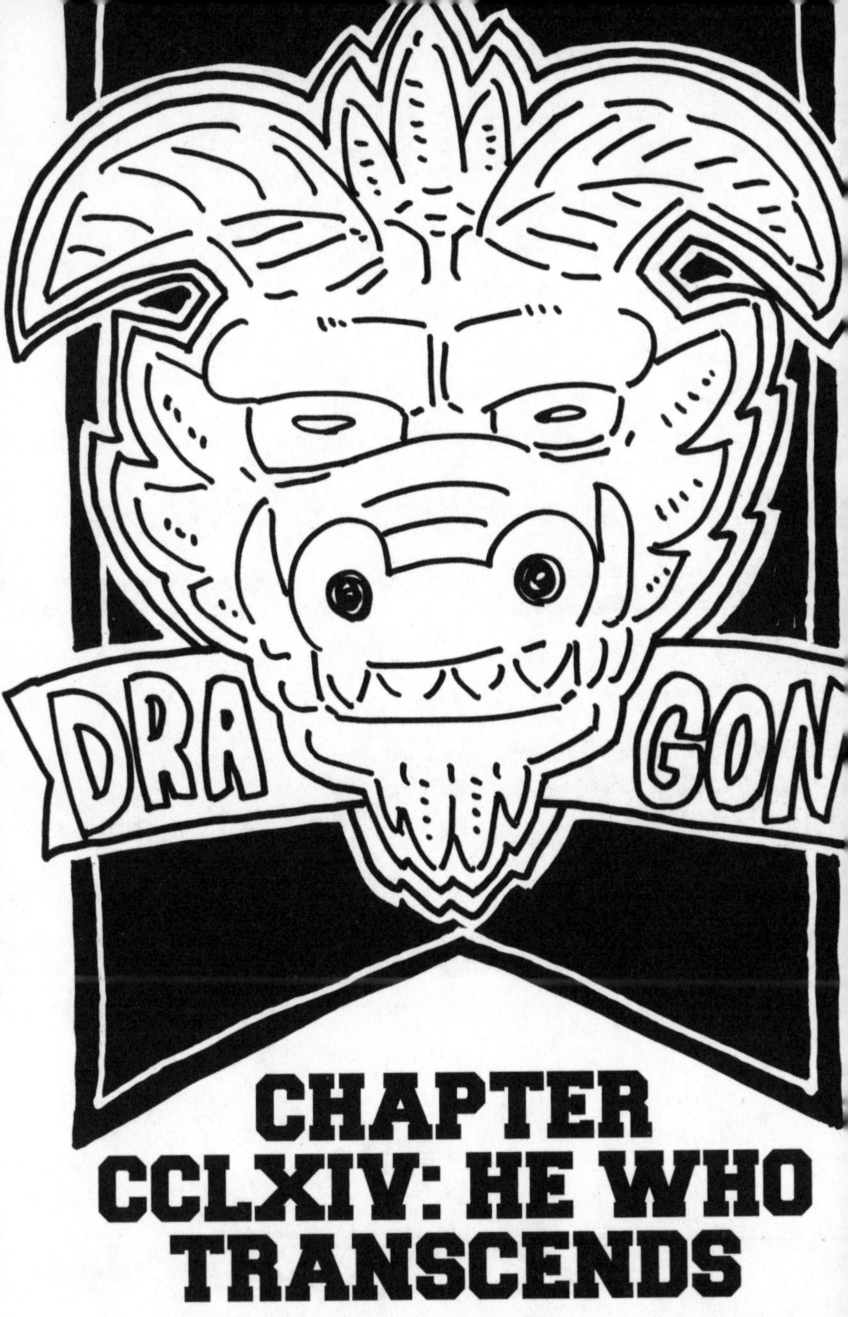
DRA GON

CHAPTER CCLXIV: HE WHO TRANSCENDS

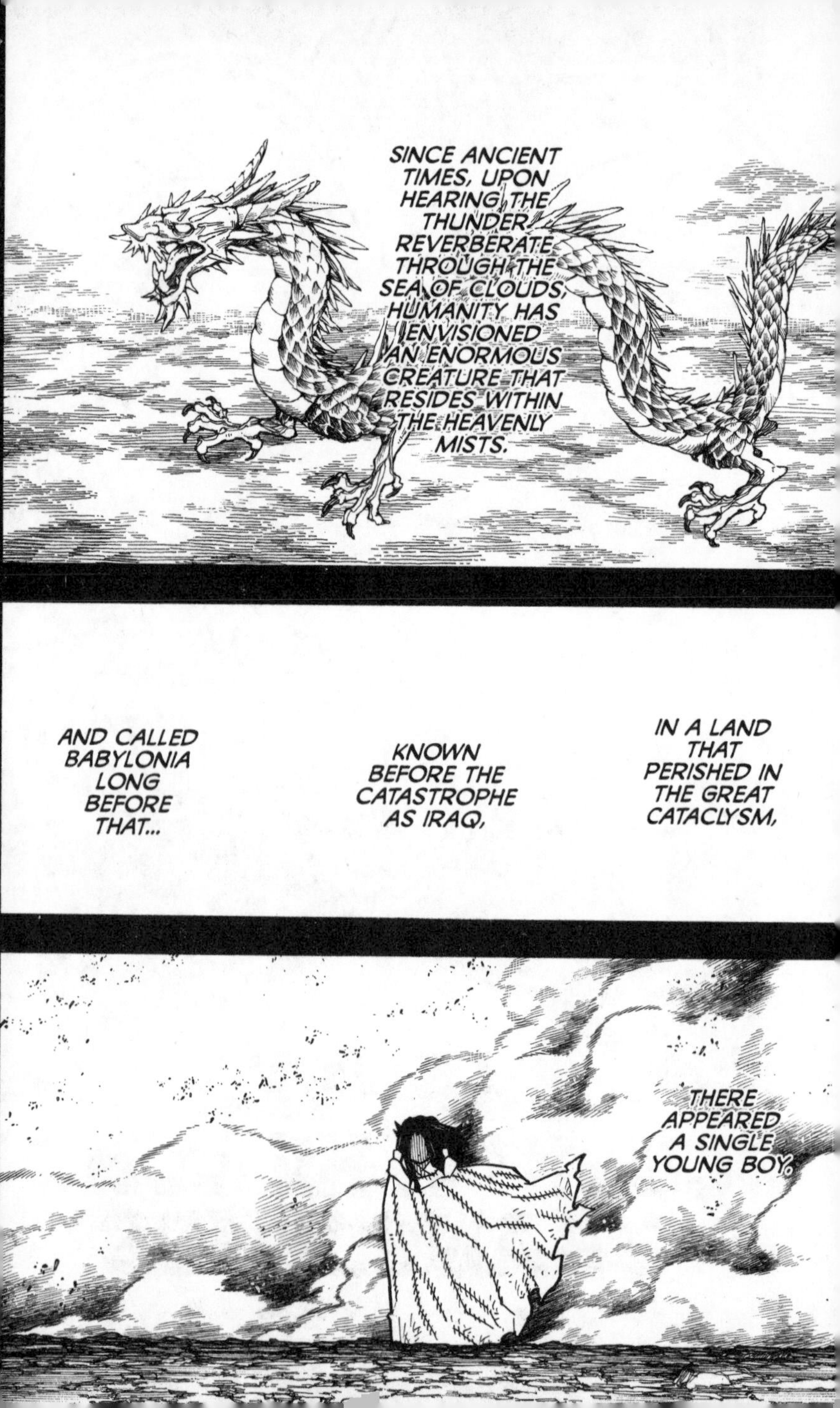
SINCE ANCIENT TIMES, UPON HEARING THE THUNDER REVERBERATE THROUGH THE SEA OF CLOUDS, HUMANITY HAS ENVISIONED AN ENORMOUS CREATURE THAT RESIDES WITHIN THE HEAVENLY MISTS.
IN A LAND THAT PERISHED IN THE GREAT CATACLYSM,
KNOWN BEFORE THE CATASTROPHE AS IRAQ,
AND CALLED BABYLONIA LONG BEFORE THAT...
THERE APPEARED A SINGLE YOUNG BOY.

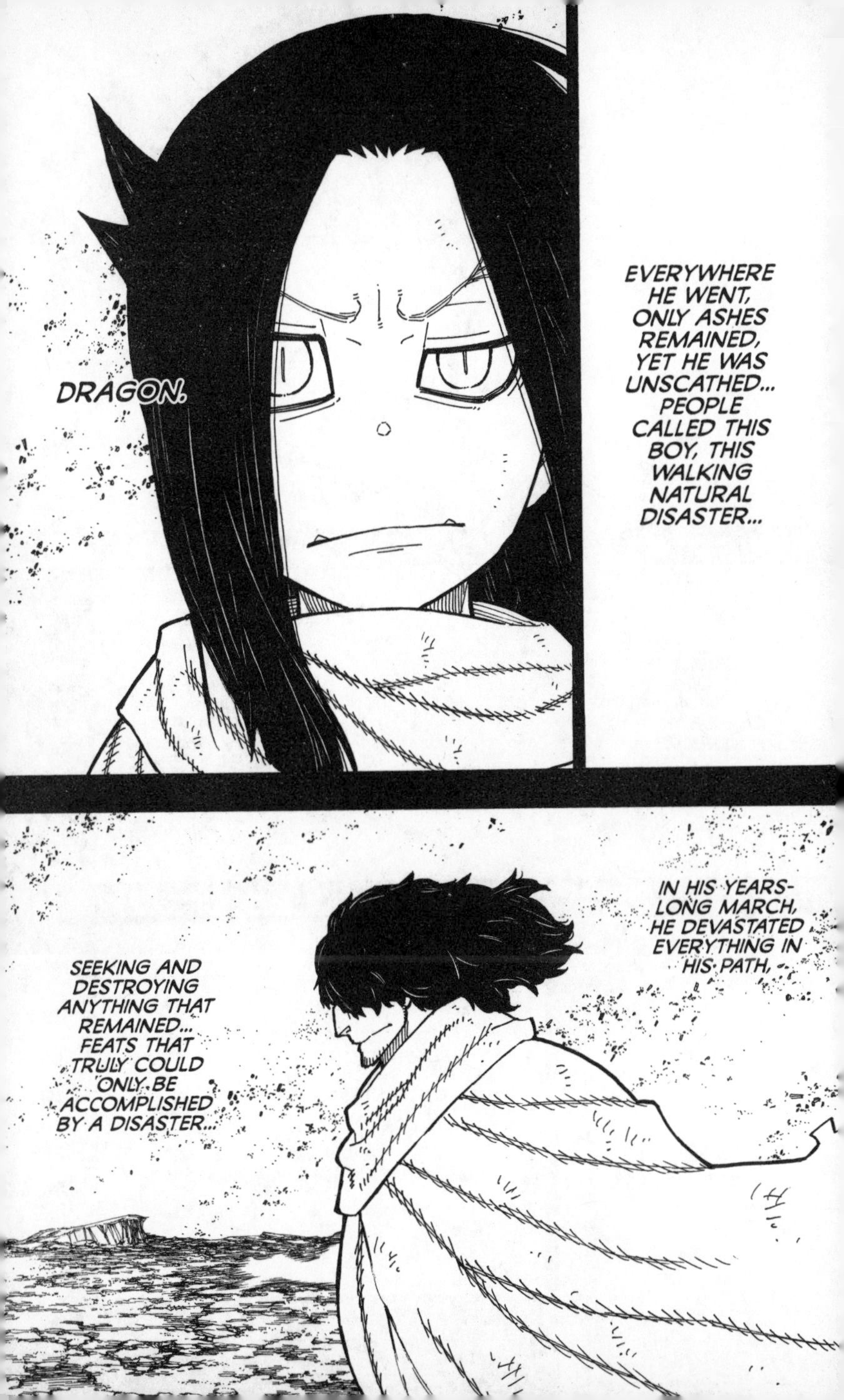
EVERYWHERE HE WENT, ONLY ASHES REMAINED, YET HE WAS UNSCATHED... PEOPLE CALLED THIS BOY, THIS WALKING NATURAL DISASTER...
DRAGON.
IN HIS YEARS-LONG MARCH, HE DEVASTATED EVERYTHING IN HIS PATH,
SEEKING AND DESTROYING ANYTHING THAT REMAINED... FEATS THAT TRULY COULD ONLY BE ACCOMPLISHED BY A DISASTER...

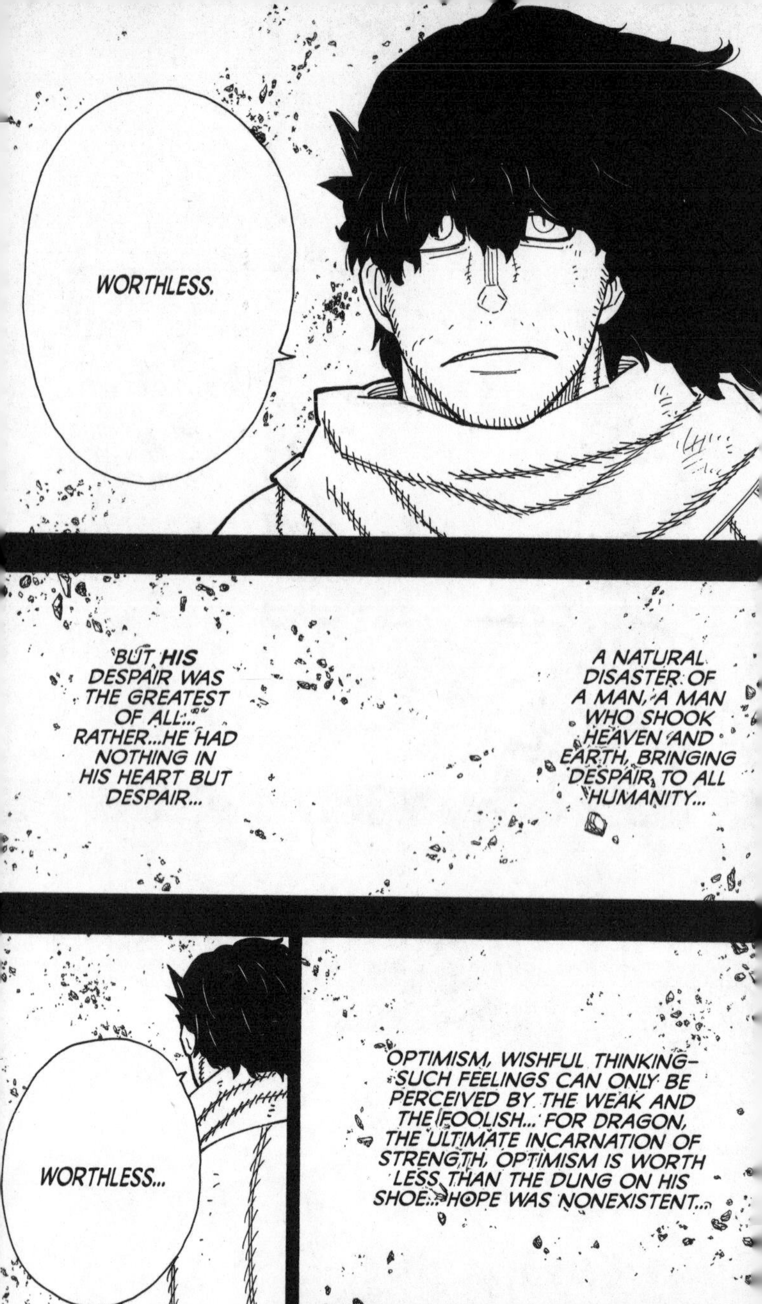
WORTHLESS.
A NATURAL DISASTER OF A MAN, A MAN WHO SHOOK HEAVEN AND EARTH, BRINGING DESPAIR TO ALL HUMANITY...
BUT **HIS** DESPAIR WAS THE GREATEST OF ALL... RATHER...HE HAD NOTHING IN HIS HEART BUT DESPAIR...
OPTIMISM, WISHFUL THINKING– SUCH FEELINGS CAN ONLY BE PERCEIVED BY THE WEAK AND THE FOOLISH... FOR DRAGON, THE ULTIMATE INCARNATION OF STRENGTH, OPTIMISM IS WORTH LESS THAN THE DUNG ON HIS SHOE... HOPE WAS NONEXISTENT...
WORTHLESS...

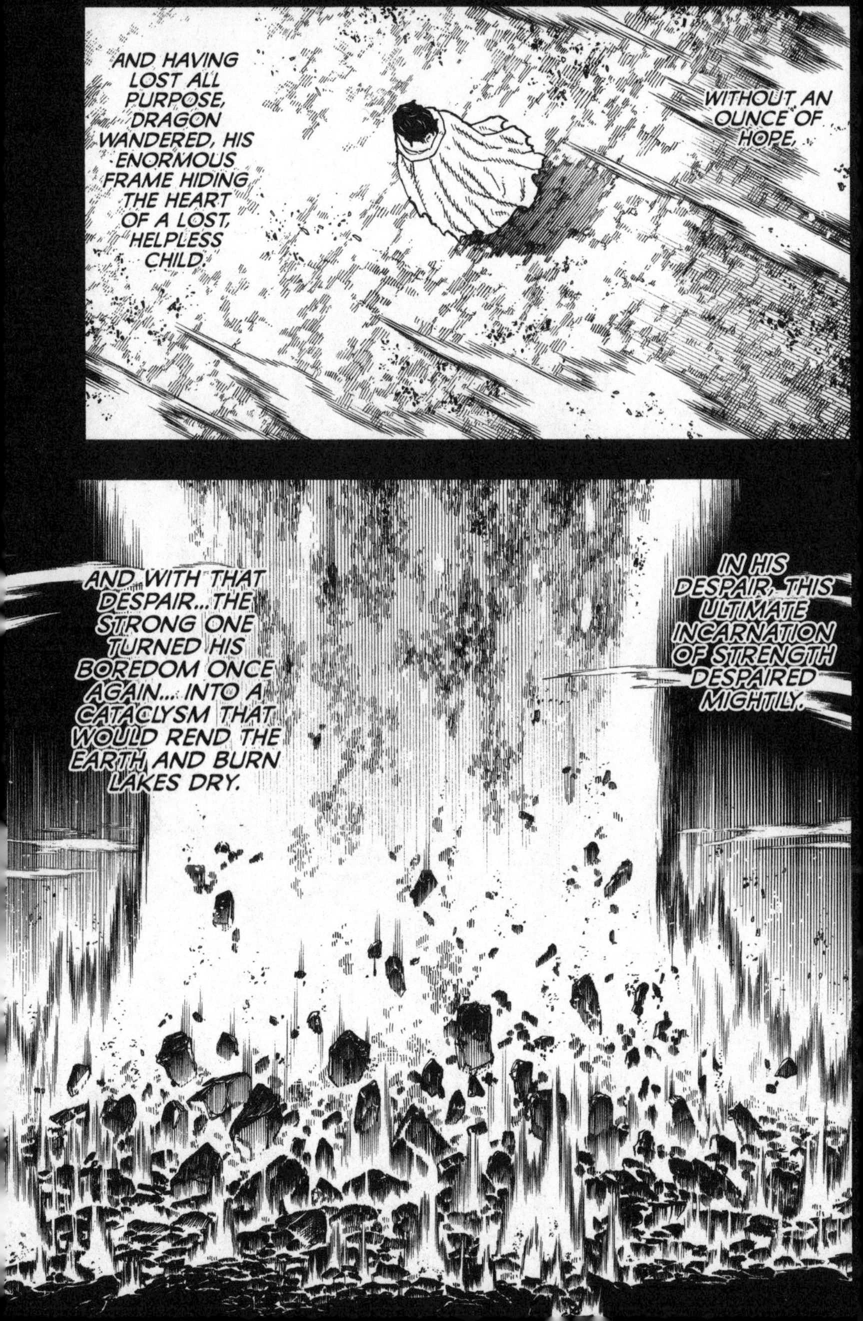
WITHOUT AN OUNCE OF HOPE,
AND HAVING LOST ALL PURPOSE, DRAGON WANDERED, HIS ENORMOUS FRAME HIDING THE HEART OF A LOST, HELPLESS CHILD.
IN HIS DESPAIR, THIS ULTIMATE INCARNATION OF STRENGTH DESPAIRED MIGHTILY.
AND WITH THAT DESPAIR...THE STRONG ONE TURNED HIS BOREDOM ONCE AGAIN... INTO A CATACLYSM THAT WOULD REND THE EARTH AND BURN LAKES DRY.

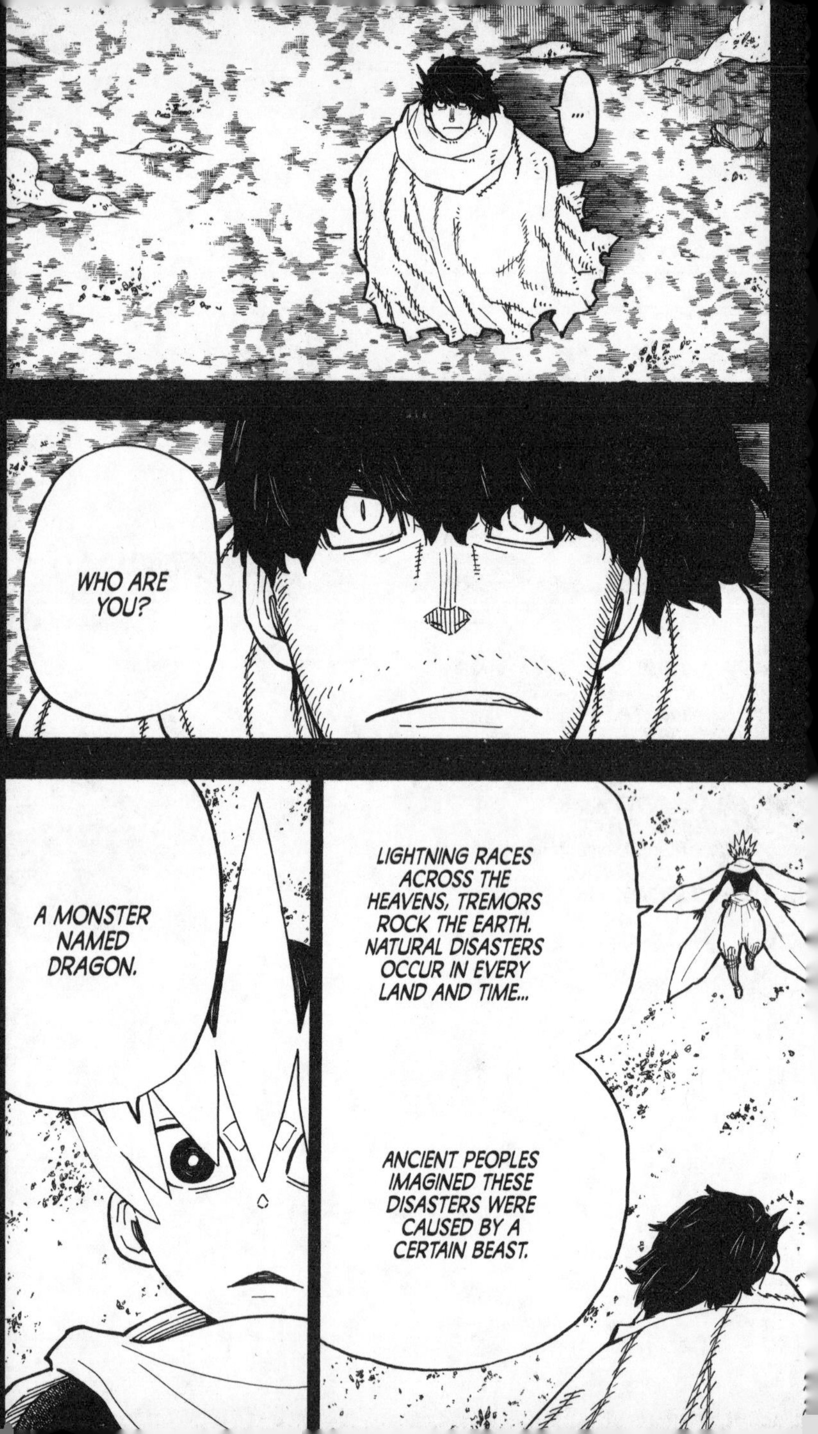
...
WHO ARE YOU?
LIGHTNING RACES ACROSS THE HEAVENS, TREMORS ROCK THE EARTH. NATURAL DISASTERS OCCUR IN EVERY LAND AND TIME...
ANCIENT PEOPLES IMAGINED THESE DISASTERS WERE CAUSED BY A CERTAIN BEAST.
A MONSTER NAMED DRAGON.

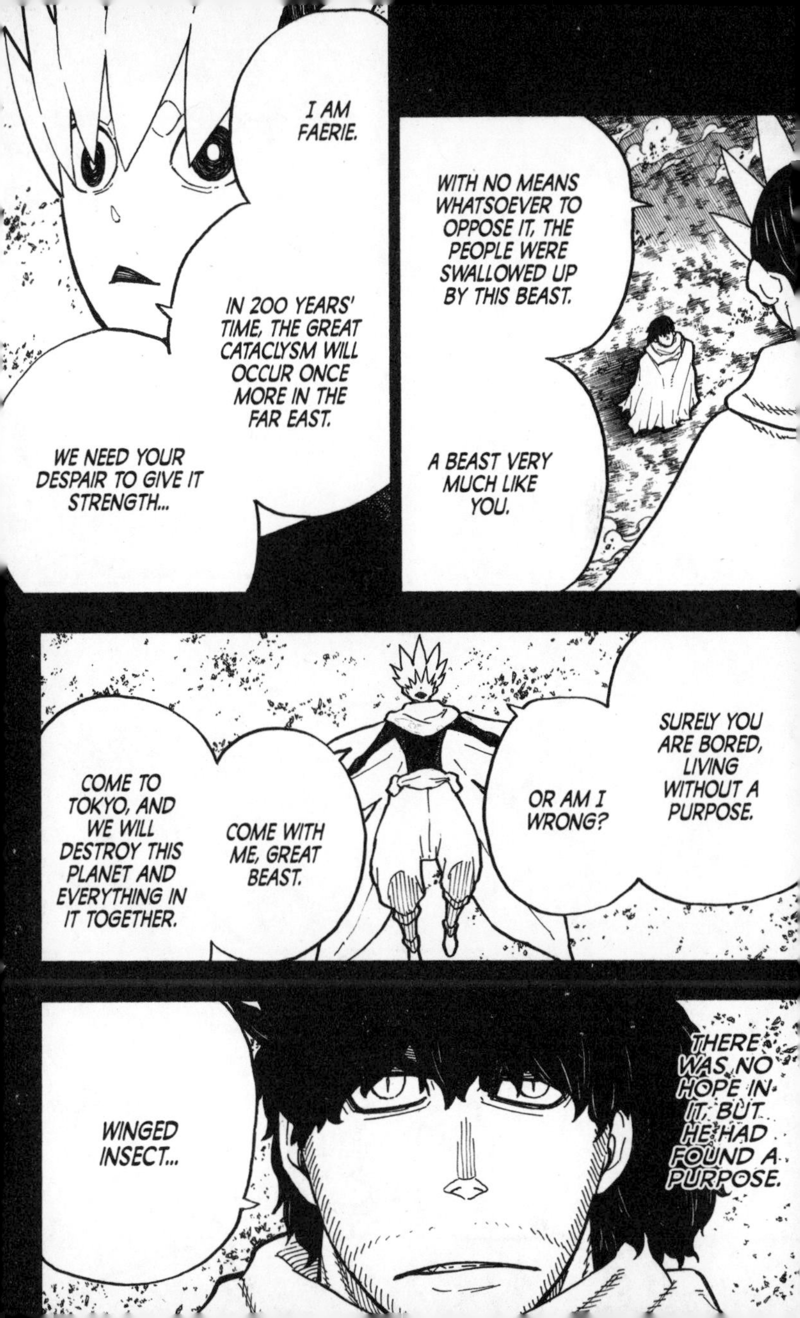
WITH NO MEANS WHATSOEVER TO OPPOSE IT, THE PEOPLE WERE SWALLOWED UP BY THIS BEAST.
A BEAST VERY MUCH LIKE YOU.
I AM FAERIE.
IN 200 YEARS' TIME, THE GREAT CATACLYSM WILL OCCUR ONCE MORE IN THE FAR EAST.
WE NEED YOUR DESPAIR TO GIVE IT STRENGTH...
SURELY YOU ARE BORED, LIVING WITHOUT A PURPOSE.
OR AM I WRONG?
COME WITH ME, GREAT BEAST.
COME TO TOKYO, AND WE WILL DESTROY THIS PLANET AND EVERYTHING IN IT TOGETHER.
THERE WAS NO HOPE IN IT, BUT HE HAD FOUND A PURPOSE.
WINGED INSECT...

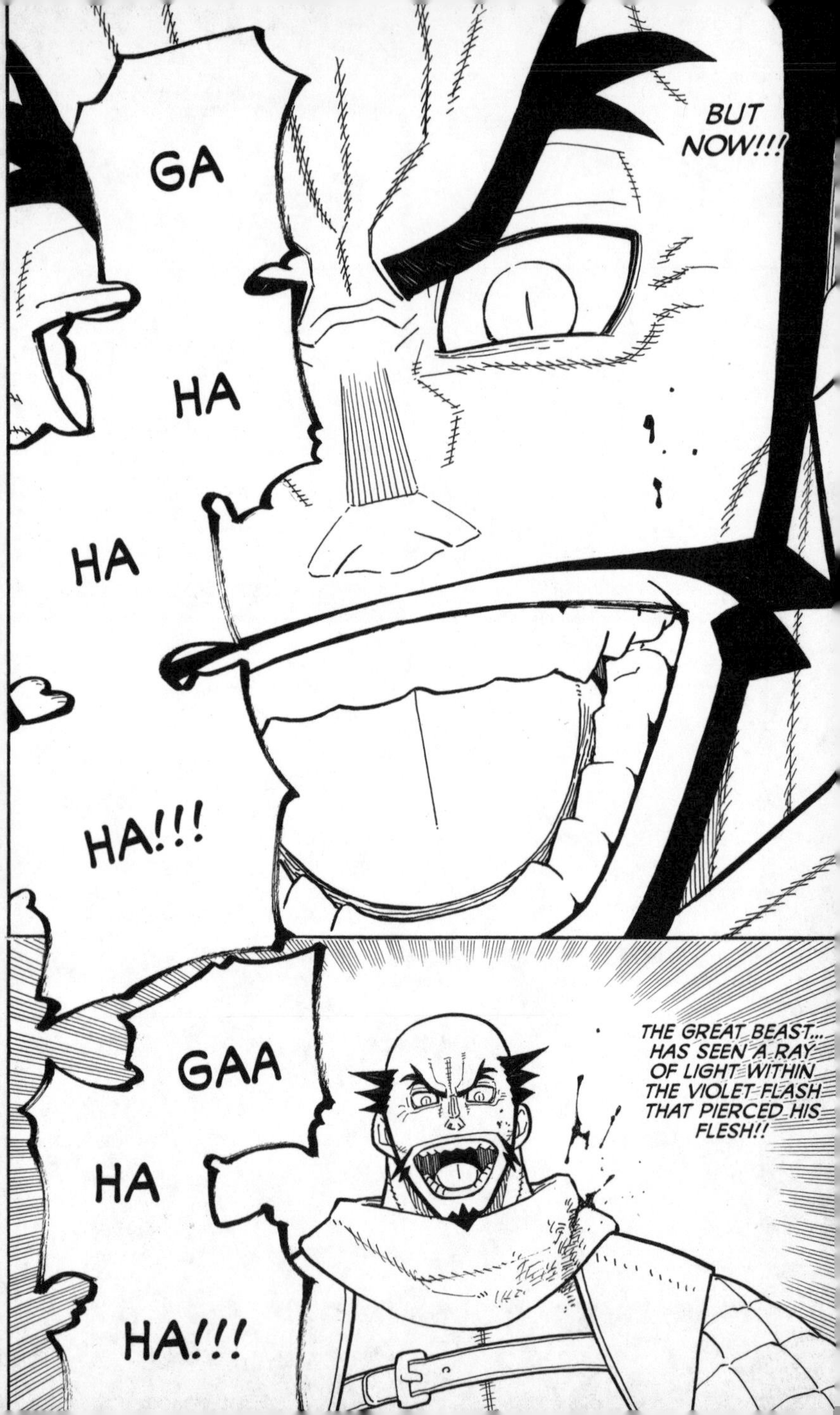
BUT NOW!!!
GA HA HA HA!!!
THE GREAT BEAST... HAS SEEN A RAY OF LIGHT WITHIN THE VIOLET FLASH THAT PIERCED HIS FLESH!!
GAA HA HA!!!

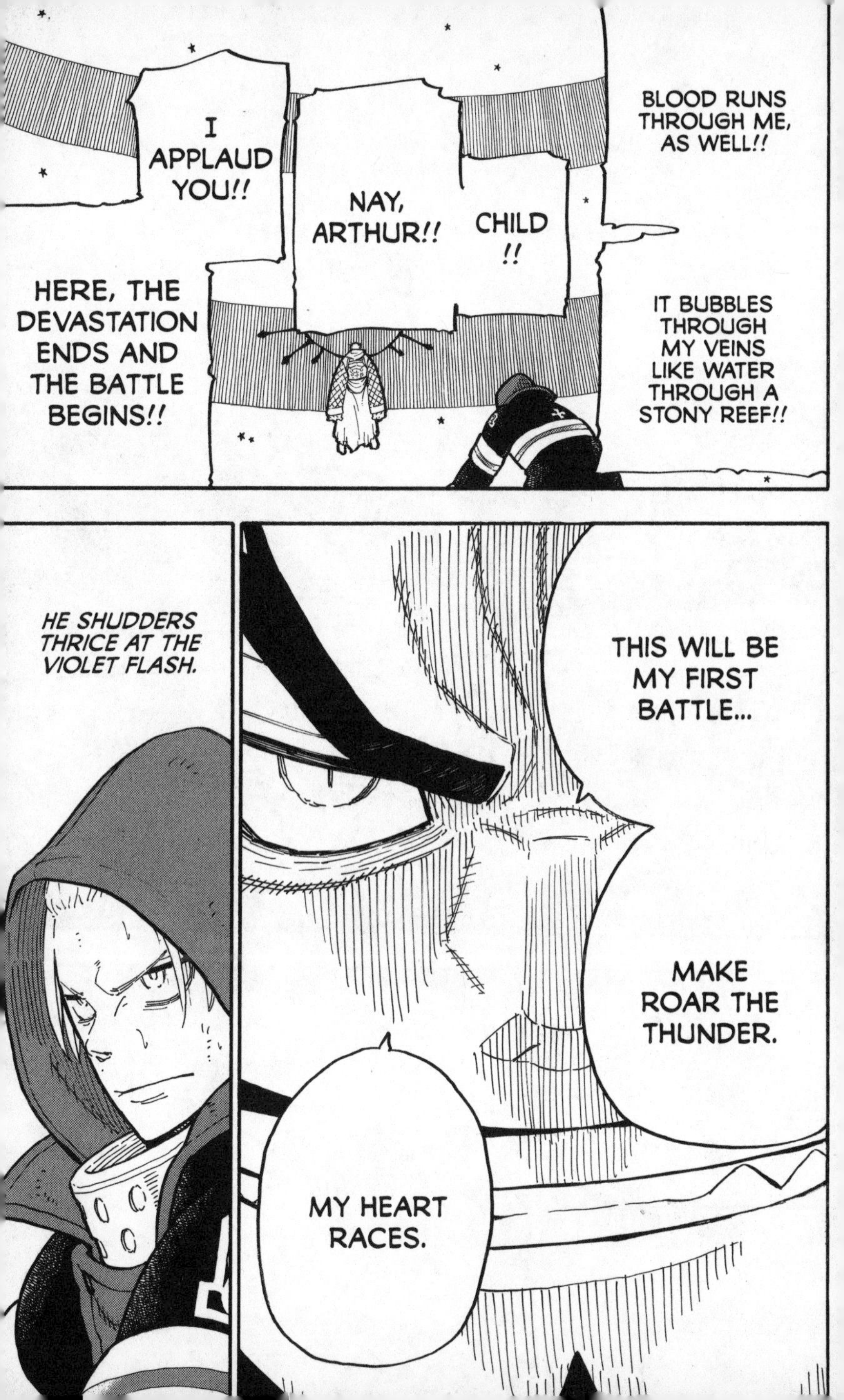
BLOOD RUNS THROUGH ME, AS WELL!!
IT BUBBLES THROUGH MY VEINS LIKE WATER THROUGH A STONY REEF!!
CHILD !!
NAY, ARTHUR!!
I APPLAUD YOU!!
HERE, THE DEVASTATION ENDS AND THE BATTLE BEGINS!!
THIS WILL BE MY FIRST BATTLE...
MAKE ROAR THE THUNDER.
MY HEART RACES.
HE SHUDDERS THRICE AT THE VIOLET FLASH.

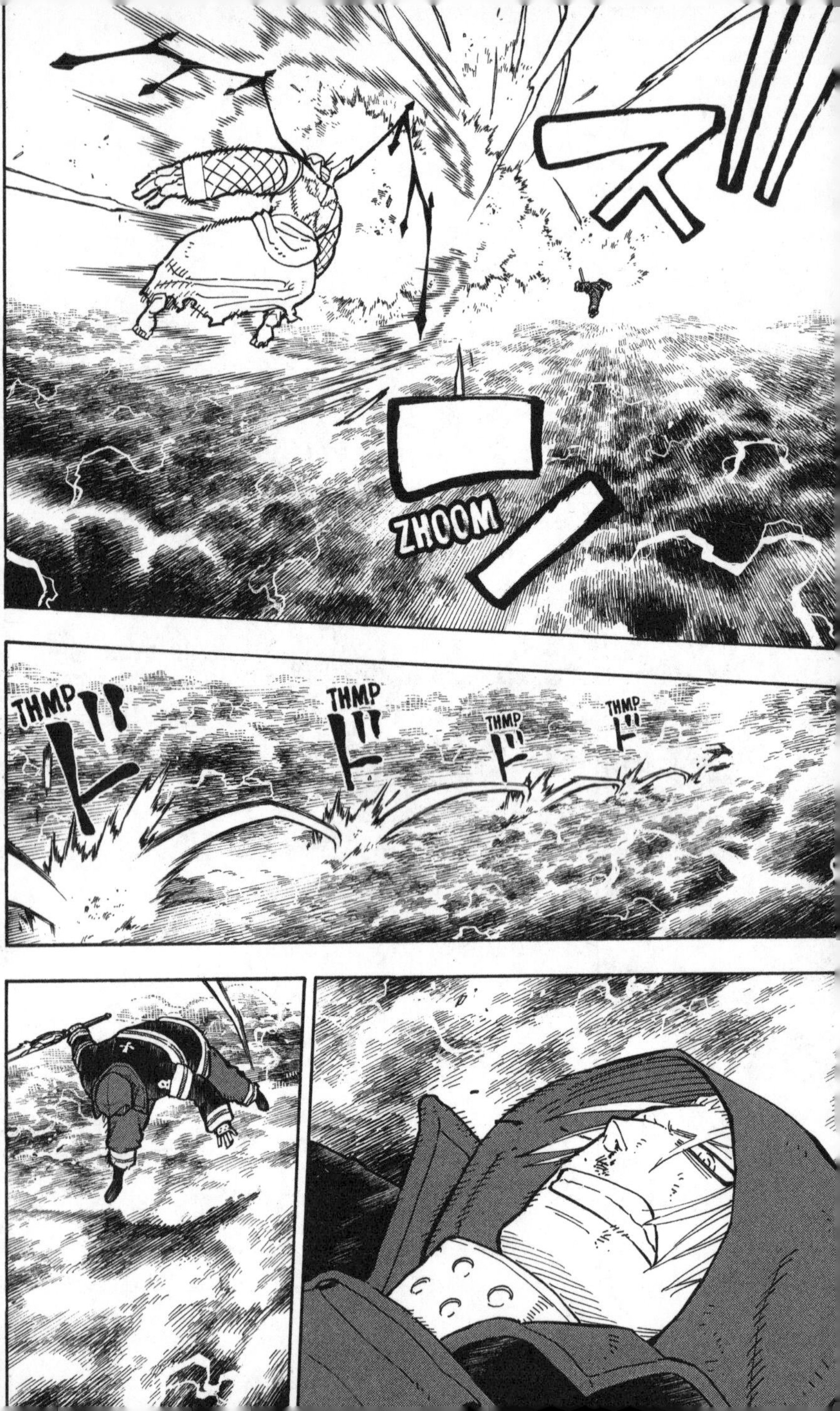

ZHOOM
THMP
THMP
THMP
THMP

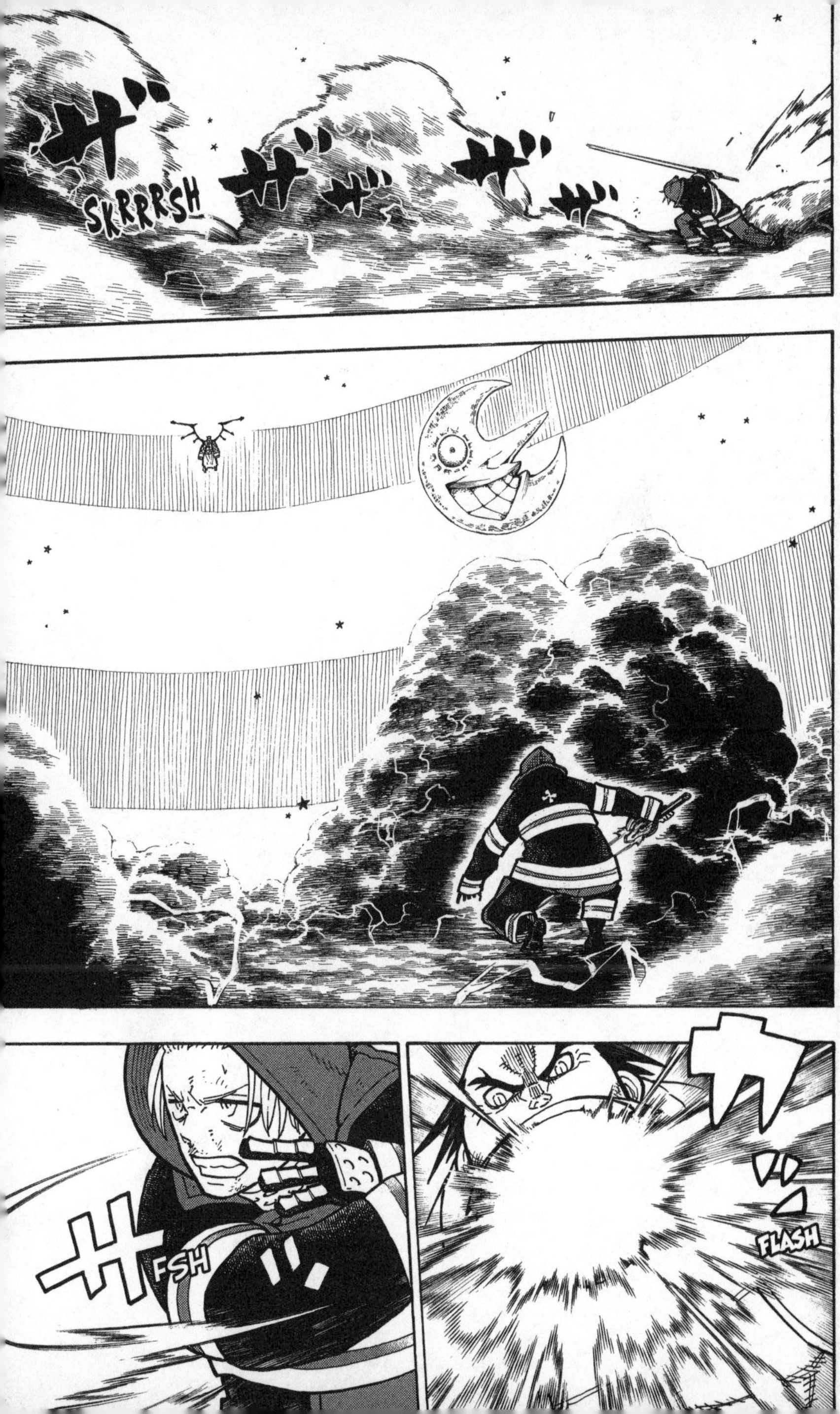
SKRRRSH
FLASH
FSH

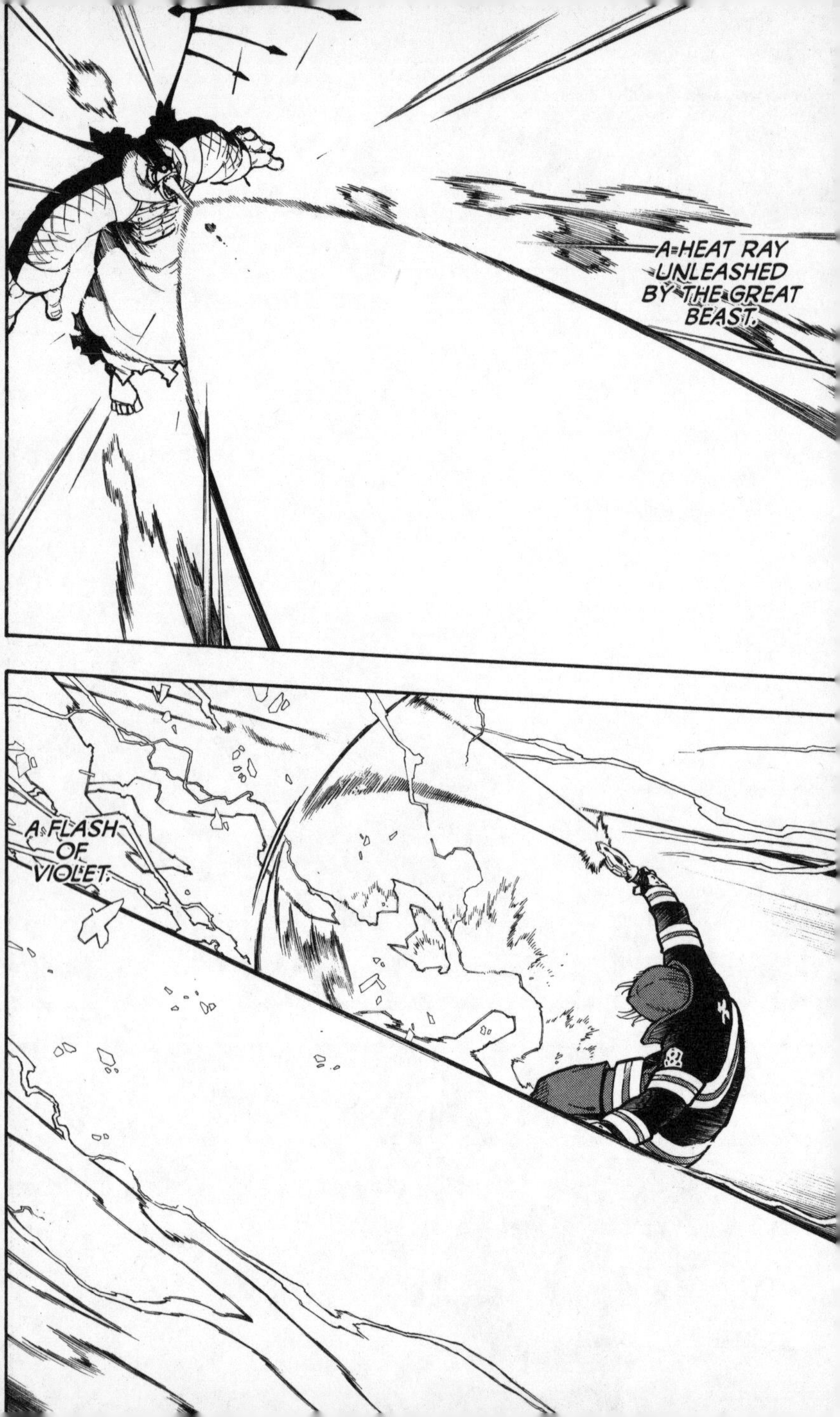
A HEAT RAY UNLEASHED BY THE GREAT BEAST.
A FLASH OF VIOLET.

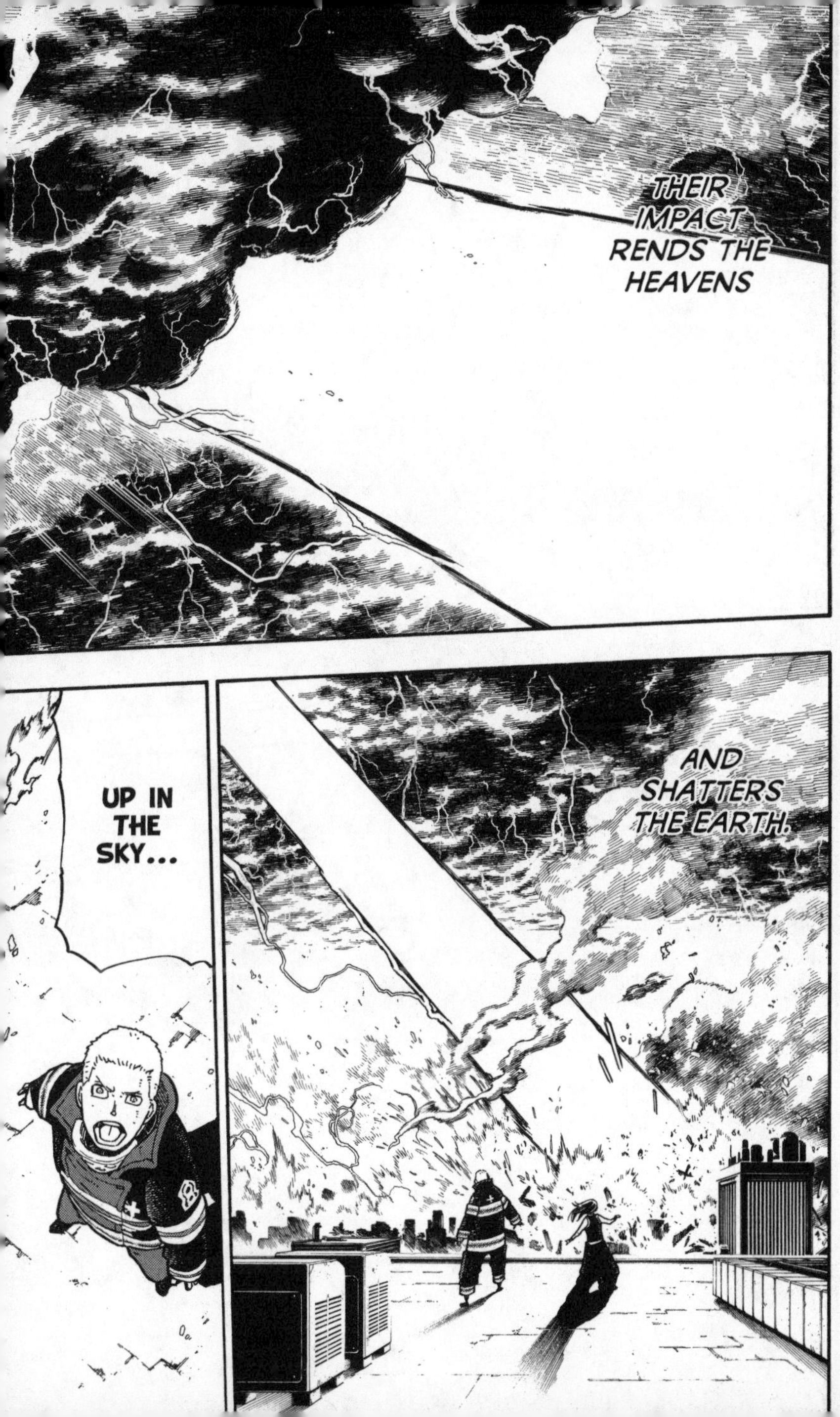
THEIR IMPACT RENDS THE HEAVENS
AND SHATTERS THE EARTH.
UP IN THE SKY...

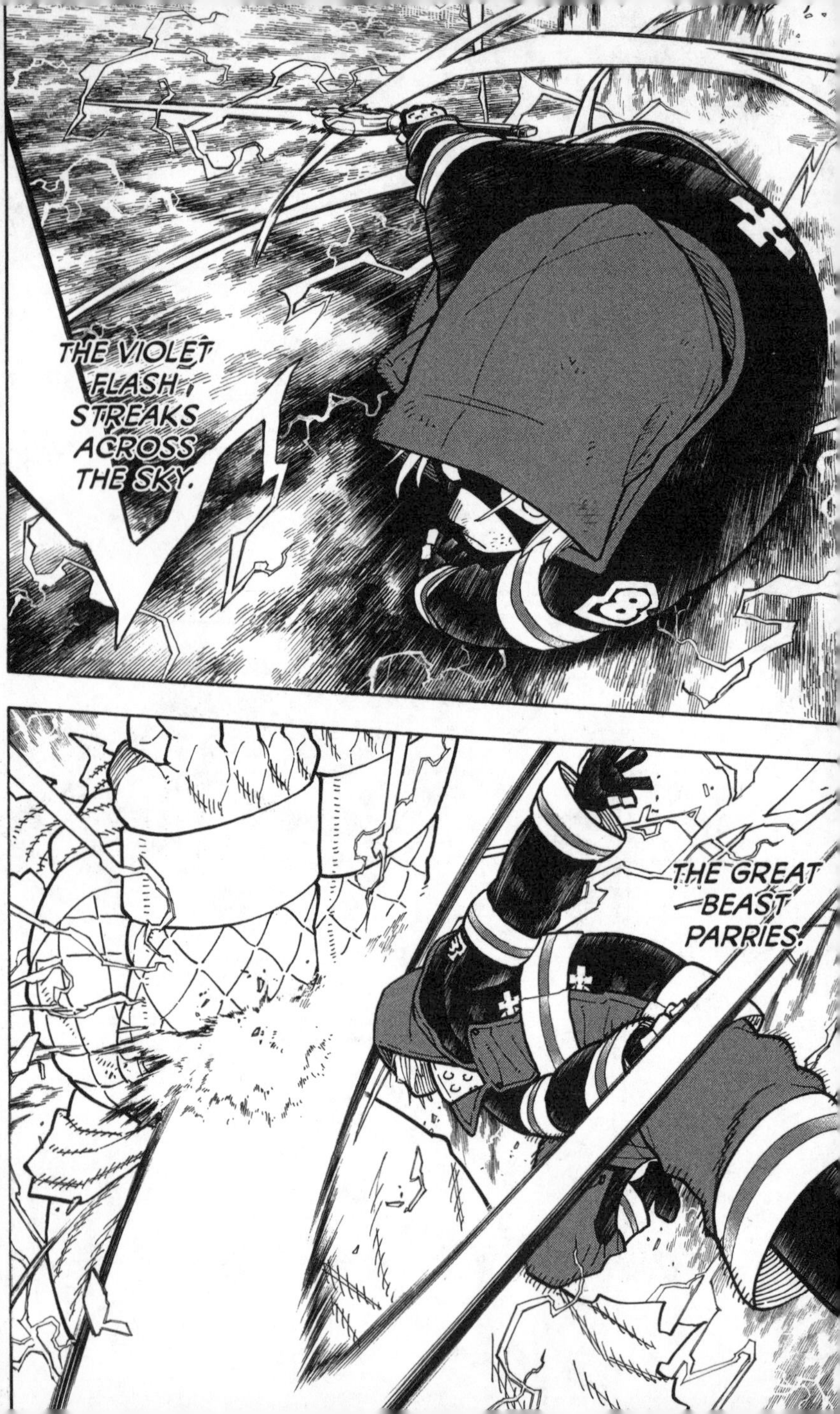
THE VIOLET FLASH STREAKS ACROSS THE SKY.
THE GREAT BEAST PARRIES.

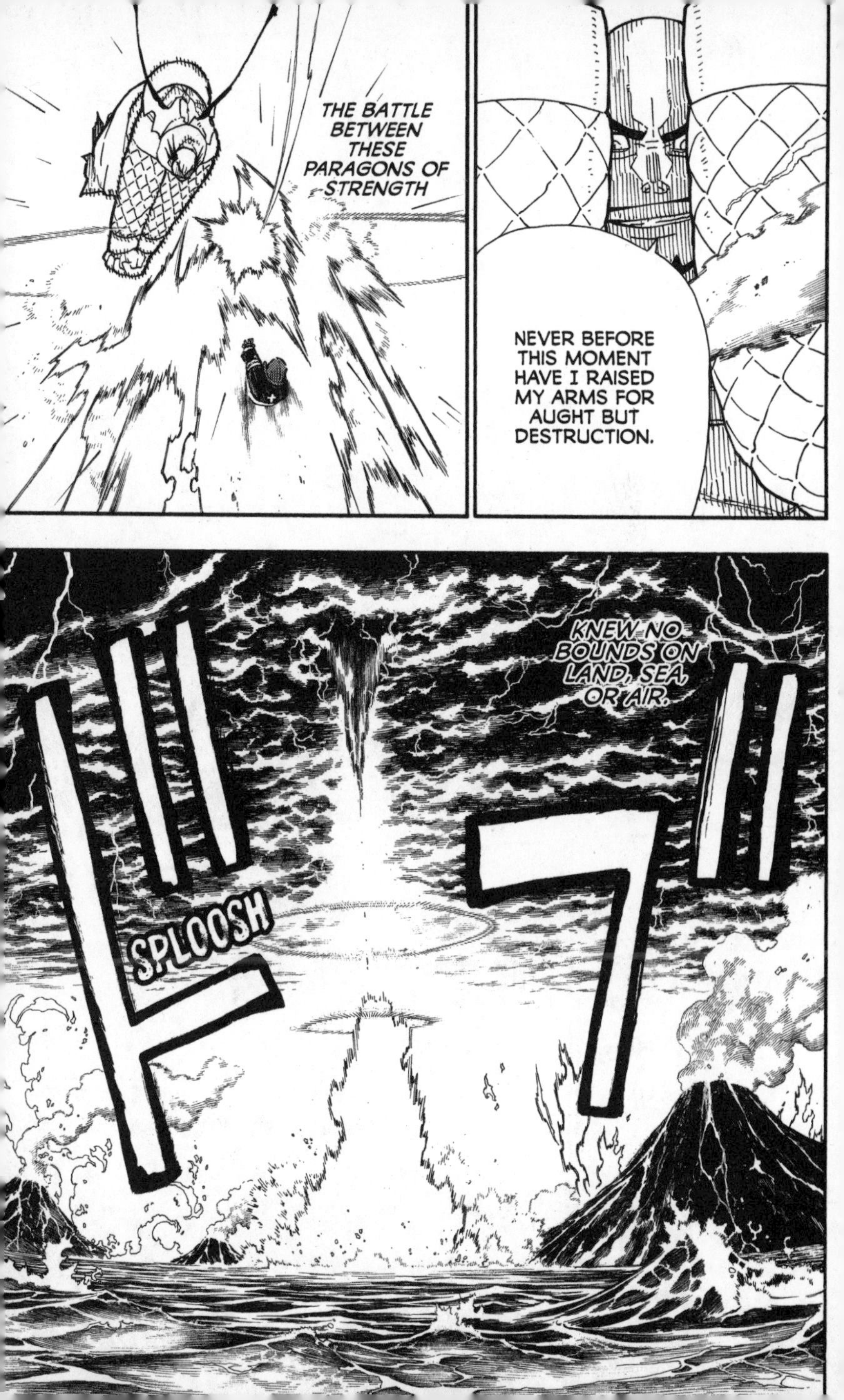
NEVER BEFORE THIS MOMENT HAVE I RAISED MY ARMS FOR AUGHT BUT DESTRUCTION.
THE BATTLE BETWEEN THESE PARAGONS OF STRENGTH
KNEW NO BOUNDS ON LAND, SEA, OR AIR.
SPLOOSH

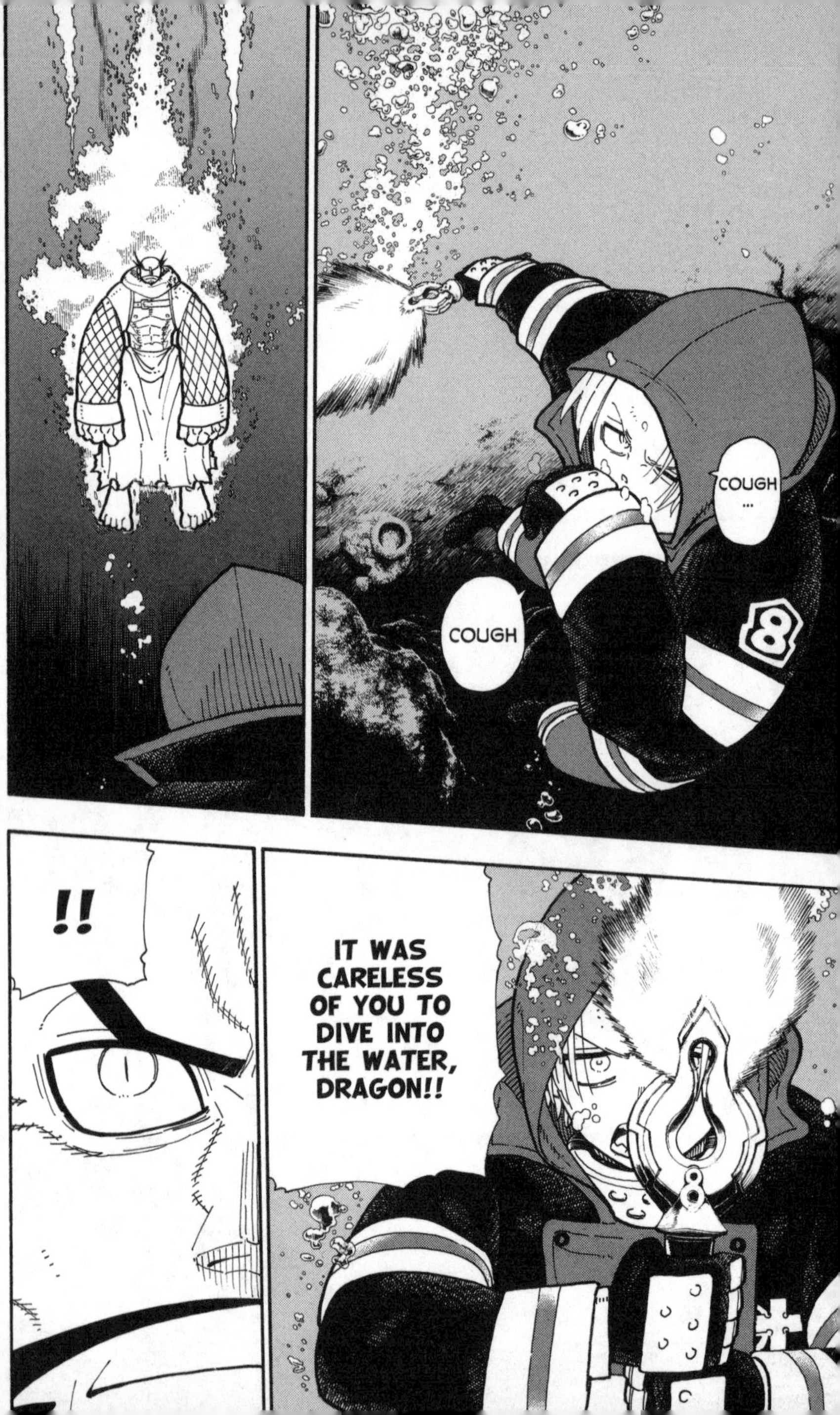
COUGH
...
COUGH
IT WAS CARELESS OF YOU TO DIVE INTO THE WATER, DRAGON!!
!!
...

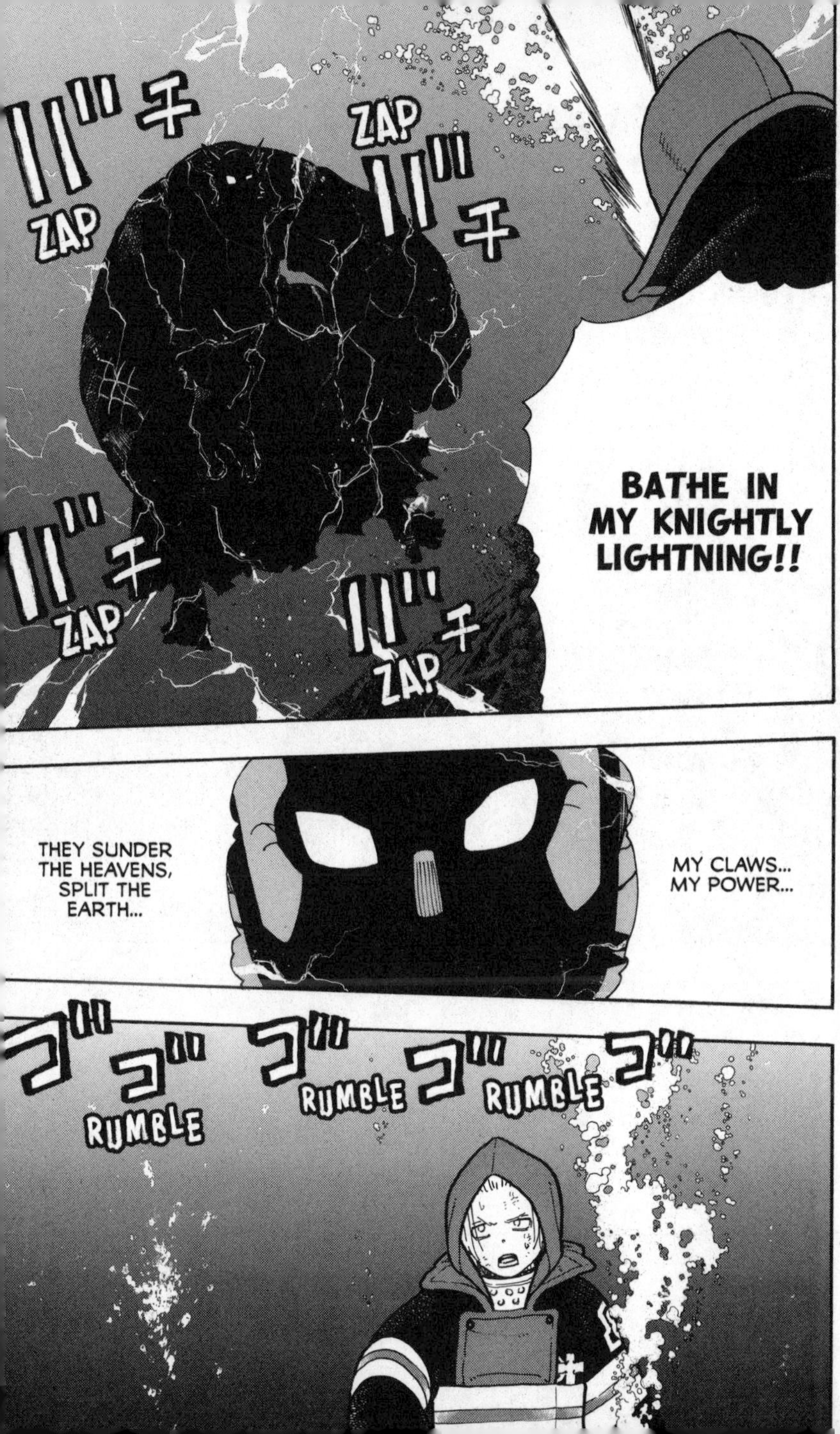
BATHE IN MY KNIGHTLY LIGHTNING!!
ZAP
ZAP
ZAP
ZAP
MY CLAWS... MY POWER...
THEY SUNDER THE HEAVENS, SPLIT THE EARTH...
RUMBLE
RUMBLE
RUMBLE

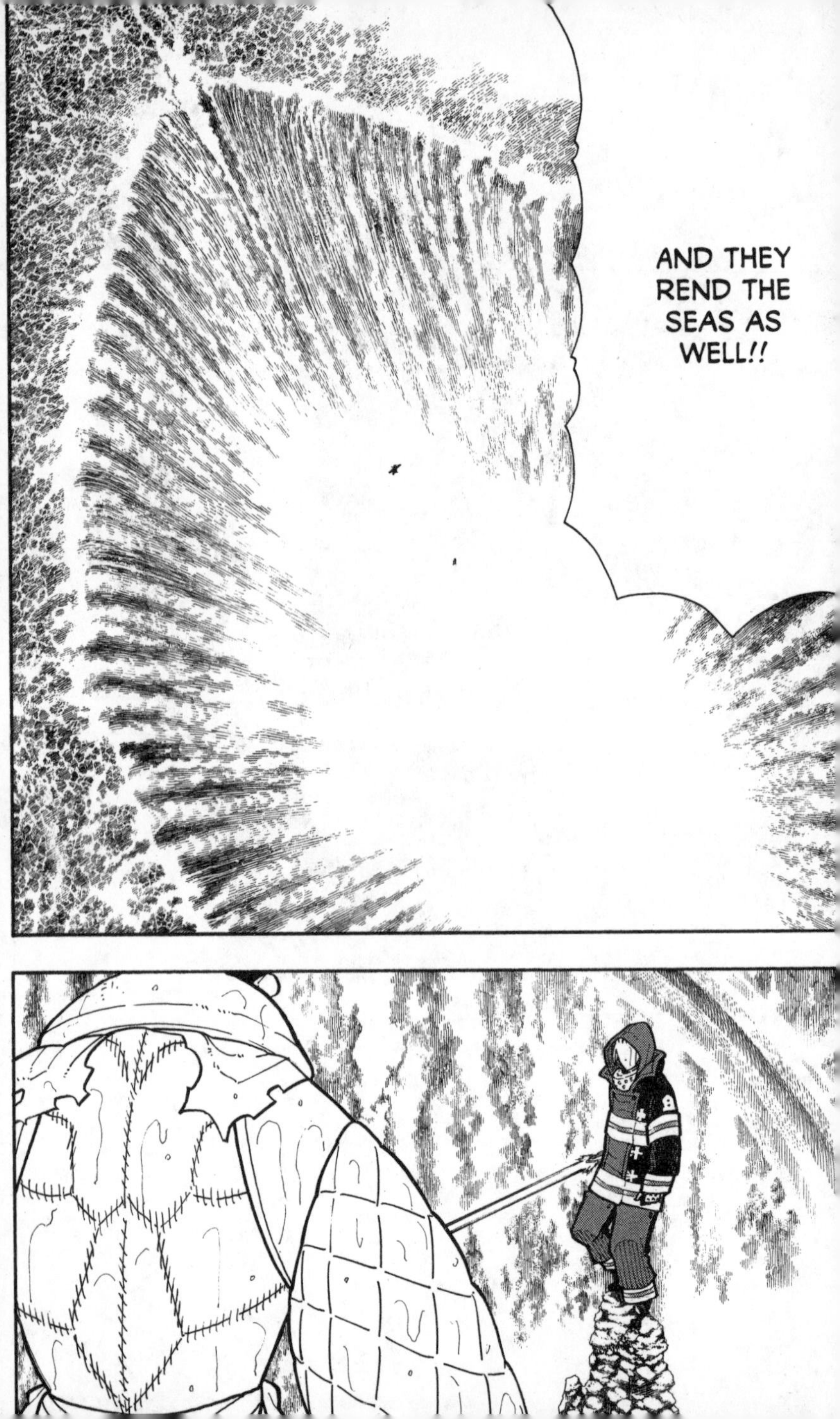
AND THEY REND THE SEAS AS WELL!!

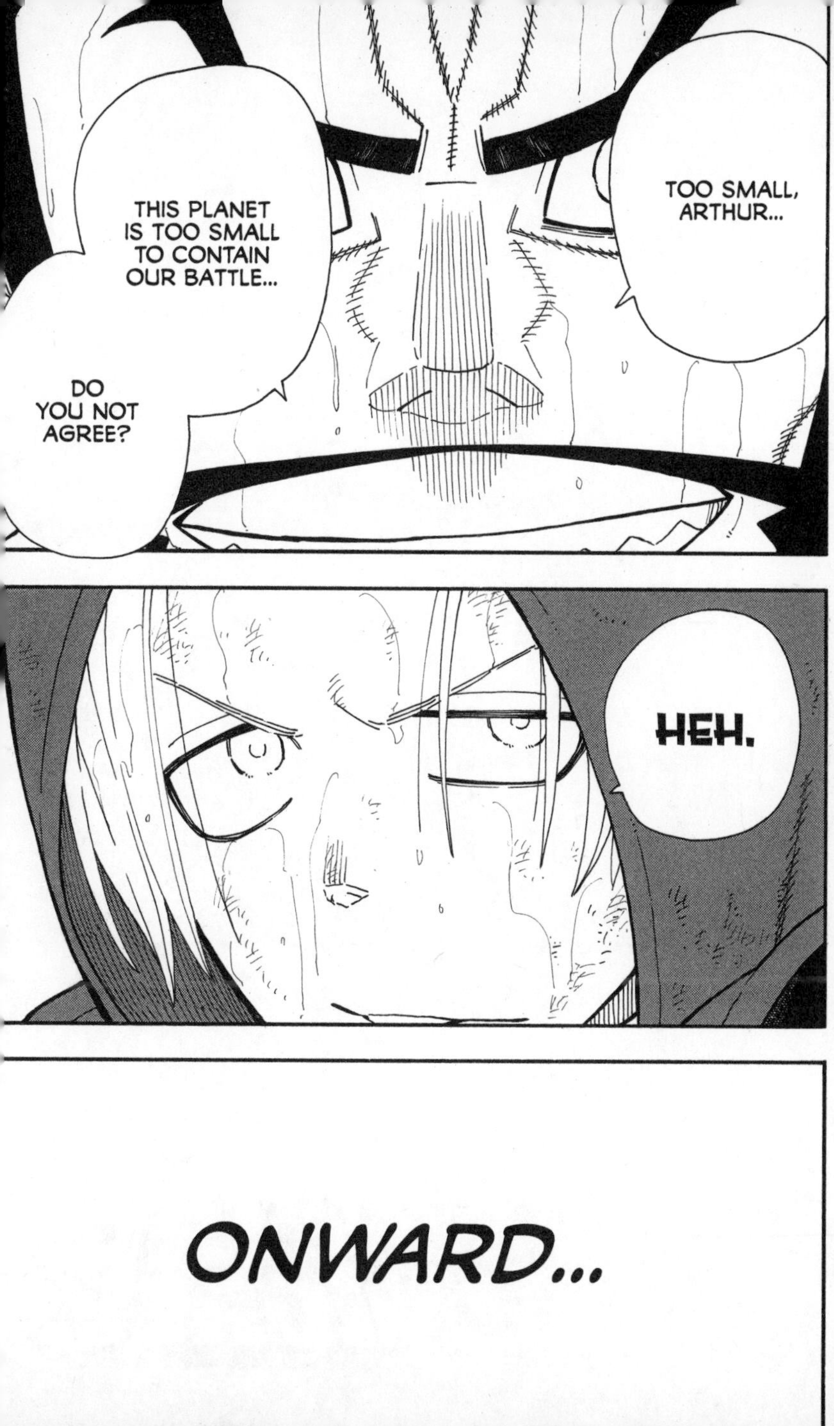
TOO SMALL, ARTHUR...
THIS PLANET IS TOO SMALL TO CONTAIN OUR BATTLE...
DO YOU NOT AGREE?
HEH.
ONWARD...

FIRE FORCE

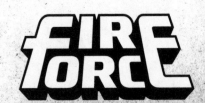

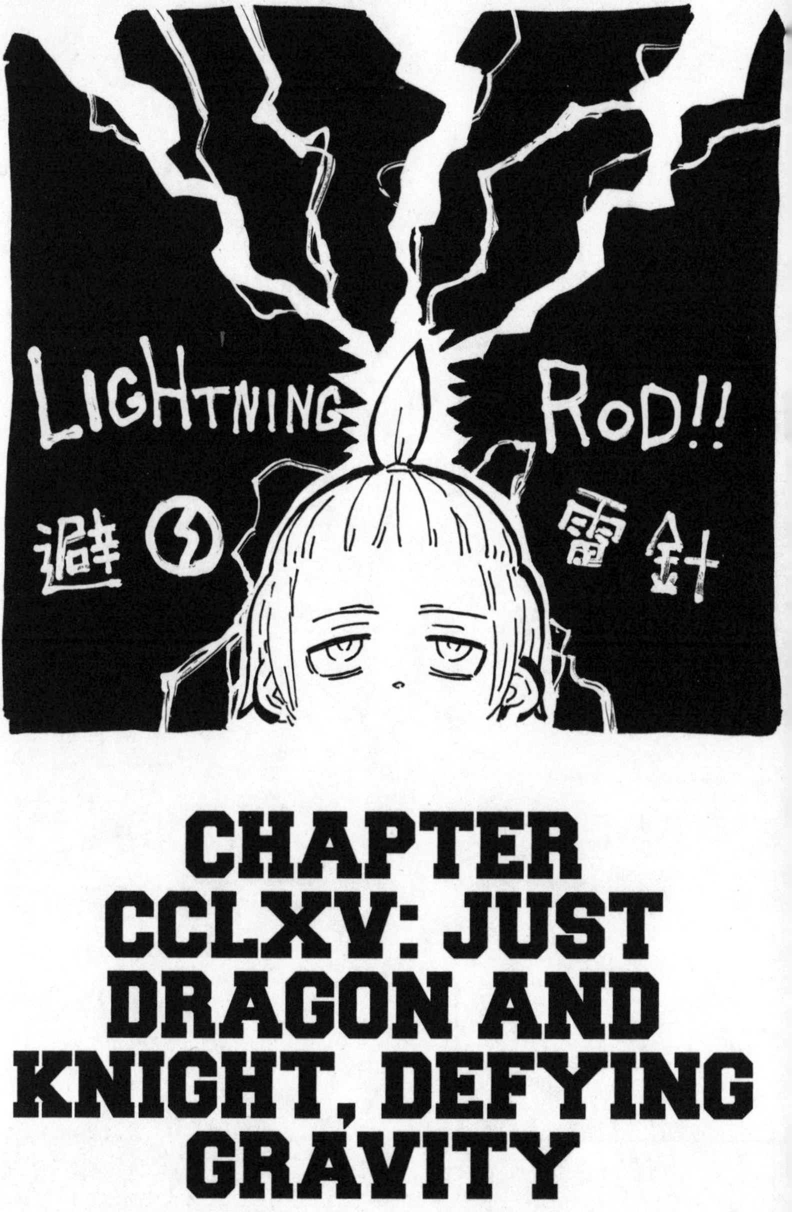
LIGHTNING ROD!!
避雷針

CHAPTER CCLXV: JUST DRAGON AND KNIGHT, DEFYING GRAVITY

ZSHHHH

SURELY THIS IS
NOT ALL YOU HAVE
TO SHOW ME!!

BOOM

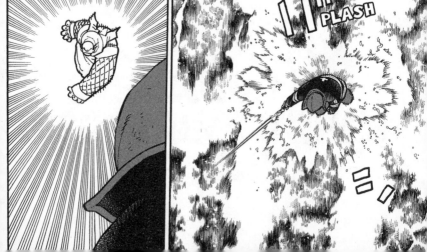

PLASH

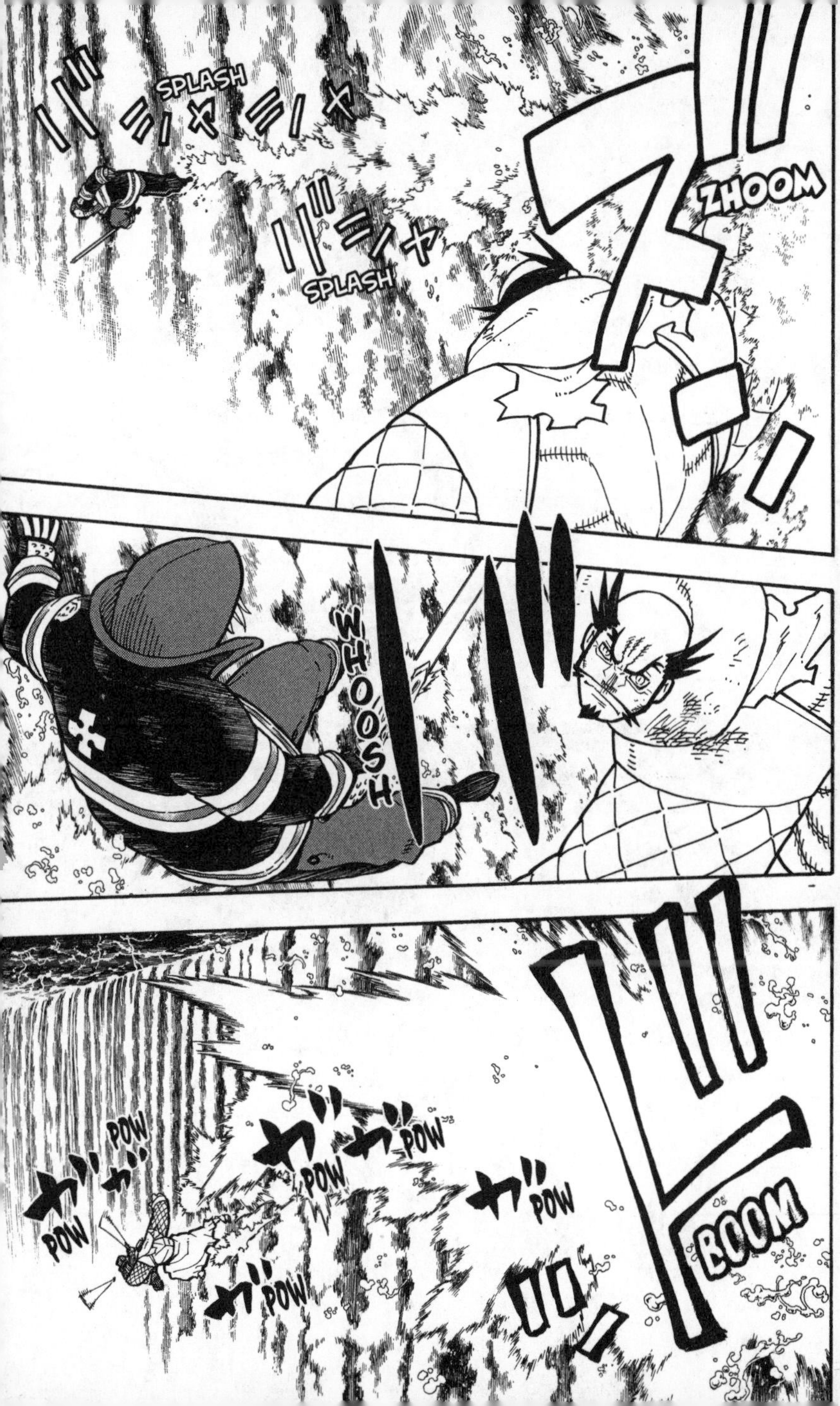

ZHOOM
SPLASH
SPLASH
WHOOSH
BOOM
POW
POW
POW
POW
POW
POW

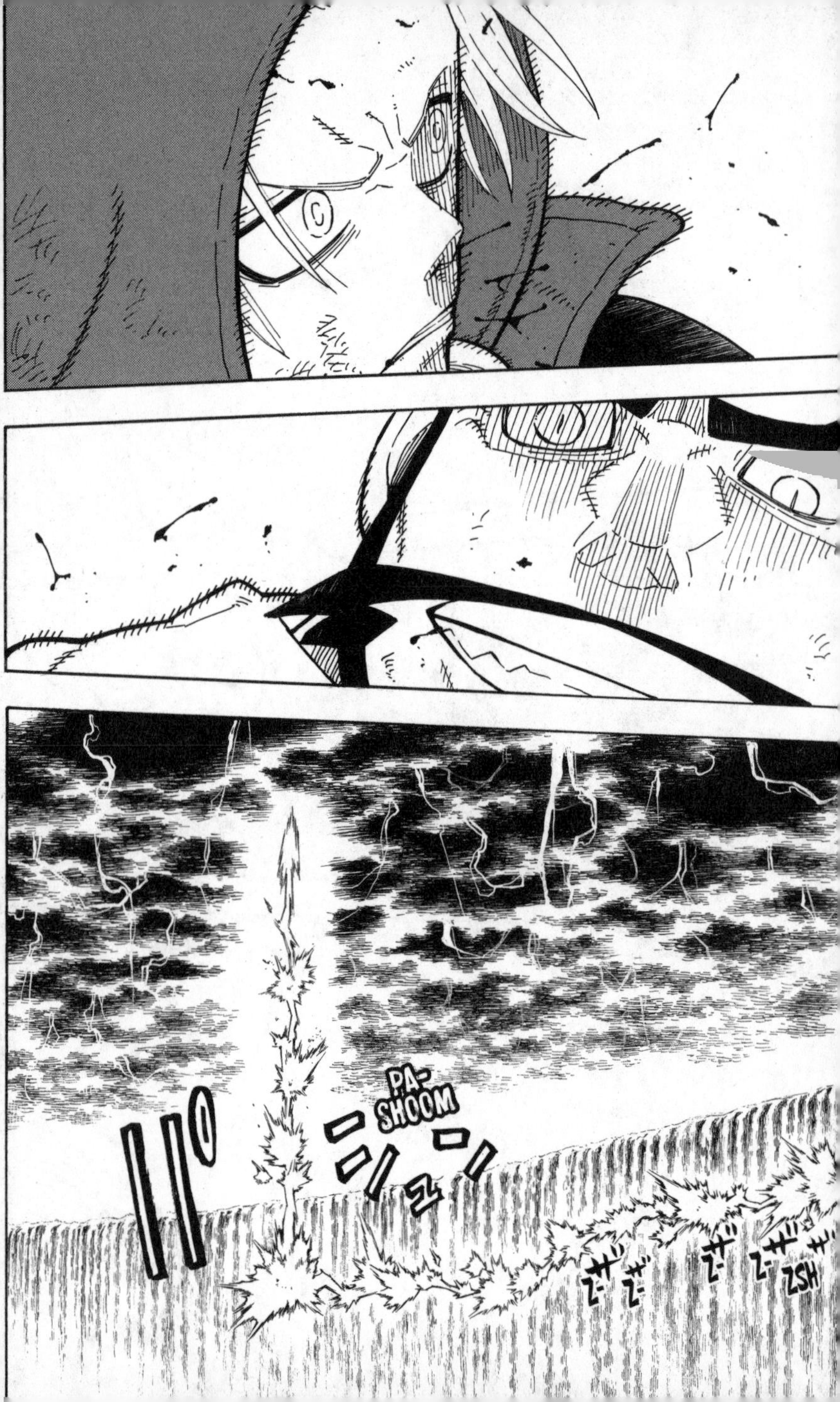
PA-SHOOM
ZSH

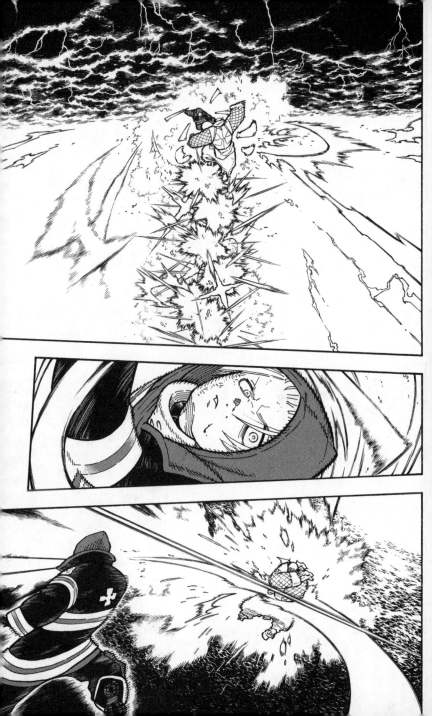

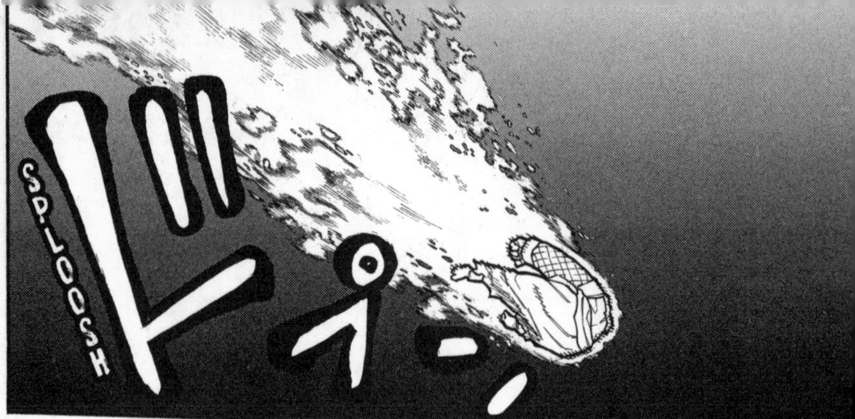
SPLOOSH
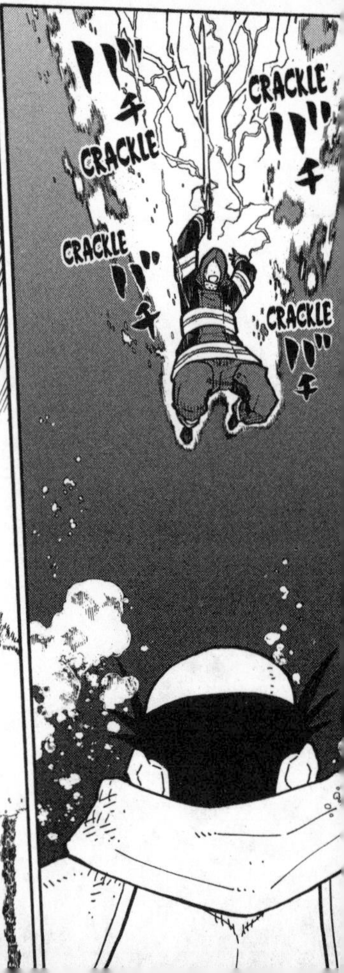
CRACKLE
CRACKLE
CRACKLE
CRACKLE
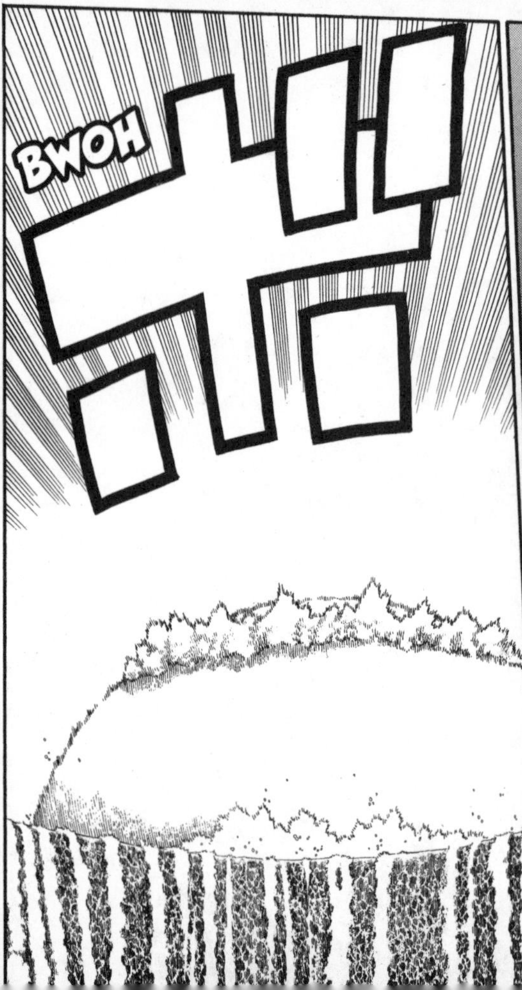
BWOH

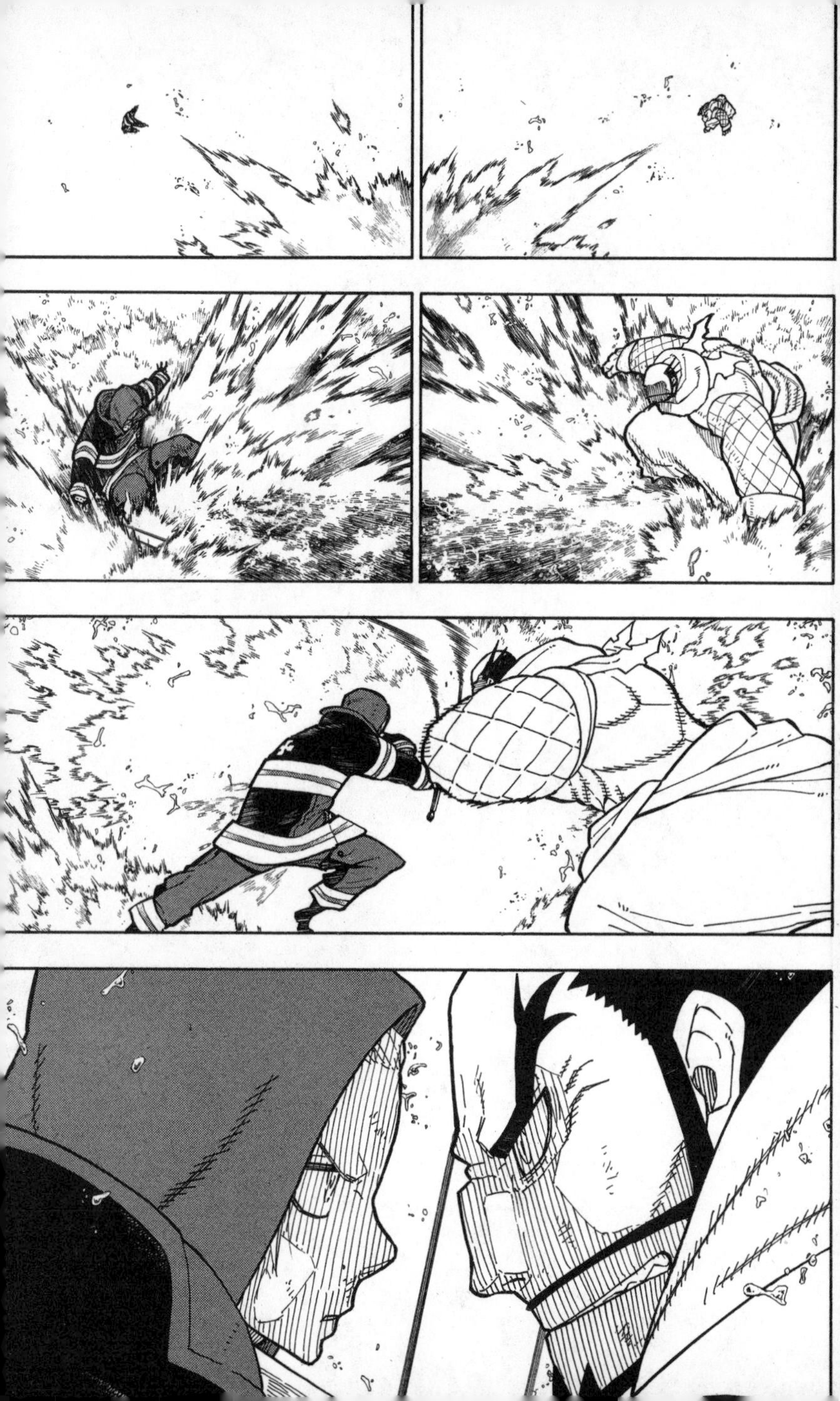

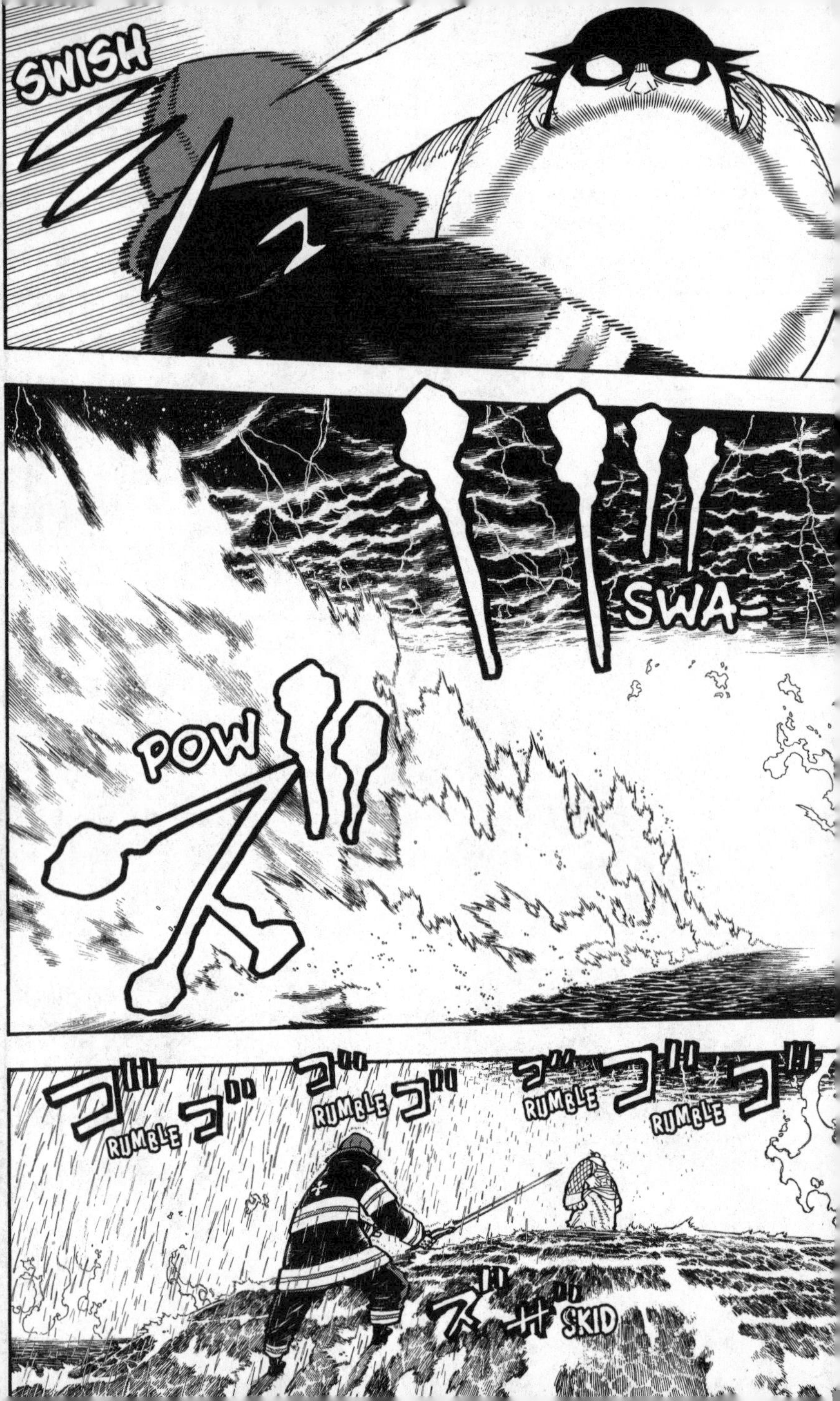
SWISH
SWA-
POW
RUMBLE
RUMBLE
RUMBLE
RUMBLE
SKID

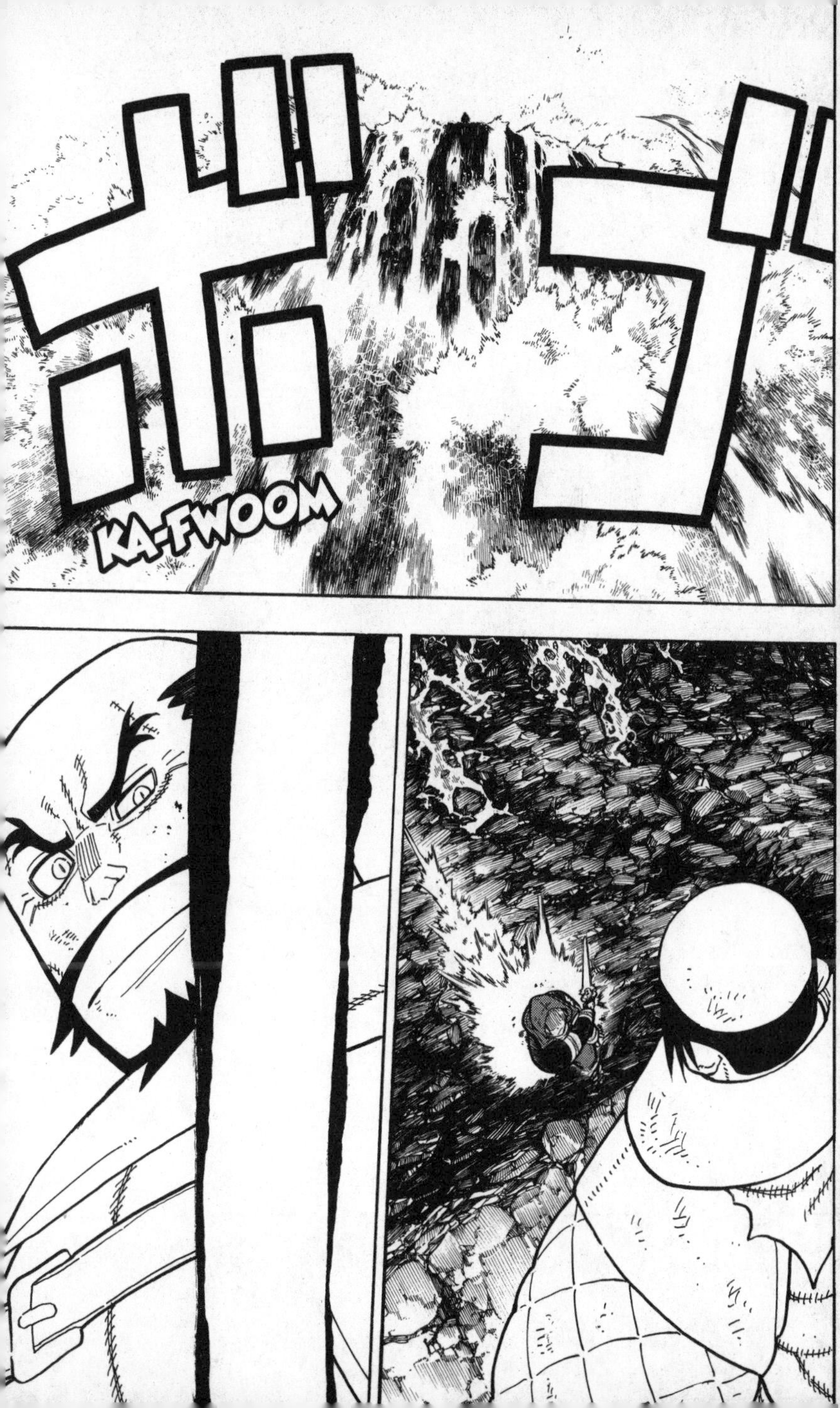
KA-FWOOM

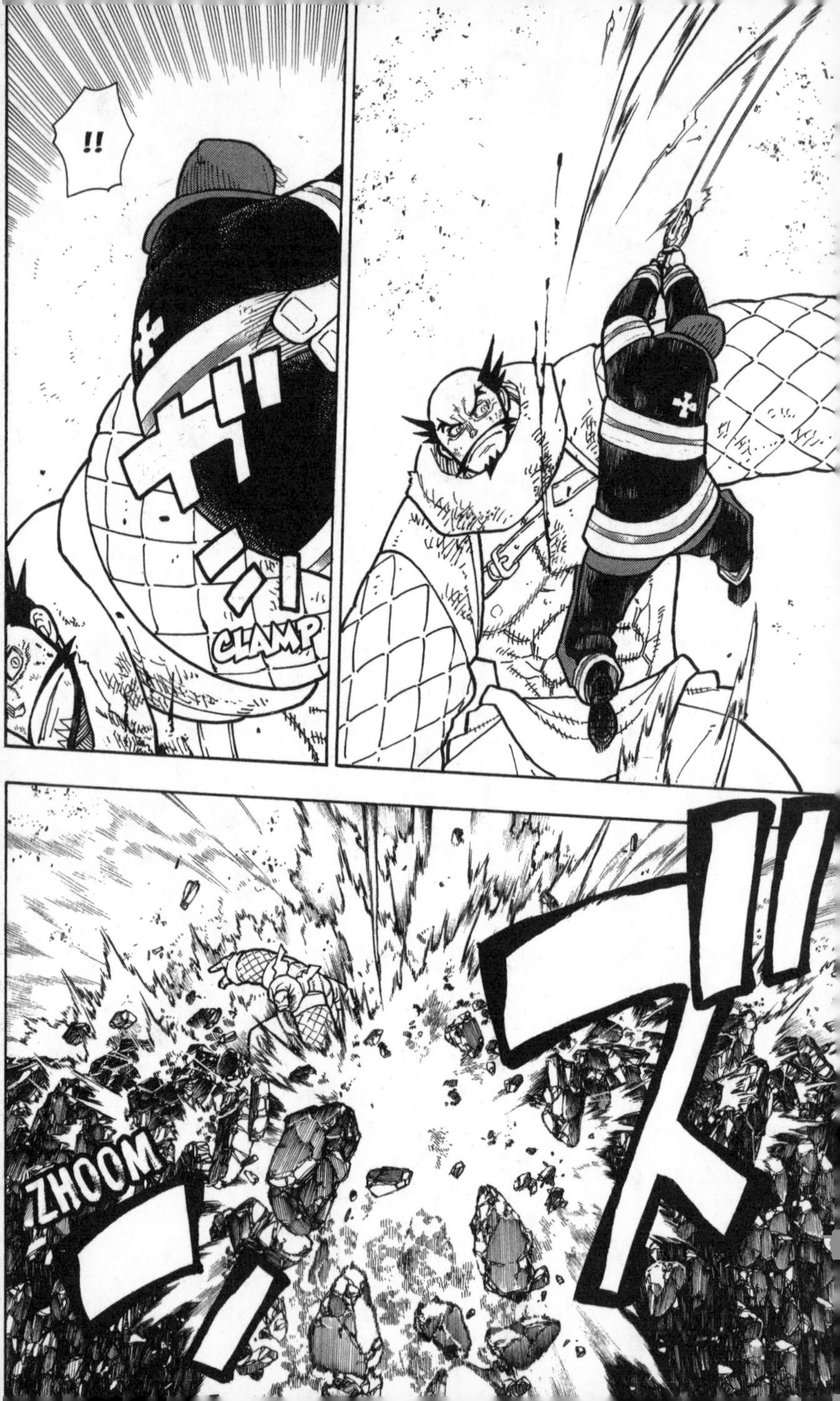
!!
CLAMP
ZHOOM

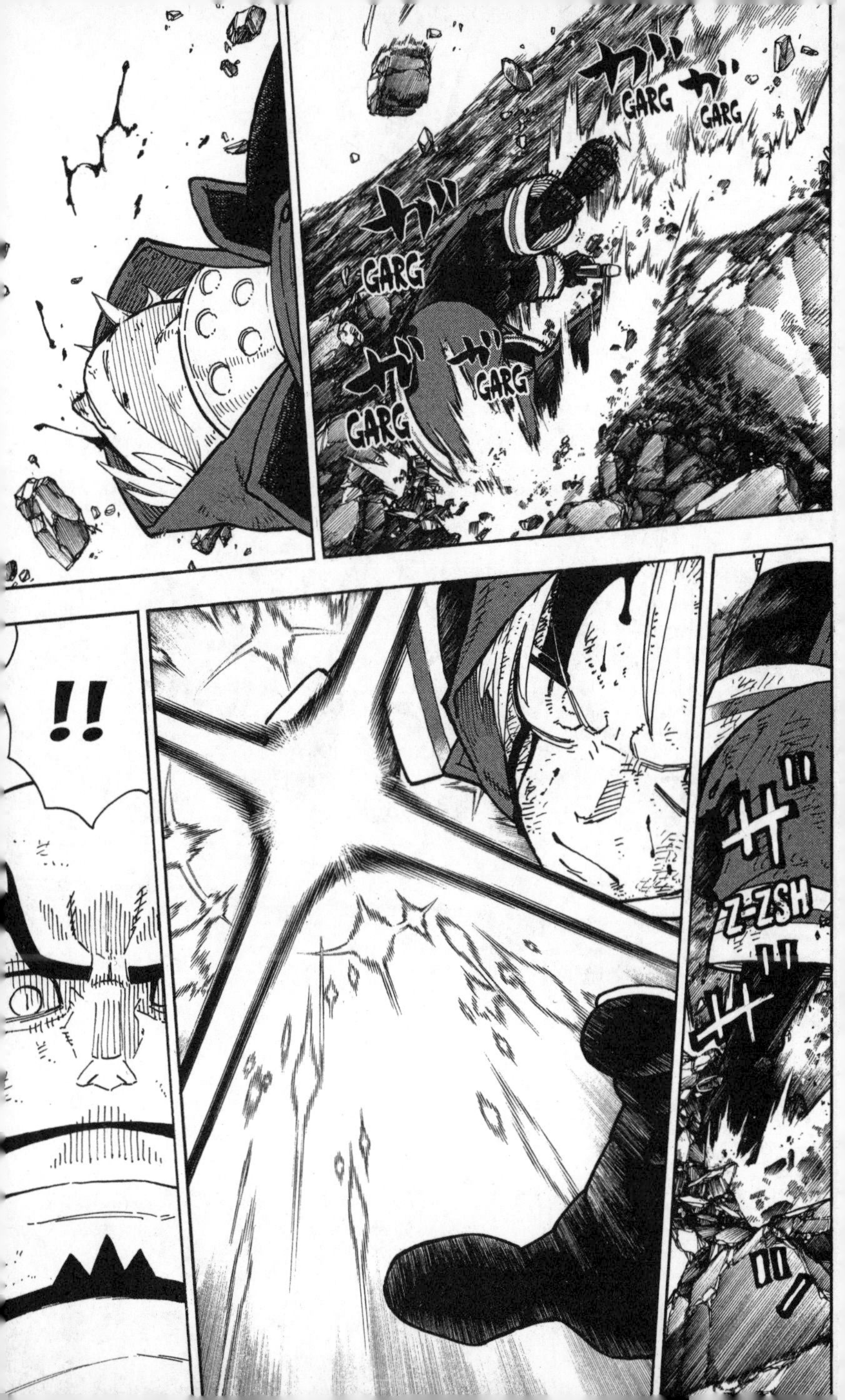
GARG
GARG
GARG
GARG
GARG
Z-ZSH
!!

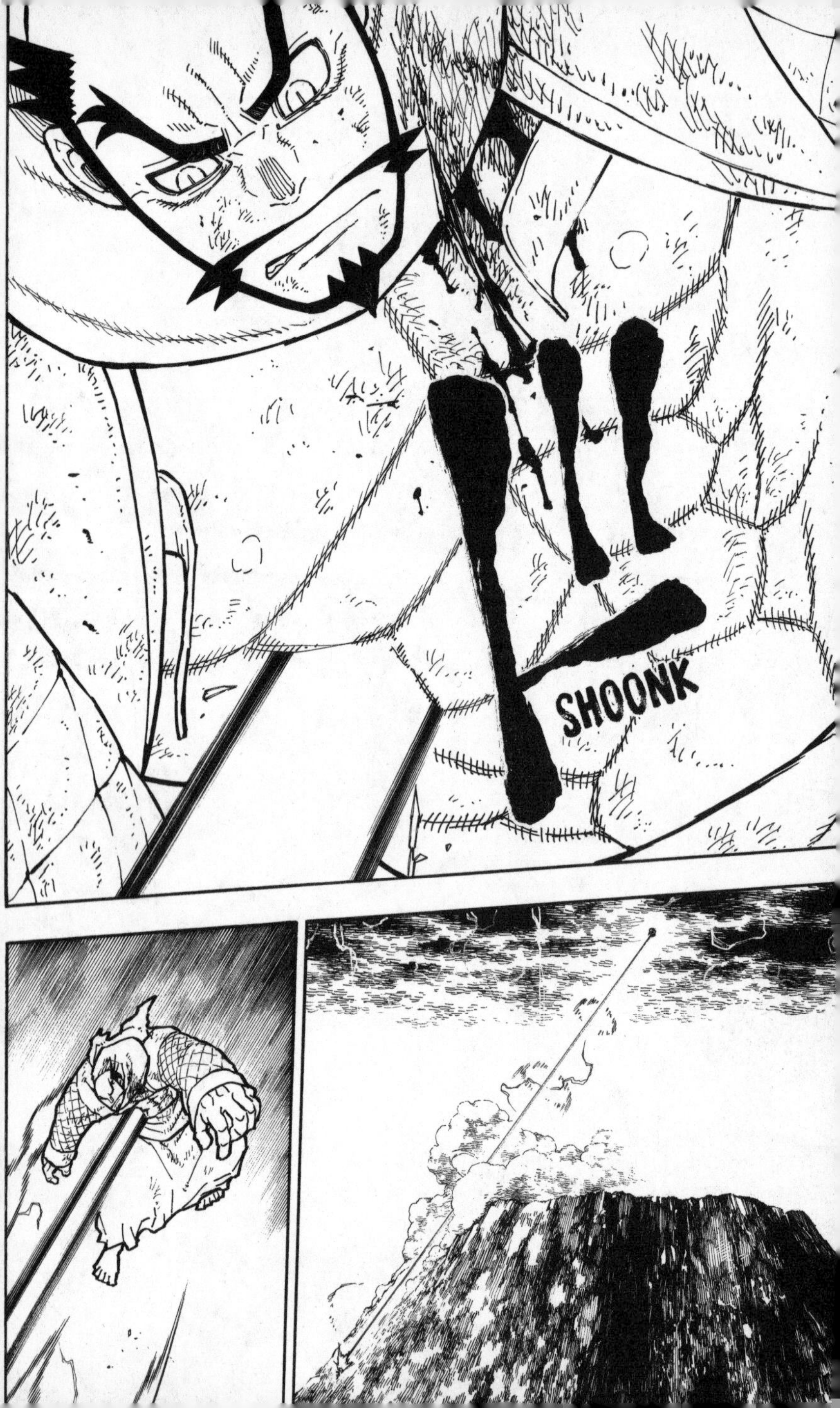
SHOONK

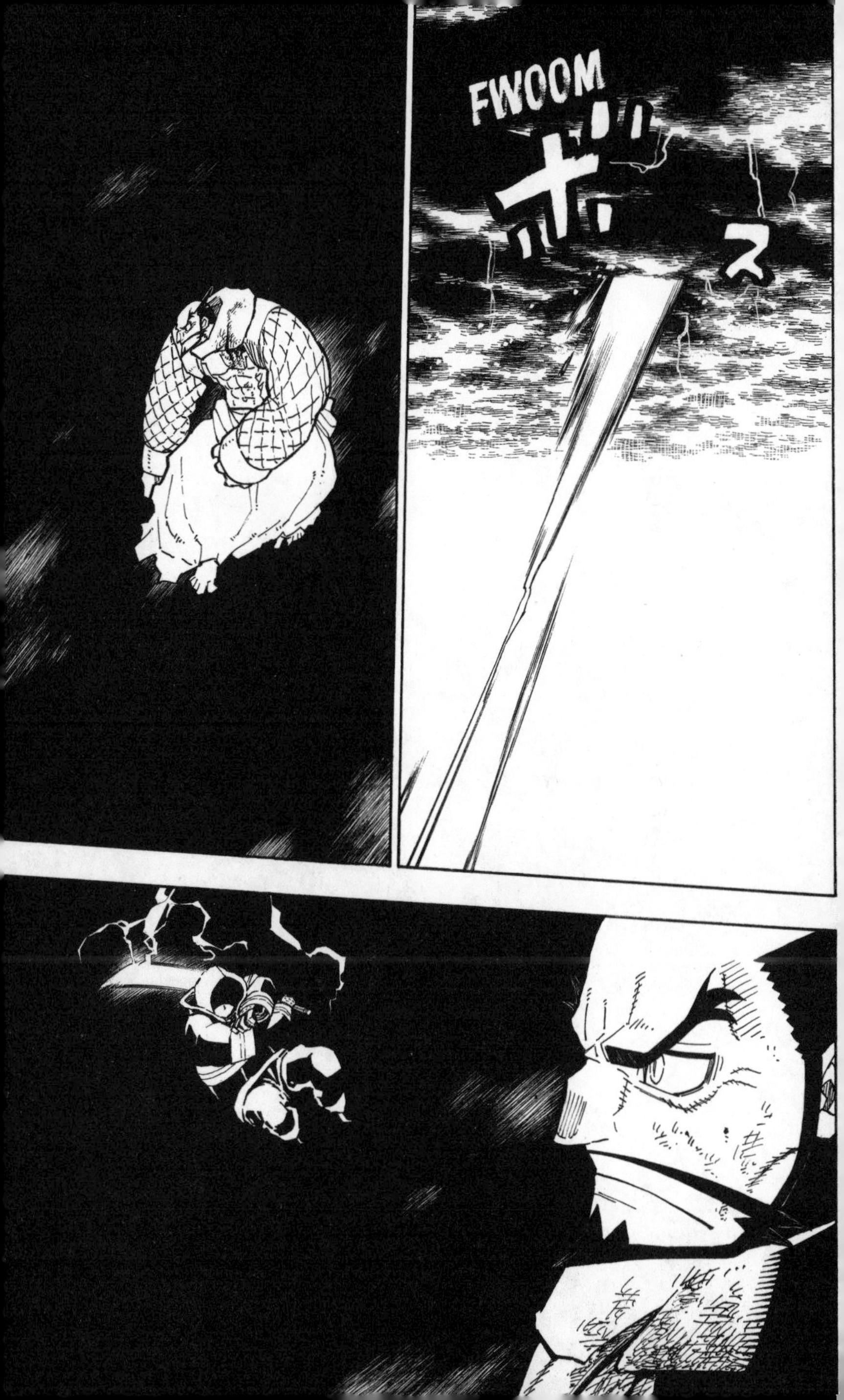
FWOOM

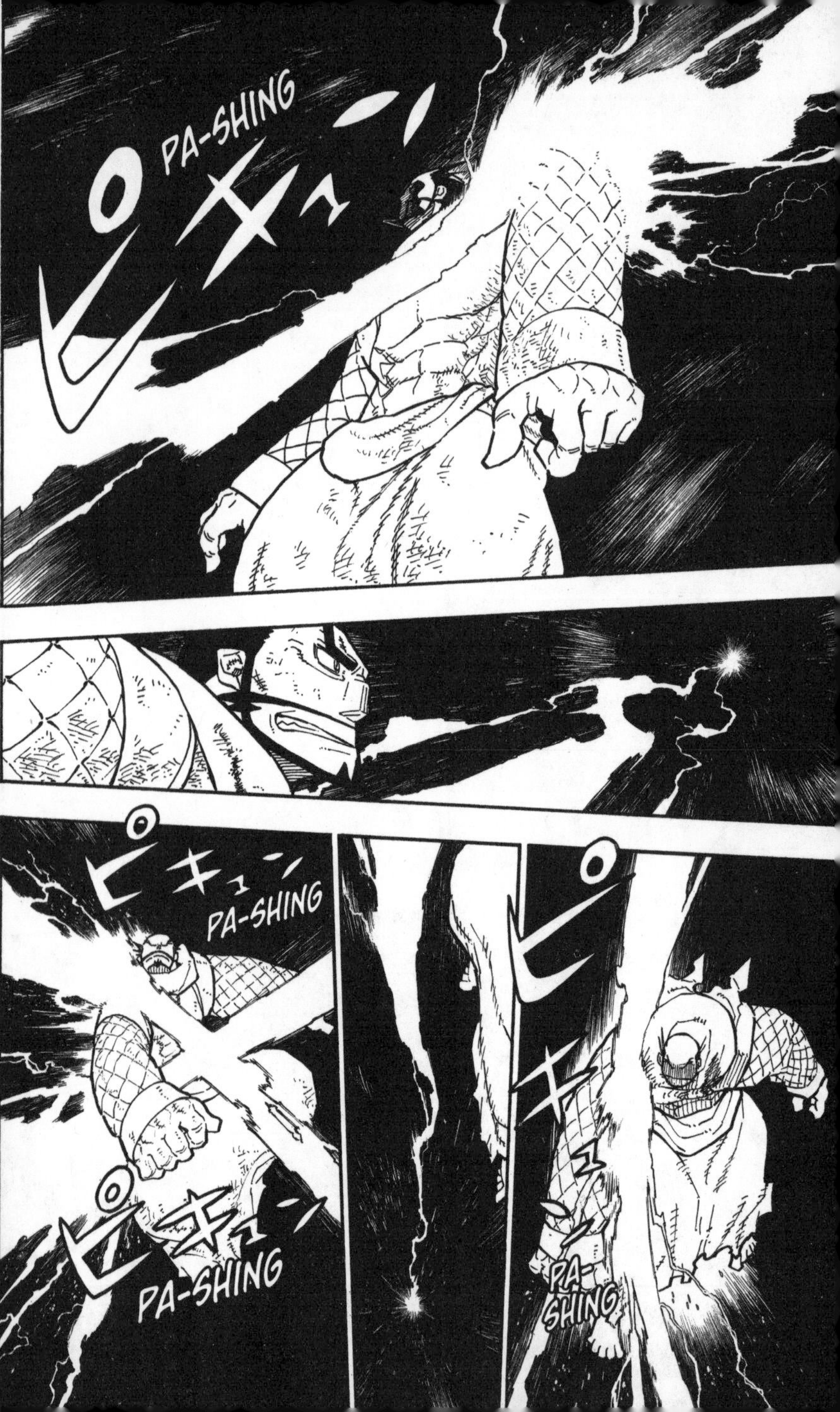
PA-SHING
PA-SHING
PA-SHING
PA-SHING

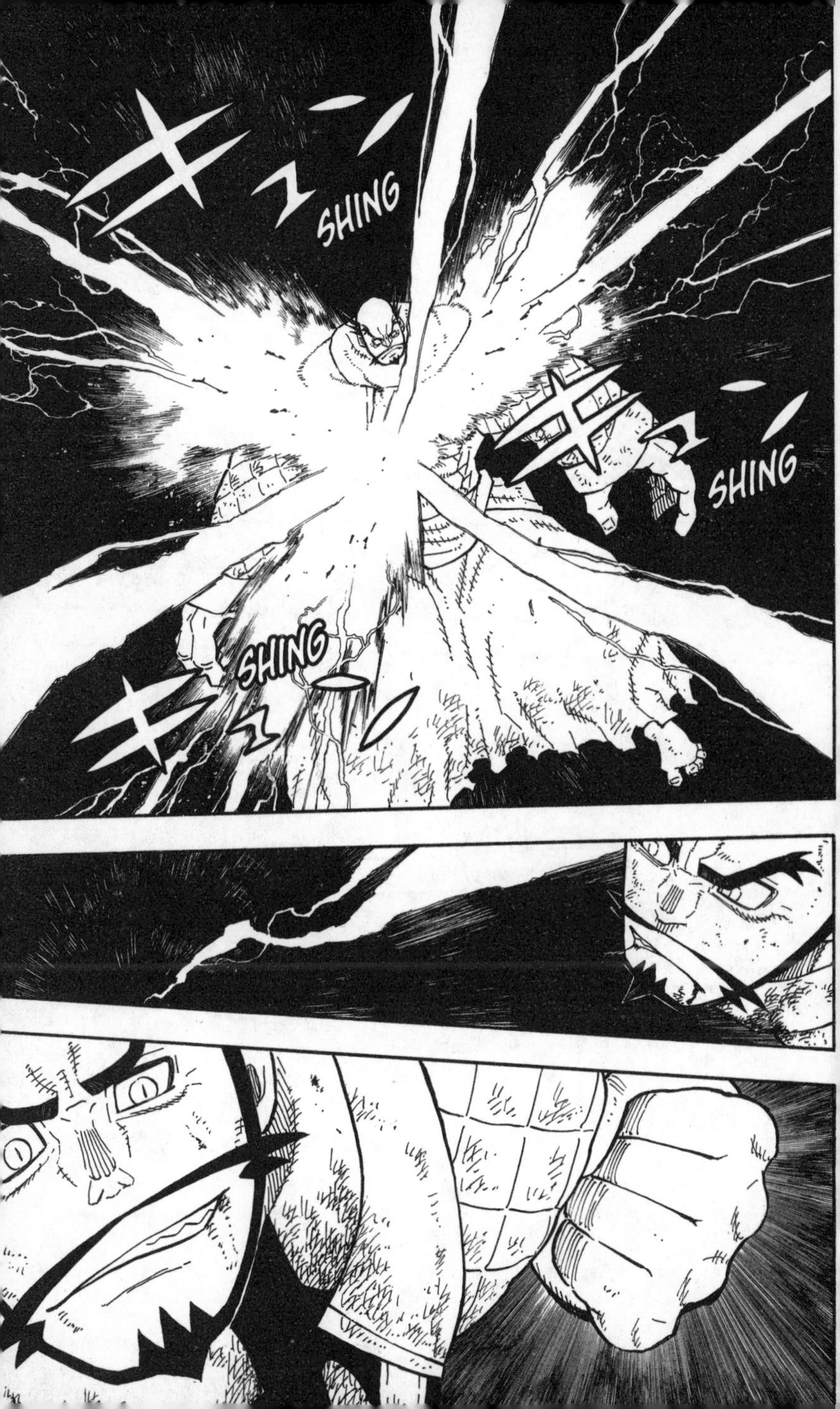
SHING
SHING
SHING

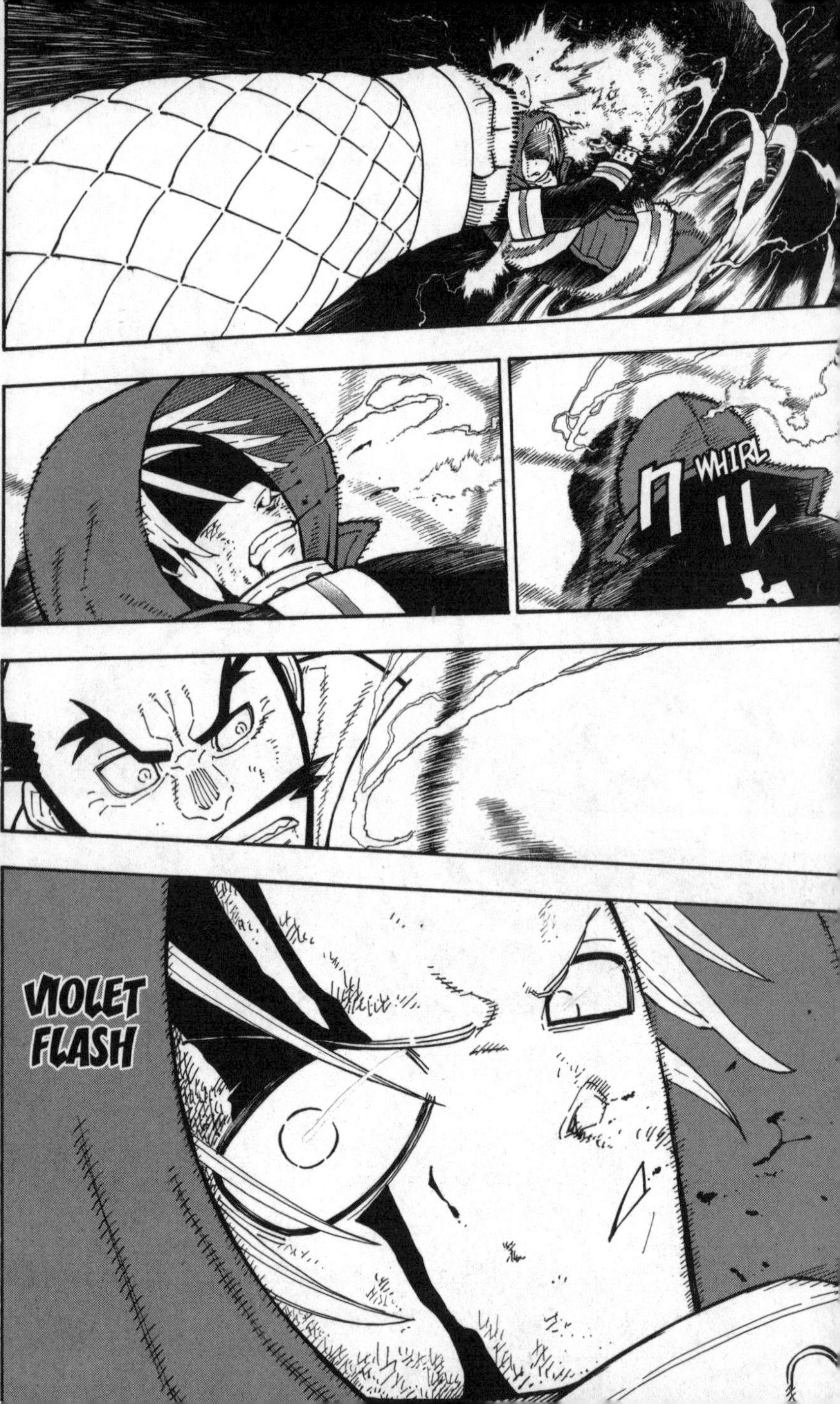
クル
WHIRL
VIOLET FLASH

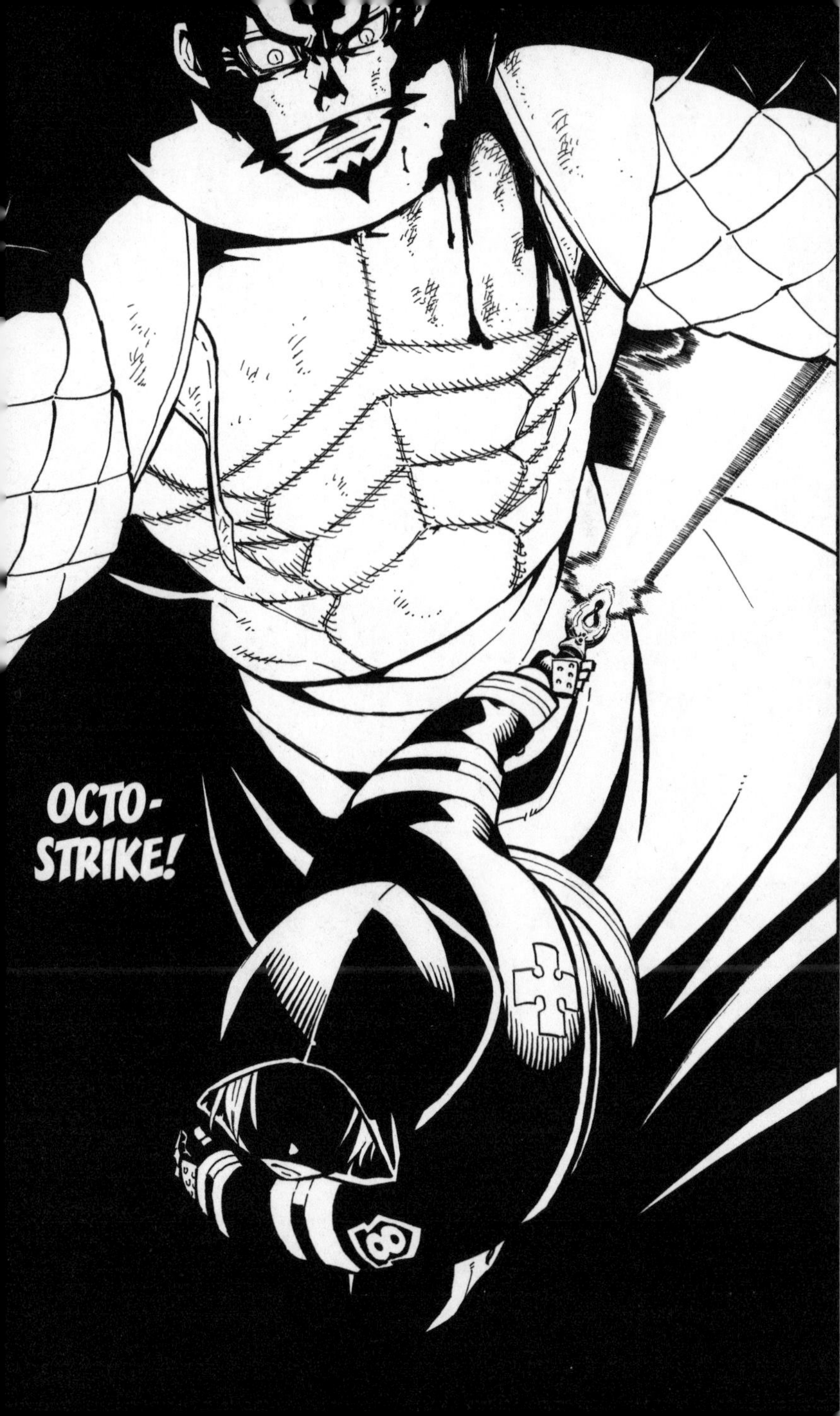
OCTO-
STRIKE!

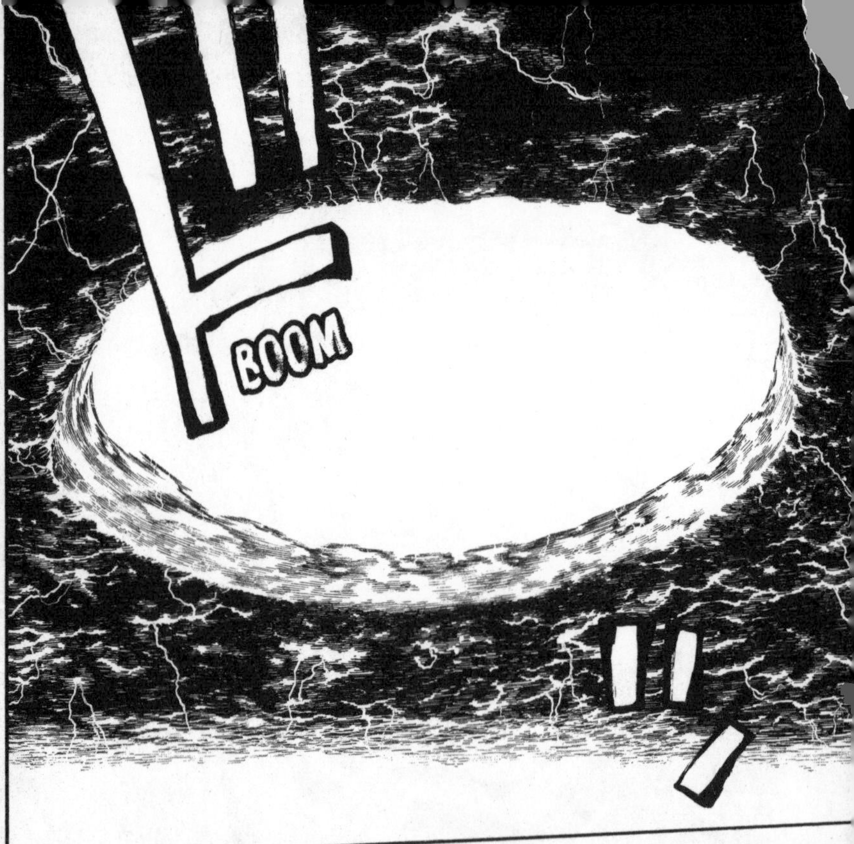
BOOM
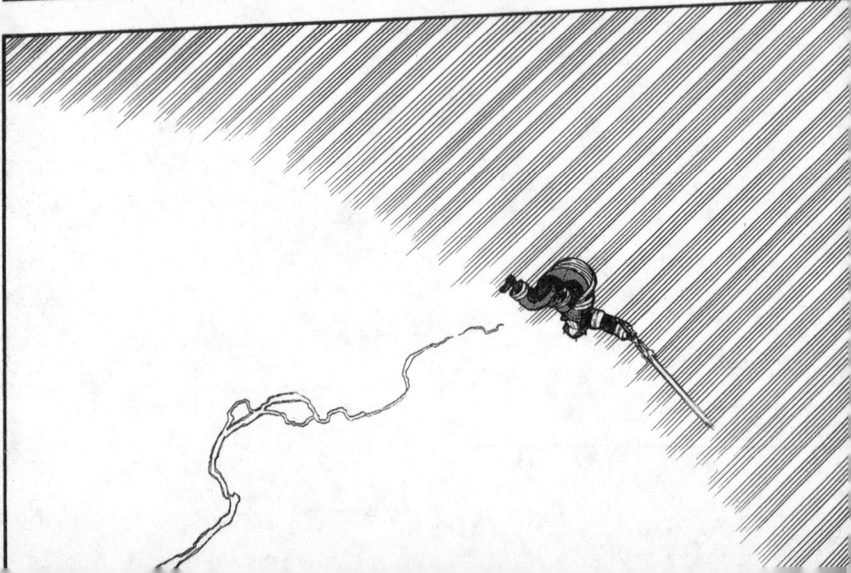

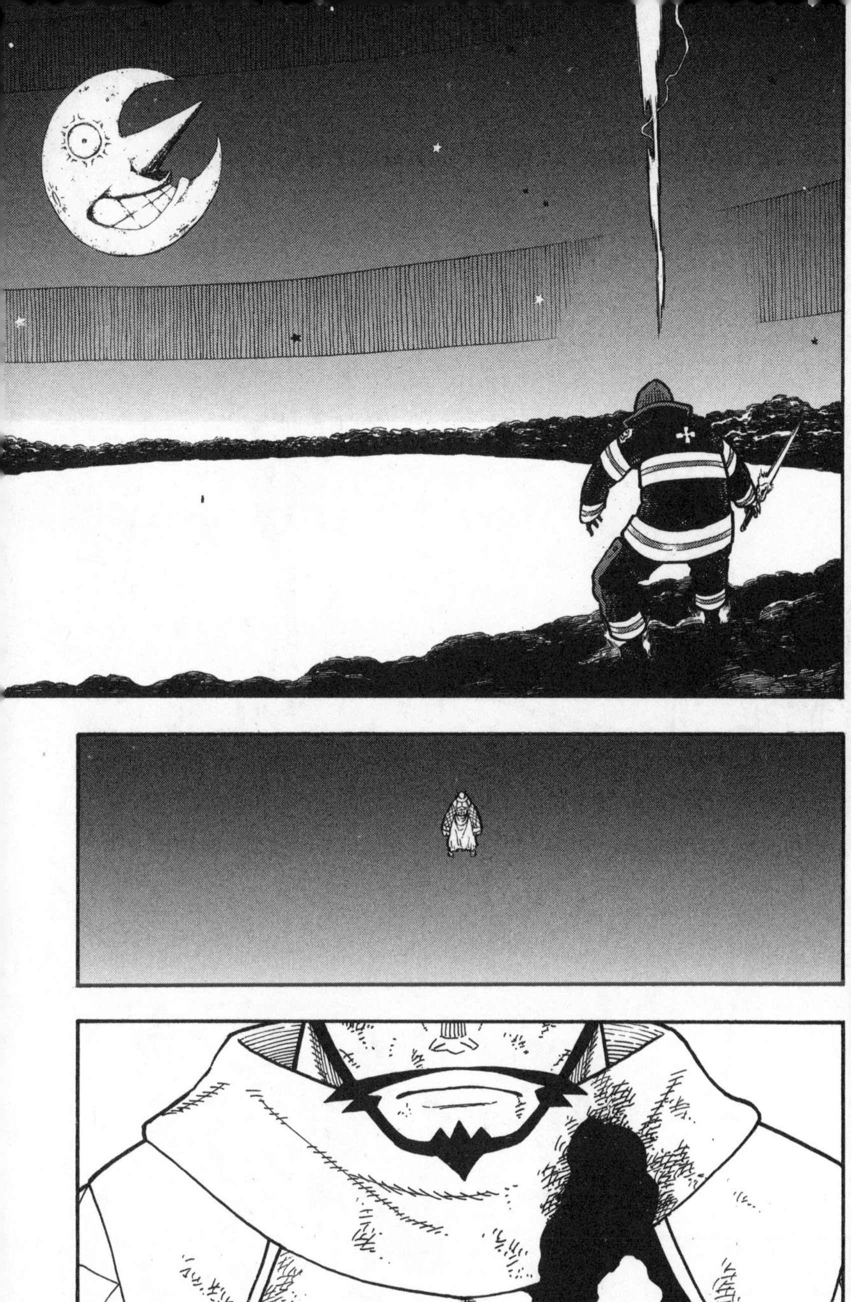

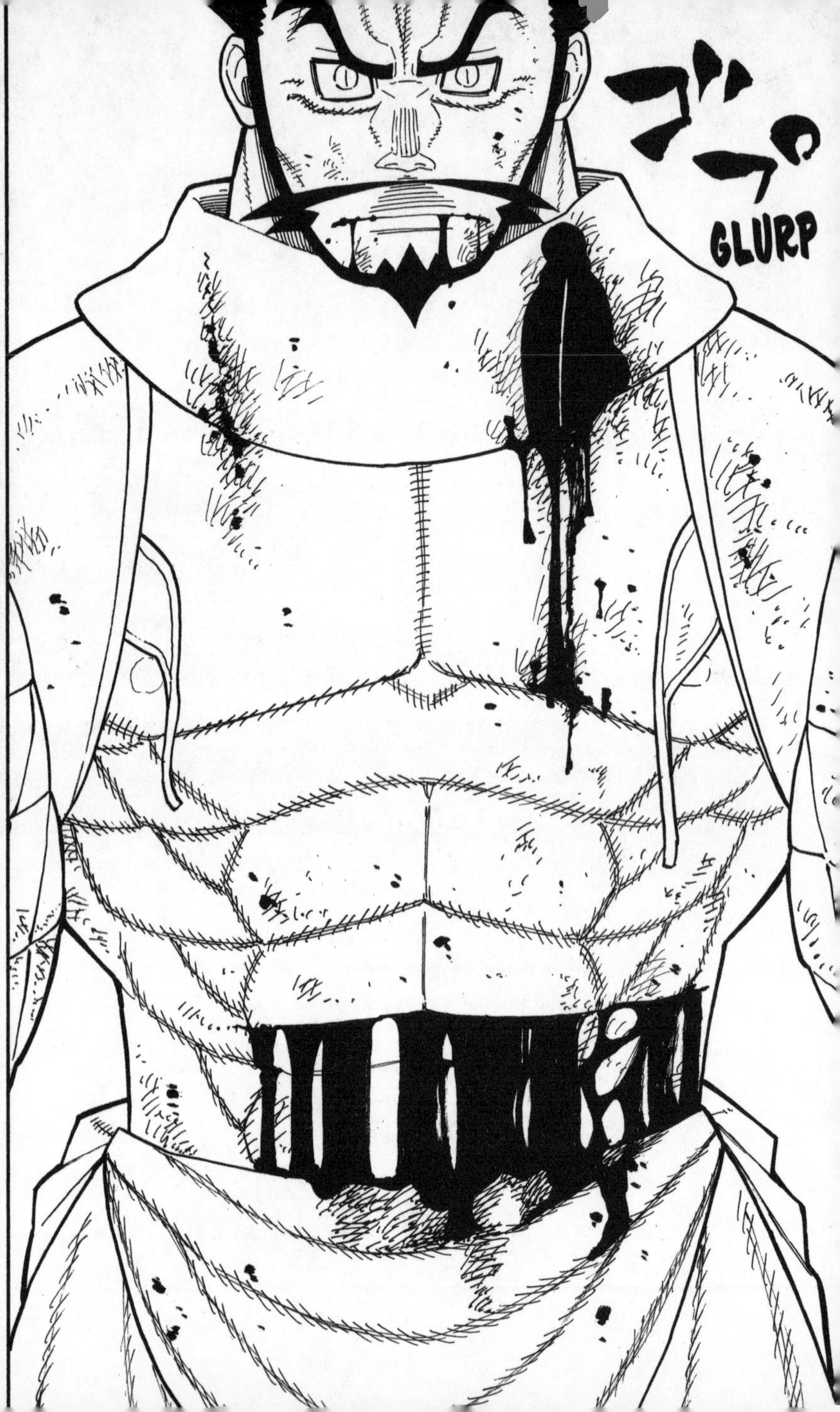
ゴクッ
GLURP

GREAT ☆ BEAST

DRAGON VS. ARTHUR

VIOLET ☆ FLASH

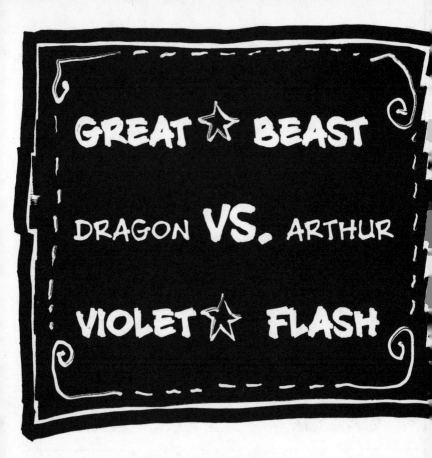

CHAPTER CCLXVI: UNRESTRAINABLE BATTLE

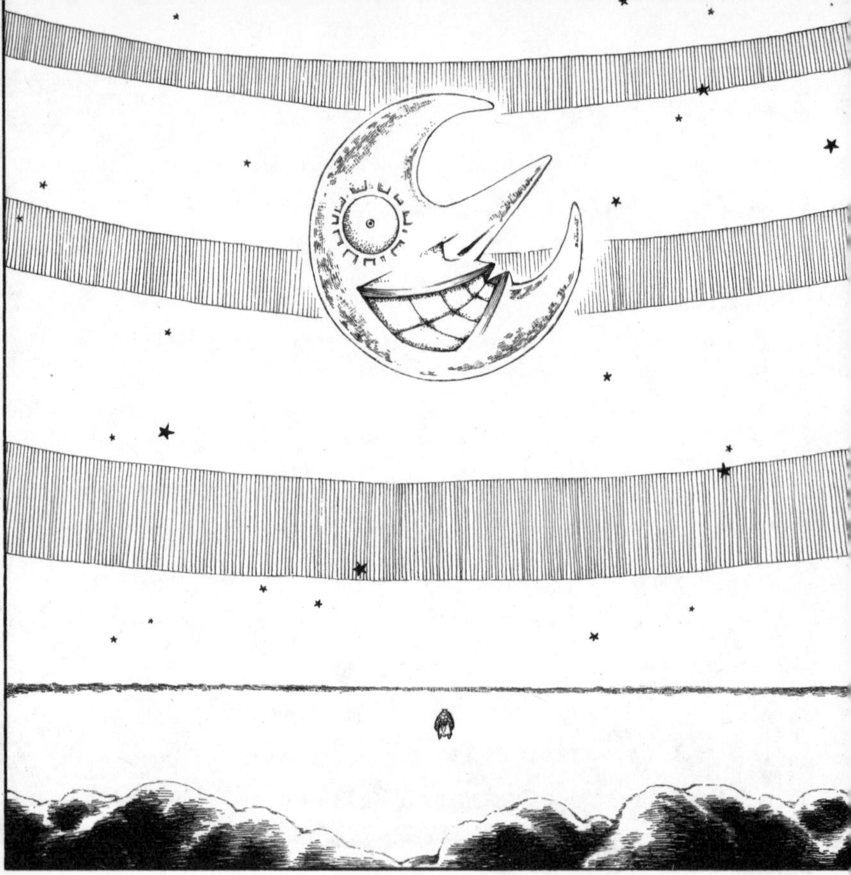

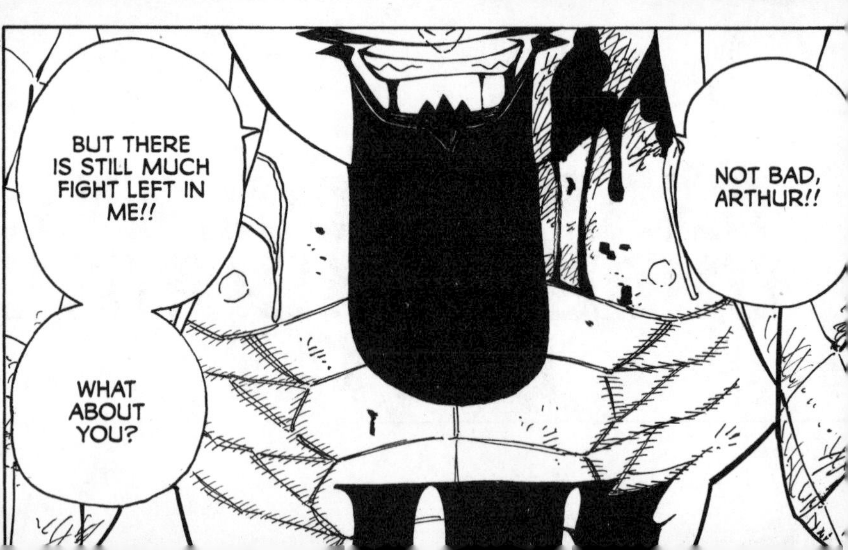
NOT BAD, ARTHUR!!
BUT THERE IS STILL MUCH FIGHT LEFT IN ME!!
WHAT ABOUT YOU?

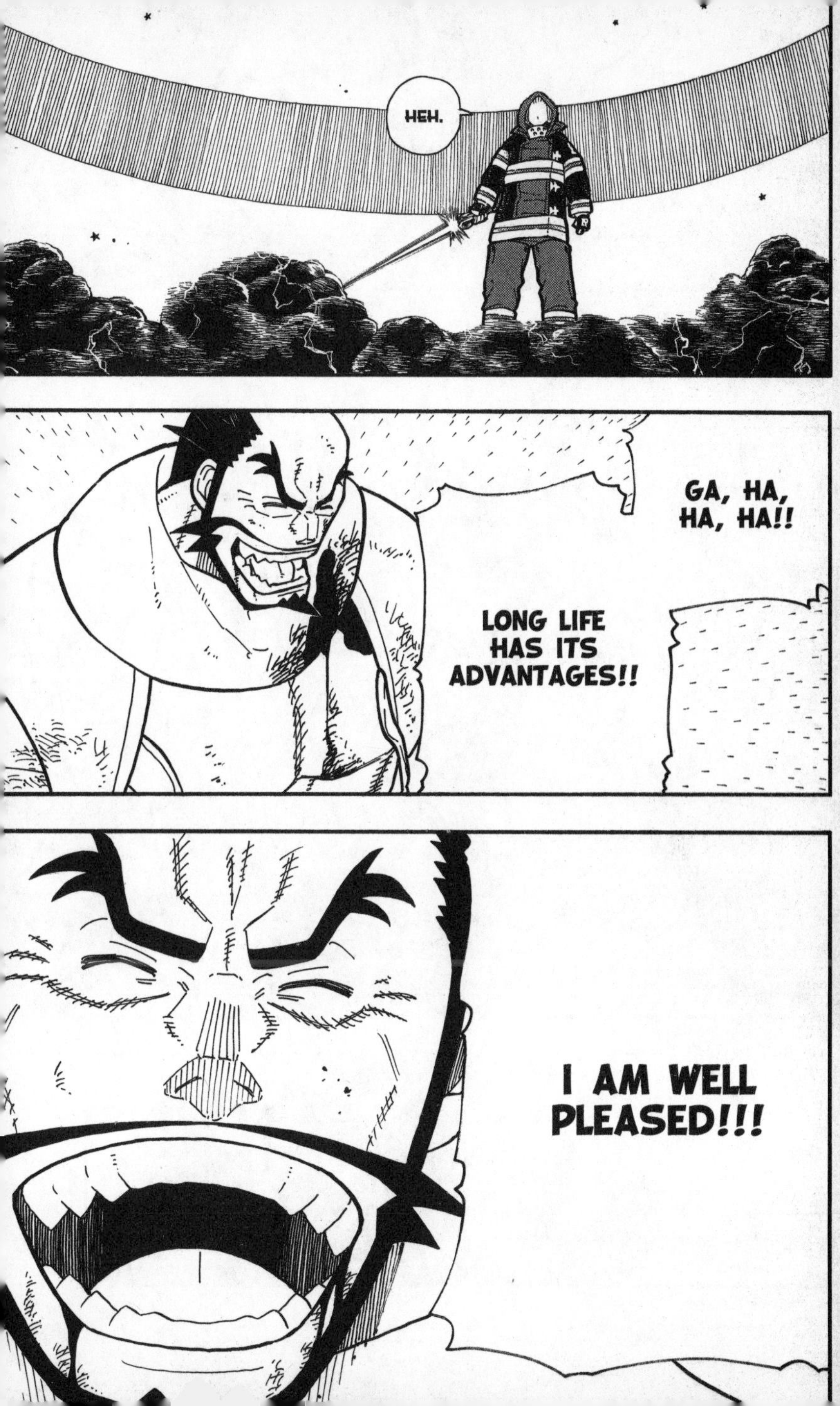
HEH.
GA, HA, HA, HA!!
LONG LIFE HAS ITS ADVANTAGES!!
I AM WELL PLEASED!!!

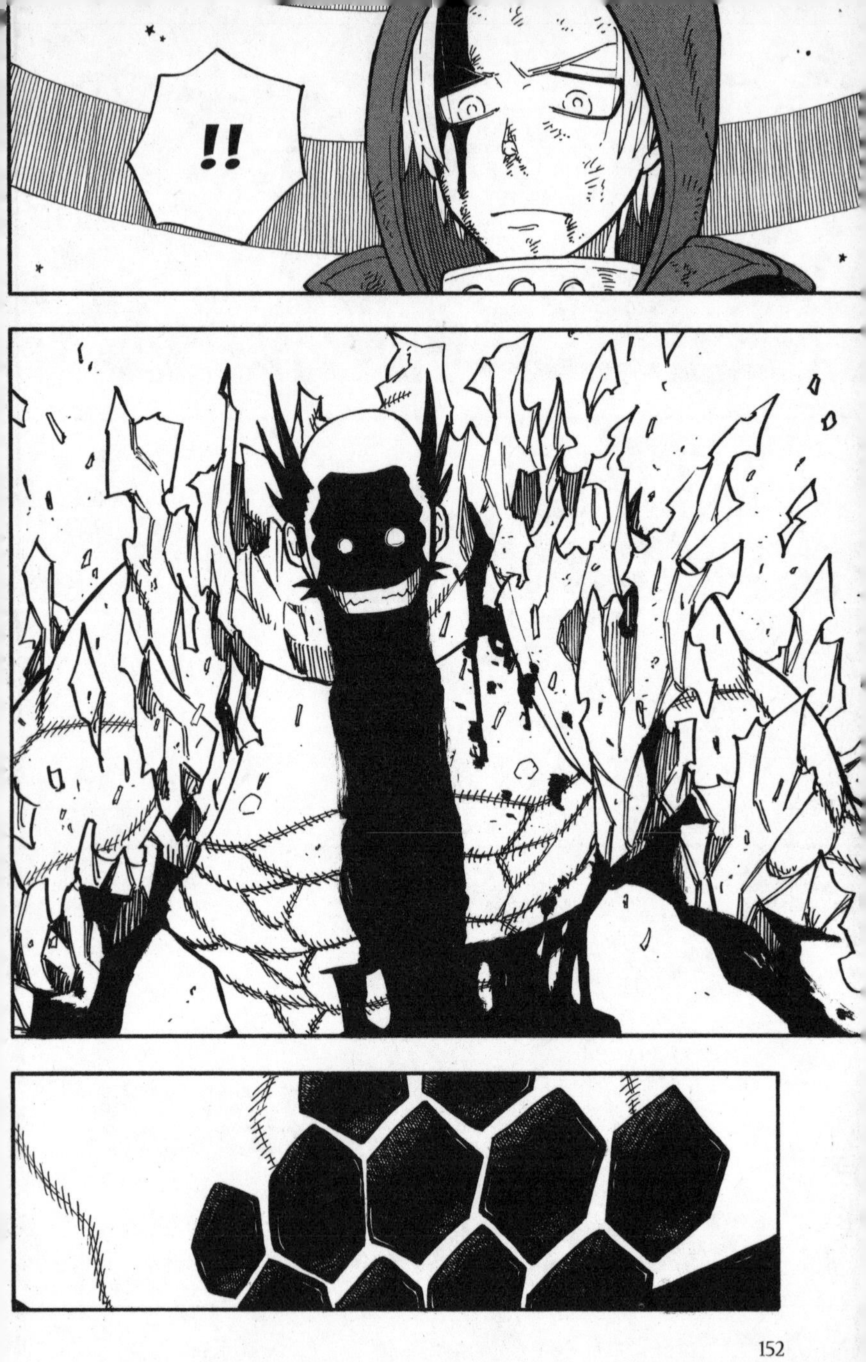
!!

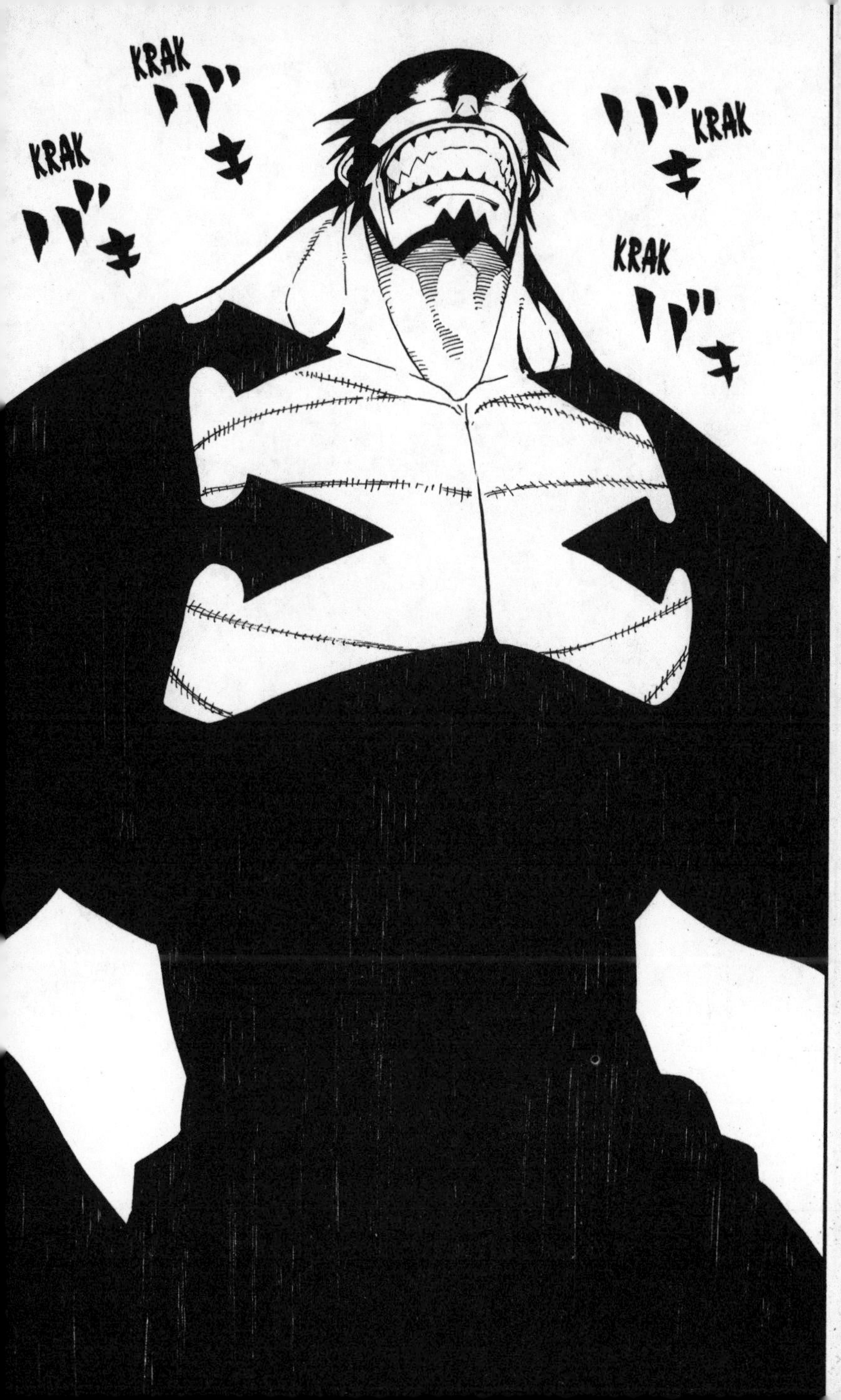

KRAK
バキ
KRAK
バキ
KRAK
バキ
KRAK
バキ

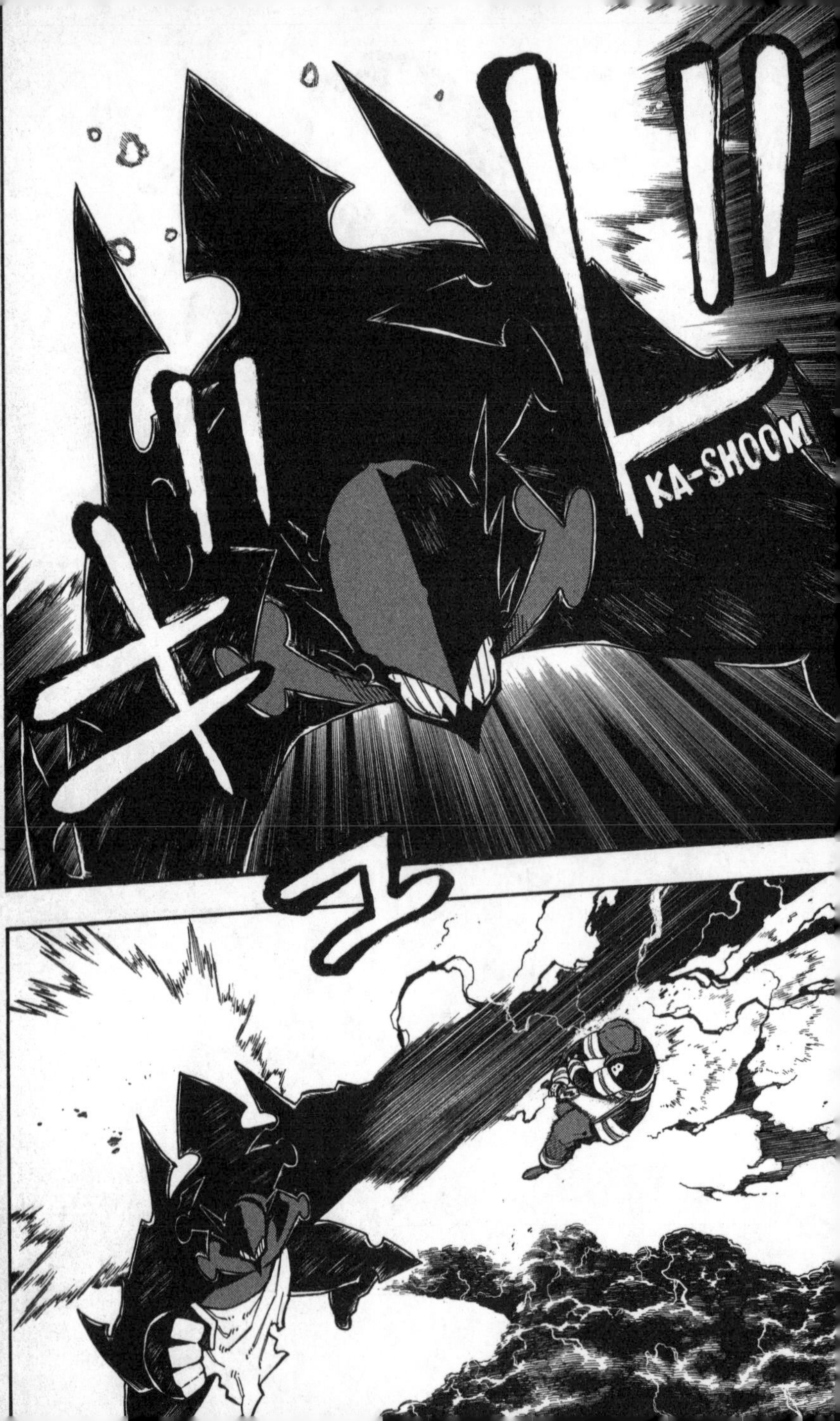
KA-SHOOM

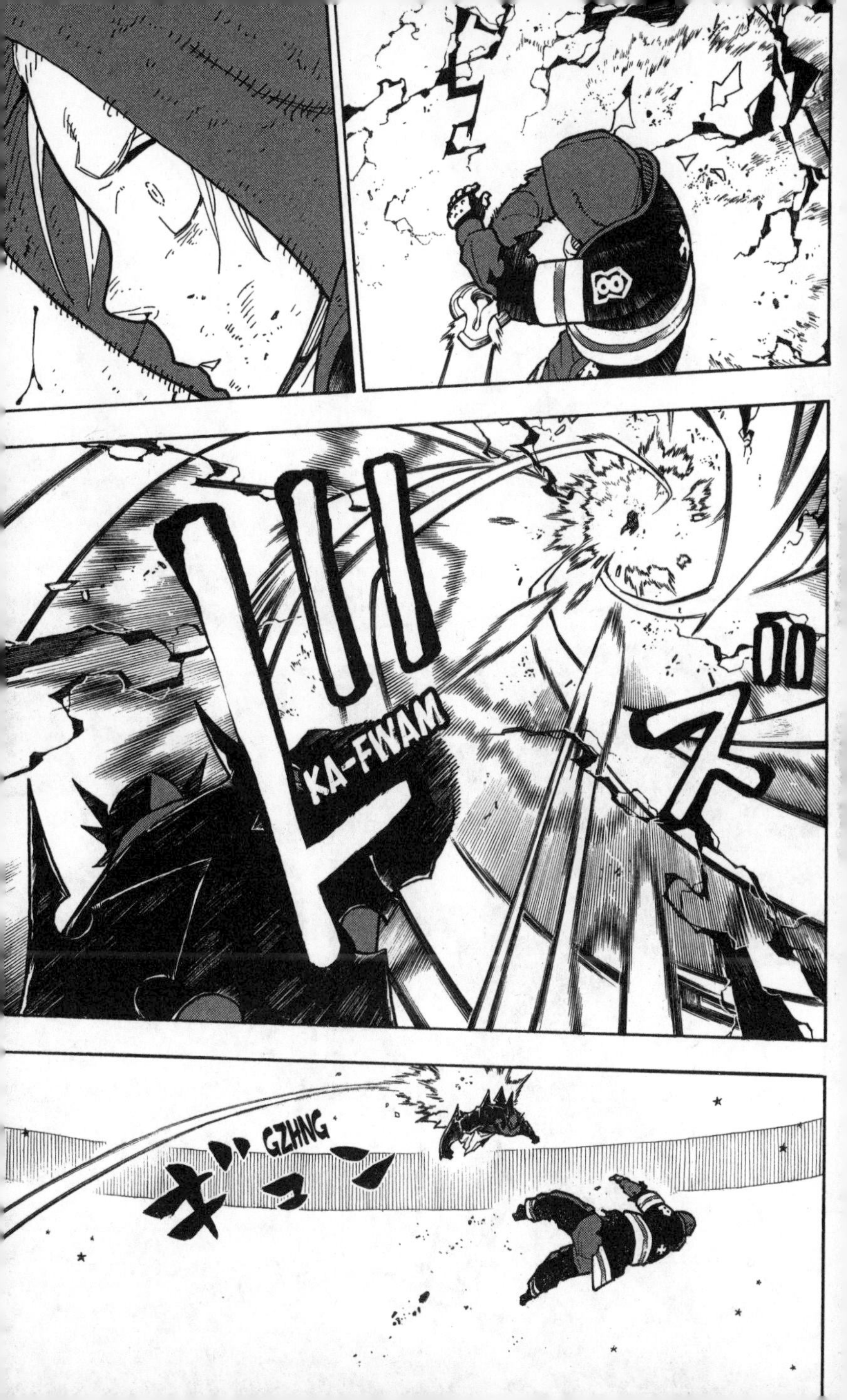
KA-FWAM
GZHNG

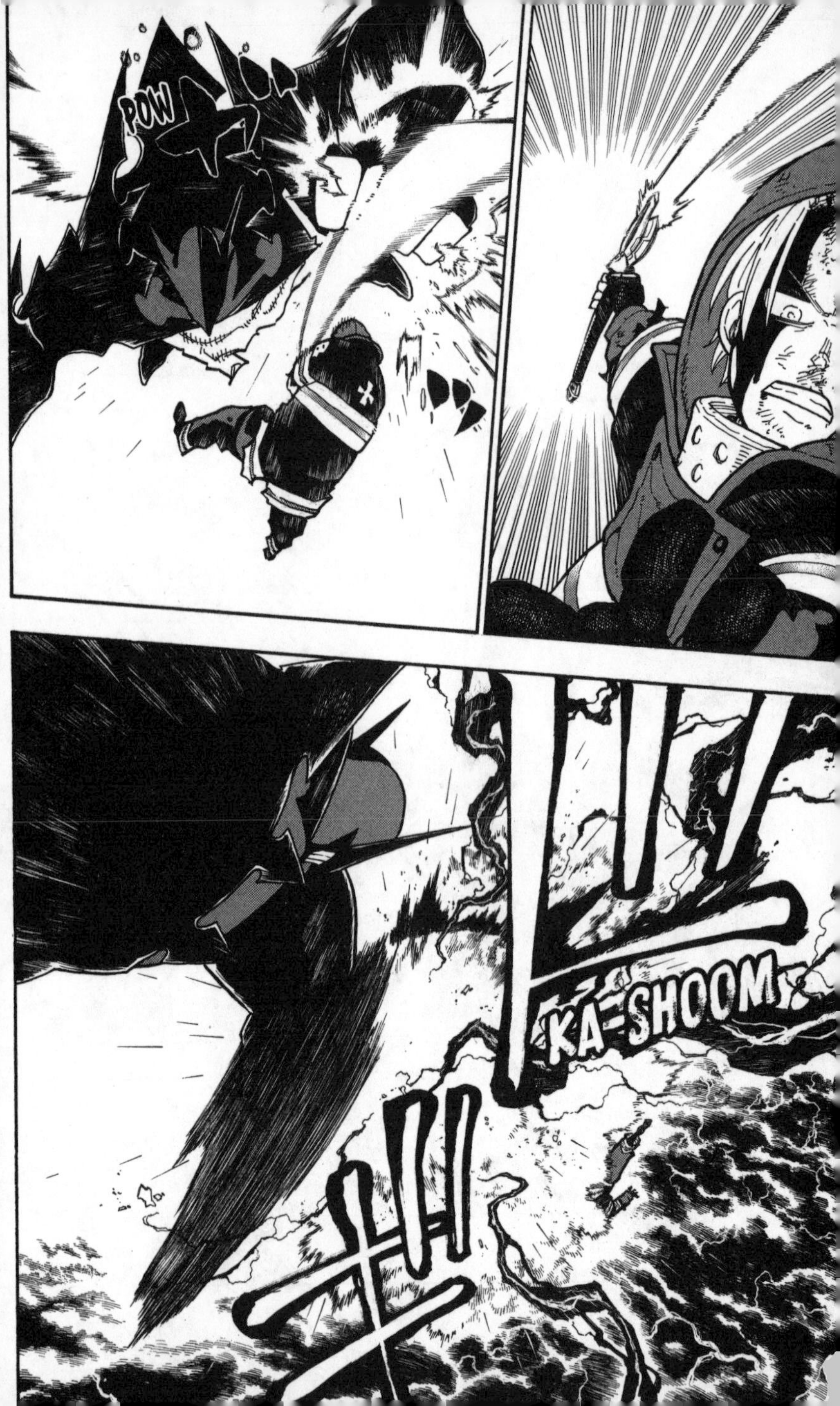
POW
KA-SHOOM

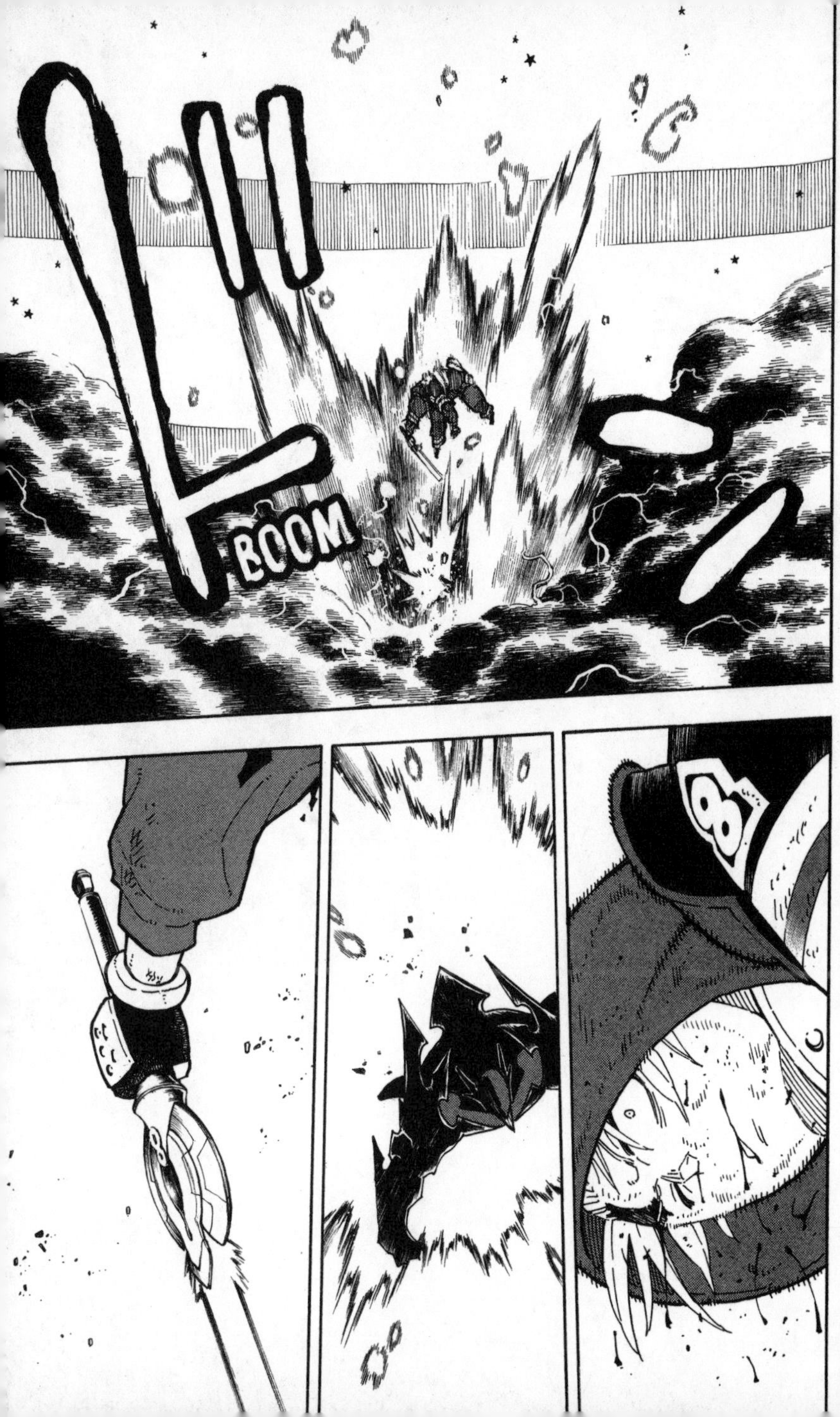
BOOM

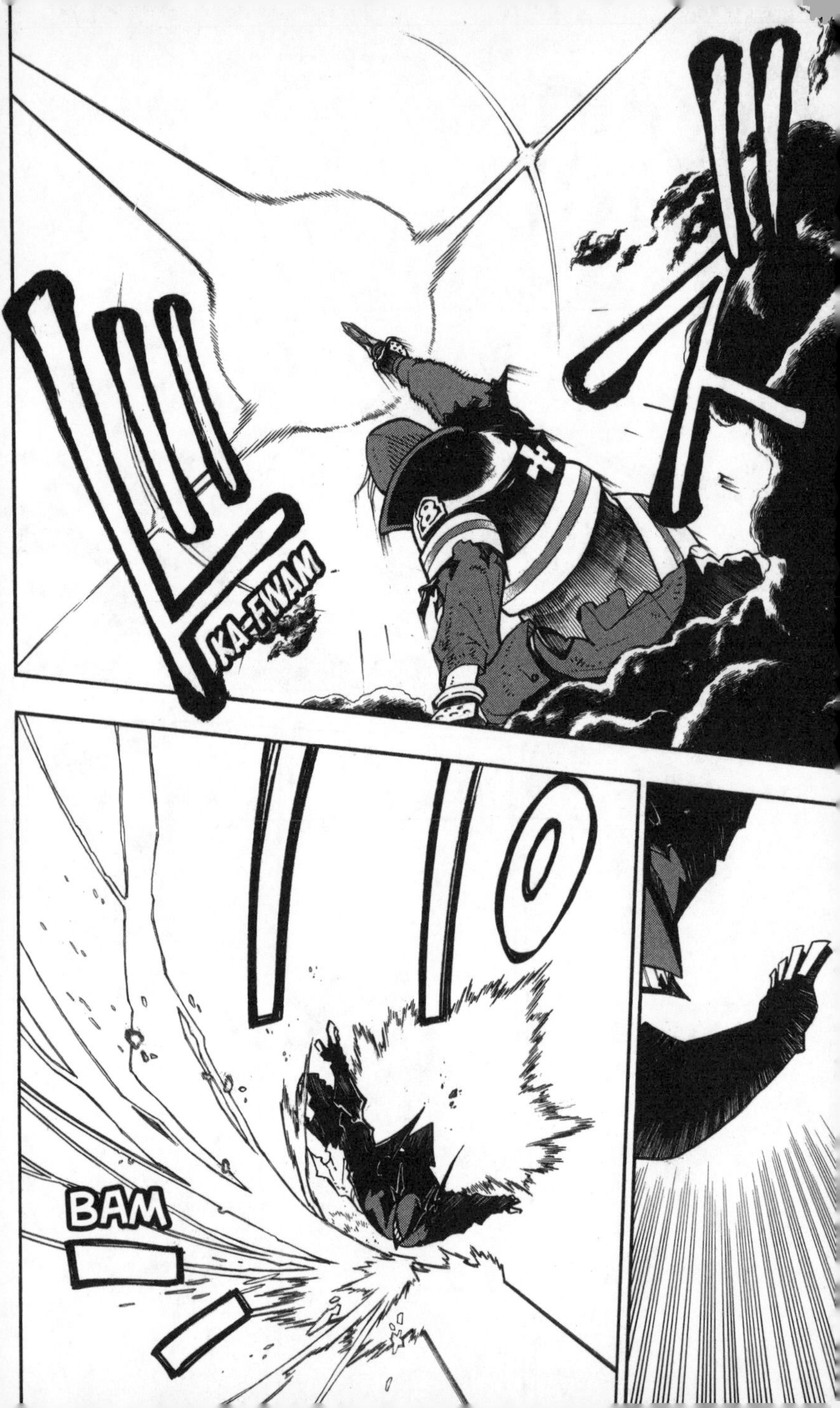
KA-FWAM
BAM

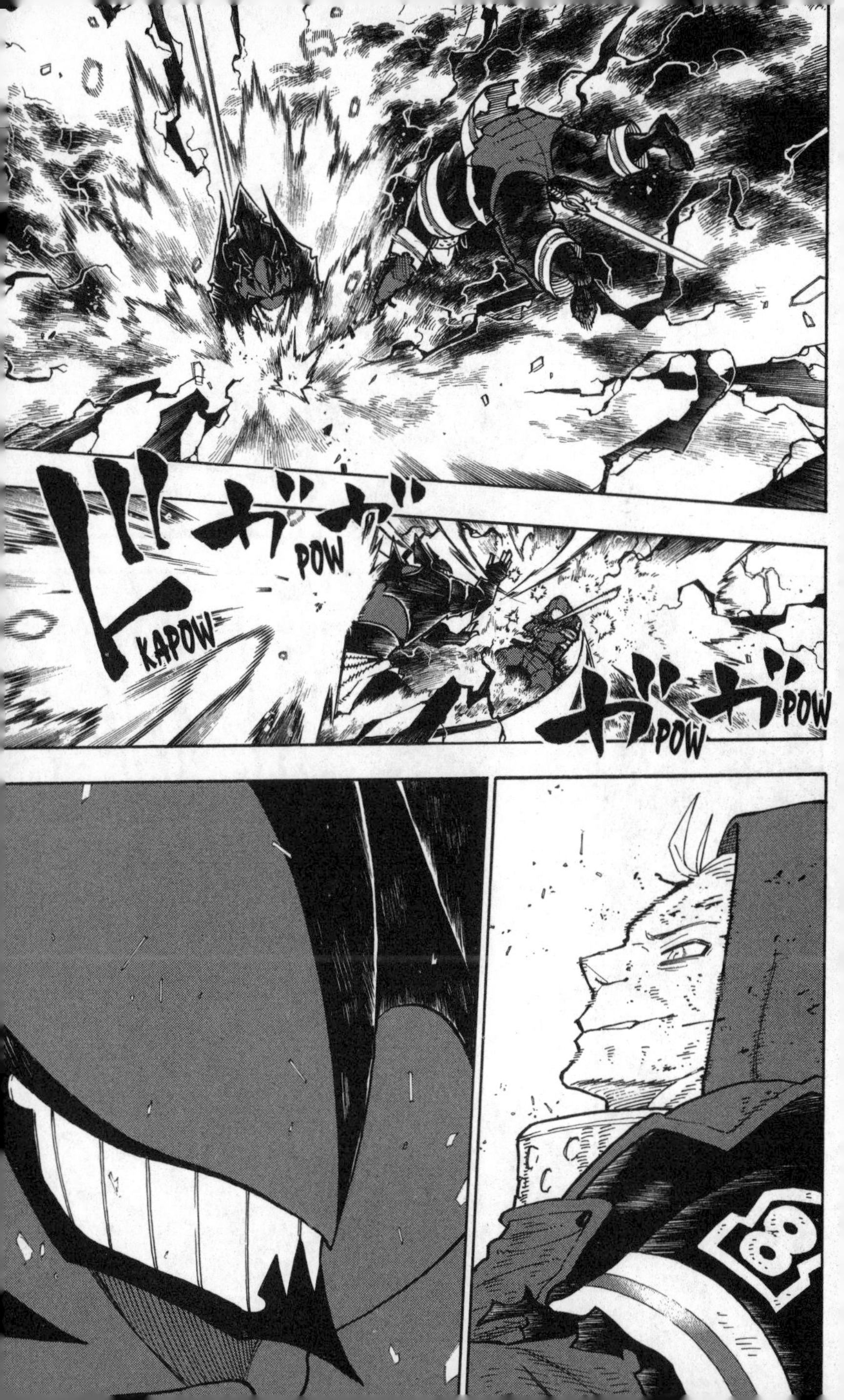
ドガガ
KAPOW
POW
ガガ
POW
POW

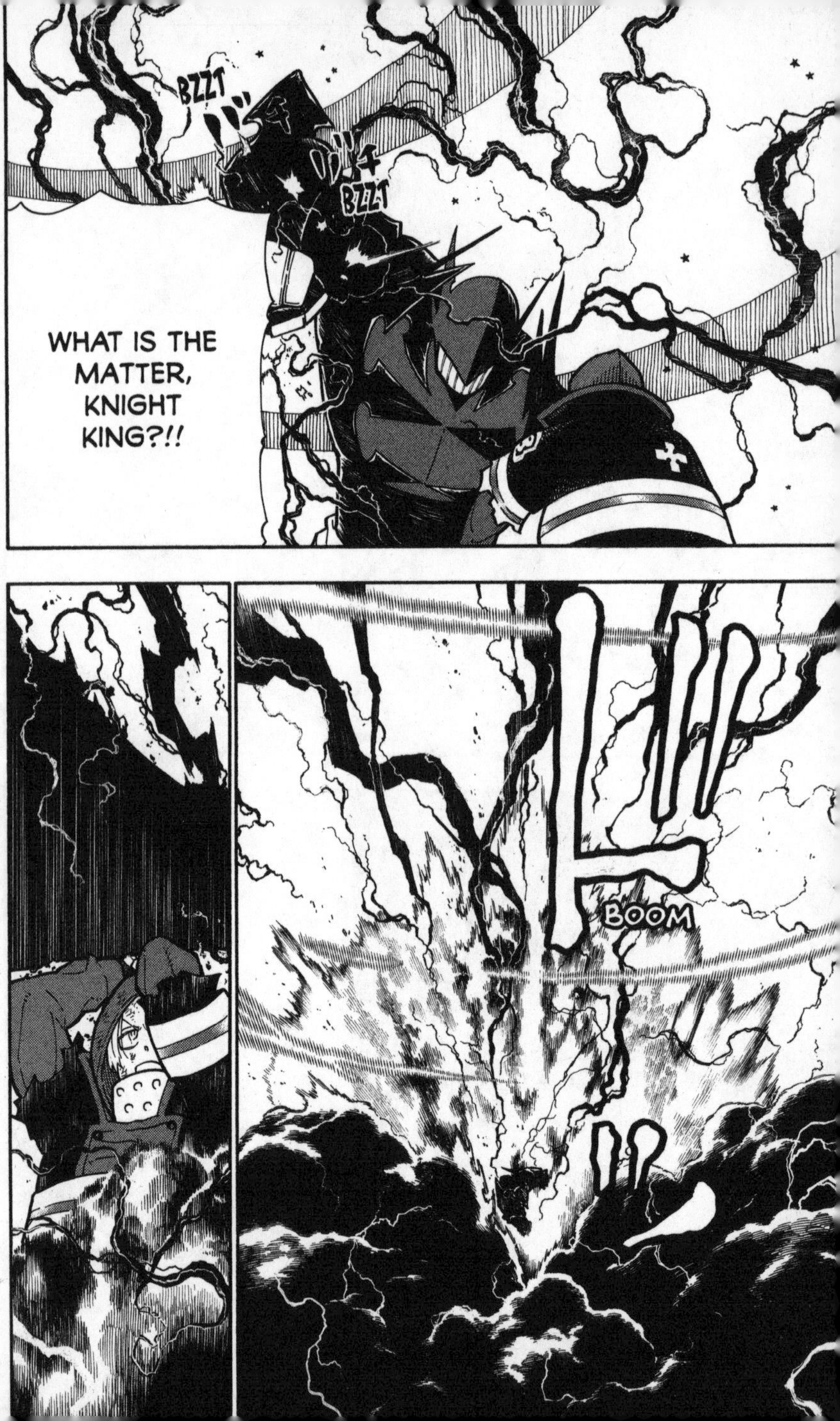
BZZT
BZZT
WHAT IS THE MATTER, KNIGHT KING?!!
BOOM

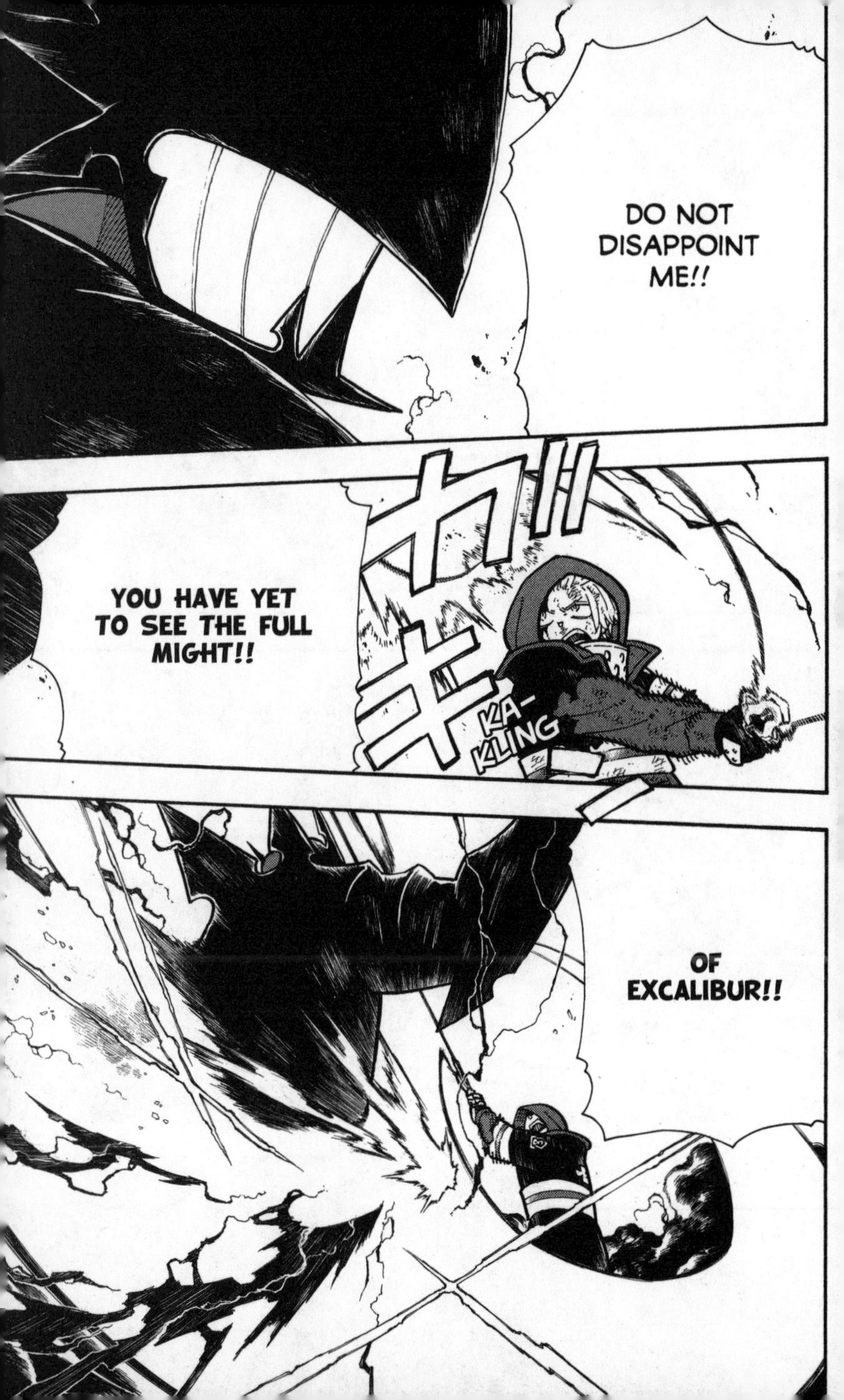
DO NOT DISAPPOINT ME!!
KA-KLING
YOU HAVE YET TO SEE THE FULL MIGHT!!
OF EXCALIBUR!!

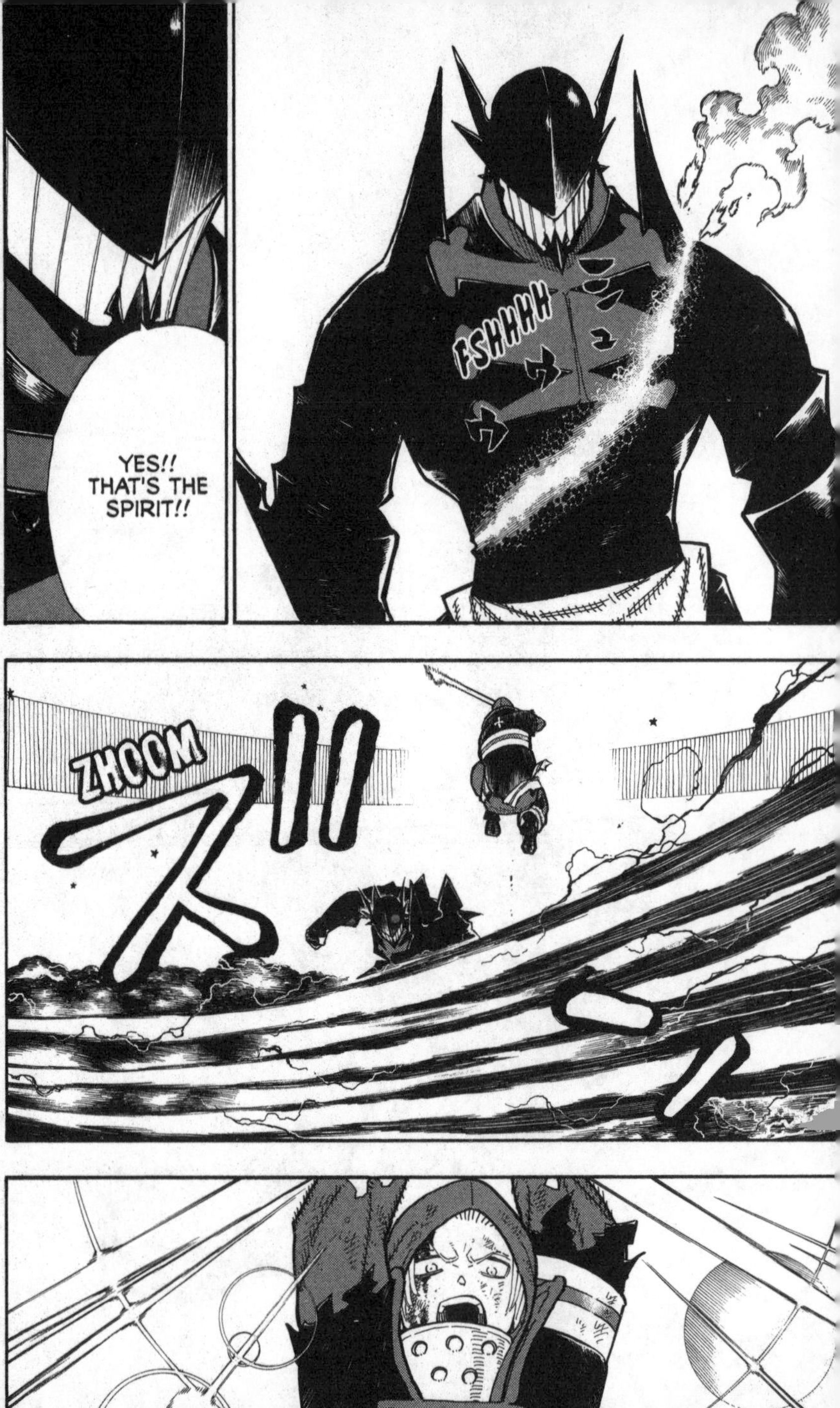
FSHHHH
YES!! THAT'S THE SPIRIT!!
ZHOOM

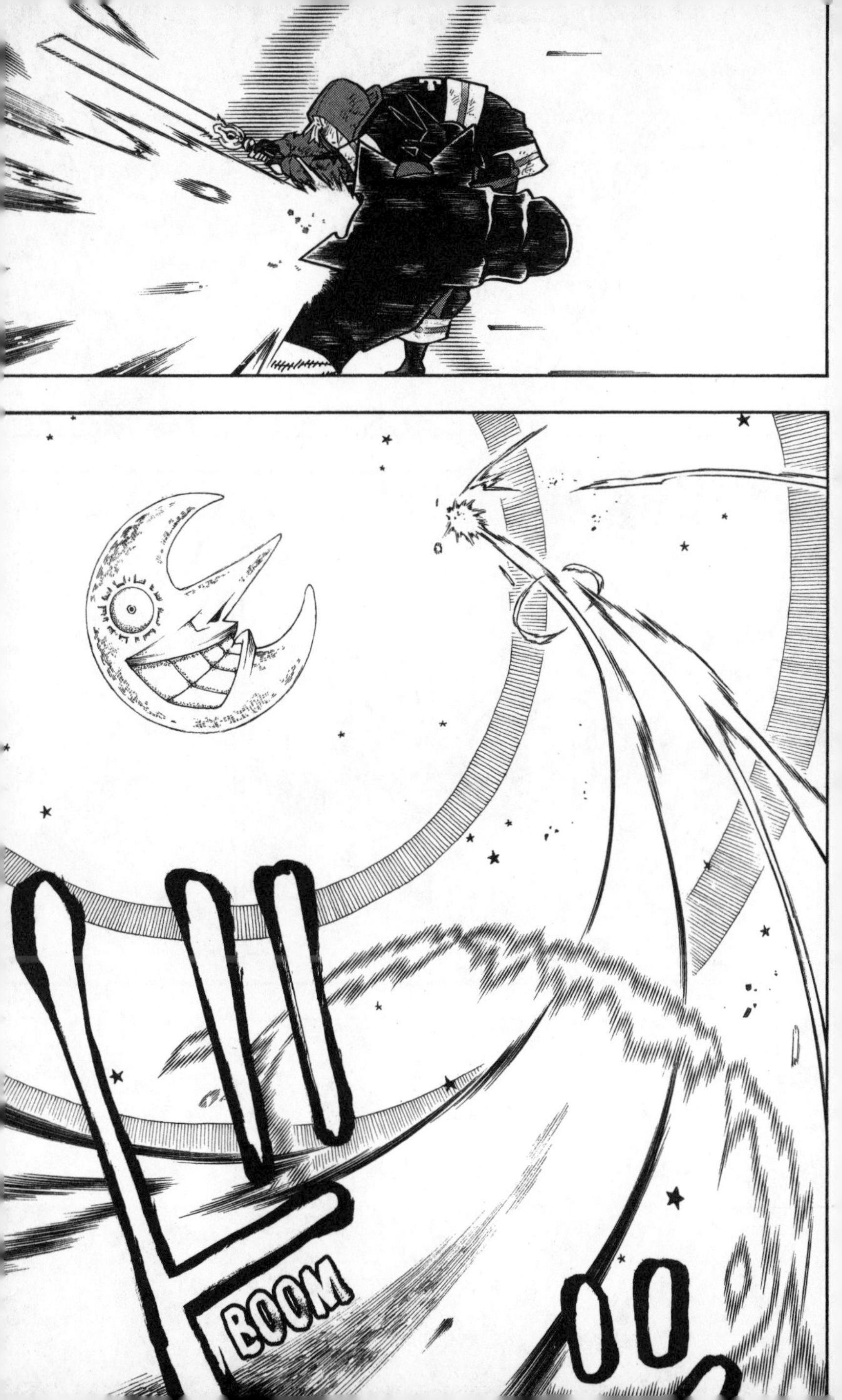
BOOM

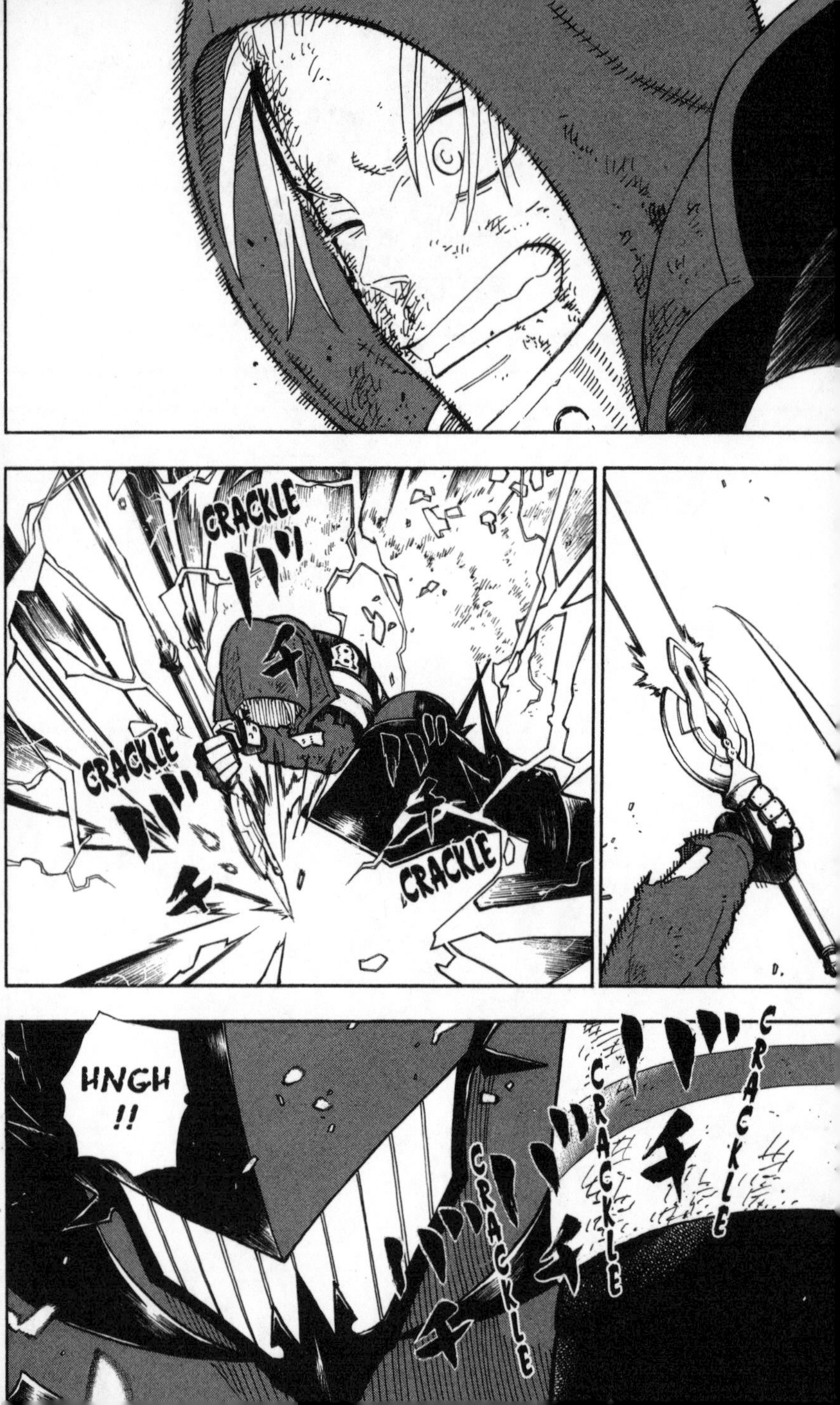
CRACKLE
CRACKLE
CRACKLE
CRACKLE
CRACKLE
HNGH !!
CRACKLE

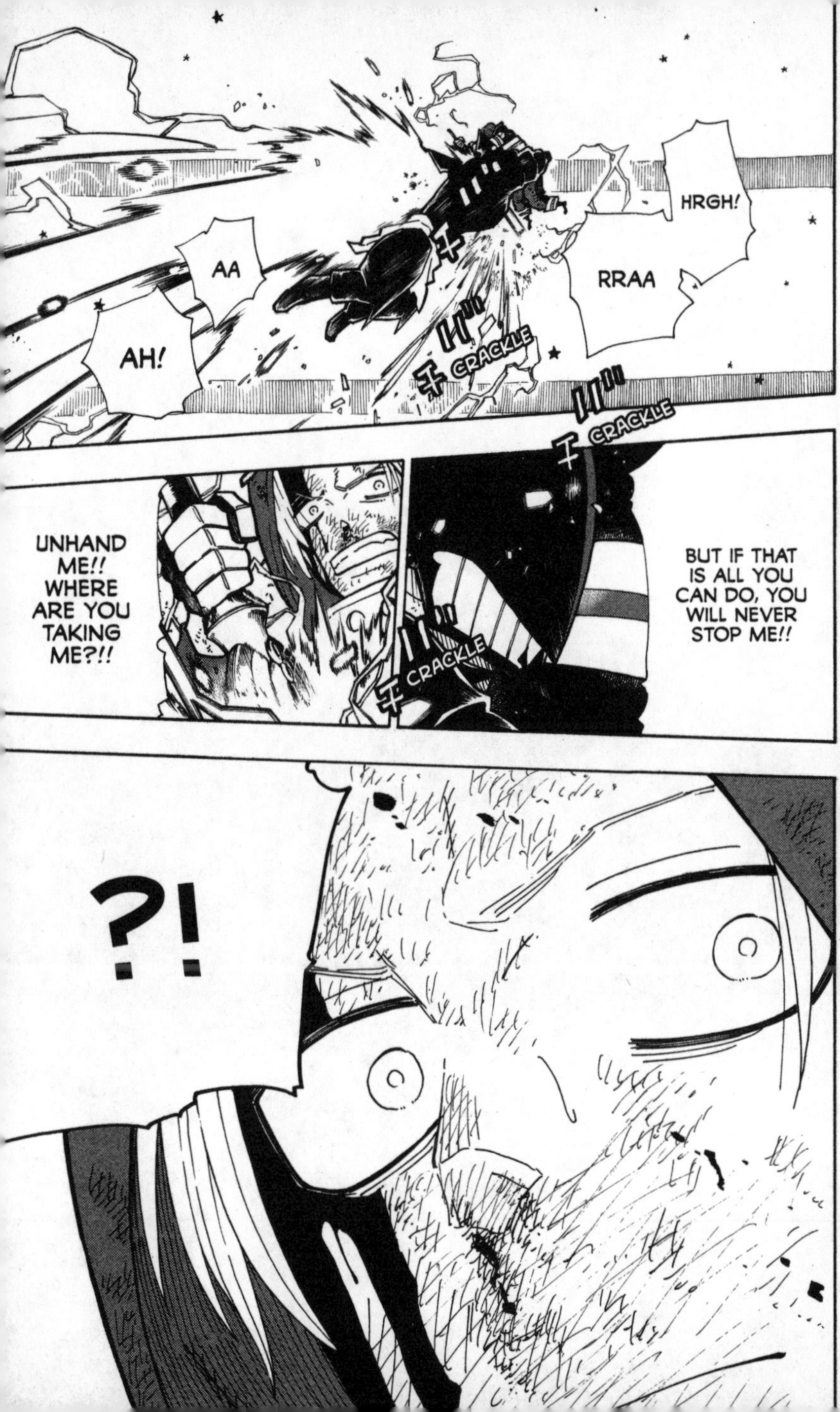
HRGH!
RRAA
AA
CRACKLE
AH!
CRACKLE
BUT IF THAT IS ALL YOU CAN DO, YOU WILL NEVER STOP ME!!
CRACKLE
UNHAND ME!! WHERE ARE YOU TAKING ME?!!
?!

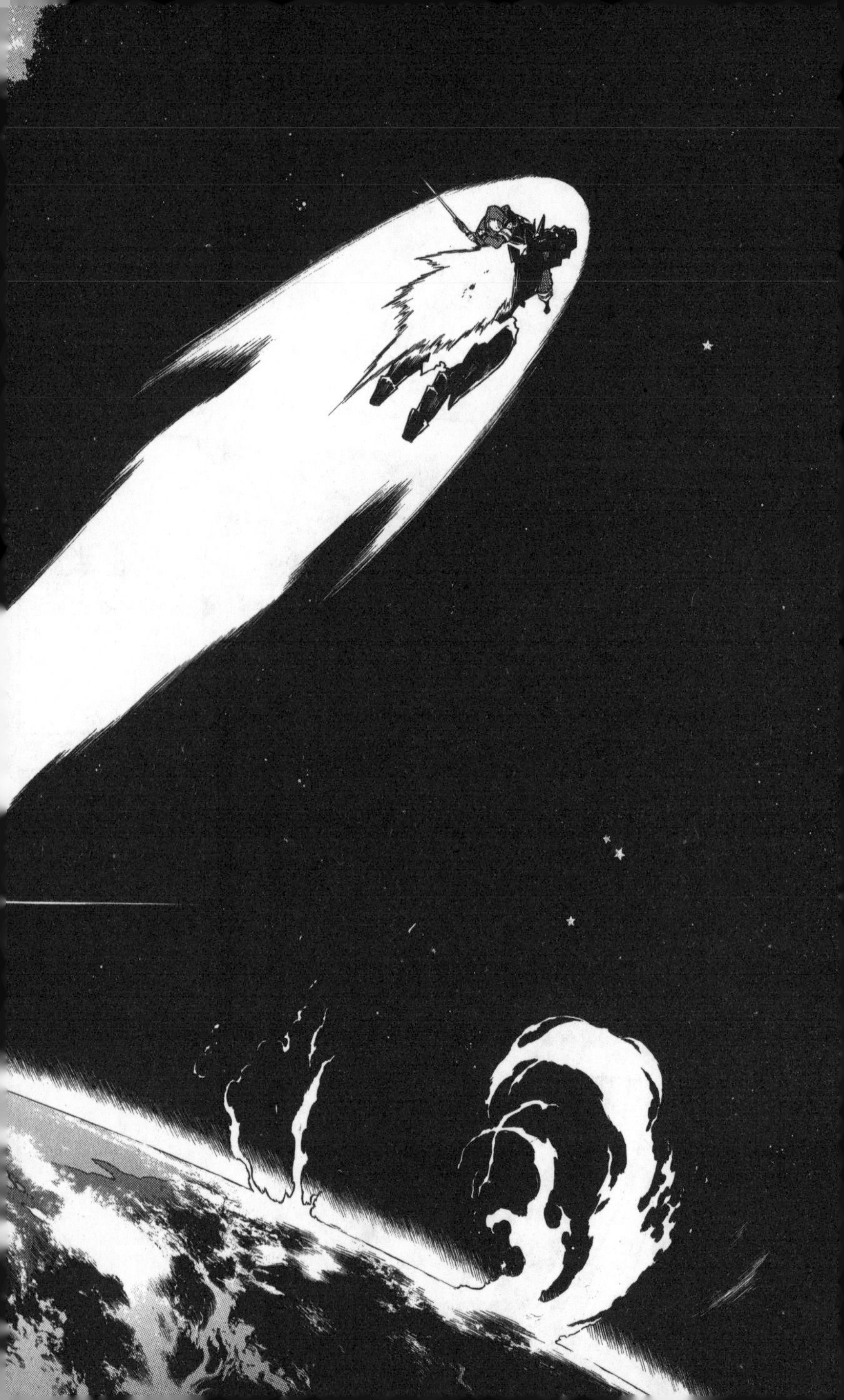

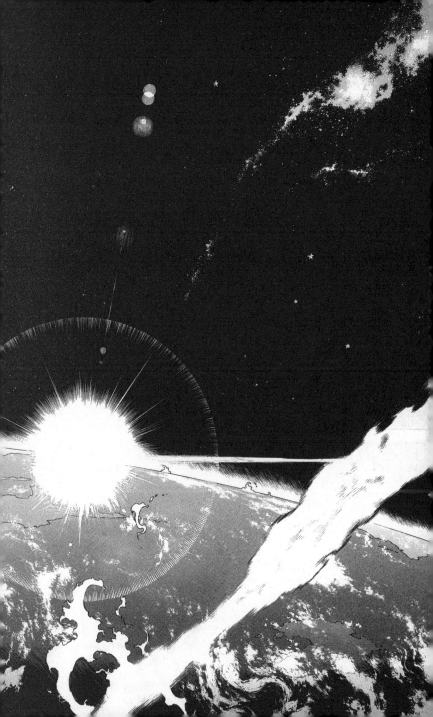

FIRE FORCE

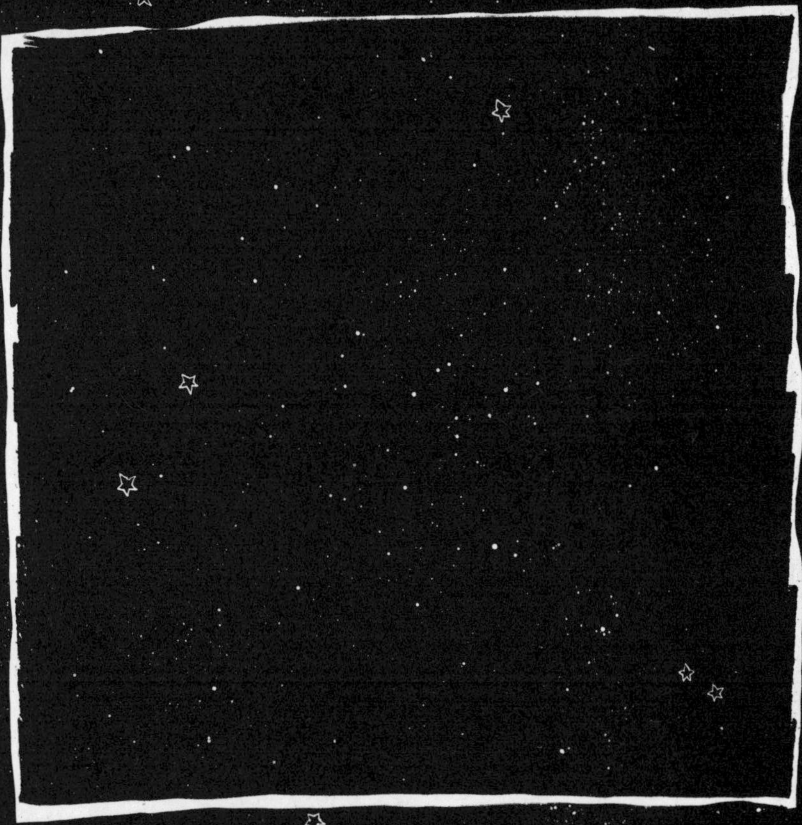

CHAPTER CCLXVII: THE KNIGHT OF THE COSMOS

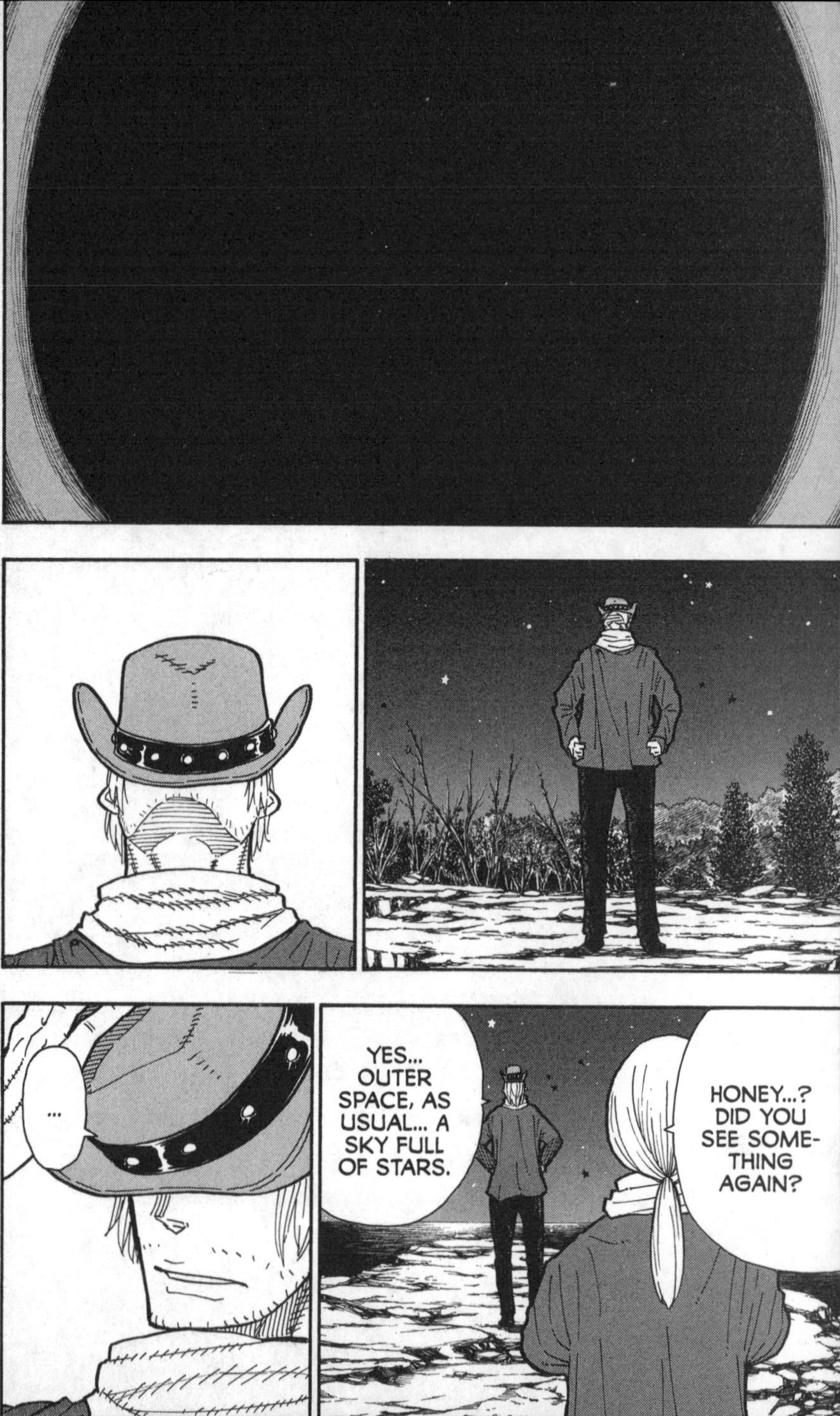
HONEY...? DID YOU SEE SOME-THING AGAIN?
YES... OUTER SPACE, AS USUAL... A SKY FULL OF STARS.
...

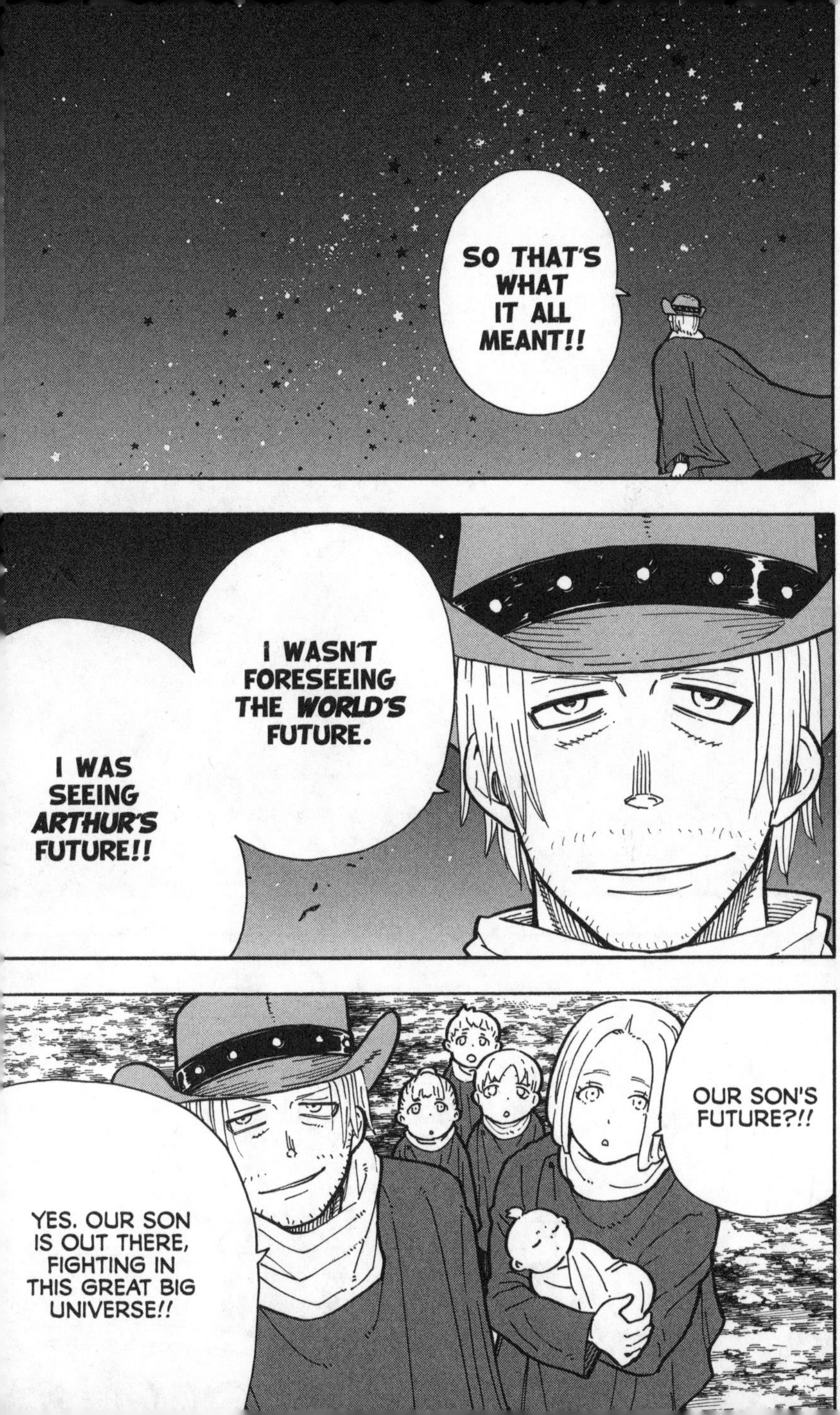
SO THAT'S WHAT IT ALL MEANT!!
I WASN'T FORESEEING THE *WORLD'S* FUTURE.
I WAS SEEING *ARTHUR'S* FUTURE!!
OUR SON'S FUTURE?!!
YES. OUR SON IS OUT THERE, FIGHTING IN THIS GREAT BIG UNIVERSE!!

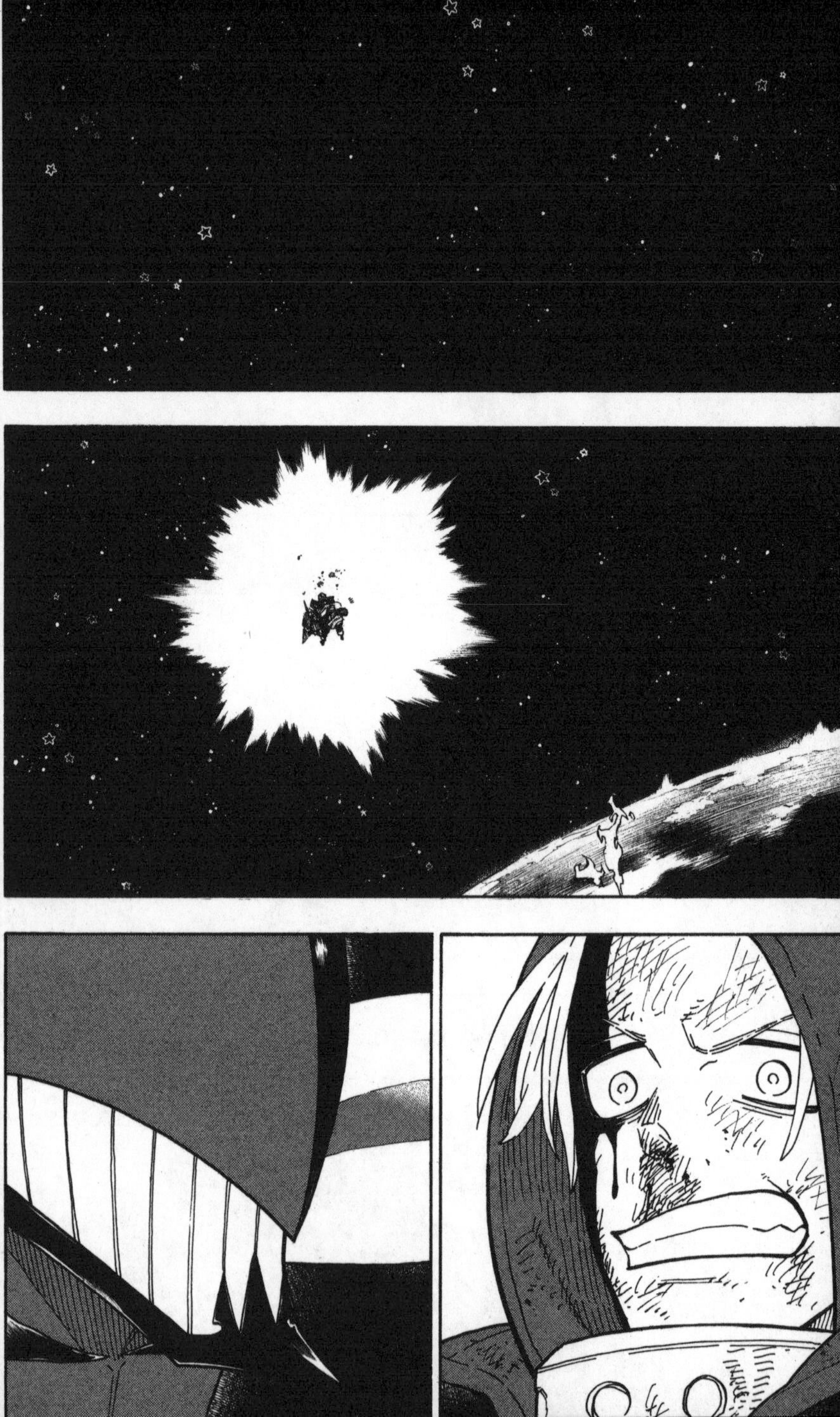

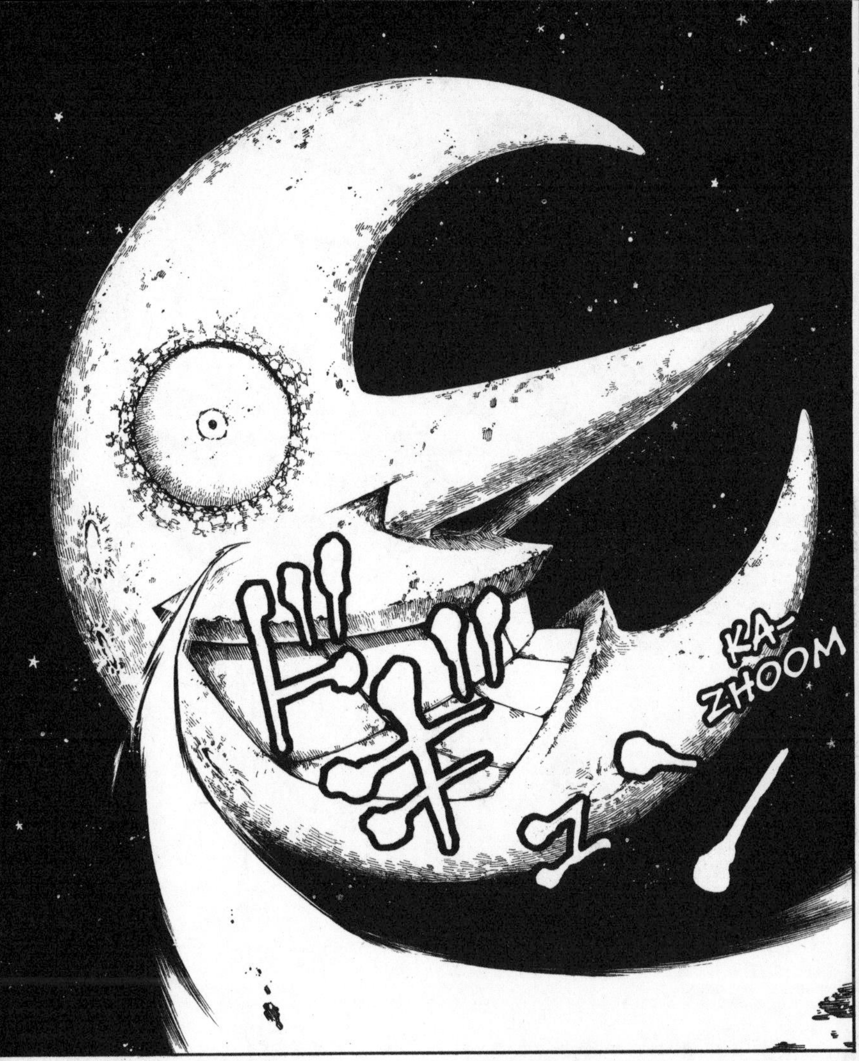
KA-
ZHOOM
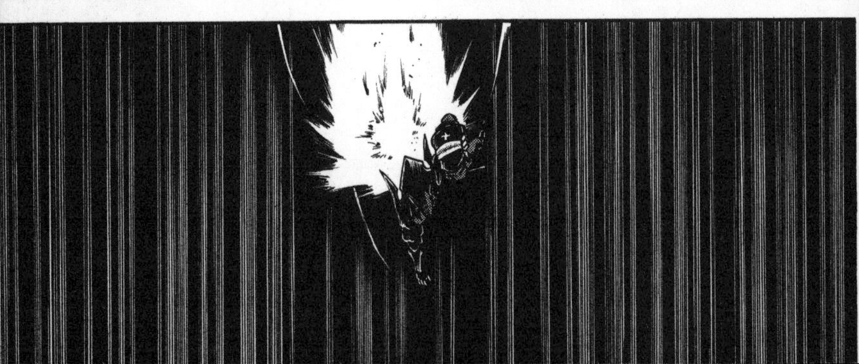

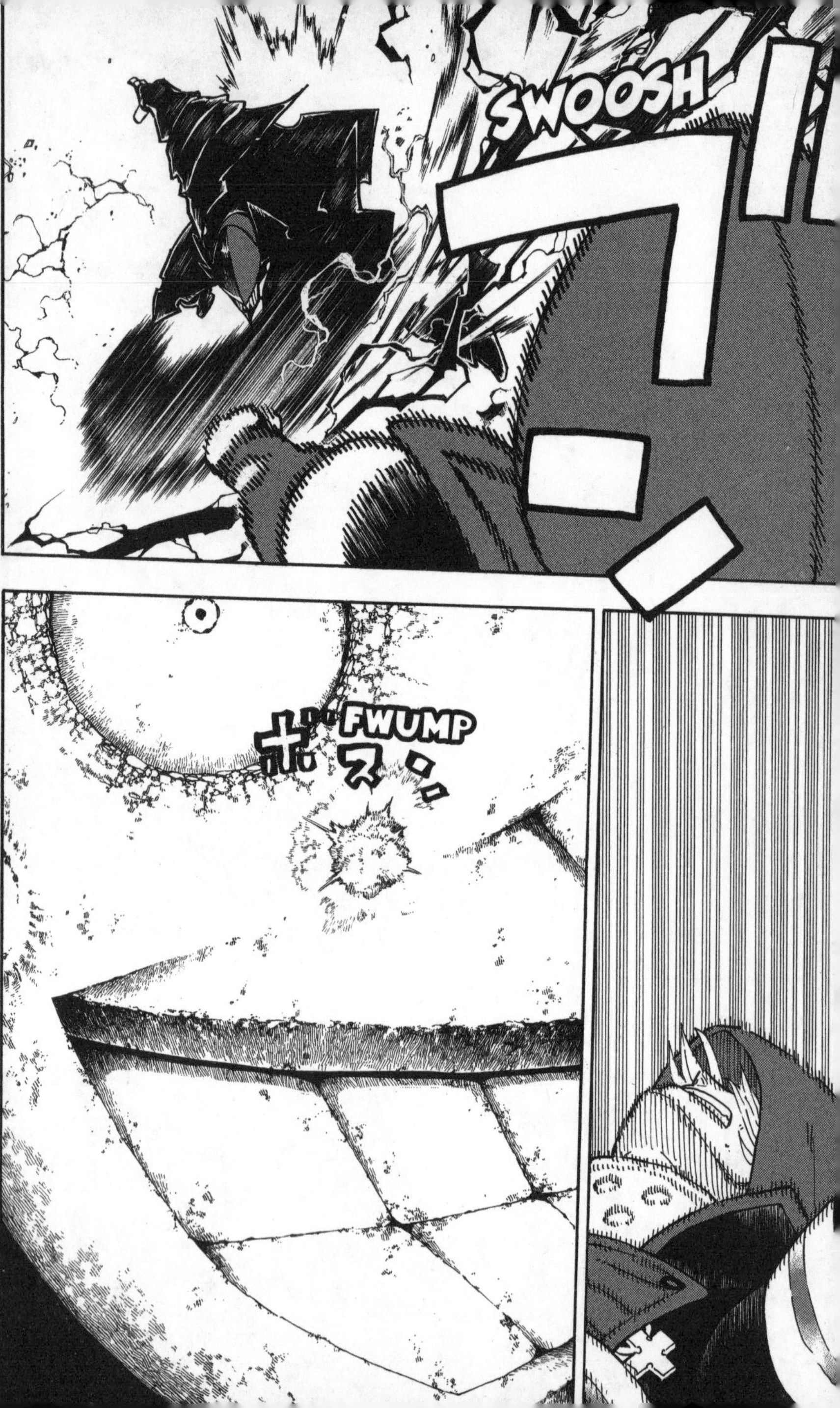
SWOOSH
FWUMP

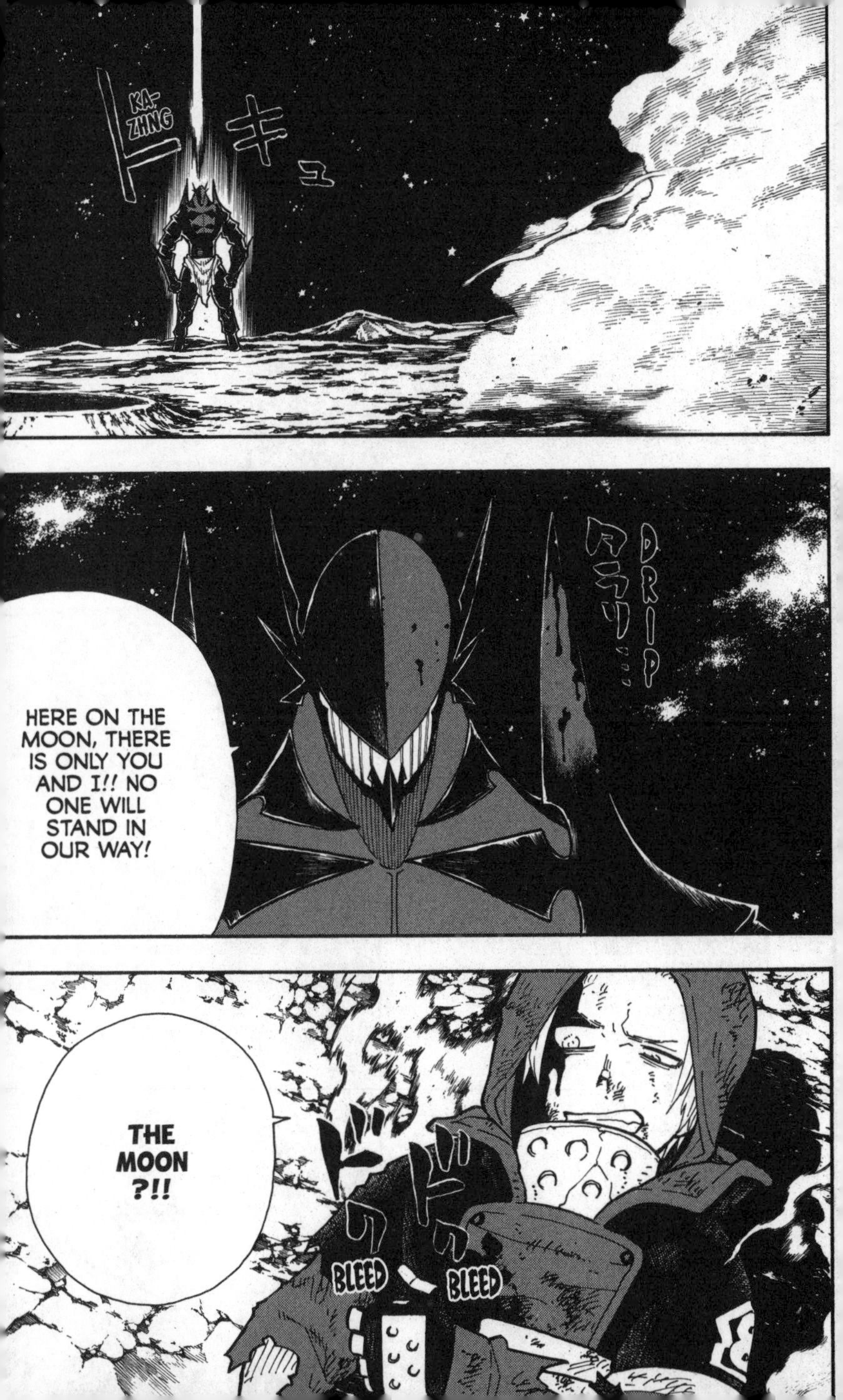
KA-ZHING
キュ
ドロ...
DRIP
HERE ON THE MOON, THERE IS ONLY YOU AND I!! NO ONE WILL STAND IN OUR WAY!
THE MOON?!!
ドクッ
BLEED
ドクッ
BLEED

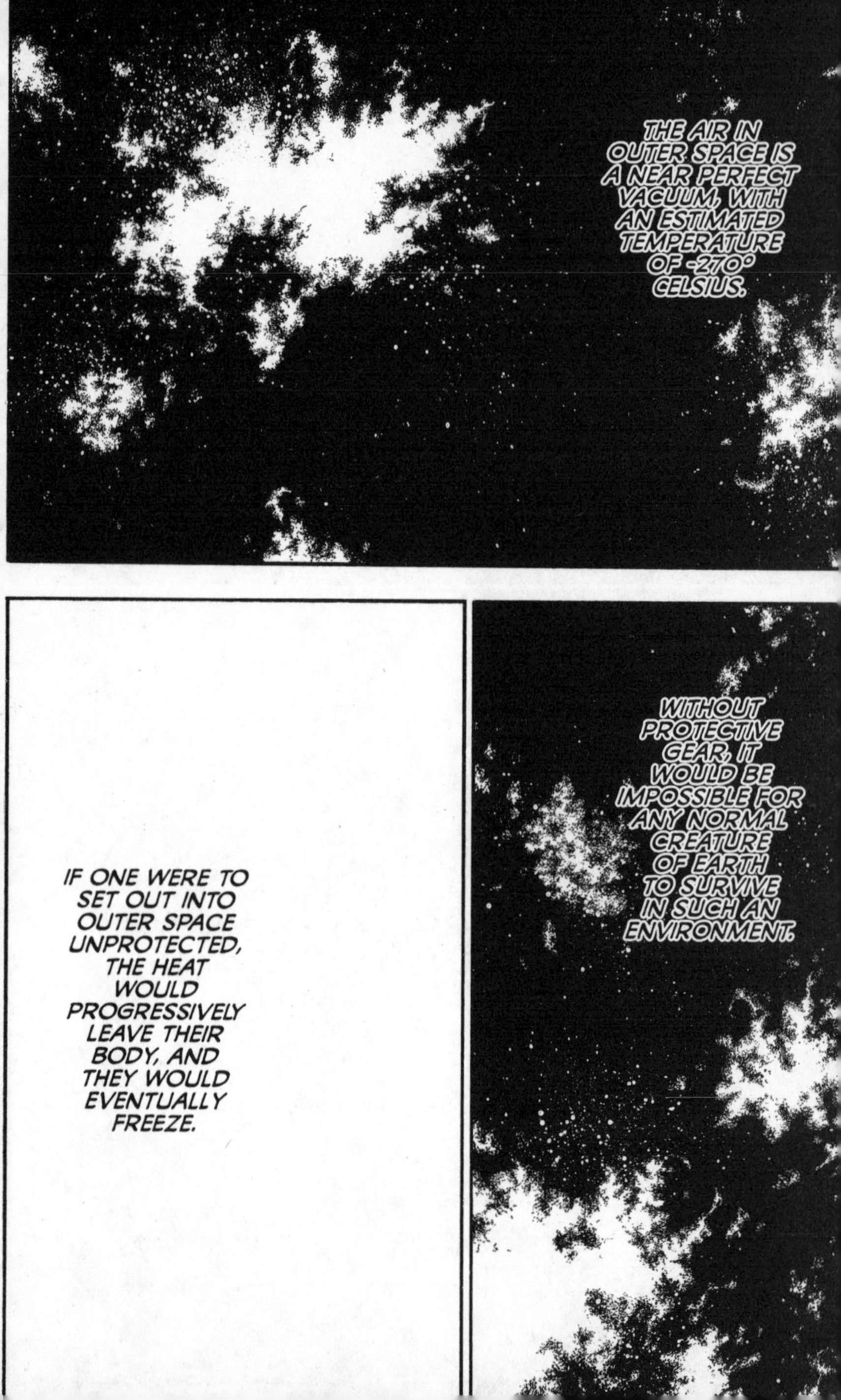
THE AIR IN OUTER SPACE IS A NEAR PERFECT VACUUM, WITH AN ESTIMATED TEMPERATURE OF -270° CELSIUS.
WITHOUT PROTECTIVE GEAR, IT WOULD BE IMPOSSIBLE FOR ANY NORMAL CREATURE OF EARTH TO SURVIVE IN SUCH AN ENVIRONMENT.
IF ONE WERE TO SET OUT INTO OUTER SPACE UNPROTECTED, THE HEAT WOULD PROGRESSIVELY LEAVE THEIR BODY, AND THEY WOULD EVENTUALLY FREEZE.

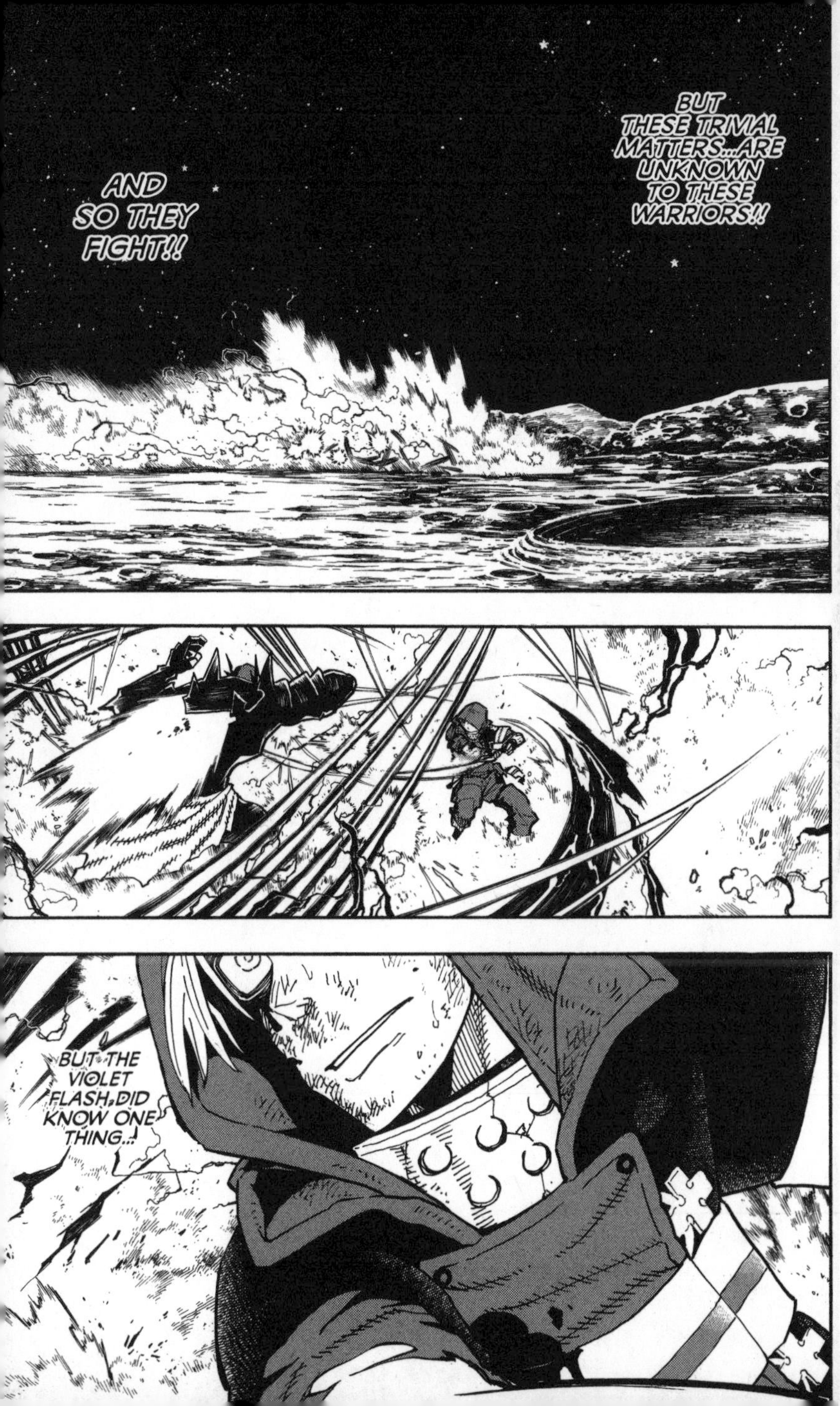
BUT THESE TRIVIAL MATTERS...ARE UNKNOWN TO THESE WARRIORS!!
AND SO THEY FIGHT!!
BUT THE VIOLET FLASH DID KNOW ONE THING...!

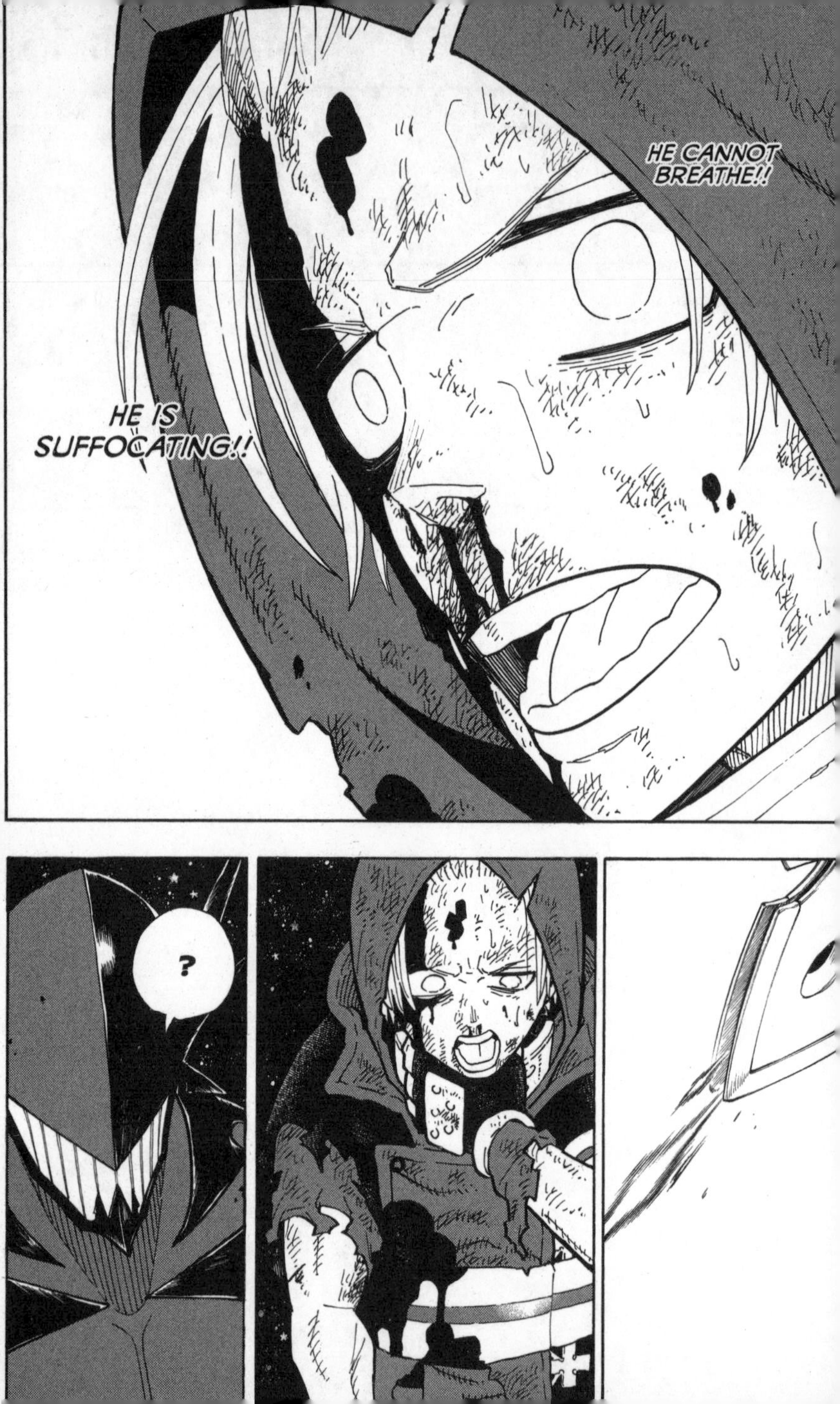
HE CANNOT BREATHE!!
HE IS SUFFOCATING!!
?

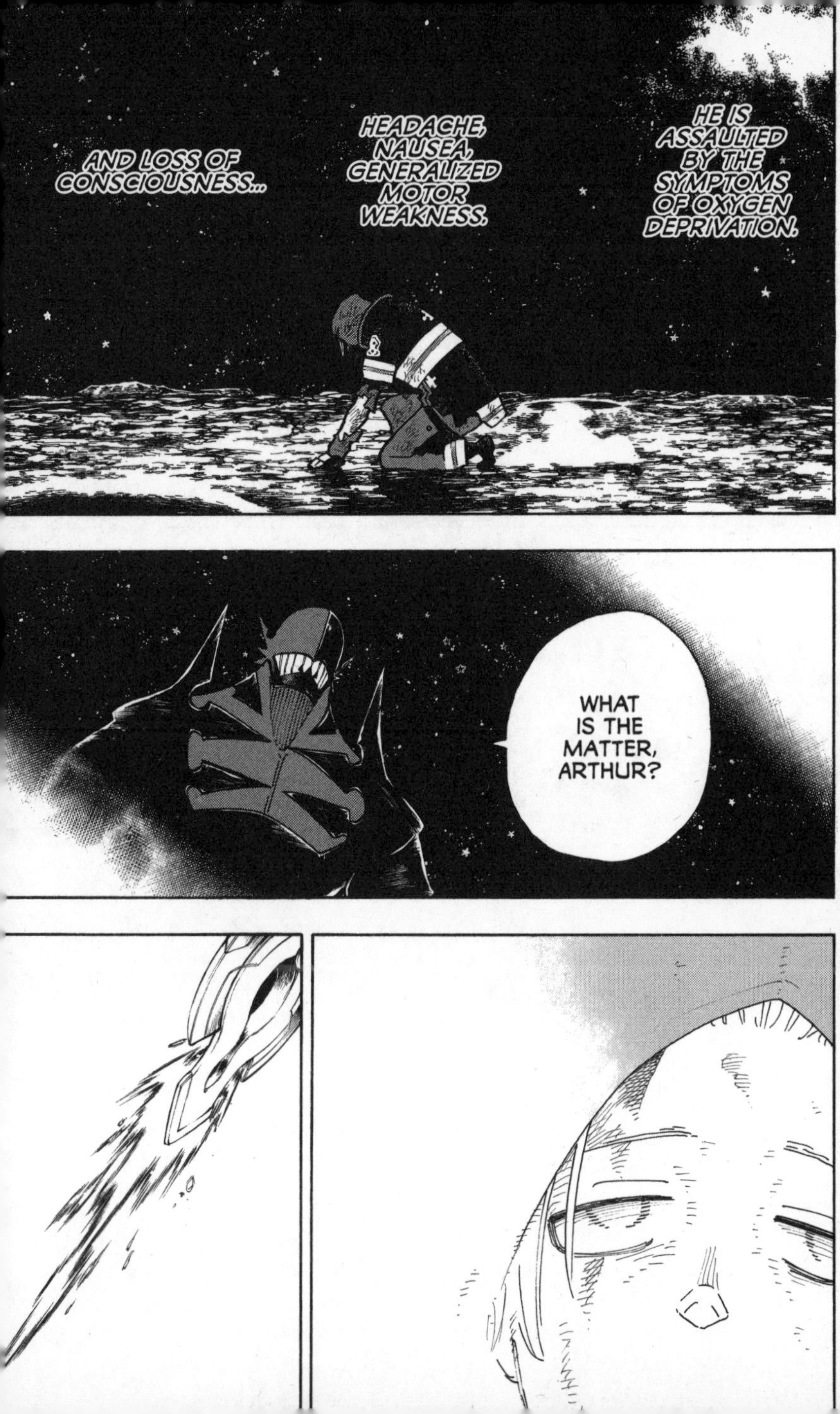
HE IS ASSAULTED BY THE SYMPTOMS OF OXYGEN DEPRIVATION.
HEADACHE, NAUSEA, GENERALIZED MOTOR WEAKNESS.
AND LOSS OF CONSCIOUSNESS...
WHAT IS THE MATTER, ARTHUR?

HE DOES NOT MOVE.

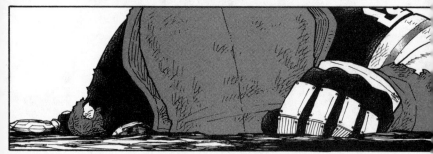

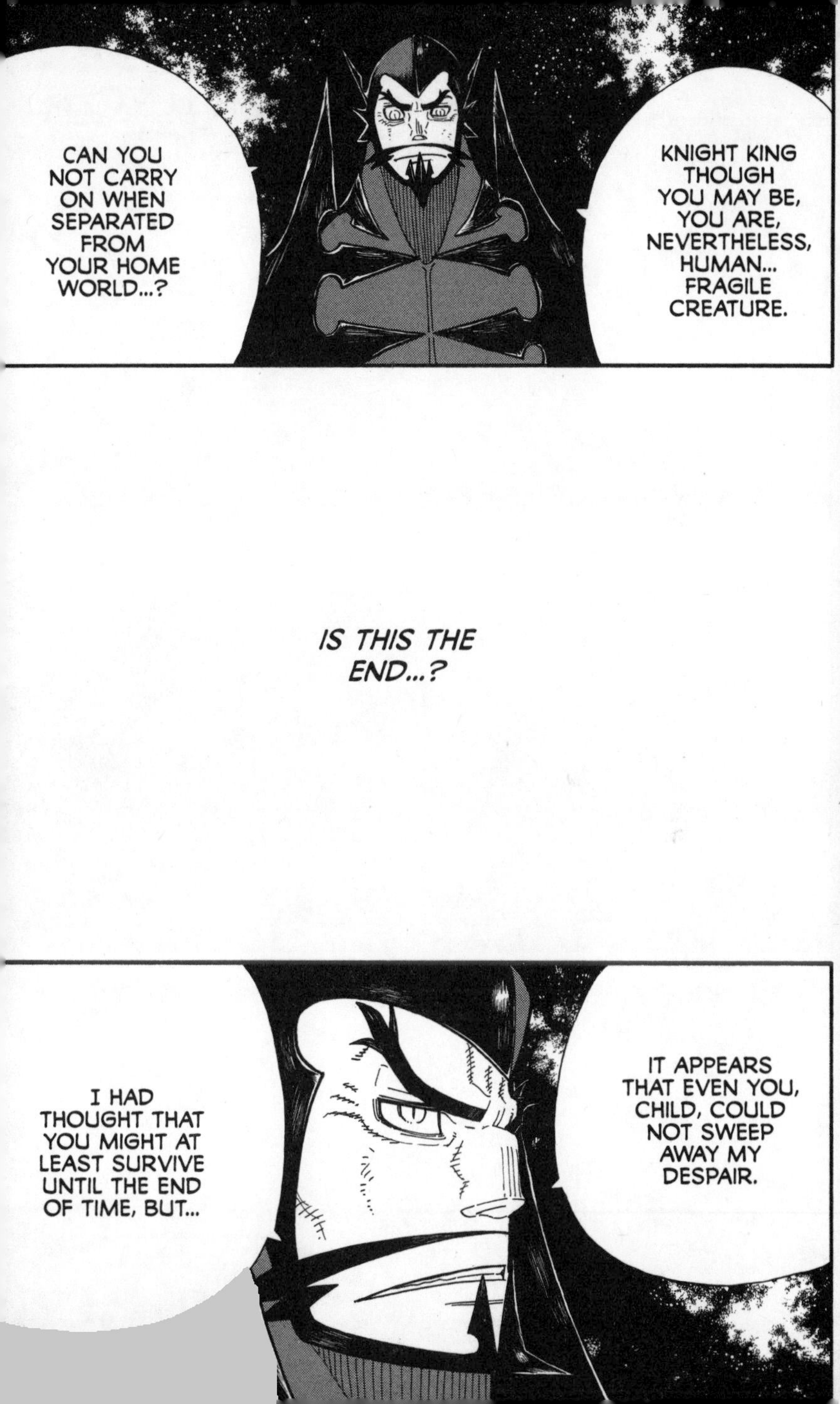
KNIGHT KING THOUGH YOU MAY BE, YOU ARE, NEVERTHELESS, HUMAN... FRAGILE CREATURE.
CAN YOU NOT CARRY ON WHEN SEPARATED FROM YOUR HOME WORLD...?
IS THIS THE END...?
IT APPEARS THAT EVEN YOU, CHILD, COULD NOT SWEEP AWAY MY DESPAIR.
I HAD THOUGHT THAT YOU MIGHT AT LEAST SURVIVE UNTIL THE END OF TIME, BUT...

CLATTER

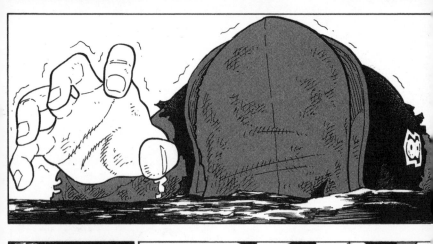

YOU WOULD ABANDON YOUR WEAPON AND BEG FOR YOUR LIFE...? I HAD THOUGHT BETTER OF YOU... DO NOT DISAPPOINT ME LIKE THIS.

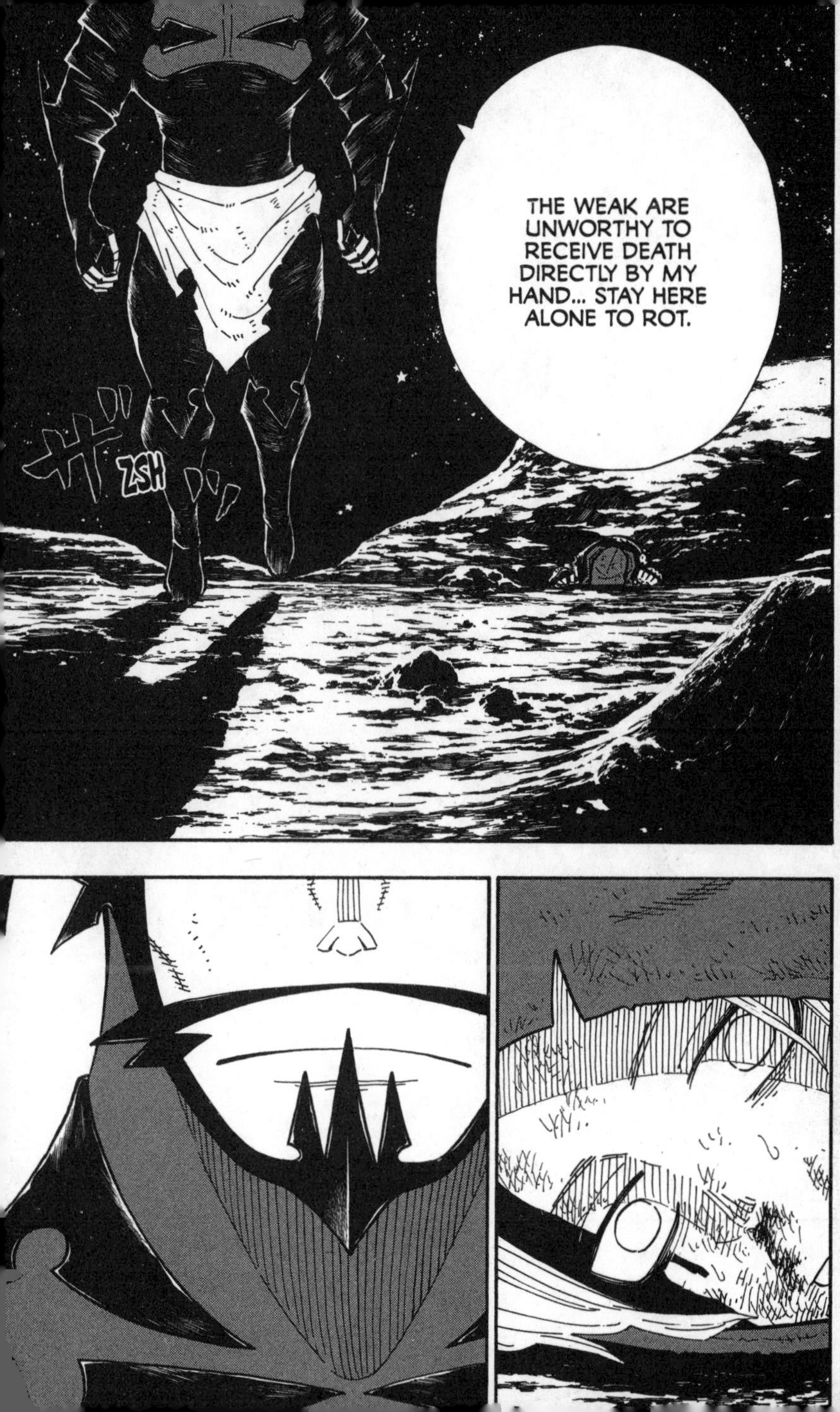
THE WEAK ARE UNWORTHY TO RECEIVE DEATH DIRECTLY BY MY HAND... STAY HERE ALONE TO ROT.
ZSH

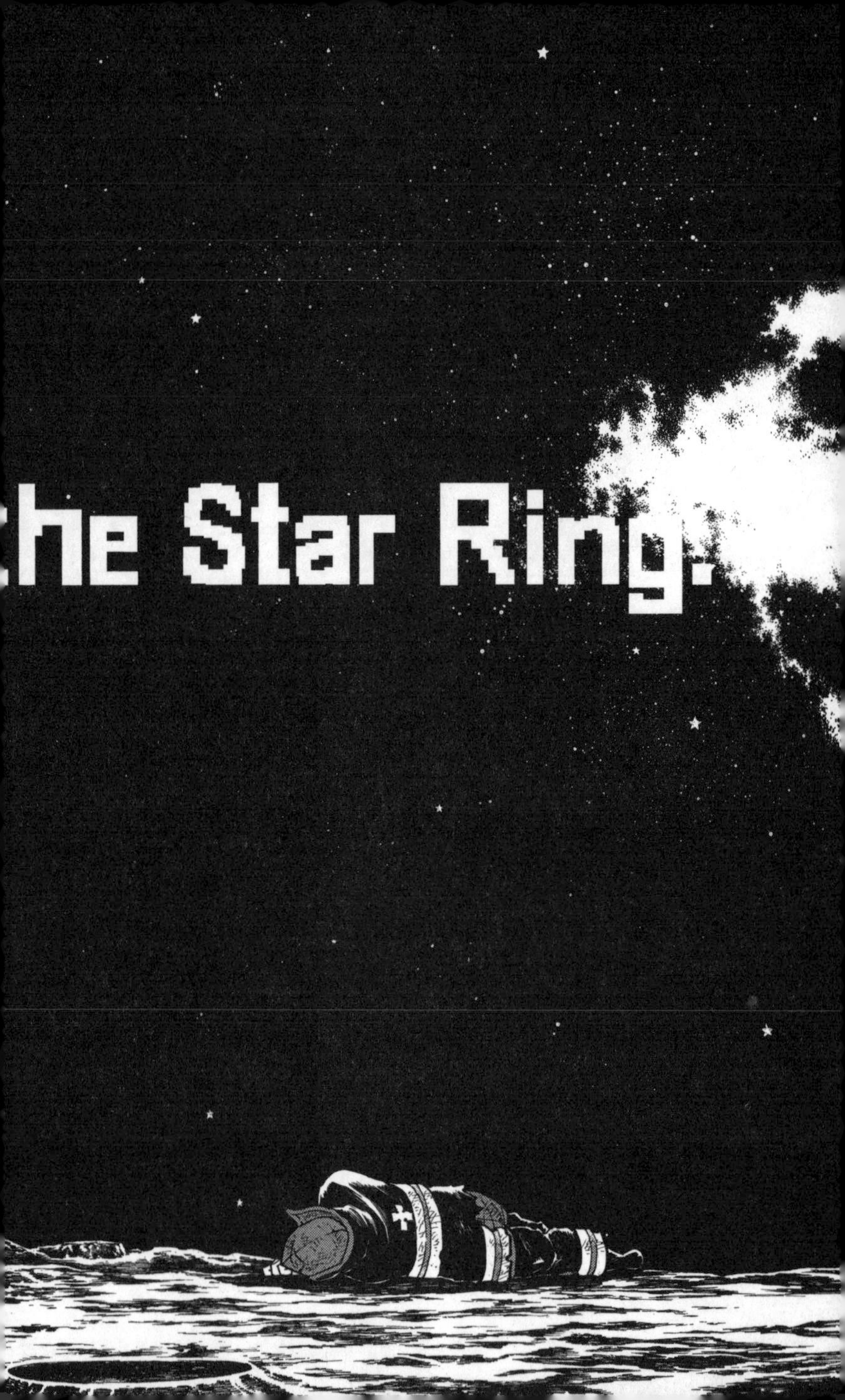
he Star Ring.

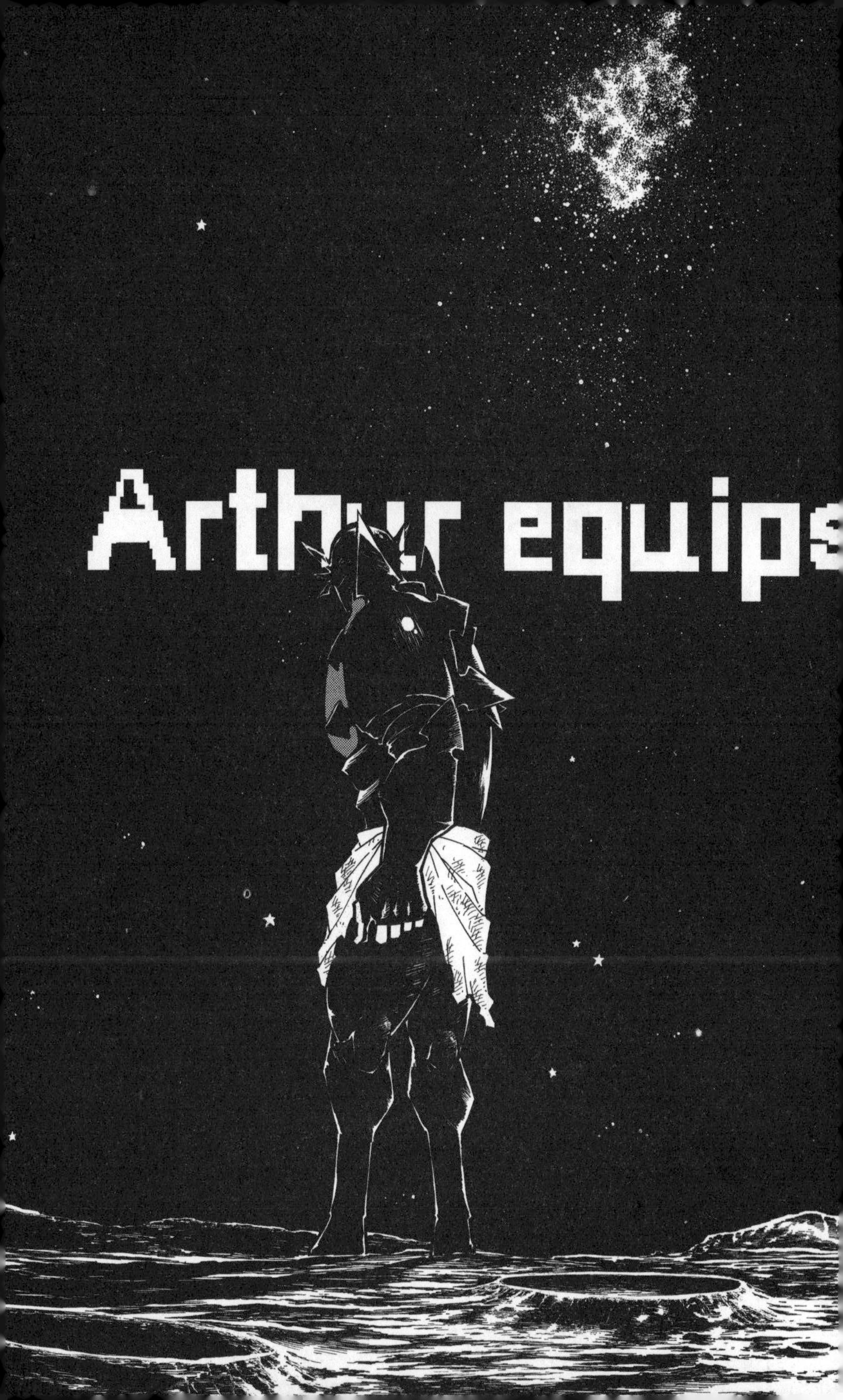
Arthur equips

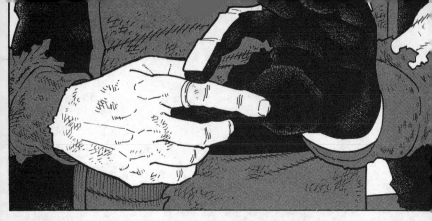

THIS IS WHAT
THE STAR RING
WAS FOR...
THANK YOU,
VULCAN...

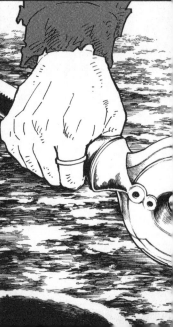

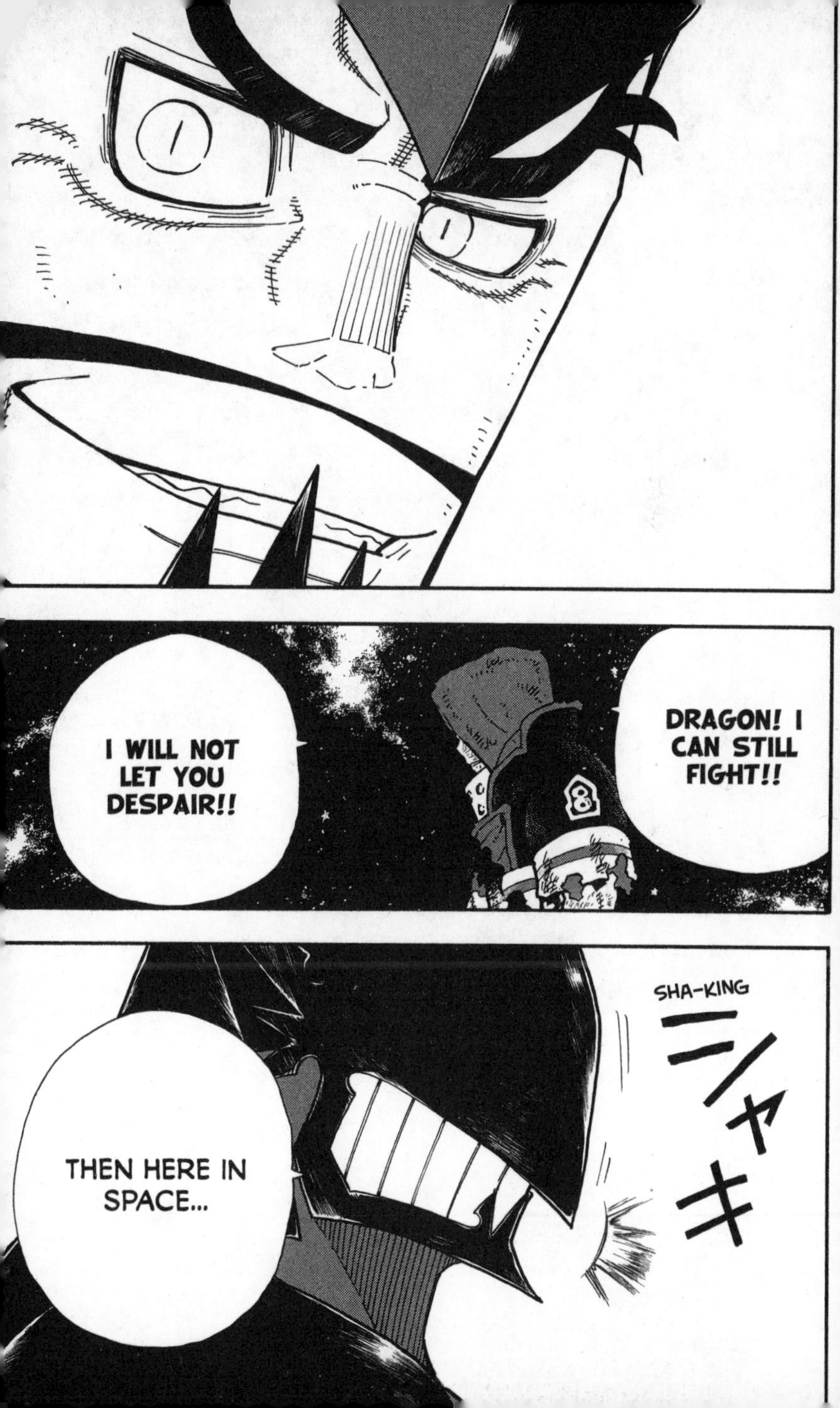
DRAGON! I CAN STILL FIGHT!!
I WILL NOT LET YOU DESPAIR!!
SHA-KING
シャキ
THEN HERE IN SPACE...

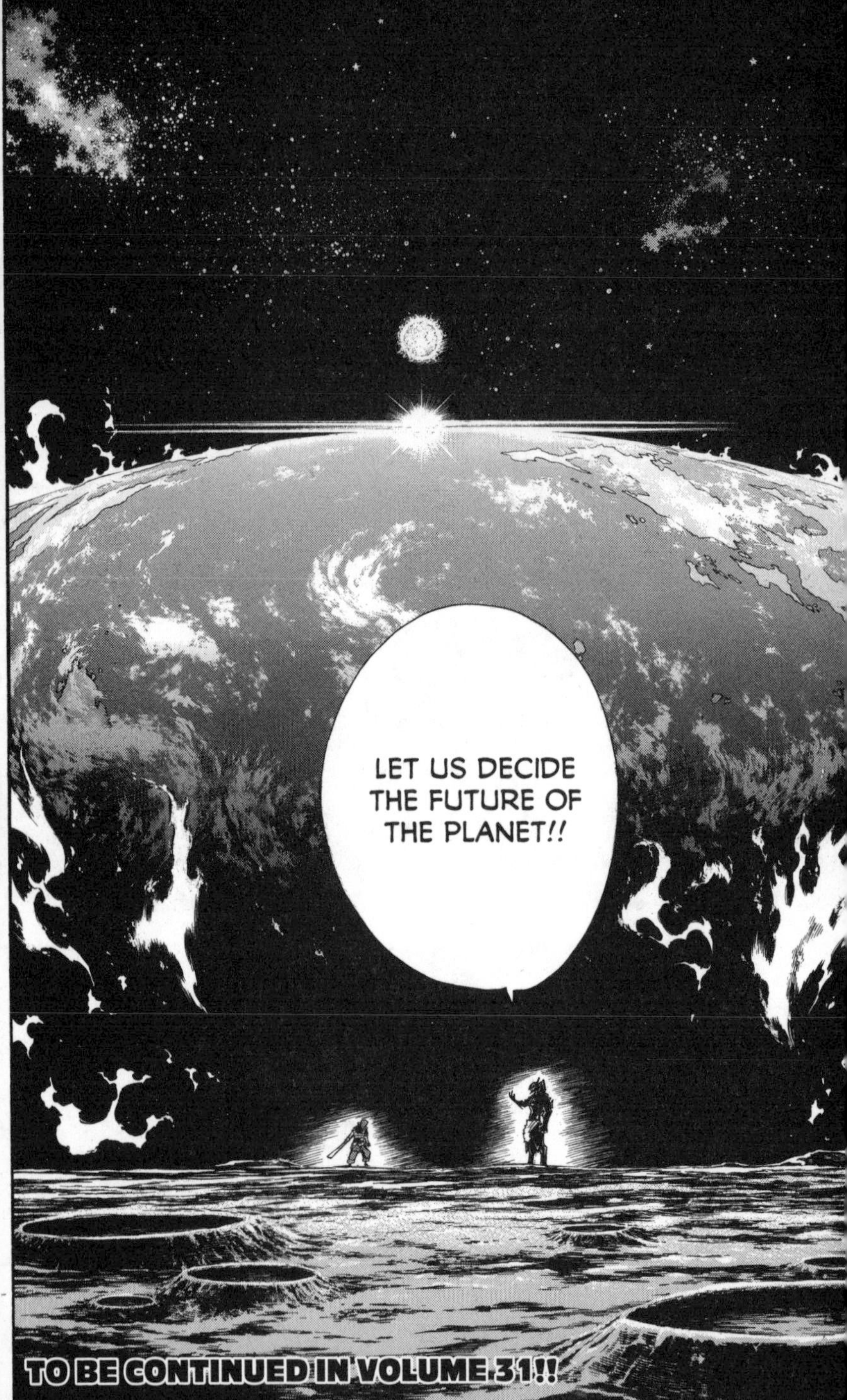
LET US DECIDE THE FUTURE OF THE PLANET!!
TO BE CONTINUED IN VOLUME 31!!

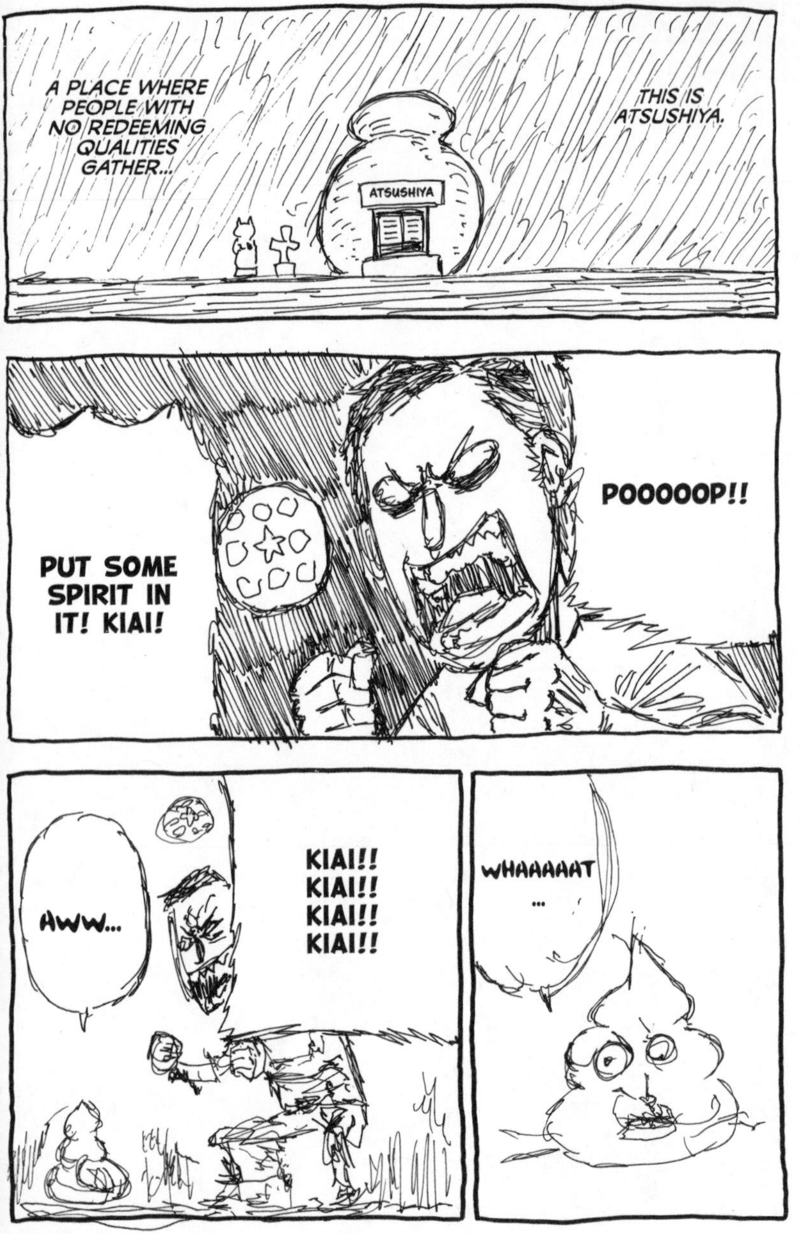
THIS IS ATSUSHIYA.
A PLACE WHERE PEOPLE WITH NO REDEEMING QUALITIES GATHER...
ATSUSHIYA
POOOOOP!!
PUT SOME SPIRIT IN IT! KIAI!
WHAAAAAT...
KIAI!! KIAI!! KIAI!! KIAI!!
AWW...

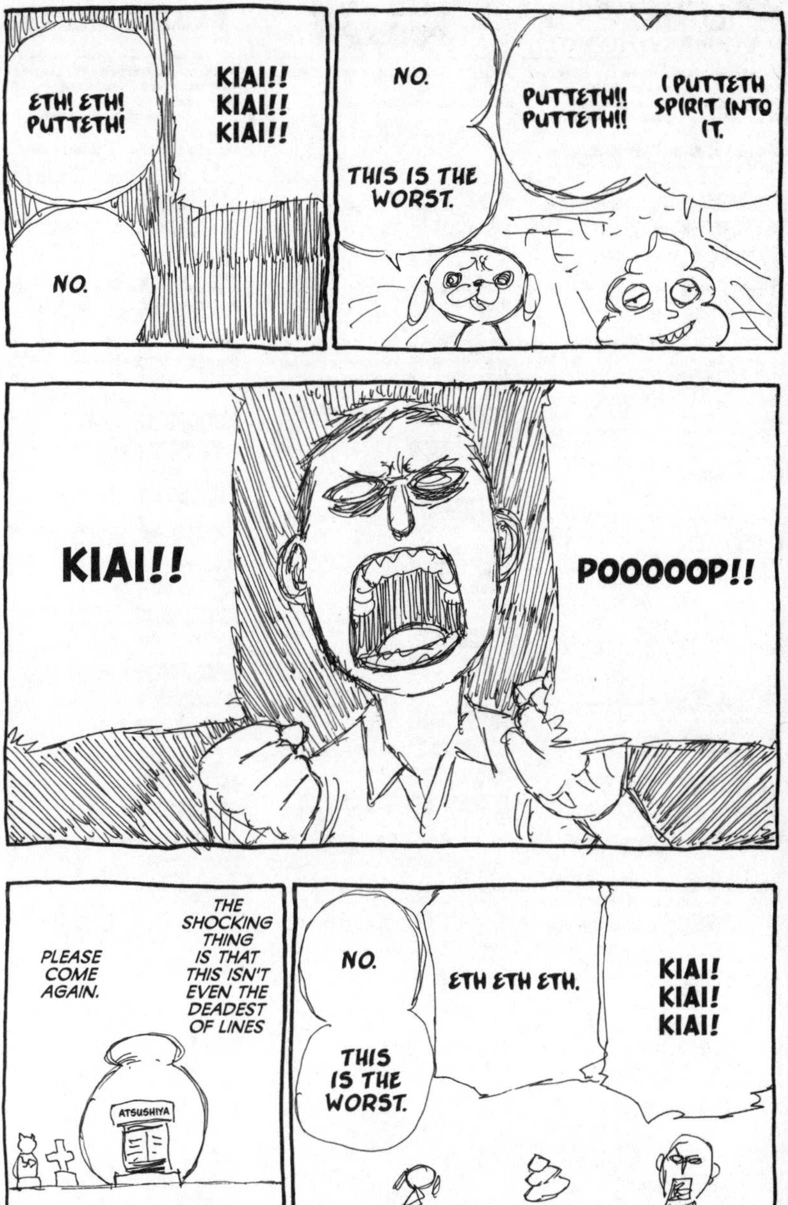
I PUTTETH SPIRIT INTO IT.
PUTTETH!! PUTTETH!!
NO.
THIS IS THE WORST.
KIAI!! KIAI!! KIAI!!
ETH! ETH! PUTTETH!
NO.
POOOOOP!!
KIAI!!
KIAI! KIAI! KIAI!
ETH ETH ETH.
NO.
THIS IS THE WORST.
THE SHOCKING THING IS THAT THIS ISN'T EVEN THE DEADEST OF LINES
PLEASE COME AGAIN.
ATSUSHIYA

DR. GIOVANNI (CURRENTLY POSSESSING YU)

AFFILIATION: SPECIAL FIRE FORCE COMPANY 3
→ WORKS FOR THE EVANGELIST
RANK: CAPTAIN (WHEN IN COMPANY 3)
ABILITY: SECOND GENERATION PYROKINETIC

Manipulates the heat energy of machines and bugs when studying them

Height	142 [4'8''] (host data)
Weight	39kg [86lbs.] (host data)
Age	Let's say 51
Birthday	Let's say June 4
Sign	Gemini
Bloodtype	B (host data)
Nickname	Plague Mask
Self-Proclaimed	He Who Transcends
Favorite Foods	Organic vegetables
Least Favorite Food	Sugar cubes
Favorite Music	Symphonic music
Favorite Animal	I only see them as test subjects
Favorite Color	I see colors differently than other humans, so whatever
Favorite Type of Girl	I hold no special emotions for living creatures
Who He Respects	Same as above
Who He Hates	Same as above
Who He's Afraid Of	Same as above
Hobbies	Observing insects
Daily Routine	Experiments
Dream	To connect myself with Adolla
Shoe Size	24cm [6.5] (host data)
Eyesight	1.5 [20/12.5] (host data)
Favorite Subject	Anyone who has forgotten the joy of learning is no better than an insect
Least Favorite Subject	

VULCAN JOSEPH

AFFILIATION: SPECIAL FIRE FORCE COMPANY 8
RANK: ENGINEER
ABILITY: NON-POWERED

Height	178cm [5'10'']
Weight	72kg [159lbs.]
Age	18
Birthday	April 18
Sign	Aries
Bloodtype	B
Nickname	Fire Soldier Loather, Haijima Hater
Self-Proclaimed	I dunno! Just call me turdface.
Favorite Foods	Lisa's cooking! Fries! Soda!!
Least Favorite Food	I wouldn't hate food!
Favorite Music	Punk! With a lot of distortion!!
Favorite Animal	All of them!
Favorite Color	Metallic!
Favorite Type of Girl	A girl who's up for anything and eats a lot!
Who He Respects	Dad and Grandpa, my ancestors who made Amaterasu
Who He Hates	Dr. Giovanni
Who He's Afraid Of	No one in particular
Hobbies	Drums!
Daily Routine	Animal watching! Mech maintenance Catch with Yū Remodeling Company 8 Cleaning up after Iris...
Dream	To revive the world!!!!
Shoe Size	28.5cm [10.5]
Eyesight	1.5 [20/12.5]
Favorite Subject	Technology! Biology!
Least Favorite Subject	The annoying ones

LISA ISARIBE

AFFILIATION: WORKED FOR THE EVANGELIST
→ SPECIAL FIRE FORCE COMPANY 8
RANK: NONE
ABILITY: THIRD GENERATION PYROKINETIC

Controls magnetic flame tentacles

Height	167cm [5'6'']
Weight	55kg [121lbs.]
Age	19
Birthday	November 3
Sign	Scorpio
Bloodtype	O
Nickname	Madonna of the Workshop (aboveground) Filthy stray (in the Nether)
Self-Proclaimed	Crybaby
Favorite Foods	Food
Least Favorite Food	Anything spicy
Favorite Music	Punk (thanks to Val's influence)
Favorite Animal	All of them
Favorite Color	Red
Favorite Type of Guy	The person I'm in love with is my type
Who She Respects	Vulcan
Who She Hates	Dr. Giovanni
Who She's Afraid Of	Dr. Giovanni
Hobbies	Karaoke
Daily Routine	Helping Vulcan
Dream	To get married and have children
Shoe Size	25cm [9]
Eyesight	1.2 [20/16]
Favorite Subject	Science
Least Favorite Subject	Math

Young characters and steampunk setting, like *Howl's Moving Castle* and *Battle Angel Alita*

A boy with a talent for machines and a mysterious girl whose wings he's fixed will take you beyond the clouds! In the tradition of the high-flying, resonant adventure stories of Studio Ghibli comes a gorgeous tale about the longing of young hearts for adventure and friendship!

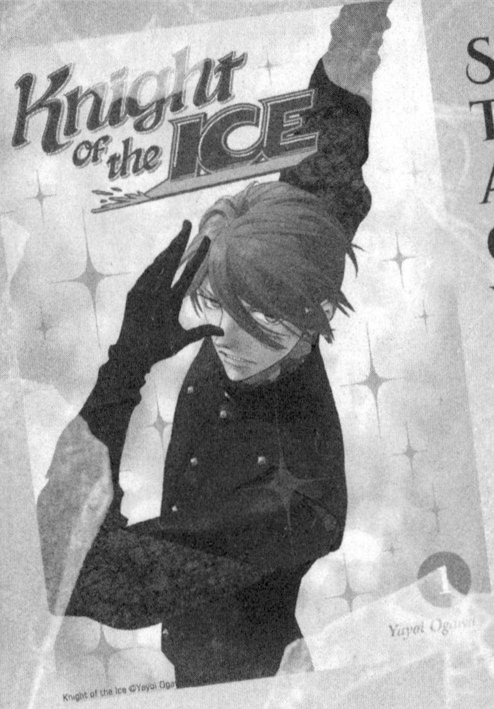
Knight of the ICE
1
Yayoi Ogawa

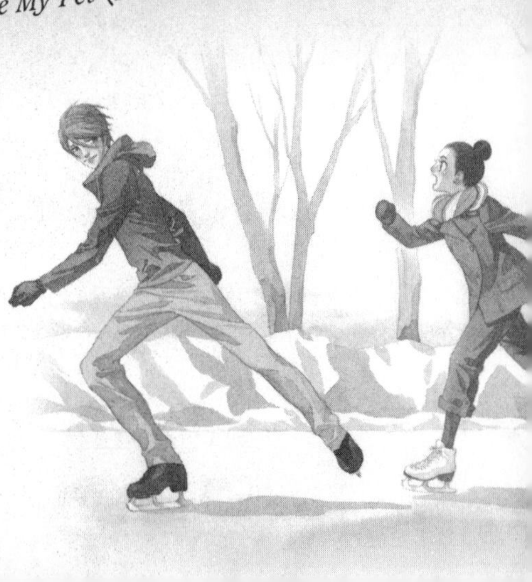

A SMART, NEW ROMANTIC COMEDY FOR FANS OF *SHORTCAKE CAKE* AND *TERRACE HOUSE!*

A romance manga starring high school girl Meeko, who learns to live on her own in a boarding house whose living room is home to the odd (but handsome) Matsunaga-san. She begins to adjust to her new life away from her parents, but Meeko soon learns that no matter how far away from home she is, she's still a young girl at heart — especially when she finds herself falling for Matsunaga-san.

PERFECT WORLD

Rie Aruga

A TOUCHING NEW SERIES ABOUT LOVE AND COPING WITH DISABILITY

An office party reunites Tsugumi with her high school crush Itsuki. He's realized his dream of becoming an architect, but along the way, he experienced a spinal injury that put him in a wheelchair. Now Tsugumi's rekindled feelings will butt up against prejudices she never considered — and Itsuki will have to decide if he's ready to let someone into his heart...

KC KODANSHA COMICS

Perfect World © Rie Aruga/Kodansha Ltd.

The boys are back, in 400-page hardcovers that are as pretty and badass as they are!

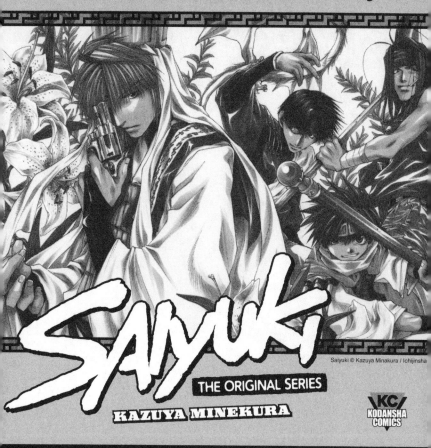

Saiyuki © Kazuya Minakura / Ichijinsha

SAIYUKI
THE ORIGINAL SERIES
KAZUYA MINEKURA

KC KODANSHA COMICS

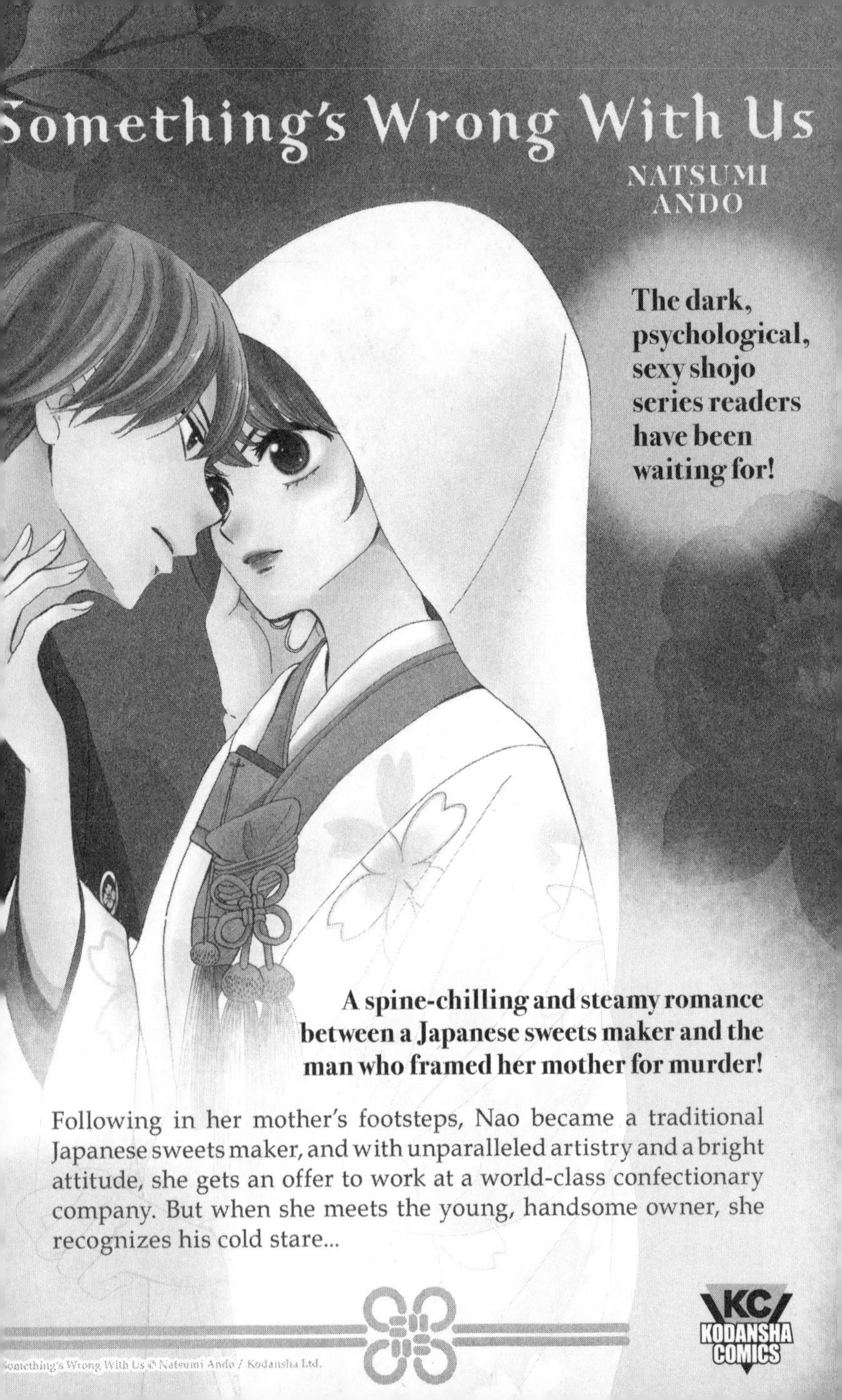
Something's Wrong With Us
NATSUMI ANDO
The dark, psychological, sexy shojo series readers have been waiting for!
A spine-chilling and steamy romance between a Japanese sweets maker and the man who framed her mother for murder!
Following in her mother's footsteps, Nao became a traditional Japanese sweets maker, and with unparalleled artistry and a bright attitude, she gets an offer to work at a world-class confectionary company. But when she meets the young, handsome owner, she recognizes his cold stare...
KC KODANSHA COMICS
Something's Wrong With Us © Natsumi Ando / Kodansha Ltd.

The adorable new odd-couple cat comedy manga from the creator of the beloved *Chi's Sweet Home*, in full color!

Praise for Chi's Sweet Home

"Nearly impossible to turn away... a true all-ages title that anyone, young or old, cat lover or not, will enjoy. The stories will bring a smile to your face and warm your heart."

—School Library Journal

Sue & Tai-chan

Konami Kanata

Sue is an aging housecat who's looking forward to living out her life in peace... but her plans change when the mischievous black tomcat Tai-chan enters the picture! Hey! Sue never signed up to be a catsitter! *Sue & Tai-chan* is the latest from the reigning meow-narch of cute kitty comics, Konami Kanata.

KC KODANSHA COMICS

THE SWEET SCENT OF LOVE IS IN THE AIR! FOR FANS OF OFFBEAT ROMANCES LIKE *WOTAKOI*

Sweat and Soap © Kintetsu Yamada / Kodansha Ltd.

In an office romance, there's a fine line between sexy and awkward... and that line is where Asako — a woman who sweats copiously — meets Koutarou — a perfume developer who can't get enough of Asako's, er, scent. Don't miss a romcom manga like no other!

CUTE ANIMALS AND LIFE LESSONS, PERFECT FOR ASPIRING PET VETS OF ALL AGES!

For an 11-year-old, Yuzu has a lot on her plate. When her mom gets sick and has to be hospitalized, Yuzu goes to live with her uncle who runs the local veterinary clinic. Yuzu's always been scared of animals, but she tries to help out. Through all the tough moments in her life, Yuzu realizes that she can help make things all right with a little help from her animal pals, peers, and kind grown-ups.

Every new patient is a furry friend in the making!

THE WORLD OF CLAMP!

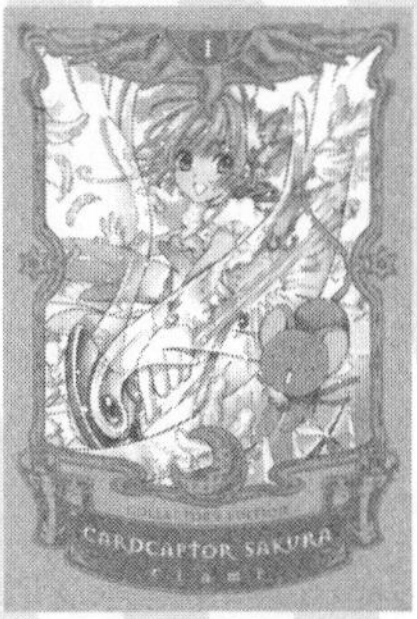
CARDCAPTOR SAKURA
CLAMP

Cardcaptor Sakura
Collector's Edition

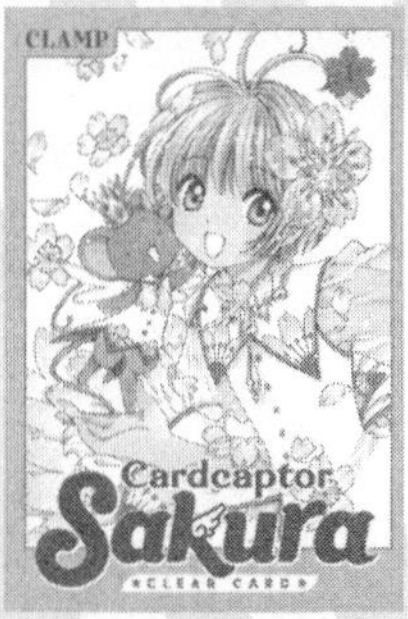
CLAMP
Cardcaptor
Sakura
CLEAR CARD

Cardcaptor Sakura:
Clear Card

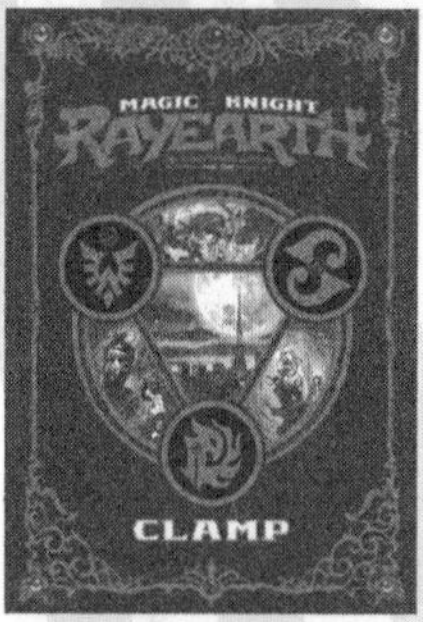
MAGIC KNIGHT
RAYEARTH
CLAMP

Magic Knight Rayearth
25th Anniversary Box Set

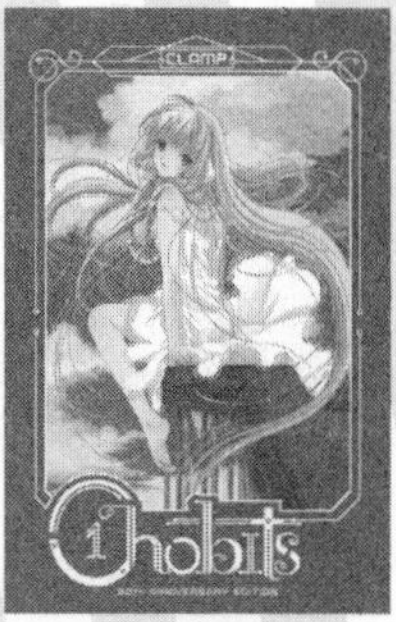
CLAMP
Chobits

Chobits

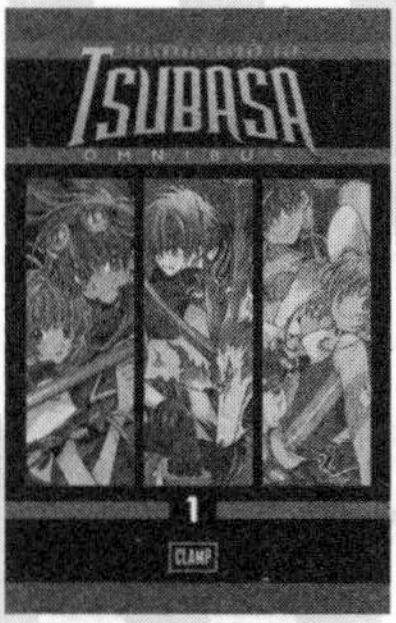
TSUBASA
OMNIBUS
1
CLAMP

TSUBASA Omnibus

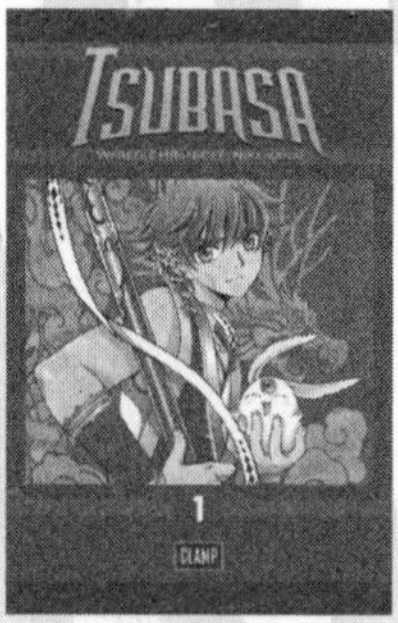
TSUBASA
1
CLAMP

TSUBASA WoRLD CHRoNiCLE

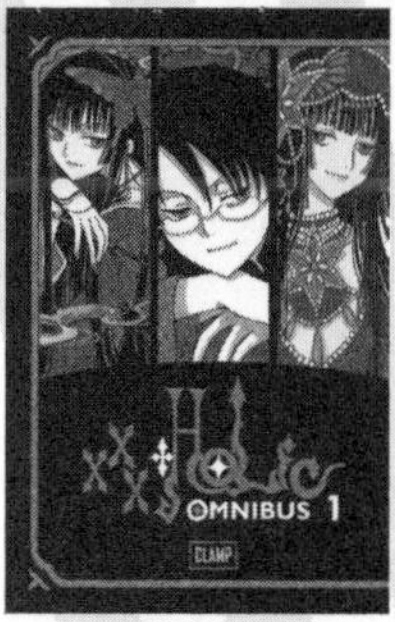
xxxHOLiC
OMNIBUS 1
CLAMP

xxxHOLiC Omnibus

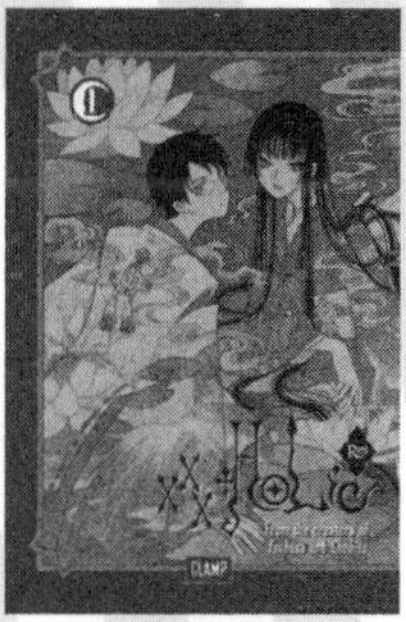
xxxHOLiC
CLAMP

xxxHOLiC Rei

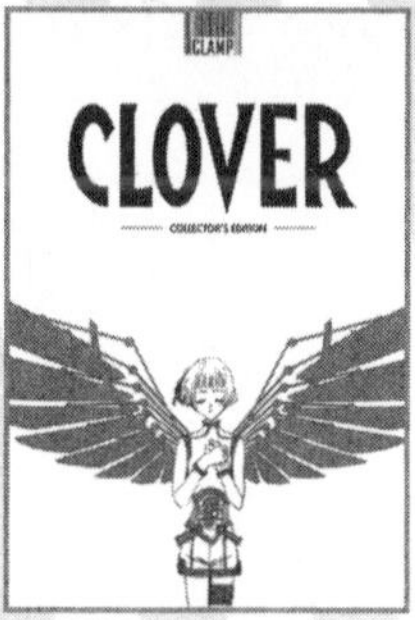
CLAMP
CLOVER
COLLECTOR'S EDITION

CLOVER Collector's Edition

KC KODANSHA COMICS

Kodansha Comics welcomes you to explore the expansive world of CLAMP, the all-female artist collective that has produced some of the most acclaimed manga of the century. Our growing catalog includes icons like *Cardcaptor Sakura* and *Magic Knight Rayearth*, each crafted with CLAMP's one-of-a-kind style and characters!

The art-deco cyberpunk classic from the creators of *xxxHOLiC* and *Cardcaptor Sakura*!

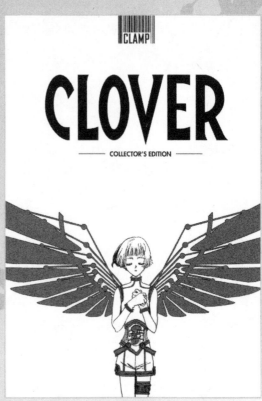

CLAMP
CLOVER
COLLECTOR'S EDITION

"Starred Review. This experimental sci-fi work from CLAMP reads like a romantic version of *AKIRA*."
—Publishers Weekly

Su was born into a bleak future, where the government keeps tight control over children with magical powers—codenamed "Clovers." With Su being the only "four-leaf" Clover in the world, she has been kept isolated nearly her whole life. Can ex-military agent Kazuhiko deliver her to the happiness she seeks? Experience the complete series in this hardcover edition, which also includes over twenty pages of ravishing color art!

KC KODANSHA COMICS

MAGIC KNIGHT RAYEARTH

25TH ANNIVERSARY EDITION

CLAMP

A BELOVED CLASSIC MAKES ITS STUNNING RETURN IN THIS GORGEOUS, LIMITED EDITION BOX SET!

This tale of three Tokyo teenagers who cross through a magical portal and become the champions of another world is a modern manga classic. The box set includes three volumes of manga covering the entire first series of *Magic Knight Rayearth*, plus the series's super-rare full-color art book companion, all printed at a larger size than ever before on premium paper, featuring a newly-revised translation and lettering, and exquisite foil-stamped covers.

A strictly limited edition, this will be gone in a flash!

KC
KODANSHA
COMICS

The beloved characters from *Cardcaptor Sakura* return in a brand new, reimagined fantasy adventure!

"[*Tsubasa*] takes readers on a fantastic ride that only gets more exhilarating with each successive chapter." —Anime News Network

In the Kingdom of Clow, an archaeological dig unleashes an incredible power, causing Princess Sakura to lose her memories. To save her, her childhood friend Syaoran must follow the orders of the Dimension Witch and travel alongside Kurogane, an unrivaled warrior; Fai, a powerful magician; and Mokona, a curiously strange creature, to retrieve Sakura's dispersed memories!

Tsubasa Omnibus © CLAMP © CLAMP·ShigatsuTsuitachi CO.,LTD./Kodansha Ltd.   Tsubasa: WoRLD CHRoNiCLE © CLAMP·ShigatsuTsuitachi CO.,LTD./Kodansha Ltd.